.NET Multithreading

.NET Multithreading

Alan L. Dennis

MANNING

Greenwich
(74° w. long.)

For online information and ordering of this and other Manning books,
go to www.manning.com. The publisher offers discounts on this book
when ordered in quantity. For more information, please contact:

Special Sales Department
Manning Publications Co.
209 Bruce Park Avenue   Fax: (203) 661-9018
Greenwich, CT 06830   email: orders@manning.com

Manning Publications Co.   Copyeditor: Elizabeth Martin
209 Bruce Park Avenue   Typesetter: Denis Dalinnik
Greenwich, CT 06830   Cover designer: Leslie Haimes

ISBN 1-930110-54-5

Printed in the United States of America
1 2 3 4 5 6 7 8 9 10 – VHG – 06 05 04 03 02

For Lara

brief contents

contents

preface

The idea for this book came out of discussions with Scott Christiansen, a leading developer using Microsoft technologies. While working together at a consulting company we spent numerous lunches kicking around ideas for a book and agreed that multithreaded development was an ideal subject. Soon after our discussions, I began a conversation with Manning Publications; this book is the end result.

Rather than focusing on abstract concepts, this book looks at the motivation behind each concept, not just the implementation. Readers of this book should know how to develop in the .NET platform. It is not assumed that you have written multithreaded applications, or programmed at a low level. All concepts beyond those required to write a single-threaded application in .NET are covered in great detail.

This book is intended primarily for architects and developers. Other players in an organization will also benefit from reading this book, but the primary focus is on designing and implementing multithreaded applications.

Since .NET does not require a single language, all examples in this book are available from the publisher's web site in both C# and Visual Basic .NET. Removing syntactical hurdles allows you to focus on the concepts. The examples alternate between the languages, showing that the fundamental issues relate to the .NET framework, not a particular language.

The code examples in the book are intentionally terse. Rather than including all code relating to an example, only the relevant elements are included. This highlights the relevant portions of code, allowing you to focus on the concept and not be drawn into the unrelated detail. All code examples are available in entirety from the publisher's web site.

about this book

How the book is organized

We begin with a discussion of operating system concepts in chapter 1. This material serves as a foundation for concepts discussed in later chapters. It's difficult, if not impossible, to write multithreaded applications without understanding what a thread is. If you've written multithreaded applications or have taken an operating systems course in college you'll likely skim this chapter.

After establishing the foundations we move into examining the .NET environment from a multithreaded viewpoint. Much can be learned by examining things from a slightly different perspective. That's the purpose of chapters 2 and 3, to look at things you've likely seen before, but from a slightly different angle.

Threads go through distinct phases of existence. Chapter 4 examines each of these in great detail. This allows you to become familiar with how threads behave. Once we've discussed the life cycle of threads we move on to controlling and communicating with threads.

While there may be a benefit to creating a thread and never interacting with it again, often multithreaded development involves interacting with, and controlling, threads. This is what chapters 5 and 6 cover.

The biggest challenge facing multithreaded development is concurrency control, something that single-threaded development doesn't need to be concerned with. Chapters 7, 8, and 9 deal with concurrency control in one form or another.

Thread pools, which provide a simplified means of concurrent execution, are used for many things in .NET. Chapter 10 discusses how to use them in your applications. Like most simple things, a thread pool can be used in some situations but not others.

In chapter 11 we discuss thread local storage, a means of associating value with a particular thread. This is followed by a discussion of delegates and exceptions in chapters 12 and 13. Each multithreaded delegate and exception is explored in detail.

In chapter 14, attention is turned to timers, a common programming construct that allows for regular execution of methods.

Windows Forms provide for a rich user experience; when combined with multiple threads highly effective interfaces can be created. Chapter 15 covers using multiple threads with Windows Forms applications along with potential pitfalls.

Chapter 16 covers the advanced topic of unmanaged code and multiple threads. Most organizations have a large number of COM objects in use. Leveraging those objects in .NET involves controlling interaction with unmanaged code.

Being able to utilize multiple threads is only part of the challenge. It is important that proper design principles be followed so that threads are used efficiently and correctly. That's what chapter 17 covers: designing with multiple threads.

We finish up by discussing multiple threads in J#, the next version of J++. Since many J++ applications are multithreaded, it's important to understand how they function, along with how a similar C# or Visual Basic .NET program might be structured.

Code conventions

All source code appears in fixed font. Within the text, the same `Courier` font is used to denote methods, classes, namespaces, programs and so forth. Annotations accompany certain segments of code. Certain annotations have further explanations that follow the code.

Source code downloads

Complete source code for the examples presented in this book is available from www.manning.com/dennis. All examples in this book are available in both C# and Visual Basic .NET.

Author Online

Purchase of *.NET Multithreading* includes free access to a private web forum run by Manning Publications where you can make comments about the book, ask technical questions, and receive help from the author and other threading experts. To access the forum and subscribe to it, point your web browser to www.manning.com/dennis. This page provides information on how to get on the forum once you are registered, what kind of help is available, and the rules of conduct on the forum.

Manning's commitment to our readers is to provide a venue where a meaningful dialogue between individual readers and between readers and the authors can take place. It is not a commitment to any specific amount of participation on the part of the author, whose contribution to the AO remains voluntary.

The Author Online forum and the archives of previous discussions will be accessible from the publisher's web site as long as the book is in print.

The author can also be contacted directly at adennis@manning.com.

acknowledgments

Without the help of many individuals, this book most likely would have never been written. I would particularly like to thank Scott Christiansen, Naveed Zaheer, Christopher Brumme, Connie Sullian, Sam Spencer, Eric Gunnerson, and Sanjay Bhansali.

The manuscript was reviewed in various stages of development by the following individuals; their input made the book you are holding a much better one: Chad Myers, Christopher Brumme, Fergal Grimes, Gary Decell, Joel Mueller, Mark Dawkins, Mitch Denny, Patrick Steele, Rob Niestockel, Santhosh Pillai, and Scott Christiansen. Special thanks to Sanjay Bhansali for a final technical review of the book, just before it went into production.

I'd also like to thank everyone at Manning Publications who worked on this book. In particular I'd like to thank Marjan Bace, my publisher; Susan Capparelle, his assistant; Ted Kennedy, review editor; as well as Mary Piergies, production editor and the entire production team: Syd Brown, design editor; Ann Navarro, developmental editor; Elizabeth Martin, copyeditor; and Denis Dalinnik, typesetter.

C H A P T E R 1

Process and thread basics

There is a great deal of value in revisiting those things we "know" and exploring them in greater depth. Every developer is familiar with what a program is (we write them, after all) and what threads and processes are.

But it is a good exercise to review the basics, those things which are part of everyday language, before tackling the somewhat daunting topic of multithreaded development.

This chapter, by way of introduction, reviews operating system (OS) concepts, with a focus on processes and threads, and covers the basics of how threads do their work and how the processor switches between them.

The examples throughout this book are written in both C# and Visual Basic .NET, alternating between the two languages. All of the examples are available from the publisher's web site at www.manning.com/dennis.

In this chapter, you'll see code that's devoted to relatively abstract concepts. The goal is to present examples that make the abstract concepts clearer and demonstrate them in a practical way.

1.1 BACKGROUND

A program, as you very well know, is typically defined as a series of instructions that are related in some way. In .NET terms, a program can be defined as an assembly, or group of assemblies, that work together to accomplish a task. Assemblies are nothing more than a way of packaging instructions into maintainable elements. An assembly is generally housed in a dynamic link library (DLL) or an executable.

> **Program** A .NET program is an assembly, or group of assemblies, that perform a task. An assembly is nothing more than a packaging mechanism where pieces of related code are grouped into a common container, typically a file.

Closely related to programs are processes and threads. A program's execution occurs on one or more threads contained with a process. Threads allow the OS to exert control over processes and the threads that execute within.

1.1.1 What is a process?

A process gives a program a place to live, allowing access to memory and resources. It's that simple.

A process is an OS object used to associate one or more paths of execution with required resources, such as memory that stores values manipulated by threads that exist within the process.

A process provides a level of isolation that keeps different applications from inadvertently interacting with each other. Think of it in terms of cans of paint. Imagine you have several different colors of paint. While each color of paint is in its own can it cannot mix with other paints. The can is similar to a process in that it keeps things in the can contained within and things outside of the can out. Every process contains one or more threads. You can think of a thread as the moving part of the process. Without a thread interacting with elements within a process, nothing interesting will happen.

1.1.2 What are threads and why should we care?

Threads are paths of execution. The threads perform the operations while the process provides the isolation. A single-threaded application has only one thread of execution.

> **Thread** A thread is the means by which a series of instructions are executed. A thread is created and managed by the OS based on instructions within the program. Every program will have at least one thread.

Let's take a step back and talk about how a program is loaded into a process. I'm not discussing Microsoft's implementation, but the things that need to occur and their likely order. When an executable is launched, perhaps by typing its name in a command window, the OS creates a process for the executable to run in. The OS then loads the executable into the process's memory and looks for an entry point, a specially marked place to start carrying out the instructions contained within the executable. Think of the entry point as the front door to a restaurant. Every restaurant has one, and front doors are relatively easy to find. Generally speaking, it's impossible to get into a restaurant without going through the front door. Once the entry point is identified, a thread is created and associated with the process. The thread is started, executing the code located at the entry point. From that point on the thread follows the series of instructions. This first thread is referred to as the main thread of the process.

Listing 1.1 contains the listing of a console application that satisfies the obligatory Hello World example.

Listing 1.1   An example of a single-threaded application (VB.NET)

```
Module ModuleHelloWorld
  Sub Main()
    Console.Write("Hello")
    Console.Write(" World")
  End Sub
End Module
```

As a console application, all input and output pass through the command-line environment. Visual Basic console applications utilize the concept of a *module*. A module is a Visual Basic construct that is identical in functionality to a C# class having all static members. This means that the method can be invoked without an instance of the class having been created.

I've found it very beneficial, when dealing with .NET, to examine the Microsoft Intermediate Language (MSIL) the compiler produces. MSIL is an assembly-like language produced by compilers targeting the .NET environment. MSIL is translated to machine instructions by the runtime. MSIL is similar to Java's bytecode. Listing 1.2 contains the MSIL that corresponds to the Main subroutine in listing 1.1.

Listing 1.2   The MSIL produced by the Hello World example (MSIL)

```
.method public static void  Main() cil managed ❶
{
  .entrypoint ❷
  .custom instance void [mscorlib]System.STAThreadAttribute::.ctor() =
    ( 01 00 00 00 )
  // Code size       25 (0x19)
  .maxstack  8
  IL_0000:  nop
  IL_0001:  ldstr      "Hello"
  IL_0006:  call       void [mscorlib]System.Console::Write(string)
  IL_000b:  nop
  IL_000c:  ldstr      " World"
  IL_0011:  call       void [mscorlib]System.Console::Write(string)
  IL_0016:  nop
  IL_0017:  nop
  IL_0018:  ret
} // end of method ModuleHelloWorld::Main
```

❶ Notice the `static` keyword. This lets the runtime know that this is a static method. Since the method is defined within a module, it is implicitly shared/static.

Console applications require a static method be the entry point. A common approach is to have the console application contain a static `Main` that creates an instance of a class and invokes a method on that instance.

❷ The `.entrypoint` directive indicates that this method is the entry point for the application. This tells the framework that this method should be invoked after the assembly is loaded into memory.

This example contains a single thread of execution that starts by entering the `Main` method and terminates when the `ret`, return, instruction executes. In this example the thread does not contain branching or looping. This makes it easy to see the path the thread will take.

Let's examine listing 1.1 in detail. Figure 1.1 shows the path the main thread of the process takes.

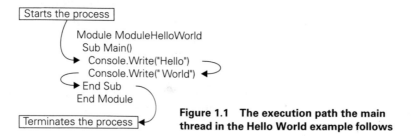

Figure 1.1   The execution path the main thread in the Hello World example follows

The arrows show the path the thread takes during execution of the Hello World program. We're covering this in such depth because, when doing multithreaded development, it is critical to understand the execution path that a thread follows. When there is more than one path, the complexity increases. Each conditional statement introduces another possible path through the program. When there are a large number of paths, management can become extremely difficult. When the path a thread takes contains branching and looping, following that path often becomes more difficult. As a review, branching occurs when a conditional instruction is encountered. Looping is accomplished by having a branching statement target an instruction that has previously been executed. Listing 1.3 contains a slightly more complex version of the Hello World example.

Listing 1.3   Hello World with a loop (C#)

```csharp
using System;
namespace HelloWorldAgain
{
  class ClassHelloWorldAgain
  {
    [STAThread]
    static void Main(string[] args)
    {
```

```
    for (int i=0;i<2;i++)
    {
      Console.Write("Hello");
      Console.Write(" World");
    }
  }
 }
}
```

It's easier to annotate the execution path by using the MSIL. Figure 1.2 contains the generated MSIL from listing 1.3 with numbered arrows indicating execution path.

This example demonstrates that code that is relatively simple can produce an execution path that is somewhat complex. The interesting part of this example is the jump that occurs at step 4. The reason for this jump is that the for loop tests to see if the test condition is true before the loop executes. The important thing to take away from this is that the main thread will execute steps 1 through 10. Those steps are the path the thread will take through the code.

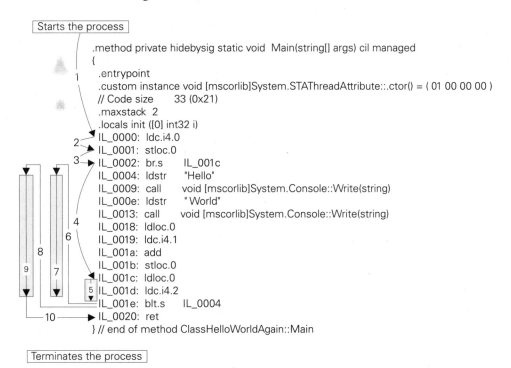

Figure 1.2   An execution path with branching

1.1.3 The cat project

It's helpful to compare abstract things, like threads and processes, to something familiar. Imagine a housecat in a typical family residence. The cat spends most of its time sleeping, but occasionally it wakes up and performs some action, such as eating.

The house shares many characteristics with a process. It contains resources available to beings in it, such as a litter box. These resources are available to things within the house, but generally not to things outside the house. Things in the house are protected from things outside of the house. This level of isolation helps protect resources from misuse. One house can easily be differentiated from another by examining its address. Most important, houses contain things, such as furniture, litter boxes, and cats.

Cats perform actions. A cat interacts with elements in its environment, like the house it lives in. A housecat generally has a name. This helps identify it from other cats that might share the same household. It has access to some or the entire house depending on its owner's permission. A thread's access to elements may also be restricted based on permissions, in this case, the system's security settings. Listing 1.4 contains a class that models a cat.

Listing 1.4 The ClassCat class models the behavior of a cat (C#).

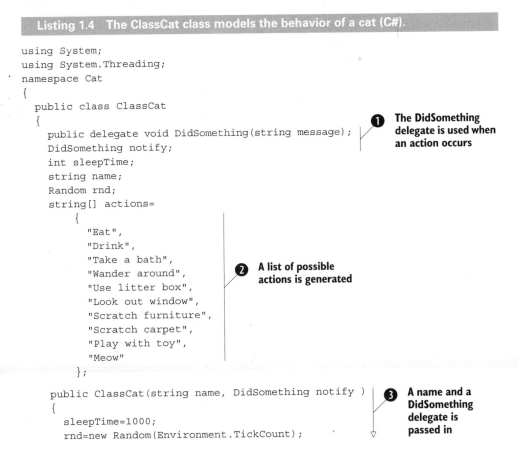

```
using System;
using System.Threading;
namespace Cat
{
    public class ClassCat
    {
        public delegate void DidSomething(string message);    ❶ The DidSomething
        DidSomething notify;                                      delegate is used when
        int sleepTime;                                            an action occurs
        string name;
        Random rnd;
        string[] actions=
            {
                "Eat",
                "Drink",
                "Take a bath",
                "Wander around",                                ❷ A list of possible
                "Use litter box",                                  actions is generated
                "Look out window",
                "Scratch furniture",
                "Scratch carpet",
                "Play with toy",
                "Meow"
            };

        public ClassCat(string name, DidSomething notify )      ❸ A name and a
        {                                                          DidSomething
            sleepTime=1000;                                        delegate is
            rnd=new Random(Environment.TickCount);                 passed in
```

```
        this.name = name;
        this.notify = notify;
    }
    private string WhichAction()        ④  A random action
    {                                       is chosen
        int which = rnd.Next(actions.Length);
        return actions[which];
    }
    public void DoCatStuff(int howMuch)   ⑤  Loop the supplied
    {                                          number of times
        for (int i=0;i< howMuch;i++)
        {
            if(rnd.Next(100) >= 80)
            {
                notify(name + ": " + WhichAction()+ " " );
            }
            else
            {
                notify(name + ": Zzz ");
                Thread.Sleep(sleepTime);
            }
        }
    }
  }
}
```

③ **A name and a DidSomething delegate is passed in**

❶ Since the cat does things, we need some way of letting the outside world know what it did. To accomplish this we use a *delegate*. A delegate is simply a way of accessing a method through a variable, similar in many ways to function pointers and callbacks. Function pointers and callbacks come from the C++ world. They provide a means of storing the information required to execute a function in a variable or parameter. This allows the function to be invoked indirectly, by accessing the variable or parameter. Cat owners may be wishing that their cat had a delegate available so that they could monitor their cat's activities.

❷ Cats do many things. I did not include sleep in this list of common feline activities since it occurs more frequently than the other activities.

❸ Unlike the normal process through which cats come into the world, our cat is created when it is allocated using the new statement. The constructor accepts the name of the newly created cat along with a reference to the delegate to call when it does something. The advantage of using a delegate in this way is that the cat class doesn't need to know anything about the class that's utilizing its functionality.

❹ The actions of a cat have always seemed pseudorandom to me. There may be a more complex algorithm they use to determine their actions but they aren't talking.

⑤ `DoCatStuff` is the main method used to simulate the cat's actions. It loops the specified number of times. Each loop has an 80 percent chance of the cat doing nothing more interesting than sleeping. The remaining 20 percent involves random selection from the list of actions we discussed earlier.

We're now ready to do something with our cat class. Listing 1.5 contains the code from a console application that utilizes `ClassCat`.

Listing 1.5   The console application that uses the ClassCat class

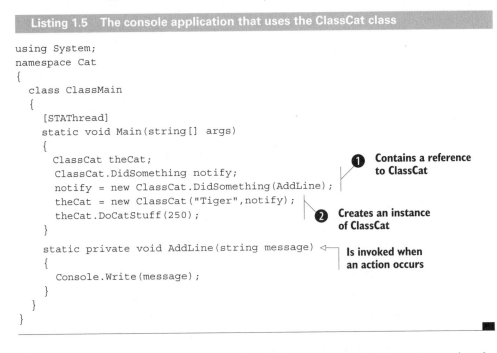

```
using System;
namespace Cat
{
    class ClassMain
    {
        [STAThread]
        static void Main(string[] args)
        {
            ClassCat theCat;
            ClassCat.DidSomething notify;
            notify = new ClassCat.DidSomething(AddLine);
            theCat = new ClassCat("Tiger",notify);
            theCat.DoCatStuff(250);
        }
        static private void AddLine(string message)
        {
            Console.Write(message);
        }
    }
}
```

① Contains a reference to ClassCat

② Creates an instance of ClassCat

Is invoked when an action occurs

❶ Our cat will perform many actions. In order for the `ClassMain` class to know that the cat has performed an action, we must supply it with a delegate. The `DidSomething` delegate that's passed in to the constructor is invoked by the instance of the cat class whenever it accomplishes some task. The instance of the `DidSomething` delegate that's passed in is associated with the `AddLine` method. This method accepts a string as its only parameter. It then writes the contents of that string to the console.

❷ When we create our cat we pass in the instance of the `DidSomething` delegate along with the cat's name. After we've created Tiger we tell it to do 250 iterations. This occurs on the main thread of the application. Once `DoCatStuff` completes, the application terminates. The following is a sample of the output produced by the program:

```
"Zzz" "Meow" "Zzz" "Zzz" "Zzz" "Play with toy" "Wander around" "Zzz" "Zzz"
"Take a bath" "Zzz" "Zzz" "Zzz" "Zzz" "Zzz" "Zzz" "Zzz" "Zzz" "Play with
toy" "Zzz"
```

We've explored a simple example of how a thread resembles a cat. In the next section we take a look at processes from the Task Manager perspective.

1.1.4   Task Manager

To see examples of processes, you need look no further than the Windows Task Manager, shown in figure 1.3.

Image Name	PID	Username	CPU	CPU Time	Mem Usage	Mem Delta	Base Pri	Handles	Threads	USER Objects	GDI Objects
ud_1066573.exe	1612	Administrator	57	11:00:59	5,020 K	0 K	Low	26	2	0	4
SnagIt32.exe	2904	Administrator	27	0:00:01	6,492 K	8 K	Normal	107	2	62	81
IEXPLORE.EXE	3048	Administrator	03	0:00:14	19,376 K	0 K	Normal	492	18	171	347
wmplayer.exe	1636	Administrator	03	0:01:45	21,988 K	(80) K	Normal	390	21	101	321
taskmgr.exe	3204	Administrator	02	0:00:22	2,208 K	0 K	High	184	8	129	138
msimn.exe	2484	Administrator	02	0:01:42	19,164 K	0 K	Normal	998	11	178	331
imontray.exe	2168	Administrator	02	0:00:35	1,880 K	0 K	Normal	62	1	9	12
WINWORD.EXE	2064	Administrator	02	0:00:27	18,700 K	0 K	Normal	271	5	110	281
DLLHOST.EXE	1972	SYSTEM	02	0:00:03	5,144 K	0 K	Normal	131	9	0	0
sqlservr.exe	868	SYSTEM	02	0:23:05	18,680 K	0 K	Normal	290	32	0	4
aspnet_wp.exe	2868	ASPNET	00	0:00:15	17,304 K	0 K	Normal	169	10	0	4
svchost.exe	2496	SYSTEM	00	0:00:00	3,928 K	0 K	Normal	201	12	2	6
UD.exe	2396	Administrator	00	0:09:47	2,380 K	0 K	Normal	158	4	25	84
sqlmangr.exe	2376	Administrator	00	0:00:19	4,452 K	0 K	Normal	110	3	86	147
AcroTray.exe	2356	Administrator	00	0:00:00	3,452 K	0 K	Normal	53	2	5	28
CTFMON.EXE	2352	Administrator	00	0:00:07	3,428 K	0 K	Normal	252	1	81	157
msmsgs.exe	2340	Administrator	00	0:00:10	5,448 K	0 K	Normal	482	19	47	124
wcmdmgr.exe	2328	Administrator	00	0:00:00	4,980 K	0 K	Low	154	5	1	4
sointor.exe	2264	Administrator	00	0:00:00	1,304 K	0 K	Normal	33	1	2	4

Show processes from all users   End Process

Processes: 62   CPU Usage: 100%   Mem Usage: 326912K / 1273724K

Figure 1.3   Windows Task Manager lists the processes that are currently executing.

Processes are assigned a priority that is used in scheduling its threads. In figure 1.3 the column Base Pri contains the priority of the process. A process itself does not execute. Instead the threads contained within a process execute. Their execution is controlled in part by their priority. The OS combines each thread's priority with that of the process containing them to determine the order in which the threads should execute. Three of the most common values for base priority—High, Normal, and Low—are listed in figure 1.3.

The columns Mem Usage, Handles, USER Objects, and GDI Objects are examples of memory and resources that a process uses. These resources include things like file handles and Graphical Device Interface (GDI) objects. A file handle is used to interact with a file system file while a GDI object is used to display graphical output, such as circles and lines, on the screen.

Processes allow the actions of one thread in a process to be isolated from all other processes. The goal of this isolation is to increase the overall stability of the system. If a thread in a process encounters an error, the effects of that error should be limited to that process.

1.2   MULTITASKING

When computers ran only one program at a time, there was no need to be concerned with multitasking. Not that long ago a computer executed only one process—a single task—at a time. In the days of DOS the computer started up to a command prompt. From that prompt you typed the name of the program to execute. This single tasking made it very difficult to interact with multiple programs. Typically users were forced to exit one program, saving their work, and start another. For many it is unimaginable that a computer could run only a single program at once, such as a word processor or spreadsheet. Today users routinely execute a relatively large number of processes at the same time. A typical user may be surfing the Web, chatting using an instant messaging program, listening to an MP3, and checking email simultaneously.

When an OS supports execution of multiple concurrent processes it is said to be multitasking. There are two common forms of multitasking: preemptive and cooperative, which we'll explore next.

1.2.1   Cooperative multitasking

Cooperative multitasking is based on the assumption that all processes in a system will share the computer fairly. Each process is expected to yield control back to the system at a frequent interval. Windows 3.x was a cooperative multitasking system.

The problem with cooperative multitasking is that not all software developers followed the rules. A program that didn't return control to the system, or did so infrequently, could make the entire system unusable. That's why Windows 3.x would occasionally "freeze up," becoming unresponsive. This occurred because the entire OS shared a common thread processing messages. When Windows 3.x started a new application, that application was invoked from the main thread. The OS would pass control to the application with the understanding it would be returned quickly. If the application failed to return control to the OS in a timely fashion, all other applications, as well as the OS, could no longer execute instructions.

Development of applications for Window 3.x was more difficult than newer versions because of the requirements of cooperative multitasking. The developer was required to process Windows messages on a frequent basis, requiring that checks to the message loop be performed regularly. To perform long-running operations, such as looping 100 times, required performing a small unit of work, and then posting a message back to yourself indicating what you should do next. This required that all work be broken up into small units, something that isn't always feasible.

Let's review the way that current Windows applications function. The main thread executes a loop called a message pump. This loop checks a message queue to see if there's work to do. If so, it performs the work. The click event, which occurs when a user clicks a control such as a button, enters work into the message queue indicating which method should be executed in response to the user's click. This method is known as an event handler. While the loop is executing an event handler, it cannot process additional messages.

Think of the message pump as a person whose job is repairing appliances. Imagine this person has an answering machine at his place of business. When people need the technician, they call the answering machine and leave a message. This is essentially what happens when an event is entered into the message queue. The technician then retrieves messages from the answering machine, and, hopefully, responds in the order they were received. Generally, while the technician is on a service call he cannot start working on additional service calls. He must finish the current job and return to the office to check for messages.

Suppose a repair is taking a long time to complete. The client might tell the technician, go back to your office, check your messages, and do one job. Once you've finished it, come back here and finish this job. This is what the `Application.DoEvents` method does. It makes a call back to the message pump to retrieve messages.

Listing 1.6 contains the class that controls the sharing of the processor in a cooperative multitasking application.

Listing 1.6   A cooperative multitasking controlling class (C#)

```csharp
using System;
using System.Collections;
namespace CooperativeMultitasking
{
  public class Sharing
  {
    public bool timeToStop=false;

    ArrayList workers;          ❶ An ArrayList is
    int current;                  used to store
    public Sharing()              the workers
    {
      workers=new ArrayList();  ❶ An ArrayList is
      current=-1;                 used to store
    }                             the workers
    public void Add(WorkerBase worker)   ❶ An ArrayList is
    {                                      used to store
      workers.Add(worker);                 the workers
    }

    public void Run()
    {
      if (workers.Count ==0)
      {
        return;
      }                                  ❷ Each worker is
      while (!timeToStop)                  given a chance
      {                                    to work
        current++;
        if (current+1 > workers.Count)
        {
          current= 0;
        }
```

```
        WorkerBase worker;
        worker=(WorkerBase)workers[current];
        worker.DoWork(this);
      }
    }
  }
}
```

❷ Each worker is given a chance to work

❶ Since multitasking involves multiple elements we need some way of storing them. In this example we use an `ArrayList` to store instances of classes derived from `Worker-Base`. An `ArrayList` is a dynamic array that manages the memory required to store its elements. To add an entry to the list you use the `Add` method. We discuss `WorkerBase` in listing 1.7.

❷ The heart of the `Sharing` class is the `Run` method which executes until the value of `timeToStop` becomes `true`. On each pass the variable `current`'s contents are incremented. This counter is used to choose which worker will be allowed to do a portion of its work. The worker is extracted from the `ArrayList` and its `DoWork` method is invoked.

    `WorkerBase` is an abstract base class. All instances of classes that are managed by the `Sharing` class must be derived from the `WorkerBase` class, either directly or indirectly. Listing 1.7 contains the `WorkerBase` class.

> **Listing 1.7 WorkerBase is the foundation for all classes controlled by the Sharing class (C#).**

```
namespace CooperativeMultitasking
{
  public abstract class WorkerBase
  {
    public abstract void DoWork(Sharing controller);
  }
}
```

Because `WorkerBase` contains an abstract method `DoWork`, all classes derived from it must implement that method. The `Sharing` class calls the `DoWork` method each time it's the worker class's turn. To perform some work we need a class that's derived from `WorkerBase` that does something. Listing 1.8 contains a class that writes out a greeting based on a string passed to its constructor.

Listing 1.8   A cooperative greeter (VB.NET)

```vb
Public Class Hello
  Inherits WorkerBase

  Private name As String

  Public Sub New(ByVal name As String)
    Me.name = name
  End Sub

  Public Overrides Sub DoWork(ByVal controller As Sharing)
    Console.Write("Hello " + name)
  End Sub
End Class
```

Notice that the DoWork method is overridden to perform a simple action. Each time an instance of this class has a chance to perform its action, it will simply write out the greeting "Hello" followed by the name passed into the constructor.

To control termination we introduce a class that limits the number of times it is invoked (listing 1.9). This keeps our example relatively simple and shows another derived worker.

Listing 1.9   A worker who signals it's time to stop all processing (C#)

```csharp
using System;
namespace CooperativeMultitasking
{
  public class Die : WorkerBase
  {
    int howManyAllowed;
    int workUnits;
    public Die(int howManyAllowed)
    {
      workUnits=0;
      this.howManyAllowed= howManyAllowed;
    }
    public override void DoWork(Sharing controller)
    {
      workUnits++;
      if (workUnits > howManyAllowed)
      {
        controller.timeToStop=true;
      }
    }
  }
}
```

The problem with cooperative multitasking is when one of the elements being controlled executes for an excessive amount of time. Listing 1.10 contains an example of a class that contains an infinite loop in its DoWork method.

```vbnet
Public Class Bad
  Inherits WorkerBase
  Public Overrides Sub DoWork(ByVal controller As Sharing)
    While (True)
    End While
  End Sub
End Class
```

We're now ready to see all the pieces tied together. The controlling part of this example is in listing 1.11. Notice that the line adding the `badWorker` is commented out.

Listing 1.11 The Sharing example main class (C#)

```csharp
using System;
namespace CooperativeMultitasking
{
  class ClassMain
  {
    [STAThread]
    static void Main(string[] args)
    {
      Sharing controller;
      controller = new Sharing();
      Hello hiNewton = new Hello("Newton ");
      Hello hiCayle = new Hello("Cayle ");
      Die terminator = new Die(10);
      Bad badWorker = new Bad();
      controller.Add(hiNewton );
      controller.Add(hiCayle );
      //       controller.Add(badWorker);
      controller.Add(terminator);
      controller.Run();
    }
  }
}
```

This program produces the following output:

```
Hello Newton Hello Cayle Hello Newton Hello Cayle Hello Newton Hello Cayle
Hello Newton Hello Cayle Hello Newton Hello Cayle Hello Newton Hello Cayle
Hello Newton Hello Cayle Hello Newton Hello Cayle Hello Newton Hello Cayle
Hello Newton Hello Cayle Hello Newton Hello Cayle
```

Notice that the greetings alternate as each worker is given a chance to do his work. When the `badWorker` is present in the collection of workers, the following output is produced:

```
Hello Newton Hello Cayle
```

Since the badWorker's DoWork method never returns, the entire cooperative system is destabilized. This kind of failure is why Windows 3.x would occasionally freeze, requiring a reboot of the computer to recover.

We've discussed the challenges of developing applications under cooperative multitasking. The biggest problem is that if one or more applications doesn't follow the rules, the entire OS is affected. It's not surprising that all modern multitasking OSs use preemptive multitasking.

1.2.2 Preemptive

Preemptive multitasking is the more common form of multitasking in use today. Instead of relying on the programs to return control to the system at regular intervals, the OS takes it. Listing 1.12 contains an example of a program that uses threads and relies on preemptive multitasking.

Listing 1.12 Using a different thread to perform the work (C#)

```
private void button1_Click(object sender, System.EventArgs e)
{
  System.Threading.WaitCallback callback;
  callback = new System.Threading.WaitCallback(Loop);
  System.Threading.ThreadPool.QueueUserWorkItem(callback);   ❶ Adds to the
}                                                                 ThreadPool

private void Loop(object state)       ❷ Defines the method
{                                         that is invoked in
  for (int i=1;i<100;i++)                 the ThreadPool
  {
    for (int k=0;k< 100;k++)
    {
      double d;
      d = (double)k/(double)i;
      SetLabel(d.ToString());         ❸ Sets the text
    }                                     of the label
  }
  SetLabel("Finished");               ❸ Sets the text
}                                         of the label

private delegate void SetLabelDelegate(string s);
private void SetLabel(string s)       ❸ Sets the text
{                                         of the label
  if (label1.InvokeRequired)
  {
    label1.Invoke(new SetLabelDelegate(SetLabel),new object[] {s});
  }
  else
  {
    label1.Text=s;
  }
}
```

The key element in this example is that the `button1_Click` method doesn't do the actual looping; instead it creates a work item that's entered into a thread pool. A thread pool is an easy way to do multithreading. As with most things, this simplicity results in a less flexible way of doing things. This execution occurs on a separate thread and is periodically interrupted by the OS to allow other threads a chance to get work done.

❶ Thread pools are a great way to perform multithreaded programming. Chapter 10 covers thread pools in detail. Thread pools perform their work using the `Wait-Callback` delegate. A method that accepts a single parameter is associated with the `WaitCallback`. That method, `Loop`, is invoked on a thread controlled by the thread pool.

❷ The `Loop` method performs the actual work. It is very similar to the method in listing 1.6. The most notable difference is that there is no call to `Application.DoEvents`. Additionally, some type casting is being performed to make the output more interesting.

❸ Instead of accessing the label directly to output the results, we use the `SetLabel` method. `SetLabel` ensures that the label is accessed on the same thread that created the form. It does this because Windows Forms are not thread-safe. The potential exists that something undesirable will occur if one thread—or more—manipulates a control on a Windows Form.

It's important to understand that this example would not work on a cooperative multitasking OS because there is no call to service the message pump or to yield control. In the next section we discuss how preemptive multitasking is done.

1.3   PREEMPTIVE MULTITASKING

When more than one application is executing, there must be some means of determining whose turn it is to execute. This is generally referred to as scheduling. Scheduling involves an element in one of two states: currently executing and waiting to execute. Under modern OSs scheduling is performed on a per-thread basis. This allows a single thread to be paused and then resumed. Only one thread can be executing at a given point in time. All other threads are waiting for their turn to execute. This allows the OS to exert a high degree of control over applications by controlling the execution of their threads.

1.3.1   Time slice, or quantum

Things are often not what they seem. When we go see a movie in a theater, the images seem to flow from one to another in a seamless way. In reality, many separate images are presented on the screen and our brain maps them together to form a continuous image.

OSs do a similar sleight of hand with threads. Multiple threads seem to execute at the same time. This is accomplished by giving each thread in the system a tiny amount of time to do its work and then switching to another one. This happens very quickly, and the user of the system is typically unaware that a switch has occurred. The amount of time a thread has to do its work is called a time slice, or quantum. The duration of the time slice varies based on the OS installed and the speed of the central processor. Listing 1.13 demonstrates that threads are periodically interrupted.

```
Module ModuleTimeSlice
    Sub Main()
        Dim whatToOutput As String
        Dim i As Integer
        Dim lastTick As Long
        Dim newTickCount As Long
        Dim opsPerTick As Long
        Dim offbyone As Long
        lastTick = System.Environment.TickCount   ❶
        opsPerTick = 0
        offbyone = 0
        whatToOutput = ""
        For i = 1 To 1000000
            newTickCount = System.Environment.TickCount
            If (lastTick = newTickCount) Then
                opsPerTick += 1
            Else
                If (lastTick = (newTickCount + 1)) Then
                    offbyone += 1
                    opsPerTick += 1
                    lastTick = newTickCount
                Else
                    Dim output As String
                    Dim numTicks As Long
                    numTicks = newTickCount - lastTick
                    output = String.Format("{0} {1}", numTicks, opsPerTick)
                    whatToOutput += output + vbCrLf
                    opsPerTick = 0
                    lastTick = newTickCount
                End If
            End If
        Next
        Console.WriteLine("OffByOne = " + offbyone.ToString())
        Console.WriteLine(whatToOutput)
    End Sub
End Module
```

❶ Retrieves the TickCount before the start of the loop

❷ Loops a large number of times

❸ Compares the current TickCount to the last one

❹ Checks to see if the last TickCount is one tick greater than the current tick

❺ Records the number of operations performed

❶ We start by retrieving the current tick from the OS. The TickCount property returns the number of milliseconds since the OS was rebooted. We store that value in the lastTick variable.

❷ To see the breaks in execution, we loop for a large number of times. Too small of a number here would not demonstrate the breaks in execution, since the task could be completed quickly.

❸ The first thing we do on each iteration is retrieve and store the current tick count. The idea is to capture how many milliseconds have passed since the last time we retrieved the value. We then check to see if the value has changed. If it hasn't we increment the number of operations that have been performed while the values were equal.

❹ If the values have changed we check to see if the new value is one greater than the old value. This would indicate that we moved from one millisecond to the next greater one. In my testing this didn't occur. This is as an indication that the amount of time the processor gives a thread is smaller than 1 millisecond.

❺ When a break of more than 1 millisecond occurs we determine the number of milliseconds that have elapsed and then record the results to a string and reset the counters. The frequency of this occurrence is a product of the load of the system, the power of the processor, and the number of iterations in the loop.

Listing 1.13 produces the following output:

	OffByOne = 0
16	177655
31	0
16	220041
15	395763

The first column contains how many milliseconds have passed when a break in the tick count occurred. The second column contains the number of iterations that were completed without a break occurring. If the thread had a processor dedicated to it there would be very even breaks, or not at all, in the tick count. As you can see, the breaks that do occur have a small amount of time between them. The amount of time a thread gets is based on the priority of the process it is executing in along with the priority associated with the thread.

A time slice is a very small unit of time. This helps provide the illusion that a thread has exclusive use of a processor. Each time that a processor switches from one thread to another is referred to as a context switch. In the next section we discuss context switching.

1.3.2 Context and context switching

There are many threads in existence in a typical system at any given point. A count of the threads from figure 1.3 yields over a hundred. Fortunately newer versions of Windows are good at dealing with multiple threads. A single processor executes one thread at a time. The thread has the processor's attention for one quantum, a time slice. After each quantum unit passes, the processor checks to see if another thread should have the processor. When the processor decides that a different thread should be executed, it saves the information the current thread requires to continue and switches to a different thread. This is called a context switch.

A high level of context switching is an indication of system load. A system that is switching excessively is said to be thrashing. The implication is that the processor is spending a great deal of time switching between threads and not performing as much work as if it were switching less frequently. High levels of context switching are generally associated with a shared resource being overutilized. When a resource isn't available, the OS pauses the thread that's requesting it. This allows other threads, which most likely aren't waiting for a resource, to execute.

One way that a context switch occurs is when a thread indicates that it has finished processing and that some other thread should be given the remainder of its time. This is accomplished using the Sleep method of the Thread class.

We'll discuss this in greater detail in section 5.3, but for now think of Sleep as a way for a thread to let the OS know that it would like to be idle for some period of time. The idea is that the thread detects that it should pause for a small amount of time to allow other things to happen. For example, if a thread is tasked with keeping a queue empty, it might pause periodically to allow multiple entries to be entered into the queue.

Sleep accepts several different types of parameters. One version of Sleep accepts an Integer indicating how many milliseconds the thread would like to be idle. If zero is passed in, it indicates that the thread wishes to yield the remainder of its time slice and continue executing on the next available time slice. This causes a context switch to occur. Listing 1.14 contains a class that uses a thread pool to execute a method on a different thread. The method continues to execute until changing the value of a Boolean flag stops it. The method calls Sleep with zero, which forces the thread to release the remainder of the current time slice to the operating system, forcing a context switch.

Listing 1.14 A class that generates a large number of context switches (C#)

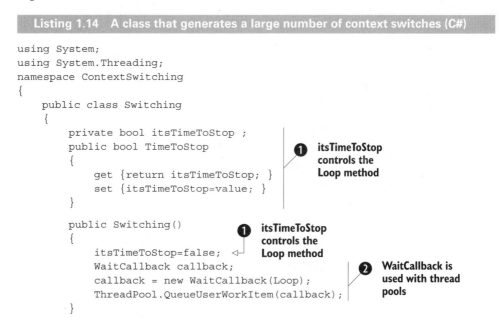

```csharp
using System;
using System.Threading;
namespace ContextSwitching
{
    public class Switching
    {
        private bool itsTimeToStop ;
        public bool TimeToStop
        {
            get {return itsTimeToStop; }
            set {itsTimeToStop=value; }
        }

        public Switching()
        {
            itsTimeToStop=false;
            WaitCallback callback;
            callback = new WaitCallback(Loop);
            ThreadPool.QueueUserWorkItem(callback);
        }
}
```

❶ itsTimeToStop controls the Loop method

❶ itsTimeToStop controls the Loop method

❷ WaitCallback is used with thread pools

```
        private void Loop(object state)
        {
            Thread.Sleep(500);
            while (!itsTimeToStop)
            {
                Thread.Sleep(0);
            }
        }
    }
}
```

❸ The Loop method executes until itsTimeToStop is true

❶ An important element of any thread is being able to control its termination. We use the `itsTimeToStop` flag to control the termination of the thread. Initially `itsTime-ToStop` is set to `false`, indicating that the `Loop` method should continue executing. To avoid interacting with the variable directly we use a property to manipulate its value. This is a good practice in general, and very important when dealing with multi-threaded development. This allows for a higher degree of control.

❷ To create a separate thread of execution we use a thread pool. These are the same steps we used in listing 1.12.

❸ The `Loop` method contains a `Sleep` statement that pauses execution for half of a second and then enters a loop where the current thread continually yields its time slice to the processor. To test the effects of this class on a system, we use a simple console application. Listing 1.15 contains the code of the console application that creates instances of the `Switching` class.

Listing 1.15   Console application that demonstrates context switching (C#)

```
using System;
namespace ContextSwitching
{
    class Class1
    {
        [STAThread]
        static void Main(string[] args)
        {
            RunTest(10);
            RunTest(5);
            RunTest(3);
            RunTest(1);
            RunTest(0);
        }
        static void RunTest(int numberOfWorkers )
        {
            string howMany;
            howMany= numberOfWorkers.ToString();
            long i;
            Switching[] switcher;
```

❶ The RunTest method is called with different parameters

❷ An array of Switching class is created

```
    switcher = new Switching[numberOfWorkers];
    for (i = 0;i <switcher.Length ;i++)
    {
      switcher[i] = new Switching();
    }
    Console.WriteLine("Created " + howMany + " workers");
      System.Threading.Thread.Sleep(5000);
    for (i = 0;i <switcher.Length ;i++)
    {
      switcher[i].TimeToStop = true;
    }
    Console.WriteLine("Stopped " + howMany + " workers");
    System.Threading.Thread.Sleep(5000);
  }
 }
}
```

❶ We call the RunTest method with a different parameter to create a different number
of workers. This demonstrates a varying level of context switching.

❷ The RunTest method creates an array of Switching objects, from listing 1.14.
We then pause the main thread for five seconds. This gives time for the other threads
to execute. After five seconds we set the TimeToStop property to false for each
Switching object.

This program writes the following output to the console:

```
Created 10 workers
Stopped 10 workers
Created 5 workers
Stopped 5 workers
Created 3 workers
Stopped 3 workers
Created 1 workers
Stopped 1 workers
Created 0 workers
Stopped 0 workers
```

We've reviewed what a context switch is; now let's examine how we can measure them.

1.3.3   Detecting context switching

The Performance Monitoring program (perfmon.exe) is useful in determining how
many context switches are occurring per second. In Windows 2000 the Performance
Monitoring program is located in the Administrative Tools group under Programs in
the Start menu. Figure 1.4 shows the impact of executing the program in listing 1.9.

The four "bumps" in the graph occurred during the time between when Created
x Workers was written to the console and when Stopped x Workers was written to the
console. Not surprisingly, the execution of zero workers did not produce a bump.

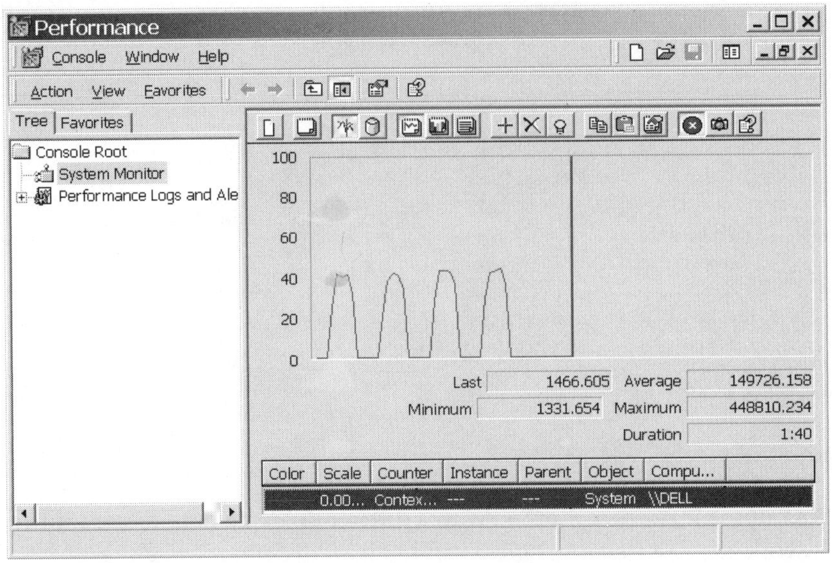

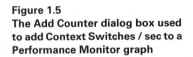

Figure 1.4 Performance Monitor during listing 1.9. The "bumps" correspond to the time between Created and Stopped.

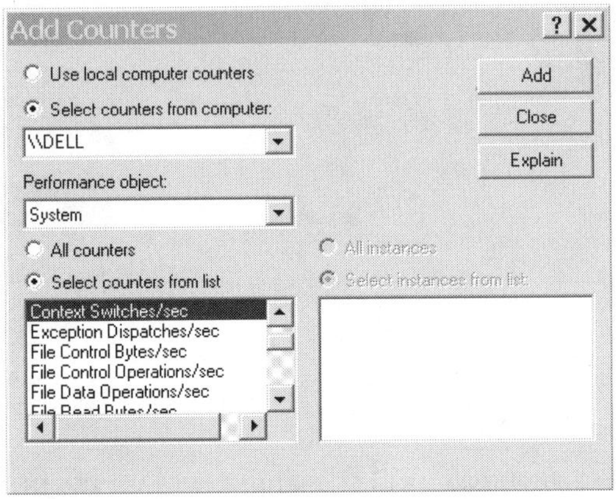

**Figure 1.5
The Add Counter dialog box used to add Context Switches / sec to a Performance Monitor graph**

Measuring the number of context switches that occur per second is a good way of troubleshooting an application. Figure 1.5 shows how to add the measure to Performance Monitor.

The OS determines when a context switch occurs. A thread can give the scheduler a hint that it has finished performing its operations, but it's up to the scheduler to determine if it will perform the context switch.

For more information on context switches, time slices, and thread scheduling, consult any book that covers the Windows platform.

CHAPTER 1   PROCESS AND THREAD BASICS

1.4   SUMMARY

This chapter serves as a review of the basic operating system concepts that relate to multithreaded development. It is by no means an exhaustive discussion but does serve to introduce the concepts. Understanding the underlying processes and threads is very important when you're doing multithreaded development. By being aware of how the OS interacts with threads you can develop programs that work with the OS rather than against it. By understanding what causes excessive context switching, you can develop programs that avoid that performance bottleneck.

In the next chapter we discuss the .NET framework from a multithreaded perspective.

C H A P T E R   2

.NET from a threading perspective

The Microsoft .NET framework was built with the knowledge that many of the applications written for it would contain multiple threads. Unlike with some platforms, where threading was an afterthought, the designers of .NET not only considered multi-threaded development needs, but also utilized multiple threads in the framework.

2.1   .NET ARCHITECTURE OVERVIEW

Throughout this book we'll examine the architecture of the .NET framework from a multithreaded perspective. Figure 2.1 shows the relationship between .NET and other elements of the OS, including Microsoft Internet Information Server (IIS).

We'll examine each of these, starting closest to the OS and working up.

2.1.1   Framework runtime

The .NET framework, which all managed applications utilize, executes on top of the OS. The runtime provides managed applications numerous services such as garbage collection, a common type system, and multithreaded support.

.NET differentiates between physical threads and logical threads because it is designed to support multiple platforms. Traditional multithreaded development on the Windows

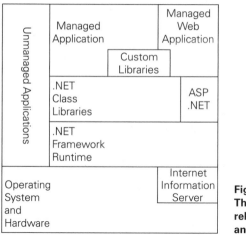

Figure 2.1
The .NET framework's relationship to OS, IIS, and unmanaged code

platform deals with physical threads. These physical threads are managed by the OS and created when the appropriate function of the Win32 application program interface (API) is called. The terms physical thread and OS thread can be used interchangeably. They both refer to the thread that's created and managed by the OS.

The .NET framework introduces the concept of a logical thread, created by the framework rather than by the OS. The framework manages logical threads. All interaction with logical threads occurs via the framework. Under the current implementation, the framework uses one physical thread for each logical thread. This could change in the future.

We revisit the services the runtime provides in later sections of this chapter.

2.1.2   .NET class libraries

The .NET class libraries provide a hierarchy of objects that encapsulate commonly needed programmatic constructs. While it is possible to write a .NET application without using the class libraries, it is unlikely, and would not be cost effective, which is why .NET applications are not presented as accessing the framework directly.

Object-oriented development relies heavily on class libraries. The majority of the learning curve associated with .NET revolves around learning the features that the class libraries provide. .NET provides support for custom multithreaded development by using the `System.Threading` namespace. Recall that a namespace is used in .NET to organize classes. Similar classes are grouped in the same namespace. We use namespaces to prevent collision of classes with the same name.

The majority of the focus of this book will be on the classes contained within the `System.Threading` namespace. One of the most frequently used classes in the `Threading` namespace is `Thread`, which allows an object to be associated with a logical thread. Just as a file object relates to an OS file, the `Thread` class relates to a thread of execution. This level of abstraction allows for easy creation and management of threads.

Many of the classes in the class library utilize multithreading in one form or another. As an example, the `WebClient` class in the `System.Net` namespace uses threads when methods such as `DownloadData` are invoked. Rather than putting the multi-threading burden on the caller of the method, the class internalizes the use of threads, providing an easy-to-use interface.

2.1.3   ASP .NET

ASP .NET is an important aspect of web development because it provides a high-performance solution to developing web applications. I've included it in the .NET class libraries section since it is essentially a subset of the library. This in no way diminishes the importance of this development environment; I view ASP .NET as the ideal web development tool. A thorough discussion of ASP .NET is outside the scope of this book.

One area where ASP.NET relates to multithreaded development is when a client application accesses an XML Web Service. XML Web Services are created using ASP .NET. Calling a method of an XML Web Service takes much longer to complete than a call to a local object. Rather than forcing the client to wait for the call to return, we can use multiple threads to continue processing other tasks. This creates a richer experience for the user of the application, as well as allowing for error recovery. XML Web Services are increasingly being used as a data access mechanism. This trend will most likely continue, increasing the need for clients that interact with them in a robust way.

2.1.4   Developing custom libraries

Custom library development is a key aspect of .NET. This is true in general, but especially so with respect to multithreaded development. By encapsulating multithreaded classes in reusable assemblies, you can achieve a high level of code reuse. Additionally, developers who are not versed in how to write multithreaded programs can use classes that utilize threads.

When developing custom libraries, it is important to consider threading implications. If the class can safely be accessed from multiple threads concurrently, the library is said to be thread-safe. Thread safety of a library should be documented. It is as important to state a library is thread-safe as it is to convey it is not. Knowing the thread safety allows developers using the library to know exactly how the classes in the library will react when manipulated by multiple threads.

2.1.5   Managed applications

Development of managed applications, that is, applications that utilize the .NET framework, is one of the most exciting ways to use multiple threads. Operations can be performed in the background while the user continues to work within the application. This is exactly what Microsoft Word does when Check Spelling As You Type is selected. As the user types, Word is checking the recently typed words against a dictionary. When the spell checker determines a word is misspelled, it places a red line under it, indicating it found something the user should examine. All of this is happening while the user continues to type.

Network operations are another area where threads are beneficial. Network operations, such as opening a file, can take a relatively long time to complete. If a single-threaded application accesses a file, all operations must pause until that operation completes. By using multiple threads, a managed application can access a remote file without suspending other operations.

There are many areas where multiple threads can be used; the key is using the new tool in an appropriate way.

2.2 GARBAGE COLLECTION

Garbage collection allows developers to focus on solving problems rather than managing memory. This section reviews garbage collection and then examines the role threads play in it. We start by discussing the need for memory management and explore the problems with traditional approaches.

Visual Basic and J++ developers take garbage collection for granted. They rightly assume that when they have finished with memory it will be disposed of correctly. For developers coming from C++ this isn't the case. Listing 2.1 is an example of a C++ program that does not free memory correctly.

Listing 2.1 Leaking program (C++)

```
#include "stdafx.h"
int main (int argc, char* argv[])
{
      for(int i=0;i< 10000000;i++)
      {
          char * c = new char[200];
      }
      return 0;
}
```

When this program executes, the memory usage grows rapidly, indicating that memory is not being freed. Figure 2.2 shows the increase in the private bytes of the process.

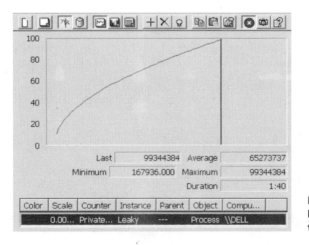

Figure 2.2
Private bytes used by the leaking program

It's easy to fix the leak in listing 2.1. Listing 2.2 contains the `delete` that should accompany the new statement.

Listing 2.2   Including the delete statement removes the leak (C++).

```cpp
#include "stdafx.h"
int main(int argc, char* argv[])
{
  for (int i=0;i< 10000000;i++)
  {
    char * c = new char[200];
    if (c != 0)
    {
      delete[] c;
    }
  }
  return 0;
}
```

Figure 2.3 demonstrates that the program no longer leaks. Notice the flat memory usage.

.NET takes care of memory management for managed applications. Listing 2.3 is the C# equivalent of listing 2.1. Notice that the memory is not released explicitly.

Listing 2.3   C# version of listing 2.1

```csharp
private void button1_Click(object sender, System.EventArgs e)
{
  for(int i=0;i< 10000000;i++)
  {
    char [] c = new char[200];
  }
}
```

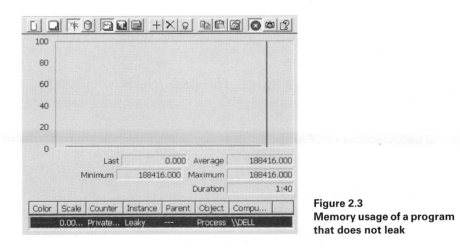

Figure 2.3
Memory usage of a program that does not leak

CHAPTER 2   .NET FROM A THREADING PERSPECTIVE

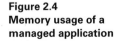

Last	0.000	Average	4827970
Minimum	1949696	Maximum	5296128
		Duration	1:40

| Color | Scale | Counter | Instance | Parent | Object | Compu... | |
| 0.00... | Private... | Allocati... | --- | | Process \\DELL | | |

Figure 2.4
Memory usage of a
managed application

Figure 2.4 shows the memory usage when the code in listing 2.3 executes. Notice that the memory used does not grow in an uncontrolled way.

Visual Basic is not immune to memory leaks; they just take a different form. Where Visual Basic has trouble is in the handling of circular references. A circular reference occurs whenever an instance of one class references an instance of another class that in turn references the original instance. Listing 2.4 is an example of a Visual Basic 6 circular reference leak.

Listing 2.4   Circular reference in Visual Basic 6

```
Private Function CreateCircular()
    Dim oA As New ClassA
    Dim oB As New ClassB
    Set oA.oClassB = oB
    Set oB.oClassA = oA
    Set oA = Nothing
    Set oB = Nothing
End Function

' Class A
Public oClassB As ClassB

Private Sub Class_Initialize()
    Debug.Print "Init A"
End Sub

Private Sub Class_Terminate()
    Debug.Print "Term A"
End Sub

' Class B
Public oClassA As ClassA
Private Sub Class_Initialize()
    Debug.Print "Init B"
End Sub
```

```
Private Sub Class_Terminate()
    Debug.Print "Term B"
End Sub
```

You can determine that the program is leaking by noticing the absence of the "Term B" and "Term A" statements in the immediate window. This is one of the reasons that the designers of .NET chose to go with garbage collection instead of reference counting as the means of managing memory. Recall that reference counting is a means of keeping track of how many objects are referencing an item. Each time an object gains a reference, it increments the reference count. When an object is finished with an item, it decrements the reference count of that item. When the reference count of an item reaches zero, it is removed from memory as part of the decrementing call.

The negative impact of garbage collection is that it introduces nondeterministic finalization. All that means is that you don't know exactly when, or even if, the Finalize method will execute.

To see that .NET really has fixed the circular reference problem, consider listing 2.5.

Listing 2.5 Circular reference in Visual Basic .NET (VB.NET)

```
Public Class Form1
    Inherits System.Windows.Forms.Form
. . .
Private Sub ButtonTestCircular_Click(ByVal sender As System.Object, ByVal e
As System.EventArgs) Handles ButtonTestCircular.Click
    MakeCircular()
    GC.Collect()
  End Sub
  Private Function MakeCircular()
    Dim oA As New ClassA()
    Dim oB As New ClassB()
    oA.oClassB = oB
    oB.oClassA = oA
  End Function
End Class

Public Class ClassA
  Public oClassB As ClassB
  Public Sub New()
    System.Diagnostics.Debug.WriteLine("New A")
  End Sub

  Protected Overrides Sub Finalize()
    MyBase.Finalize()
    System.Diagnostics.Debug.WriteLine("Finalize A")
  End Sub
End Class

Public Class ClassB
  Public oClassA As ClassA
```

```
  Public Sub New()
    System.Diagnostics.Debug.WriteLine("New B")
  End Sub

  Protected Overrides Sub Finalize()
    MyBase.Finalize()
    System.Diagnostics.Debug.WriteLine("Finalize B")
  End Sub
End Class
```

One thing you will notice is the addition of the GC.Collect to the testing method. GC.Collect tells the garbage collector to recover any unused memory. Typically there's no reason to call Collect. A better practice is to allow the framework to determine when garbage collection should be performed. The output from this program is as follows:

```
New A
New B
Finalize B
Finalize A
```

If you run it a few times you'll see that sometimes Finalize B is displayed before Finalize A. Other times it will reverse itself. This is an indication of the nondeterministic finalization we discussed earlier. The important thing to notice is that both Finalize methods execute.

2.2.1   Finalization

Finalization is another area where threads play an important role. If a class contains a Finalize method, it is invoked on a thread dedicated to that purpose. For this reason the Finalize method should not rely on thread local values. Listing 2.6 contains an example of a class with a Finalize method.

> **Listing 2.6   Example of using the Finalize method (C#)**

```
using System;
using System.Threading;
using System.Collections;
namespace Dennis
{
  public class
Data
  {
    static public void MakeData()   ❶   Creates and starts
    {                                    the thread
      Thread t= new Thread(new ThreadStart(ThreadMethod));
      t.Name="Data Thread";
      t.Priority = ThreadPriority.BelowNormal;
      t.IsBackground=true;
      t.Start();
    }
```

```
static long instanceIdCounter=0;
long instanceId;
ArrayList myData;
public Data()           ❷ Defines the class
{                          constructor
  instanceId = Interlocked.Increment(ref instanceIdCounter);
  myData =new ArrayList();
  Random rnd = new Random(System.Environment.TickCount);
  String s;
  s= new String('c',rnd.Next(5000,60000));
  myData.Add(s);
}

~Data()       ❸ Method invoked when
{                the class is destroyed
  Thread finalThread;
  finalThread = Thread.CurrentThread;
  string message;
  message=string.Format(
    "Finalize: Id={0} Name={1} Priority={2}",
    instanceId,finalThread.Name,
    finalThread.Priority);
  Console.WriteLine(message);
}

static private void ThreadMethod()   ❹ Method the new
{                                       thread executes
  string message;                       initially
  message=string.Format(
    "{0} Enter Thread Method",
    Thread.CurrentThread.Name);
  Console.WriteLine(message);
  for (int i=0;i<10;i++)
  {
    Data tmpData = new Data();
  }
  message=string.Format(
    "{0} Exit Thread Method",
    Thread.CurrentThread.Name);
  Console.WriteLine(message);
}
  }
}
```

It's not important to understand all of the things that are happening in listing 2.6.
What is important is to understand that the method named ~Data is the Finalize
method. It will be invoked when the garbage collector frees the class it is associated
with. We'll briefly go over each of the methods of the Data class.

❶ The static `MakeData` method makes it easy to test the `Data` class. It creates an instance of the `Thread` class and associates it with the `ThreadMethod`. It then starts the new thread. The following is an example of how `MakeData` is called:

```
System.Threading.Thread.CurrentThread.Name="Main";
Data.MakeData();
Console.WriteLine("Hit Enter to Exit");
Console.ReadLine();
```

Notice that an instance of the `Data` class is not required to call the method. That's because the method is static.

❷ The `Data` constructor increments a static counter. This allows each instance of the `Data` class to be assigned an instance ID. Since the instance ID is monotonically increasing, we know that an instance with a higher value was created after one with a smaller value. This helps demonstrate that the order of invocation of the finalization methods is not the same as the order of creation. The `Interlocked` class allows for operations that are guaranteed to complete safely in a multithreaded environment.

❸ The `Finalize` method is invoked when the memory the class uses is reclaimed. Notice that C# uses the ~{class name} approach to identify the `Finalize` method. In Visual Basic .NET overrides the `Finalize` method. The following is the Visual Basic .NET version of the `Finalize` method:

```
Protected Overrides Sub Finalize()
    MyBase.Finalize()
    Dim finalThread As Thread
    finalThread = Thread.CurrentThread
    Dim message As String
    message = String.Format( _
      "Finalize: Id={0} Name={1} Priority={2}", _
      instanceId, finalThread.Name, finalThread.Priority)
    Console.WriteLine(message)
End Sub
```

❹ The `ThreadMethod` is associated with the thread that is created by the static `Make-Data` method. It creates ten instances of the `Data` class and then exits. When this program is executed, it produces results similar to the following:

```
Hit Enter to Exit
Data Thread Enter Thread Method
Data Thread Exit Thread Method
Finalize: Id=4 Name= Priority=Highest
Finalize: Id=2 Name= Priority=Highest
Finalize: Id=1 Name= Priority=Highest
Finalize: Id=3 Name= Priority=Highest

Finalize: Id=10 Name= Priority=Highest
Finalize: Id=9 Name= Priority=Highest
Finalize: Id=8 Name= Priority=Highest
Finalize: Id=7 Name= Priority=Highest
```

```
Finalize: Id=6 Name= Priority=Highest
Finalize: Id=5 Name= Priority=Highest
```

Each time the program executes, the results will likely vary:

```
Hit Enter to Exit
Data Thread Enter Thread Method
Data Thread Exit Thread Method
Finalize: Id=5 Name= Priority=Highest
Finalize: Id=4 Name= Priority=Highest
Finalize: Id=3 Name= Priority=Highest
Finalize: Id=2 Name= Priority=Highest
Finalize: Id=1 Name= Priority=Highest

Finalize: Id=10 Name= Priority=Highest
Finalize: Id=9 Name= Priority=Highest
Finalize: Id=8 Name= Priority=Highest
Finalize: Id=6 Name= Priority=Highest
Finalize: Id=7 Name= Priority=Highest
```

Notice that the thread name is empty. The thread name property lets us assign a name to a thread that makes it easier to identify a thread during debugging. The main thread is named "Main" and the thread that creates the data is named "Data Thread," so where does this unnamed thread come from? The thread is created by the runtime and is dedicated to calling the Finalize method of objects that are freed. Notice that the priority of the thread is set to Highest. The Finalize thread is intended to execute Finalize methods. Those methods should be designed to execute very quickly. A Finalize method should only be used to free resources that are not managed. Finalization should only be used when needed. It adds a considerable amount of overhead to the cleanup of elements that are no longer needed.

2.3 SECURITY

One area in which .NET has made considerable improvements is security. Under .NET not only are users restricted based on their access rights, but code is only allowed to access resources based upon a set of rules called a security policy. A policy takes into consideration evidence that is gathered about code. This evidence includes things such as where the code came from, if it is signed or not, and so on, which is then evaluated against security policies. Evidence-based security allows the runtime to exert a high degree of control over threads accessing resources.

The level of trust associated with an assembly is dependent upon the location it is loaded from. Recall that an assembly is nothing more than a way of packaging up pieces of code, generally into a DLL. If you think about it, you generally trust programs that are on your computer more than you do things that are on a web server of a different company. Additionally, you trust programs that are in certain directories more than you do others. For example, if a program is installed in "Program Files" you generally feel more secure about it than you do a program installed in a Temp or Download directory.

When a thread is created, it is bound by the same restrictions as the thread that creates it. This ensures that malicious code does not circumvent the security policy of a machine and gain access to restricted resources, such as a hard disk drive.

Often more than one assembly is included in a program. Suppose you had one assembly that processed credit cards. The assembly itself is very well trusted. Suppose you also had an assembly that was trusted very little. If that untrusted assembly called a method in the credit card assembly, the trust level would be based on the untrusted assembly. Otherwise malicious code could manipulate trusted code and gain access to resources that were restricted by the security policy. When a function in an assembly calls one in another assembly, the security of the called function will be based on the trust level and security of the calling assembly. This level of trust will be the minimum of the two levels.

Security is a complex topic, and complete coverage of it is beyond the scope of this book.

2.4 SUMMARY

We've seen how .NET is built from the ground up with support for multithreading. This makes writing multithreaded applications easier than was previously possible. The runtime itself uses multiple threads to perform concurrent actions. One area where multiple threads are used is in the garbage collection system.

Garbage collection frees developers from managing memory within an application. This allows them to focus on solving problems rather than allocating and freeing memory. Traditionally, the majority of software defects occur as a result of memory management issues. .NET eliminates memory-related defects by utilizing garbage collection, resulting in high-quality code.

Security in applications is becoming increasingly important. .NET has robust security features that help developers produce applications that protect their users from malicious code. One way this is accomplished is through the use of evidence-based security. We briefly discussed the types of evidence and saw how they are combined with a security policy to determine what resources are available during execution.

In the next chapter we discuss multithreading in .NET in greater detail.

C H A P T E R   3

Multithreading in .NET

Microsoft's .NET framework is an exciting new platform for software development, with extensive support for multithreaded development. But, as we said in chapter 1, before we launch into a new area, we should examine the basics. In this case, we'll begin by examining the concept of an application domain and how it relates to a process. Once we have that under our belts, we'll look at the two classes of threads—logical and physical—and then examine the use of delegates to perform asynchronous execution.

3.1 APPLICATION DOMAIN

In .NET every application executes within an application domain. Application domains are similar to Win32 processes in many ways but differ in several important areas. The next section compares application domains to Win32 processes.

3.1.1 An application domain vs. a process

Historically a process has been used to isolate one application from another. As we discussed in chapter 1 a process is a collection of physical threads of execution manipulating resources. When one process terminates it generally does not affect another process. Just as .NET extended the concept of a physical thread to a logical thread, it takes the concept of a process and extends it to an application domain. One or more application domains are housed within a single Win32 process. One or more logical threads

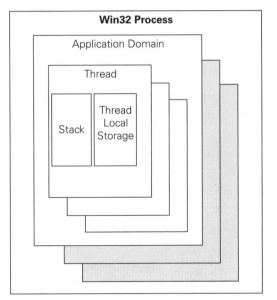

Win32 Process

Application Domain

Thread

Stack

Thread Local Storage

Figure 3.1
A Win32 process contains one
or more application domains.

execute within the application domain, just as one or more physical threads execute within a process. Figure 3.1 shows the relationship of an application domain to a process.

The `AppDomain` class is used to access application domains in .NET.

3.1.2   The AppDomain class

The `AppDomain` class allows for manipulation of the current application domain as well as creation of additional application domains. There are times that the current application domain needs to be retrieved, such as when a value is being stored at an application level using `GetData` and `SetData`. These functions give all assemblies contained within an application domain the ability to retrieve and set global values. One situation where this would be extremely beneficial is when an application should behave differently when in a development environment versus a production environment.

There are two ways of retrieving the current domain. `System.AppDomain.CurrentDomain` and `System.Threading.Thread.GetDomain` both allow access to the domain in which the statements are executed. The following example demonstrates that the `CurrentDomain` property is equal to the domain returned by the `GetDomain` method:

```
AppDomain appDomain1 = AppDomain.CurrentDomain;
AppDomain appDomain2 = System.Threading.Thread.GetDomain();
if (AppDomain.ReferenceEquals(appDomain1,appDomain2))
{
  Debug.WriteLine("The same");
}
```

Once we've retrieved a domain we can utilize some of its more commonly used methods and properties:

- `BaseDirectory`—Contains the starting location at which .NET will look for assemblies

- `DynamicDirectory`—Specifies where .NET should look for dynamically created assemblies

- `FriendlyName`—Equates to the filename of the assembly

- `RelativeSearchPath`—Specifies a path where .NET should look for private assemblies

- `ShadowCopyFiles`—Controls if dependent assemblies are copied to the domain's cache

- `SetupInformation`—Contains a reference to an `AppDomainSetup` object that contains information about the installation of the application

- `Evidence`—Contains a reference to an instance of the `Evidence` class that is used by the security policy

- `CreateDomain`—Creates an application domain within the current Win32 process

- `SetData`—Associates a value with a specified name

- `GetData`—Retrieves a value based on a supplied name

3.1.3 CreateDomain

A Win32 process can contain more than one application domain. `CreateDomain` is a static method of the `AppDomain` object that creates a domain within the Win32 process. It's important to note that this does not create a new thread within the process but instead only creates a domain where a thread can execute. Listing 3.1 uses `CreateDomain` and also creates a logical thread to execute in the new domain.

Listing 3.1 An example of using CreateDomain

```
using System;
using System.Threading;
using System.Security.Policy;
namespace AppDomainTest1
{
  class ClassAppDomainTest
  {
    [STAThread]
    static void Main(string[] args)           ❶ Static entry point
    {                                            to the program
      Console.WriteLine("Enter Main");
      ClassAppDomainTest c = new ClassAppDomainTest();
      c.Main();
    }
    void Main()
    {
      AppDomain current;
      current = AppDomain.CurrentDomain;
```

```
   Thread.CurrentThread.Priority = ThreadPriority.BelowNormal;
   object o= current.GetData("autostart");
   if (o == null)
   {
      Thread otherThread;
      otherThread = new Thread(new ThreadStart(NewThread));
      otherThread.Start();
      current.SetData("autostart",false);
      current.ExecuteAssembly("AppDomainTest1.exe");
   }
   Thread.Sleep(1000);
   string message;
   message=string.Format(" {0}",current.FriendlyName);
   Console.WriteLine(message);
   }
   void NewThread()
   {
      AppDomain otherDomain;
      otherDomain = AppDomain.CreateDomain("otherDomain");
      otherDomain.SetData("autostart",false);
      otherDomain.ExecuteAssembly("AppDomainTest1.exe");
   }
 }
}
```

❷ **Method that creates a domain**

This program produces the following output:

```
Enter Main
Enter Main
Enter Main
 AppDomainTest1.exe
 otherDomain
 AppDomainTest1.exe
```

❶ The first `Enter Main` statement occurs when the program is initially loaded. The first thing the main thread does is create an instance of the class containing the static `Main` method and invokes the instance's `Main` method. This is a common way of overcoming the need for a static entry point into a console-based program.

❷ The `CreateDomain` method that creates a domain and names it the specified name. In this case the new domain inherits its security and evidence from the current domain.

3.2   THREADS

A thread is a path of execution. Every program contains at least one thread. .NET differentiates between logical and physical threads. As we discussed in chapter 2, a physical thread is an OS thread. Just as the OS manages other resources it manages physical threads. .NET introduces the concept of a logical thread. A logical thread is managed by the .NET framework and provides additional functionality beyond a physical thread.

3.2.1 Logical threads

Under the Win32 implementation of .NET there is a one-for-one mapping between physical threads and logical threads. When additional platforms are supported by .NET it is very possible that there may be more than one logical thread associated with each physical thread. For example, if an OS didn't provide support for multiple physical threads in a process, the .NET runtime might supply that functionality using logical threads. Logical threads in .NET are accessed using the `System.Threading` namespace.

Threading namespace

The `Threading` namespace contains the classes associated with creating threads under managed code.

Table 3.1 contains the most important classes in the `Threading` namespace.

Table 3.1 Commonly used classes in the Threading namespace

Class	Description	Section/Chapter Discussed
AutoResetEvent	A synchronization mechanism that resets itself from the signaled state.	8.2
Interlocked	A class that provides access to simple atomic operations.	7.2
ManualResetEvent	A synchronization mechanism that stays in the signaled state until it is explicitly reset.	8.4
Monitor	One of the most commonly used synchronization mechanisms. It allows for restriction of access to an object.	7.4
Mutex	A class that allows for the creation of mutually exclusive blocks of code.	8.5
ReaderWriterLock	A class that allows for multiple readers and a single writer. This allows for high-performance solutions when the majority of the access to a data element is to read a value.	9
SynchronizationLockException	An exception that's raised when an attempt is made to access a Monitor class method that requires synchronization while not in a synchronized block of code.	13.2.4
Thread	A class that contains methods for creating and manipulating logical threads.	4
ThreadAbortException	An exception that's raised when a thread is terminated using the Abort method of the Thread class.	13.2.1
ThreadExceptionEventArgs	A class that contains data used when a ThreadException occurs.	12.4
ThreadInterruptedException	An exception that's raised when a thread is interrupted using the Interrupt method of the Thread class.	13.2.2

continued on next page

Table 3.1   Commonly used classes in the Threading namespace *(continued)*

Class	Description	Section/Chapter Discussed
ThreadPool	A class that provides an easy way of performing multithreaded operations by reusing multiple threads.	10
ThreadStateException	An exception that's raised when the thread is in a state that is invalid for a particular method.	13.2.3
Timeout	A class that contains a static public field used to represent an infinite wait.	5.3.1
Timer	A means of executing a method at a regular interval.	14.3
WaitHandle	A base class that provides a means of restricting access to a resource by having one or more threads wait for it to become available.	8.1
LockCookie	A structure used to store lock information when a lock is converted from a reader lock to a writer lock.	9.2.3
ThreadStart	A delegate used to represent a method that is the entry point for a new thread.	3.2.1
TimerCallback	A delegate used with the Timer class to define the method that's executed when the Timer's timeout occurs.	12.3.1
WaitCallback	A class that is used with a ThreadPool class to enter a work item into the queue.	12.3.2
WaitOrTimerCallback	A class that is used with a WaitHandle derived class. It is invoked when the WaitHandle class becomes signaled or a timeout occurs.	12.3.3
ApartmentState	An enumeration that indicates the threading state of an apartment.	16.2.1
ThreadPriority	An enumeration that contains the priorities a thread can be assigned.	5.7.1
ThreadState	An enumeration that contains the valid states a thread can be in.	4.4

This is an overview of the classes in the `Threading` namespace. The `Thread` class and the `ThreadStart` delegate are critical to managed threading. Without them it would be impossible to create multithreaded managed programs in the .NET framework.

Thread class

The `Thread` class represents a managed thread. The `CurrentThread` property is used to retrieve a reference to the currently executing managed thread. This is similar to the `AppDomain.GetDomain` method we discussed earlier. The following is an example of using the `CurrentThread` property:

```
Dim thisThread As System.Threading.Thread
thisThread = System.Threading.Thread.CurrentThread
```

Table 3.2 contains the frequently used properties and methods of the `Thread` class and where they are described in this book.

Table 3.2   The Thread class's properties and methods

Property/Method	Description	Section Discussed
ApartmentState	Controls how a thread interacts with COM objects	16.2.1
CurrentThread	Retrieves the instance of the Thread class that is associated with the currently executing logical thread	3.2.1
IsAlive	Indicates if a thread is in an active state	4.4.1
IsBackground	Used to determine if a thread executing will cause its application domain to continue to exist	5.4
IsThreadPoolThread	A Boolean that indicates if a thread is managed by a thread pool	10.3.2
Name	Used to help identify a thread	5.2
Priority	Used to control the scheduling of a thread	5.7.1
ThreadState	Returns a value indicating the state of a thread	4.4.2
Abort	Signals a thread that it should terminate	4.3
AllocateDataSlot	Used to allocate thread local storage that is not associated with a name	11.2
AllocateNamedDataSlot	Used to allocate thread local storage that is associated with a name	11.3
FreeNamedDataSlot	Used to free thread local storage that is associated with a name	11.3
GetData	Retrieves a value from thread local storage	11.2
GetDomain	Retrieves the application domain the thread is contained within	3.1.2
GetNamedDataSlot	Allows access to a named thread local storage location	11.3
Interrupt	Signals a thread that is in the Sleep state that it should become active	5.3.2
Join	Causes the calling thread to wait until a timeout occurs or the requested thread terminates	4.3.3
ResetAbort	Cancels a call for a thread to Abort	4.3.2
Resume	Allows a thread that has been suspended to resume	5.5.2
SetData	Used to store values in thread local storage	11.2
Sleep	Causes the current thread to pause its execution for a period of time	5.3.1
Start	Invokes the thread delegate creating an new logical thread	4.2
Suspend	Signals a thread to pause its execution	5.5.1

ThreadStart delegate

The `ThreadStart` delegate is used to associate a method with a newly created thread. As we discussed in chapter 1, a delegate is a way to associate a thread with a method that is to be executed on that thread. Delegates are a powerful construct in .NET.

3.2.2 Physical threads

Managed threads provide a high degree of flexibility and control. There are times that access to the physical thread is required. In those cases we use `System.Diagnostics.Process` and `System.Diagnostics.ProcessThread`.

System.Diagnostics.Process

The `Process` class represents a Win32 process. To retrieve an instance of the `Process` class that's associated with the currently executing Win32 process, we use the static method `GetCurrentProcess`. The following is an example of using the `GetCurrentProcess` method:

```
Process thisProcess= Process.GetCurrentProcess();
```

Once we have an instance of the current process, we can examine it. For our purposes the most important property of the `Process` object is the `Threads` property. The `Threads` property is a `ProcessThreadCollection`. The `ProcessThreadCollection` supports the `GetEnumerator` method. This means it can be used with C#'s `ForEach` operator. The following displays the IDs of each thread to the debug window:

```
Process thisProcess= Process.GetCurrentProcess();
foreach (ProcessThread aPhysicalThread in  thisProcess.Threads)
{
  Debug.WriteLine( aPhysicalThread.Id.ToString());
}
```

Notice there are a considerable number of threads, the majority of which were created to display the threads in the process. When using the `Diagnostics` namespace, remember that inspecting a portion of the system may change the behavior of that part of the system.

System.Diagnostics.ProcessThread

A physical thread is represented using the `ProcessThread` object. Table 3.3 contains selected `ProcessThread` properties and methods.

Table 3.3 The ProcessThread Class's Properties and Methods

Property/Method	Description	Section Discussed
BasePriority	Used to calculate the CurrentPriority of a thread.	5.7.1
CurrentPriority	The priority that the thread is currently operating at based on any priority boosts and the priority of the containing process.	5.7.1
Id	Each thread has an operating system assigned unique identifier. The Id property exposes that value.	5.7.3
PriorityBoostEnabled	Determines if a thread is eligible for a temporary boost in priority.	5.7.1
PriorityLevel	Used to set a thread to a predefined range of priority levels contained within the ThreadPriorityLevel enumeration.	5.7.1
ThreadState	An indication of the thread's state.	5.6
Ideal Processor	Used to give the operating system scheduler a hint as to which processor the thread should be executed on.	5.7.3
Processor Affinity	Used to restrict a thread to a particular processor or processors.	5.7.2
ResetIdealProcessor	Clears any previously assigned ideal processors.	5.7.3

The `ProcessThread` class allows for relatively low-level manipulation of threads. It should be used with care since misusing it may result in poor performance, or even system instability.

3.3 BENEFITS OF .NET TO MULTITHREADING

There are many benefits to doing multithreaded development in the .NET environment. Since a thread is a managed element, the amount of effort required to create and manage threads is greatly reduced. As with all managed resources, the framework ensures threads are disposed of properly. Additionally, any resources utilized by a thread are also managed by the runtime.

3.3.1 Advantages of objects

Knowing exactly when a thread comes into existence and when it terminates is a very important aspect of multithreaded development. For example, suppose you were tasked with developing a server that processes requests. One or more threads will be tasked with processing those requests. It is important that the thread-processing requests be created before those requests arrive, or soon after, to ensure the entries are handled in a timely fashion.

In traditional Win32 software development, a thread was created using a Win32 API call. A handle was returned from the call that was used to interact with the control. In .NET we use the `Thread` class to create a new thread. The `Thread` class contains all methods and properties required to manage a thread. This provides a single point for finding all `Thread`-related methods.

A fundamental object-oriented concept is that an object should contain the methods that are related to it. That's what the `Thread` class does. It contains those methods required to interact with a logical thread. By having an object that represents a logical thread, it becomes very easy to write multithreaded applications.

3.3.2 Asynchronous execution of delegates

There are several ways of executing methods on a different thread. One way is to use asynchronous execution of a delegate. This has the benefits of the method executing on a different thread while requiring one of the lower levels of effort. In the next chapter we discuss the more flexible way of utilizing multiple threads. Listing 3.2 contains an updated version of the `Cat` object we discussed in chapter 1.

Listing 3.2   A modified ClassCat that utilizes a delegate's BeginInvoke method (VB.NET)

```
Imports System.Threading
Public Class ClassCat
    Private Delegate Sub DoStuff(ByVal howMuch As Integer)
    Private async As DoStuff
    Public Delegate Sub DidSomething(ByVal message As String)
    Private notify As DidSomething
    Private sleepTime As Integer
    Private name As String
    Private rnd As Random
    Private actions() As String = {"Eat", "Drink", "Take a bath", _
        "Wander around", "Use litter box", "Look out window", _
        "Scratch furniture", "Scratch carpet", "Play with toy", "Meow"}
    Private callback As AsyncCallback
    Public Sub New(ByVal name As String, ByVal notify As DidSomething)
        sleepTime = 1000
        rnd = New Random(Environment.TickCount)
        Me.name = name
        Me.notify = notify
    End Sub

    Private Function WhichAction() As String
        Dim which As Integer
        which = rnd.Next(actions.Length)
        Return actions(which)
    End Function

    Public Sub DoCatStuff(ByVal howMuch As Integer
        Dim i As Integer
        For i = 0 To howMuch - 1
```

Defines a delegate that is used to perform asynchronous execution ①

```
                If (rnd.Next(100) > 80) Then
                    notify(name + ": """ + WhichAction() + """ ")
                Else
                    notify(name + ": ""Zzz"" ")
                    Thread.Sleep(sleepTime)
                End If
            Next
        End Sub
        Private Sub Finished(ByVal ar As IAsyncResult)
            notify(name + ": Finished")
        End Sub
        Public Sub Go(ByVal howMuch As Integer)
            Dim state As Object
            callback = New AsyncCallback(AddressOf Finished)
            async = New DoStuff(AddressOf DoCatStuff)
            async.BeginInvoke(howMuch, callback, state)
        End Sub
    End Sub
End Class
```

❷ Creates an instance of the DoStuff delegate and then calls BeginInvoke

❶ To take advantage of asynchronous delegate execution, we need a delegate to associate with the method we wish to execute. The `DoStuff` delegate is private to the `Class-Cat` class. We need an instance of the `DoStuff` delegate to utilize. The `async` private data member is used to store the reference to the instance.

❷ The public method `Go` is used to create an instance of the `DoStuff` delegate. Part of the creation process is to associate the delegate with a method to execute. Visual Basic uses the `AddressOf` keyword to differentiate between a method and a reference to that method. Once the `async` variable contains a reference to a new `DoStuff` dele-gate, we can use the `BeginInvoke` method to start the asynchronous execution of the `DoCatStuff` method.

Listing 3.3 contains code of the main module that utilizes the `ClassCat` class.

Listing 3.3   The main module that uses ClassCat (VB.NET)

```
Module Module1
    Sub Main()
        Dim notify As ClassCat.DidSomething
        notify = New ClassCat.DidSomething(AddressOf OutputLine)

        Dim oTiger As ClassCat
        oTiger = New ClassCat("Tiger", notify)
        oTiger.Go(10)

        Dim oGarfield As ClassCat
        oGarfield = New ClassCat("Garfield", notify)
        oGarfield.Go(10)

        Console.WriteLine("Press enter to exit")
        Console.ReadLine()
    End Sub
```

❶ One instance of ClassCat named Tiger

❷ Another named Garfield

```
Sub OutputLine(ByVal message As String)
    Console.WriteLine(message)
End Sub
End Module
```

❶ This example is very similar to that in chapter 1. One major difference is that the execution of the `DoCatStuff` method occurs on a different thread. The `oTiger` variable is a reference to an instance of the `ClassCat`. When the `Go` method of the `oTiger` method is invoked, an instance of the `DoStuff` delegate is created and `BeginInvoke` is called on it. The `Go` method returns as soon as it has invoked the `BeginInvoke` method. This will be before the `DoCatStuff` method has completed.

❷ To see that the execution occurs on different timelines it helps to have two instances of `ClassCat`. The second instance has a different name but shares the same `DidSomething` delegate.

The program produces the following output:

```
Press enter to exit
Tiger: "Zzz"
Garfield: "Zzz"
Tiger: "Zzz"
Garfield: "Drink"
Garfield: "Zzz"
Tiger: "Zzz"
Garfield: "Zzz"
Tiger: "Zzz"
Garfield: "Zzz"
Tiger: "Take a bath"
Tiger: "Zzz"
Garfield: "Zzz"
Tiger: "Zzz"
Garfield: "Zzz"
Tiger: "Zzz"
Garfield: "Zzz"
Tiger: "Meow"
Tiger: "Zzz"
Garfield: "Zzz"
Tiger: Finished
Garfield: "Zzz"
Garfield: Finished
```

Notice that the two "cats'" output is commingled. If the execution were occurring on the same thread, the Tiger output would be separate from the Garfield output.

Asynchronous delegates are an easy way to execute methods on different threads. There are limitations on how this should be used. The source of these limitations is related to asynchronous delegates using a thread pool to do their asynchronous execution. Thread pools are limited in size. Because the number of threads that can exist in a thread pool is restricted, methods invoked in thread pools should be short-lived. This restriction is often too severe for many problems. Because not every problem can be solved using asynchronous delegates, it's important to understand how to do multi-threading using the `Thread` class in the `Threading` namespace. That's where we pick up in the next chapter.

3.4 SUMMARY

This chapter has introduced some fundamental elements of multithreading in the .NET framework. Application domains provide the framework with a way of determining the boundaries of an application. Application domains are very similar to the Win32 process within which they live. Each application domain contains one or more logical threads that execute a series of instructions.

Logical threads are represented in the .NET framework using the `System.Threading.Thread` class. This class is used to create, control, and manage logical threads. There are times that it is necessary to manipulate physical threads; to do so the .NET framework includes the `System.Diagnostics.Process` and `System.Diagnostics.ProcessThread` classes. These classes allow access to all physical threads on a system, not just those related to the .NET framework.

.NET provides many benefits to developers. This is especially true with regards to multithreaded development. Since the .NET framework is object-oriented, all methods needed to manipulate a logical thread are contained in the `System.Threading.Thread` class. This grouping makes it very easy to find the methods to manipulate a thread.

The `System.Threading.Thread` class is not the only way to execute a method on a different thread. We discussed the asynchronous execution of delegates. While this approach is simpler to implement than using the `System.Threading.Thread` class, it lacks flexibility.

In the next chapter we dig into the means of creating, destroying, and interacting with logical threads.

CHAPTER 4

Thread life cycle

So far we have talked about multithreading concepts and how they relate to .NET. We are now going to explore how threads are created, why they go away, and how we can make them go away. At the end of the chapter we will look at how we can determine what a thread is doing. All examples, available in both VB.NET and C#, are available from the publisher's web site.

We will alternate between C# and VB.NET, showing how close the languages are to each other with regard to the use of threads. Also, we will examine the differences that exist. To demonstrate, we will use an implementation of a bubble sort to sort an array of randomly generated numbers. The bubble sort algorithm is easily understood and inefficient, which is good. Because it is inefficient it allows us time to examine it during execution.

In this chapter all examples will be console applications, allowing us to focus on the concepts rather than be distracted by unrelated implementation issues. Each example includes at least two classes per section. One will contain the main entry point associated with console applications. The other will contain the code relating to the array of values and the creation of the threads that operate on those values.

In general, threads should be associated with the data elements they operate on, supporting the object-oriented concepts of data protection and abstraction. The user of the class need not be concerned with the creation of the thread. Instead the user calls methods on the class and allows the class to keep track of the threading information. Including threads as elements of a class is a powerful concept, which is why we introduce it this early in the discussion.

4.1 CREATING A THREAD

The process of launching a new thread can be broken down into three steps:

1 Define the method that will serve as the entry point for the thread.

2 Declare and create an instance of a thread start delegate that is used to associate the entry point with the thread.

3 Create an instance of the Thread class, passing in the thread start delegate to the constructor.

4.1.1 Defining the thread's entry point

Suppose that you wanted to sort an array of numbers from smallest to largest. For demonstration purposes we will use a simple bubble sort since it is an algorithm most developers are familiar with. The process starts by creating a method that will be the entry point for the new thread, in this case SortAscending. This means that the method will be invoked, much as if it had been called directly; however, the method will execute on a different thread than its caller. We will discuss this in greater detail in the next section. The method can either be static or an instance method associated with an instance of a class (listing 4.1).

Listing 4.1 Defining a thread's entry point (C#)

```
public class ClassThreadExample_1
{
  long[] NumbersToSort;          ← Declares an
  . . .                             array of longs
  private void SortAscending()   ← Defines a method associated
  {                                 with the new thread

    for (int i= 0;i < NumbersToSort.Length ;i++)
    {
      for (int j=0;j<i;j++)
      {
        if (NumbersToSort[i] < NumbersToSort[j])
        {
          Swap(ref NumbersToSort[i],ref NumbersToSort[j]);
        }
      }
    }
  }
  private void Swap(ref long First,ref long Second)
  {
    // Swap the values in First and Second
    long TempNumber = First;
```

```
   First = Second;
   Second = TempNumber;
 }

. . .
```

In listing 4.1 it is an instance method. This means that the thread will have access to all instance and static/shared variables contained within a particular instance of `ClassThreadExample_1`.

4.1.2 Creating an instance of the ThreadStart delegate

The way that the method is associated with a thread is through the use of the `ThreadStart` delegate that is located in the `System.Threading` namespace. Chapter 12 discusses delegates in detail. For now, assume that the `ThreadStart` delegate is the way that a method is associated with a thread. When the delegate is created, the name of the method to execute is passed in to the constructor. Before we can create an instance of the delegate, we should declare a variable to allow us to reference the new delegate.

```
ThreadStart ThreadStartDelegate;
```

We're now ready to create an instance of the `ThreadStart` delegate and associate it with a method to execute:

```
ThreadStartDelegate = new ThreadStart(SortAscending);
```

The name of the method is not included in quotes. `ThreadStart` expects a method name, not a string, as the parameter to its constructor. The method cannot have parameters nor can it have a return value. This is the type of method that the `ThreadStart` delegate is expecting. Chapter 6 discusses communication between threads. Since the method associated with the thread cannot accept a parameter, it is not possible to pass any information to the new thread during its construction. Instead, if the thread is associated with an instance method, it will have access to all instance variables contained within the instance of the class it is contained within.

> **ThreadStart** `ThreadStart` is a delegate that is used to associate a method with a `Thread`. An instance of the delegate is passed in to the thread constructor so that the thread knows what delegate to invoke.

In the body of the thread method it is acceptable, and desirable, to call other methods. This generally makes the code more readable and reusable. Remember that these methods will execute on the thread from which they are called.

4.1.3 Creating an instance of the Thread class

Now we need to create an instance of the `Thread` class. Before we can do that we need to have a declaration of a variable to associate with that new instance. This will allow us to interact with the class after it is created. The following declares an instance of the `Thread` class:

```
Thread ExampleThread;
```

We're now ready to create an instance of the `Thread` class. The constructor of the class expects that a `ThreadStart` will be passed in. When we create an instance of the `Thread` class, we supply the newly instantiated `ThreadStart` delegate:

```
ExampleThread = new Thread(ThreadStartDelegate);
```

This tells the `Thread` object what delegate it should invoke when we tell the thread to start executing. Note that so far we have not created an OS thread. What we have created is an instance of the `Thread` class that will allow us to create the OS thread in the next section.

We can simplify the thread object creation code in C# by doing the following:

```
Thread ExampleThread = new Thread(new ThreadStart(SortAscending));
```

VB.NET does this automatically, so all you need to pass in to the `Thread` constructor is the address of the method you wish to associate with the new thread. Unless there is a reason to assign the instance of the `ThreadStart` delegate to a variable, the creation can be done inline.

> **TIP** Under most circumstances the `ThreadStart` delegate is not needed once it is passed in to the `Thread` constructor. Instead of you assigning a variable its value, it can be passed to the `Thread` constructor inline.

As an example, you might need to assign the delegates to variables when a different delegate may be assigned depending on a runtime condition. For instance, if the number of elements is less than 10,000, sort them in ascending order; otherwise sort them in descending order:

```
if (HowMany < 10000)
  ThreadStartDelegate = new ThreadStart(SortAscending);
else
  ThreadStartDelegate = new ThreadStart(SortDescending);
```

Until we start the thread, neither `SortAscending` nor `SortDescending` will execute. All we have done is create an instance of the `Thread` class and associated it with a delegate that is in turn associated with the method. We are now ready to start the threads.

4.2   STARTING THREADS

Since we are dealing with the .NET framework instead of language constructs, the VB.NET example is very similar to the C# example from the previous section. The most obvious difference is how the `ThreadStart` delegate is created. In the VB.NET example the `ThreadStart` delegate seems to be missing. In its place the `AddressOf` operator precedes the name of the method that will be the entry point for the new thread. The reason: the `AddressOf` operator creates a delegate that accesses the `SortAscending` method.

AddressOf The AddressOf operator is the mechanism that VB.NET uses to create a delegate for a method.

Since the VB.NET compiler can determine which of the possible delegates it should produce, it uses the results of the AddressOf operator in place of the delegate. In C# the name of the method resolves to the address of the method and the ThreadStart delegate is required to convert this address into a delegate. Unless there are other considerations, such as assigning the ThreadStart delegate to a variable based on runtime conditions, VB.NET developers should use the AddressOf operator in the Thread constructor. C# developers should use an inline ThreadStart delegate as discussed in the previous section.

Start Start is a method of the Thread class that signals a managed thread to begin execution. This generally creates an OS thread.

Now that we have created our instance of the Thread class, we are ready to launch the thread. Starting a thread is much like calling a method, except the calling thread continues execution. The following example includes the addition of the call to the Start method:

```
Sub CreateThreadExample(ByVal HowMany As Integer)
  . . .
  Dim ExampleThread As System.Threading.Thread
  ExampleThread = New System.Threading.Thread(AddressOf SortAscending)
  ExampleThread.Start()
End Sub
```

In the example, StartThreadExample will probably exit before SortAscending has finished executing. If the line containing the Start method was replaced with

```
SortAscending()
```

execution would continue on the same thread. This means that StartThread-Example would pause until the SortAscending method completed its calculations. Once those calculations are complete the SortAscending method exits, then the StartThreadExample method exits.

This is a new concept to many developers, and a key one, so we will spend some time exploring it. Figure 4.1 displays a visual representation of how this works. At the point ExampleThread.Start() executes, a thread is created and the SortAscending method begins to execute on that thread. This increases the number of threads associated with the process by one. In our example the thread will continue until SortAscending completes execution and returns. In the next section we will cover another way that threads can end. The important concept is that when the method associated with the ThreadStart delegate terminates, the thread associated with it also terminates. Remember that even though we did not declare a ThreadStart delegate in the VB.NET example, one was created for us.

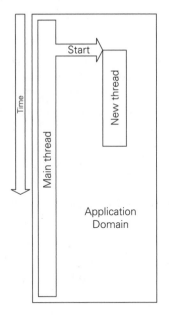

Figure 4.1
Creation of a thread

The first thread created in a process is called the main thread. It is a foreground thread and it is possible to have multiple foreground threads in the same process. So far all of our examples have contained only foreground threads. In the next chapter we will explore all forms of thread control, one of which is setting a thread to be a background thread.

Debugging multithreaded applications is a little different than debugging traditional applications. In our example, stepping through the code does not step into the `SortAscending` method. Instead control goes from the invocation of the `Start` method and returns to the calling method. The way to see what happens on the new thread is to use a breakpoint in the `SortAscending` method. When debugging a multithreaded application, you should focus on one thread at a time because it is often difficult, if not impossible, to determine the exact order of execution of multiple threads. This is one of the challenges associated with multithreaded development.

4.3 ENDING THREADS

Suppose that you wanted a thread to end. One way to do that is to have the method the thread is executing end. For some applications this is sufficient. One way of telling a thread it is time to end is through the use of instance variables associated with the class the thread method is a member of. The thread method generally has a loop of some sort and a test for a change in the value of the variable. When the variable changes, it is an indication that the method should exit. In listing 4.2, if `TimeToStop` is true the method exits and the thread terminates.

Listing 4.2 Ending a thread (VB.NET)

```
public class ClassThread_End_1
{
  long [] NumbersToSort;
  public bool TimeToStop = false;          Controls the
  . . .                                    termination of
  public void CreateDataAndStartThread(int HowMany)   the thread
  {
  . . .
    ExampleThread = new Thread(new ThreadStart(Sort));
    TimeToStop = false;
    ExampleThread.Start();
  }
  public void StopThread()
  {
    TimeToStop =true;
  }
. . .
  void SortAscending()
  {
    for (int i= 0;i < NumbersToSort.Length ;i++)
    {
      if (TimeToStop) return;      Determines if the
                                   thread method
      for (int j=0;j<i;j++)        should return
      {
        if (NumbersToSort[i] < NumbersToSort[j])
        {
          Swap(ref NumbersToSort[i],ref NumbersToSort[j]);
        }
      }
    }
  }
. . .
}
```

A different thread changes the value of TimeToStop by calling its method, signaling that it is time to terminate execution. This demonstrates one of the problems with this approach: the inner loop must complete before the test is performed. This also relies on the thread method checking this value, and being in a state that it can check the value.

TIP   One way of ending threads is to have the thread check a variable that signals when the thread should stop.

While this approach works for many situations, there are times that a more direct method must be used. Fortunately we have a means of signaling the thread that it is time to end. The Abort method signals a thread that it should terminate. When an abort is signaled a ThreadAbortException is raised on the thread.

Abort   Abort is a method on the Thread class that raises a ThreadAbortException on the related thread. Abort is used to stop a thread from processing.

The Thread class also contains a method, Sleep, that will suspend execution of a thread for a set period of time. It accepts a parameter that indicates how long the thread should be idle, in milliseconds. This allows a thread to pause itself for a period of time.

Sleep   Sleep is a method on the Thread class that causes the current thread to
pause execution for a period of time.

We will discuss the Sleep method in more detail in the next chapter. In the Main method of our example, we have the following:

```
void Main()
{
  ClassThread_Exceptions_1 Example = new ClassThread_Exceptions_1();
  Example.CreateDataAndStartThread(10000);
  System.Threading.Thread.Sleep(1000);
  Example.StopThread();
  System.Threading.Thread.Sleep(4000);
}
```

We create an instance of the class associated with this example called Example. We then call the CreateDataAndStartThread method, passing in HowMany elements we want in our array. This creates and populates the array with random values and starts the ExampleThread.

```
public void CreateDataAndStartThread(int HowMany)
{
  . . .
  ExampleThread = new Thread(new ThreadStart(Sort));
  ExampleThread.Start();
}
```

We then pause the main thread using the Sleep method, indicating that we wish to sleep for 1,000 milliseconds, or one second. After the main thread has slept for one second it calls the StopThread method, which calls Abort() on the Example-Thread, raising an exception on the ExampleThread.

```
public void StopThread()
{
  ExampleThread.Abort();
}
```

We then sleep for an additional four seconds and then exit the Main method. Anytime an unhandled exception occurs on a thread, that thread will terminate. To achieve the desired results, you must understand thread-related exceptions.

4.3.1 Introducing the ThreadAbortException exception

Exceptions are likely a new concept for VB developers. They are a means of handling runtime conditions that if not dealt with become runtime errors. In chapter 13 we will discuss thread-related exceptions in greater detail.

Exceptions   Exceptions are a type of error handling that allows for dealing with unexpected runtime conditions.

As we saw in the previous section, when `Abort()` is called on a thread a `ThreadAbortException` is raised. The thread may not be terminated immediately. The runtime waits until the thread reaches a safe point before terminating it. Safe points are locations in code where the .NET runtime can take control of a thread and perform needed actions. Terminating a thread is one of those actions.

The way that exceptions are generally handled involves `try`, `catch`, and `finally` clauses. The `try` block contains a series of instructions that are to be executed and that might raise an exception. `catch` handles the exceptions that have not been handled by a more specific clause. When an exception is handled by a `catch` clause, execution generally continues. The `ThreadAbortException` is unlike most exceptions because execution does not continue after the `catch` clause. `finally` clauses are always executed, regardless of whether or not an exception is raised. A `try` block must be followed by `finally`, `catch`, or both.

**ThreadAbort-   The `ThreadAbortException` generally does not allow execution to
Exception**   continue after the exception has been handled.

Listing 4.3 shows how a method can be written to handle exceptions.

Listing 4.3   Example of handling ThreadAbortException (VB.NET)

```
Private Sub Sort()
  Dim i, j As Integer
  Try
    For i = 0 To NumberOfElements
      For j = 0 To i
        If NumbersToSort(i) < NumbersToSort(j) Then
          Swap(NumbersToSort(i), NumbersToSort(j))
        End If
      Next
    Next
  Catch ex As Threading.ThreadAbortException
    Console.WriteLine("Caught ThreadAbortException:" + ex.Message)
  End Try
End Sub
```

When `Abort` is called on the `ExampleThread`, the following line is written out to the console:

```
Caught ThreadAbortException:Thread was being aborted.
```

Suppose that you wanted to determine why the thread was being aborted. This would allow the cleanup code to perform different operations depending on the message sent. A version of the Abort method accepts a single parameter called a stateInfo. This allows an object to be passed to the thread via the ThreadAbortException. The object that is passed to the Abort method will be available by accessing the Exception-State property. So if we change our StopThread method to pass a string, that string will be passed on to the catch clause that catches the ThreadAbortException.

```
Sub StopThread()
  Dim StateInfo As String
  StateInfo = "It's time to stop executing."
  ExampleThread.Abort(StateInfo)
End Sub
```

If we change our catch clause to the following:

```
Catch ex As Threading.ThreadAbortException
  Console.WriteLine("Caught ThreadAbortException:")
  Console.Write("Message=")
  Console.WriteLine(ex.Message)
  If Not ex.ExceptionState Is Nothing Then
    Console.Write("ExceptionState=")
    Console.WriteLine(ex.ExceptionState)
  End If
```

the following output will be generated on the console:

```
Caught ThreadAbortException:
Message=Thread was being aborted.
ExceptionState=It's time to stop executing.
```

Notice the test to see if ExceptionState is Nothing. If state information is not passed into the Abort method, then ExceptionState will be Nothing.

The finally clause will always execute, whether or not an exception occurs. It allows for a series of statements that should be executed regardless of outcome, such as closing any open ports or files, and releasing any resources. If we add

```
Finally
  Console.WriteLine("The Sort has ended")
```

to our exception-handling code, then the output of the execution would be:

```
Caught ThreadAbortException:
Message=Thread was being aborted.
ExceptionState=It's time to stop executing.
The Sort has ended
```

If the Abort did not occur, the results would be:

```
The Sort has ended
```

4.3.2 The ResetAbort method

It seems a shame to blindly stop sorting the elements of our array when an `Abort` occurs. Suppose that we are 99 percent finished and received an `Abort`. Wouldn't it be nice if we could choose to ignore it? That is exactly what the `ResetAbort` method lets you do.

```
...
catch(ThreadAbortException ex)
{
  Console.WriteLine("Caught ThreadAbortException: "+ ex.Message);
  if (ex.ExceptionState != null && (bool)ex.ExceptionState)
  {
    if (i > NumberOfElements/2)
    {
      Console.WriteLine("Ignoring the abort");
     Thread.ResetAbort();
    }
  }
}
finally
{
  Console.WriteLine("finally");
}
...
```

In the example if more than half of the elements are in order, we let the sort complete:

```
void Sort()
{
  int i = 0;
  bool ContinueProcessing = true;
  while (ContinueProcessing)
  {
    try
```

This requires reworking the `Sort` method so that an `Exception` can be handled and processing can continue. Without this modification we would call `ResetAbort`. We would then be able to stay in the thread's method. Next we would exit the `catch` clause, and execute the `finally` clause. Next we would exit the `try` block, exit the method, and end the thread. We would have ignored the `Abort` but the thread would have ended anyway. We use the `stateInfo` parameter of the `Abort` method to pass in a Boolean indicating if it is permissible for the `Abort` to be ignored. This allows the caller of the `Abort` to permit the thread to ignore the abort.

The first thing we need to do is change the outer loop from a `for` loop to a `while` loop and change where the counter was initialized. Additionally we added a `while` loop to allow us to resume our sorting:

```
while (i < NumberOfElements )
```

By initializing the outer loop index before the `while` loop, we ensure that the index value will be preserved when an exception occurs. We also need to have a way of indicating that we have finished with the sorting. When the outer loop finishes, we execute the following line:

```
ContinueProcessing = false;
```

This indicates that we have finished sorting the data and the thread can exit. We also change the way we call `Abort` to pass in a Boolean that indicates if the thread can choose to ignore the abort:

```
public void StopThread()
{
  bool CanResetAbort = true;
  ExampleThread.Abort(CanResetAbort);
}
```

This approach allows for robust handling of different states. It also adds complexity to the solution. The idea that a thread can determine how it should behave is both powerful and dangerous. Threads should respond as expected, unless they are given permission to do otherwise. This gives the designer of the solution the ability to make things more complex. Keep in mind that if the thread is a foreground thread and it ignores an `Abort`, it may cause the thread to keep executing after the main thread has completed its execution. While this might be desired under some circumstances, generally it is not a good idea. If the thread is not a foreground thread, the runtime terminates the thread without considering if the `ResetAbort` method is invoked. The next chapter discusses foreground and background threads in depth.

Notice that the `finally` clause executes more than once. It is important to remember that the `finally` clause indicates exit from a `try`, `catch`, `finally` block. As we've seen in this example, it is possible to exit and reenter a `try/catch/ finally` block numerous times.

An important concept here involves signaling an `Abort` and assuming that it occurred. Before you signal a thread to abort, you need to know its state. Second, if you need to know that the thread actually ended, you should wait for it to end. We will cover these two topics in the following two sections of this chapter.

4.3.3   The Join method

So far we've created, started, and requested a thread to stop executing. Until now we've had no way of knowing that the thread actually stopped executing. The `Thread` class provides the `Join` method that lets us wait until the specified thread stops executing. We call `Join` on the instance of the `Thread` class we wish to wait on. Figure 4.2 is a graphical representation of how `Join` works. A key element is that the main thread will wait until the new thread terminates before continuing.

The next example is similar to those we've done before. We create an instance of the class that contains the instance of the `Thread` class. We create an array of 10,000 elements and assign random values. We then start the thread. The main thread sleeps for one second and then signals that the thread should stop. Next, instead of sleeping for an arbitrary amount of time, we wait, indefinitely, for the thread to terminate.

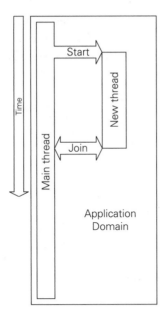

Figure 4.2
Graphical representation
of the Join method

```
Sub Main()
    Dim Example As New JoinThread()
    Example.CreateDataAndStartThread(10000)
    System.Threading.Thread.Sleep(1000)
    Example.StopThread()
    Example.WaitForThread()
End Sub

Sub WaitForThread()
    ExampleThread.Join()
End Sub
```

At the point ExampleThread terminates, the Join method returns and the WaitForThread method continues executing. Join is termed a blocking method, meaning it does not return until it has finished waiting for some event to occur, thereby blocking the thread it is executed on.

Join   Join is a method of the Thread class that causes the current thread to pause until the thread associated with the instance of the Thread class terminates or a timeout occurs. If a parameter is supplied to the Join method, it indicates how long the runtime should wait before timing out. If no parameter is supplied, it means to wait indefinitely for the thread to terminate.

One issue with using Join as we have here is that it waits indefinitely for Example-Thread to terminate. If ExampleThread never terminates, Join never returns. There are cases where that is exactly what you want to do. However, sometimes you want to wait for the thread to end; if it doesn't, you do something else. This is often associated with polling the state of the thread.

Suppose that you wanted to let the sorting method run for ten seconds, and if the sort had not completed, call `StopThread`. Recall that `StopThread` may not result in the thread stopping, since the thread can choose to call `ResetAbort` and continue processing. The `WaitForThread` method is now more complex:

```
Sub WaitForThread(ByVal HowLongToWait As Integer)
   Dim KeepGoing As Boolean
   Dim ThreadDied As Boolean
   Dim NumberOfSeconds As Integer
   NumberOfSeconds = 0
   KeepGoing = True
   While (KeepGoing)
     ThreadDied = ExampleThread.Join(1000)
     If ThreadDied Then
       Console.WriteLine("Dead")
       KeepGoing = False
     Else
       NumberOfSeconds += 1
       Console.WriteLine("Alive " + NumberOfSeconds.ToString)
       If NumberOfSeconds > HowLongToWait Then
         Console.WriteLine("Calling StopThread")
         StopThread()
       End If
     End If
   End While
End Sub
```

The version of `Join` we are using here accepts a single integer parameter that indicates a timeout value. The parameter indicates how many milliseconds `Join` should wait for the thread to end, in this case 1,000, or one second. If `Join` returns true then the thread terminated in the time allowed by the timeout parameter. If it returns false, the thread is still alive. The logic of this method is pretty straightforward. While the thread is executing we keep attempting to `Join` it, waiting one second each time. After `HowLongToWait` attempts to join, we start requesting that the thread die, which causes an `Abort` to be called on the thread. Depending on how far along the thread is in its processing, it may either die or continue sorting its elements.

We can modify our main procedure to remove any `Sleep` calls as follows:

```
Sub Main()
    Dim Example As New JoinThread2()
    Example.CreateDataAndStartThread(20000)
    Example.WaitForThread(10)
End Sub
```

Another version of `Join` accepts a `TimeSpan` parameter, instead of an integer parameter, indicating how long to wait before timing out. The `TimeSpan` structure allows for greater flexibility. The smallest unit of time that can be assigned using a `TimeSpan` object is one hundred nanoseconds, known as a tick. The return value behaves the same: true if the thread ended, false if not.

4.4 DETERMINING A THREAD'S STATUS

Being able to determine the condition of a thread is very useful. There are two properties that provide insight into the condition of a thread. IsAlive returns a Boolean value indicating if the thread is in a state where it is executing. ThreadState returns a bitmasked value that provides more detail into the exact states a thread is in at any point.

4.4.1 The IsAlive property

So far we know how to tell if a thread is alive only by waiting for it to die. We could ask to Join a thread and specify a very small timeout, such as 1 millisecond. But this doesn't express what we are trying to do; we want to know if the thread is alive, not if it is going to die in the next millisecond. To do this we use the IsAlive property of the Thread class. Our next example uses IsAlive instead of Join.

A key concept here is that IsAlive returns immediately with either true or false. It is intended to check the state of a thread. We will discuss the other states that threads go through in the next section. IsAlive is an easy way to determine if a thread is executing.

One area where IsAlive can be useful is during thread startup. We have seen that calling Abort does not terminate the thread immediately; the same thing is true of calling Start. Start is a request for the runtime to start the thread. Depending on machine load and performance, the thread may or may not be started by the time the next instruction executes. If it is critical to know if a thread is started, checking its state using IsAlive is a good idea. It's worth noting that under typical conditions threads start very quickly, and it is not generally necessary to check to see when a thread actually started.

Suppose that we needed to know if the ExampleThread actually started. If it did, we display the message "Thread is alive"; if not, "Thread is not alive." If a thread does not start after a sufficiently long period, an error message should be logged. This will likely be due to a machine being in an unhealthy state. Attempting to start the thread again most likely will not help.

```
public void CreateDataAndStartThread(int HowMany)
{
  CreateData(HowMany);
  ExampleThread = new Thread(new ThreadStart(Sort));
  ExampleThread.Start();
  int IsAlivePollCount = 0;
  while (!ExampleThread.IsAlive)
  {
    IsAlivePollCount++;
    if (IsAlivePollCount > 100)
    {
      // Do something drastic
      throw new Exception("ExampleThread would not start");
    }
```

```
        Console.WriteLine("Thread is not alive");
        Thread.Sleep(1000);
    }
}
```

Let's examine the value of IsAlive at each point through the thread creation process:

```
public void TestIsAlive(int HowMany)
{
    Thread OurThread;
    CreateData(HowMany);
    OurThread= new Thread(new ThreadStart(Sort));
    Console.WriteLine(OurThread.IsAlive);  // False
    OurThread.Start();
    Thread.Sleep(1000);
    Console.WriteLine(OurThread.IsAlive);  // True
    Thread.Sleep(1000);
    Console.WriteLine(OurThread.IsAlive);  // True
    OurThread.Abort();
    Console.WriteLine(OurThread.IsAlive);  // True
    OurThread.Join();
    Console.WriteLine(OurThread.IsAlive);  // False
}
```

We start by declaring and assigning an instance of the Thread class, associating it with a method that will serve as the entry point to the thread. IsAlive returns false at this point, since we haven't started the thread. The next step is to start the thread. If a small amount of time has passed, IsAlive returns true, assuming the runtime was able to start the thread. If we signal an Abort, the value of IsAlive stays true, in part because the thread method chooses to ignore the call, but also because Abort is a request for an Abort so it is unlikely that it would be processed immediately. After we Join the thread, IsAlive returns false.

We've now seen a way to check if a thread is alive. This is somewhat useful but there is a lot more we can know about the state of the thread.

4.4.2   The ThreadState property

Threads go through several states. A state is a condition that is either true or false. A thread is either in a state or it is not. One way to see the states a thread goes through is to create another thread whose sole purpose is to watch the thread we care about. The following example creates a thread to keep track of the thread we want to watch:

```
Imports System.Threading
Public Class ThreadStateWatcher
    Private ThreadToWatch As Thread
    Private WatchingThread As Thread
    Public Sub WatchThread(ByRef ThreadToWatch As Thread)
        Me.ThreadToWatch = ThreadToWatch
        WatchingThread = New Thread(AddressOf Watch)
        WatchingThread.IsBackground = True
        WatchingThread.Start()
    End Sub
```

```
   Private Sub Watch()
      Dim LastState As ThreadState
      While True
         Dim CurrentState As ThreadState
         CurrentState = ThreadToWatch.ThreadState
         If CurrentState <> LastState Then
            LastState = CurrentState
            Trace.Write(ThreadToWatch.IsAlive.ToString)
            Trace.Write(" ")
            Trace.WriteLine(CurrentState.ToString())
            Thread.Sleep(5)
         End If
      End While
   End Sub
   . . .
End Class
```

Every five milliseconds the thread wakes up and checks if the thread it is watching has changed state. If it has, it outputs the new state. It also outputs the value for IsAlive. When we create the thread we set the IsBackground property to true. When designing systems it isn't uncommon to dedicate a single thread to monitoring the activities of the other threads. It wouldn't be very efficient to create a monitoring thread for each thread that needed to be monitored.

ThreadState The ThreadState property is a bitmasked value that indicates the current state(s) the thread is in. A thread can be in more than one of the ten states at the same time. Certain states are mutually exclusive, such as Running and Stopped.

Threads start out as Unstarted. Once started, threads transition from Unstarted to Running. If the thread method exits, the thread transitions from the Running state to Stopped. If an Abort is called on a thread, it transitions to AbortRequested. If the thread then chooses to ignore the Abort using ResetAbort, it returns to the Running state. Otherwise the thread transitions to the Aborted state and then to the Stopped state.

   Notice in the sample output that ThreadState can have multiple values at the same time. For instance it can be WaitSleepJoin and AbortRequested at the same time. This is accomplished by using bit-masked values. A bitwise AND must be used to determine if a thread is in a certain state. For example:

```
If CurrentState And ThreadState.Unstarted Then
```

Since a thread can be in more than one state at the same time, the values must be checked individually. In the current implementation, the Running state is associated with the integer value zero. This means that a test to see if a thread is in the Running state cannot be accomplished using a simple bitwise comparison. Instead, if the thread is not in the Unstarted state or is not stopped, then it must be running.

```
Public Function MyAlive() As Boolean
  Dim UnstartedOrStopped As ThreadState
  UnstartedOrStopped = ThreadState.Unstarted Or ThreadState.Stopped
  Return ThreadToWatch.ThreadState And UnstartedOrStopped = 0
End Function
```

The first column contains the value of `IsAlive`, the second the `ThreadState`:

```
False Unstarted
True Running
True AbortRequested
True WaitSleepJoin, AbortRequested
True AbortRequested
True WaitSleepJoin, AbortRequested
True Running
False Stopped
False Aborted
```

Figure 4.3 shows the states and transitions that we've covered so far. Don't be overly concerned if it seems complex; we will discuss it in more detail in the next chapter.

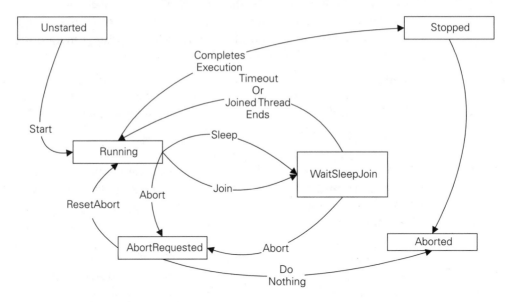

Figure 4.3   ThreadState transition diagram

Table 4.1 contains the current values for each of the thread states. As we discussed earlier, `Running` is associated with zero. Notice that the values are powers of two. This allows bitwise logic to be applied. We will discuss each of these states in detail in later chapters.

Table 4.1 ThreadState Descriptions and Values

State	Description	Value
Aborted	The thread is in the Stopped state as a result of an Abort request.	256
AbortRequested	An abort has been signaled.	128
Suspended	A thread has called Suspend on the thread. It can only leave the suspend state when some other thread calls Resume.	64
WaitSleepJoin	The thread is idle. It is either waiting for a resource, for another thread to terminate, or for a sleep timeout to expire.	32
Stopped	The thread is no longer executing.	16
Unstarted	The thread object has been created but the OS thread has not been started.	8
Background	The thread is executing in background mode, meaning it will be terminated when all other nonbackground threads terminate.	4
SuspendRequested	A Suspend request has been signaled.	2
StopRequested	A stop has been requested.	1
Running	The thread is currently executing.	0

Suppose you had a thread that was a `Background` thread in the `WaitSleepJoin` state. The value returned by `ThreadState` would be 4 plus 32 which would equal 36. One of the interesting properties of combining bitmask values with a bitwise OR is that it is equivalent to addition. Table 4.2 demonstrates how this is occurring at a bit level.

Table 4.2 Explanation of Bitwise OR

2^8	2^7	2^6	2^5	2^4	2^3	2^2	2^1	2^0	Decimal Value
0	0	0	0	0	0	1	0	0	4
0	0	0	1	0	0	0	0	0	32
Logical OR									
0	0	0	1	0	0	1	0	0	36

To determine if a bit is on, we use a logical AND. In Table 4.2 the resulting row has both the 2^5 and 2^2 bits on. This yields a resulting decimal value of 36. Table 4.3 shows how a logical AND can be used to see if a bit is turned on. The first line contains the value 36, the same as the result from Table 4.2. When it is compared to the constant for `WaitSleepJoin`, 32, using a logical AND, the result is 32.

Table 4.3 Explanation of Bitwise AND

2^8	2^7	2^6	2^5	2^4	2^3	2^2	2^1	2^0	Decimal Value
0	0	0	1	0	0	1	0	0	36
0	0	0	1	0	0	0	0	0	32
Logical AND									
0	0	0	1	0	0	0	0	0	32

The majority of the time you do not care what the actual value returned by the logical AND is; you only care if it is greater than zero. This indicates that at least one bit is on.

4.5   SUMMARY

After we learned how to create a thread and how it can be started, we saw how this creates an OS thread. When the method associated with the thread's `ThreadStart` delegate exits, the thread terminates. Alternatively, we can use the `Abort` method on the instance of the `Thread` class associated with the thread to trigger a `Thread-AbortException` that results in the termination of the thread. We can use the `ResetAbort` method to cancel an abort.

CHAPTER 5

Controlling threads

As a general rule, anything that is allowed to happen without a certain degree of control is a bad thing. I'm reminded of a wedding I once attended. A youngster was in an over-stimulated state. At one point during the festivities the child was running at full speed directly toward the wedding cake. Fortunately his alert grandmother intercepted him and got him under a certain degree of control.

Threads that are not controlled can potentially be just as dangerous.

In the last chapter we covered creating threads, determining their state, and stopping them. While this is a good foundation, you'll often need to exercise more control over threads. One of the things we generally want to do with a thread is be able to identify it from another. If I have a thread that is performing a certain task, say a calculation, it is more convenient to refer to that thread as the "Calculating Thread" rather than as thread 2412. The `Thread` class allows us to assign a name to a thread so that we can more easily identify it during debugging.

Like the child running toward the cake, threads that don't have a proper amount of pause during their execution can cause some very bad things to happen. To help slow them down, we can use the `Sleep` method. Sometimes we want to interrupt a thread while it is sleeping, which is exactly what the `Interrupt` method does.

Just as his grandmother caused the child to stop what he previously was doing, running toward the wedding cake, we sometimes want to stop a thread from doing what

69

it is doing. This is what the `Suspend` method allows us to do. Once a thread has entered the `Suspended` state we are likely going to want to have it exit that state. The `Resume` method causes a thread that is in the `Suspended` state to exit it and continue its execution.

This chapter uses a web site monitoring application for demonstration purposes. A site monitoring application fits many of the concepts we'll be covering. When possible the concepts will be associated with that example. Occasionally a simple example will be introduced when it can more clearly convey the information.

This chapter also covers advanced topics, such as processor affinity. These advanced mechanisms generally should not be used when dealing with managed code. It is a good idea to be familiar with them, but in general the methods in the `System.Diagnostics.Process` class should not be used to tune multithreaded applications. If the need arises, you will be familiar with the concepts and able to determine when you need the features they provide.

5.1 EXAMPLE: WEB SITE MONITORING

When a web site stops working correctly, the time it is unavailable can often be measured in dollars. The example we'll use in this chapter is a web site monitor, a program used to ensure that a web site is in a state such that it can service user requests in a timely manner. One approach to web site monitoring is to have a predefined page that returns an indication of health. The page is retrieved at regular intervals. This page often exercises various objects or assemblies, perhaps accesses a database, and returns a reasonable estimation of the health of the web server the page resides on. Listing 5.1 uses the `System.Net.WebClient` object to retrieve a page referenced by a URL.

Listing 5.1 Retrieving a web page using WebClient (VB.NET)

```
Imports System.Net
Imports System.Threading

Public Class WebSiteMonitor

  Private URL As String
  Private MonitorThread As Thread
  Private SleepTime As Integer
  Private LastRequestHowLong As TimeSpan

  Public Sub New(ByVal URL As String, ByVal SleepTime As Integer)
    Me.URL = URL
    Me.SleepTime = SleepTime
    MonitorThread = New Thread(AddressOf ThreadMethod)
    MonitorThread.Name = "WebSiteMonitor"
  End Sub
. . .

  Private Sub ThreadMethod()
    Dim Notify As Boolean
```

```
    While True
        Notify = False
        Dim client As New WebClient()    ←┐  Creates a simple
                                           ┘  HTTP client
        Dim data As Byte()
        Dim StartTime As DateTime = System.DateTime.Now
        ' Retrieve the Page                             Retrieves
        data = client.DownloadData(URL)    ←┐           the page
        Dim StopTime As DateTime = System.DateTime.Now
        LastRequestHowLong = StopTime.Subtract(StartTime)
        Dim Results As String
        Results = System.Text.Encoding.ASCII.GetString(data)
        If Results.IndexOf("OK") < 0 Then
          Notify = True
        End If
        If Notify Then
          ' Let someone know
        End If
        Thread.Sleep(SleepTime)
    End While
  End Sub
End Class
```

Processing begins by creating an instance of the `WebClient` class. The current time is recorded so that the time required to retrieve the page can be calculated. The `DownloadData` method is used to return the contents of the page as an array of `Bytes`. Once the page is downloaded, the time is recorded. In order to easily interact with the contents page, we must convert it from a `Byte` array to a string using the `GetString` method of the `System.Text.Encoding.ASCII` class. If the resulting string does not contain `"OK"` the `Notify` flag is set to true, indicating that someone should be notified that the web site is in an unhealthy state. The idea is that a dynamic page will return the status of the web site. If the system is in a healthy state, the page will return. Notification could be through the addition of an entry to the NT Event Log, or some other means. Figure 5.1 gives a high-level view of how the application logically functions.

When we monitor a web site, we generally pause between each check. If the pause is too short, we have written a web site stress-testing tool instead of a monitor. If we pause too long, we may miss something important. We've seen the `Sleep` method in previous chapters. It causes a thread to pause for a period of time. We will examine

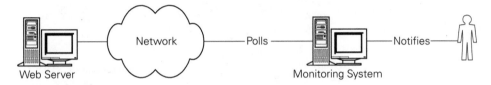

Figure 5.1 Web site monitoring logical flow

the Sleep method in detail in section 5.3.1. At times we wish to check the state of the site immediately; perhaps someone has reported that the web site is down. In threading terms, this is accomplished using the Interrupt method.

When the connection from the monitoring machine to the Internet goes down, often the best approach is to stop checking the site until the connection has been reestablished. This relates to the Suspend and Resume methods that we cover in section 5.5. At the point it becomes apparent that the connection is down, the thread polling the site should be suspended. Once it is determined that polling should continue, Resume should be called on the suspended thread.

When multiple sites are being checked, some are likely more important than others. We may want to ensure that the thread that is checking the more important site is given the opportunity to do its work first. In section 5.6.1 we cover how to adjust the thread's priority. We most likely will want to have a thread whose job is to notify someone when there is a problem. That notification is important and needs to happen at a higher priority than the monitoring.

Often the computer doing the monitoring is not dedicated to that task. In that case it is desirable to control how many of the resources of the computer are used. We may wish to control what processors in a multiple-processor machine can be used to check the status of the web sites. In this case processor affinity lets us control what processors a process utilizes. Processor affinity is an advanced topic, and not something generally done. We'll cover it in section 5.7 since it relates to thread control. If you limit what processor a process uses, you've also limited what processor a thread can use.

5.2   NAMING THREADS

Sometimes you need to keep track of what a particular thread is doing. To help you do this, the Thread class supports the Name property. This allows us to assign a name to an instance of a thread. So rather than referencing threads by their identification number, we can then refer to them by name.

Name   Name is a property of the Thread object that allows a developer to assign a name to a thread. The Name property can be assigned a value only once; any additional attempts will result in an exception.

In Listing 5.2 we assign the main thread of the process the name Main. This enables us to easily identify that thread.

Listing 5.2   Example of naming a thread (C#)

```
void InstanceMain(string[]args)
{
  Thread.CurrentThread.Name = "Main";                        Associates "Main"
  Console.WriteLine(Thread.CurrentThread.Name);              with the main thread
  WebSiteMonitor SiteMonitor;
  SiteMonitor = new WebSiteMonitor("http://localhost/test.htm", 1000);
  SiteMonitor.Start();
```

CHAPTER 5   CONTROLLING THREADS

```
    Thread.Sleep(15000);
    SiteMonitor.Abort();
    SiteMonitor.Join();
}
```

When we stop execution using a breakpoint, we can examine what threads are in the application domain and what their names are. To see the value of Name before assignment, set a breakpoint on the line that assigns the value "Main" to the Name property and run the program. Before the line executes, select Debug \ Windows \ Threads, or press Ctrl+Alt+H, to bring up the window shown in figure 5.2.

Figure 5.2   The Thread window before the main thread is named

Notice that the Name column contains an entry that is set to <No Name>. This lets you know that the thread currently does not have a name. The Location column contains the method the selected thread is currently executing. The small arrow on the left side indicates the current thread that the debugger is viewing. Since we have not started any other threads there is only one thread in the process, so it makes sense that it would be the active thread. The ID column contains the operating system thread identifier. This identifier is unique to a thread and will likely change on each execution. We will cover Priority and Suspend in sections 5.5 and 5.6 respectively. As you can see in figure 5.3, once we've assigned the Name property the value of "Main" the Thread window updates.

	ID	Name	Location	Priority	Suspend	
⇨	2188	Main	ThreadName.WebSiteMonitorConsole.InstanceMain	Normal	0	

Figure 5.3   The Thread window after the main thread is assigned a name

After the Sleep statement is executed (listing 5.2), there are four additional threads listed. Notice in figure 5.4 that the WebSiteMonitor is the thread that is currently visible in the debugger.

The last three threads are related to the WebClient object. This demonstrates that many things in the .NET framework are themselves multithreaded. Having named the two threads we are primarily concerned with, we can now easily identify them during debugging.

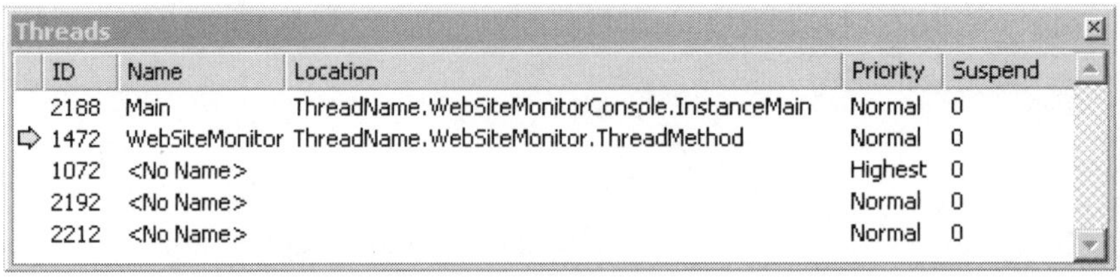

Figure 5.4 The Thread window after the `WebClient` object creates additional threads

The following rules govern thread names:

- Once a thread's name has been set, it cannot be changed.
- Thread names do not need to be unique within an application domain.
- Thread names can contain any character.
- Thread names should be as long as needed to make it easy to recognize the thread; there is no limit to the length of the thread name.

The `Name` property of the `Thread` object allows both `Get` and `Set`. This means that the thread's name can be retrieved programmatically. Once a name is associated with a thread, it cannot be changed. The danger here is that a developer might assume that a thread's name is unique and attempt to do some sort of logic based upon it. Nothing prevents two threads from having the same name. If a thread needs to be uniquely identified, and the reference to the `Thread` object isn't sufficient, then using the `GetHashCode` method will return an integer that will be unique within an application domain.

> **GetHashCode** `GetHashCode` is a method that returns an integer value that will be unique within an application domain.

Thread names are great for what they are intended, which is associating an easily recognizable value with a thread. Assigning a thread a name can greatly improve and simplify the debugging process.

5.3 USING SLEEP AND INTERRUPT

What's the difference between a web site stress-testing tool and a web site monitor? The short answer is the amount of time between requests. The goals of the two products are very different. Both applications repeatedly request pages from a web server, but a stress-testing tool is designed to request as many pages as possible; a web site monitor requests its pages at a much slower rate. To slow down the requesting of pages, we can use the `Thread` class's `Sleep` method.

Threads go through many different states, one of which is `WaitSleepJoin`. As you might guess, a thread enters this state when it executes the `Wait`, `Sleep`, or `Join` methods. This section discusses how the `Sleep` method of the `Thread` class affects the state of a thread. It also discusses how a thread can be triggered to exit the `WaitSleepJoin` state by using the `Interrupt` method.

5.3.1   The Sleep method

Imagine how much you could accomplish if you never rested. The same is very true of threads. Since a computer's processor and memory are finite shared resources, if one thread doesn't rest other threads may not be able to get their work done. Many applications rely on a relatively large amount of time passing between actions. For example, if the web site monitor were to constantly request pages, it would put an unnecessary stress on the web site that it was monitoring. Fortunately, we can use the Sleep method to suspend the execution of a thread for a period of time.

Sleep   Sleep is a method on the Thread class that enables the current thread to pause its execution for a period of time. Alternatively, it can be used to yield the remainder of its time to the OS.

A thread can put only itself to sleep. This means that one thread cannot cause a different thread to sleep by calling its Sleep method. Because Sleep is such a useful method, we've been working with it for some time now. Listing 5.3 shows Sleep in a number of forms.

Listing 5.3   Example of using various forms of Sleep (VB.NET)

```
Sub Main()
    Thread.CurrentThread.Name = "Main"
    Console.WriteLine(Thread.CurrentThread.Name)
    Dim SiteMonitor As New WebSiteMonitor("http://localhost/test.htm", 1000)

    Dim ThreadWatcher As ThreadStateWatcher
    ThreadWatcher = New ThreadStateWatcher()
    ThreadWatcher.WatchThread(Thread.CurrentThread)

    SiteMonitor.Start()
    Dim D, H, M, S, MS As Integer
    D = 0   ' Days
    H = 0   ' Hours
    M = 0   ' Minutes
    S = 20  ' Seconds
    MS = 0  ' Milliseconds
    Thread.Sleep(1000)
    Thread.Sleep(0)
    Thread.Sleep(New TimeSpan(100))
    Thread.Sleep(New TimeSpan(H, M, S))
    Thread.Sleep(New TimeSpan(D, H, M, S))
    Thread.Sleep(New TimeSpan(D, H, M, S, MS))
    Thread.CurrentThread.Interrupt()
    Thread.Sleep(System.Threading.Timeout.Infinite)
    SiteMonitor.Abort()
    SiteMonitor.Join()
End Sub
```

❶ Sleeps for one second

❷ Gives up the remainder of the time slice

❸ Sleeps for 100 ticks

❹ Sleeps until a different thread calls Interrupt

Sleep is a way for a thread to yield control to the OS. Naming the method Sleep is fairly accurate. You can think of it as the thread taking a nap. During naps, we don't consume many resources; we're still alive, and generally pretty easy to wake up. That applies equally well to threads that have invoked their Sleep method.

❶ There are different versions of the Sleep method. The version we have seen so far takes an integer parameter that indicates the maximum number of milliseconds the current thread should be allowed to sleep. In listing 5.3, the thread sleeps for one second, or one thousand milliseconds.

❷ This version passes zero to the Sleep method. When the parameter to Sleep is 0 this indicates that the current thread should yield the remainder of its time slice to the operating system and continue executing on the next time slice. There are times when this is a good idea. The thread watching class we discussed in section 4.5.2 is a good example of when this approach should be used. Instead of calling Sleep with five milliseconds, it would have been better to call it with zero. This would indicate that as soon as the thread had finished the current iteration of inspecting the other thread, it should yield the remainder of the current time slice. If the thread takes longer than one time slice to do its work, it will be interrupted and a context switch will occur. Using the thread watching class, we can see that calling Sleep on a thread causes it to enter the WaitSleepJoin state.

❸ This version of the Sleep method accepts a TimeSpan object as its parameter. The TimeSpan object can be created numerous ways and offers an easy way to indicate the length of time that a thread should sleep. One way to create a TimeSpan object is to pass in the number of ticks the span should account for. A tick is the smallest unit of time in .NET. There are 10,000,000 ticks in a second.

TimeSpan   TimeSpan is an object that represents a unit of time. There are various constructors that allow for a highly flexible means of representing time durations. One version of the Sleep method accepts a TimeSpan object as its parameter.

The TimeSpan object also allows for the span to be denoted in terms of days, hours, minutes, seconds, and milliseconds. The following statement causes the current thread to sleep for one hour, two minutes, and three seconds:

```
Thread.Sleep(New TimeSpan(1, 2, 3))
```

For threading purposes, sleeping for multiple days probably is not the best approach. Instead, the Schedule component is likely a better fit. However, for those cases where it is needed, the capability does exist. The following causes the current thread to sleep for one day, two hours, three minutes, four seconds, and five milliseconds:

```
Thread.Sleep(New TimeSpan(1, 2, 3, 4, 5))
```

             CHAPTER 5   CONTROLLING THREADS

❹ If the `Sleep` method is called with `System.Threading.Timeout.Infinite` passed in as the parameter, the thread will remain in the `WaitSleepJoin` state until a different thread wakes it by using the `Interrupt` method.

```
Thread.Sleep(System.Threading.Timeout.Infinite)
```

One reason you might want to do this is if a thread determines that it is in a state where the best thing it can do is nothing. This may be an alternative to ending the thread by using the `Abort` method, or simply exiting the thread's method. Once a thread ends, there is no way to restart it. However, if a thread calls the `Sleep` method and passes in `Infinite` for the timeout value, it is possible to exit that state at a later time.

This concept is similar to calling `Join`. When `Join` is called and no parameter is passed in, the current thread will wait indefinitely for the thread to end. When `Join` is called with a timeout value, the `Join` method will block for at most that period of time and then return a value indicating if the thread of interest ended. A key difference is that `Join` is called on a different thread while `Sleep` is called on the current thread. `Join` also causes the current thread to pause for a period of time, but with the idea that it is waiting for some other thread to terminate. At the point the thread being joined terminates, the `Join` method returns. Later we will see how to pause a different thread's execution.

5.3.2   The Interrupt method

Suppose that you're tasked with making sure your company's web site is functioning correctly. Your boss calls and asks, "Is the web site down?" In this case, you don't want to wait until the thread finishes sleeping to find out if the web site is not well. The `Interrupt` method on the instance of the `Thread` object allows one thread to wake up another.

Interrupt   The `Interrupt` method can be called on a thread that is in the `Sleep-WaitJoin` state. It raises a `ThreadInterruptedException` that causes the thread to exit the `SleepWaitJoin` state.

`Interrupt` is similar to `Abort` in that it causes an exception to be raised in the thread's method. If the exception is not handled, the thread will terminate. This is a recurring theme; always wrap a thread's main method with a `try catch` block to capture any exceptions that might arise. The `ThreadInterruptedException` is raised whenever another thread calls `Interrupt`. Notice in listing 5.4 that we aren't declaring a variable to reference the exception being caught in the case of the two thread exceptions.

Listing 5.4 Using the Interrupt method (C#)

```
private void ThreadMethod()
{
  while (true)
  {
    try
```

```
        {
            CheckSite();
            Thread.Sleep(sleepTime);
        }
        catch(ThreadInterruptedException)   ◁─┐  Raised when a thread
        {                                      │  calls Interrupt
            status = "Interrupted";
            System.Diagnostics.Trace.WriteLine(status);
        }
        catch(ThreadAbortException)
        {
            status = "Aborted";
            System.Diagnostics.Trace.WriteLine(status);
        }
        catch(Exception ex)
        {
            status = "Caught " + ex.ToString() + " " + ex.Message;
            System.Diagnostics.Trace.WriteLine(status);
        }
    }
}
```

The exception's message contains information on where the exception was generated. In our example we don't care where the `Abort` or `Interrupt` was initially triggered. We only care that they were triggered, so we can safely ignore the information.

To allow for easier user interaction let's move our example from the console-based world to the Windows Forms world. A screenshot of the application can be seen in figure 5.5. The class being called is basically the same as in previous examples except that instead of writing out to the console the state of the last request, we record the state in a status variable. This isn't ideal—in the future we'll save the output to a database—

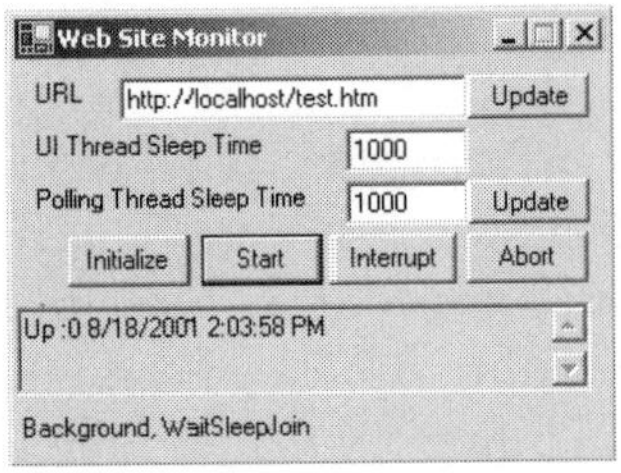

Figure 5.5 Our web site monitoring application

but for now, it's sufficient. We're now using properties to change the URL that is being checked, along with the time to sleep between requesting a download of the page referenced by the URL. The use of properties is always a good idea, but it becomes even more important when doing multithreaded development. Because properties restrict access to data elements, it is much easier to determine when a variable can change value. Since multiple threads may act upon a value, it is a good idea for them to go through a property to do so. We will discuss this more in future chapters.

We update the values displayed in the window of the application on a variable rate using a thread dedicated to that purpose. Because the native Windows controls are not thread-safe, we must use the control's `Invoke` method, passing in a delegate. We will discuss this more in chapter 15.

By changing the value of UI Thread Sleep Time you can change the responsiveness of the application. When the Initialize button is clicked, a new instance of WebSiteMonitor is created and assigned to the SiteMonitor variable. Clicking Start causes the URL and sleep time properties on SiteMonitor to be updated and invokes SiteMonitor's Start method. Clicking the Interrupt button causes the following code to be executed:

```
if (SiteMonitor != null)
{
  SiteMonitor.Interrupt();
}
else
{
  MessageBox.Show("Not Initialized");
}
```

SiteMonitor.Interrupt simply invokes the Interrupt method on the instance of the Thread class:

```
MonitorThread.Interrupt();
```

When the interrupt is signaled, a ThreadInterruptedException is generated. The exception likely will occur during the Thread.Sleep statement; however, since the WebClient object uses threads it is possible that the exception will occur during the DownloadData call. Exceptions should always be handled, and ideally as close to the source of the exception as possible. Chapter 13 covers thread-related exceptions in detail.

When we create the threads in this example, we set the IsBackground property to true. In the next section we'll explore that property and why we use it.

5.4 USING BACKGROUND AND FOREGROUND THREADS

Suppose that you had a thread that calculates the running average time to download a given web page. At the point the web site monitor is shutting down, there is no reason for that thread to continue to exist. To simplify application termination, you can mark the thread as a background thread. This is accomplished by using the IsBackground property.

IsBackground IsBackground is a property of the Thread object that controls termination of the process. When a thread is a background thread, it will be terminated at the point all foreground threads terminate.

In previous examples, we have assigned true to the IsBackground property. IsBackground controls how termination of a process is carried out. The application domain will continue to exist as long as there is at least one foreground thread executing. This means that if the main thread of the process exits and another foreground thread is executing, the process will continue to exist and the foreground thread will continue to execute.

In the following example we set UIThread's IsBackground property to true to indicate that the thread associated with UIThread is a background thread:

```
Private Sub Form1_Load (ByVal sender . . .)
  Thread.CurrentThread.Name = "Main"
  UIThreadSleepTime = 1000
  UIThread = New Thread(AddressOf UpdateUIMethod)
  UIThread.Name = "UIThread"
  UIThread.IsBackground = True     ◁─┐  Makes UIThread a
  UIThread.Start()                    │  background thread
End Sub
```

Suppose you have a process that has two threads in it: one is a foreground thread, while the other is a background thread. If the background thread ends, the foreground thread will continue to execute, as you would expect (figure 5.6). The ending of background threads has no effect on the life of the process where the thread lives.

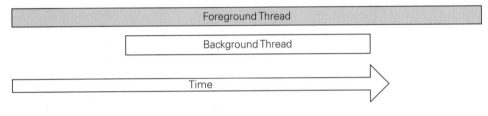

Figure 5.6   Background thread ending before foreground thread

If the foreground thread terminates before the background thread, the background thread's execution is also ended. Figure 5.7 shows an example where the termination of the foreground thread causes the background thread to be terminated. When the last foreground thread ends, the process also ends. When the background thread is ended, no exceptions are raised in the background thread's methods. This means that the background thread is not given the chance to gracefully exit. If some operation is partially completed, it will be interrupted and the thread will terminate.

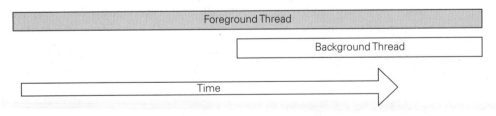

Figure 5.7   Foreground thread ending before background thread

A common mistake that developers new to multithreaded development make revolves around foreground threads and process termination. A process will continue to exist as long as there is at least one foreground thread. Figure 5.8 demonstrates this.

CHAPTER 5   CONTROLLING THREADS

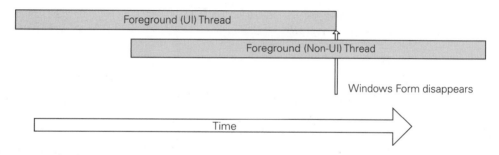

Figure 5.8 Multiple foreground threads

When a Windows Form application starts up, the only thread that exists is the thread that creates the user interface elements, such as buttons, text boxes, and the form itself. During the execution of the main thread, another foreground thread is created. When the main, user interface oriented thread exits, the visual portion of the application disappears. However, the application continues to execute because there is still at least one foreground thread executing. The application will terminate when the last foreground thread exits, or when the process is terminated.

The mistake is that the non-UI foreground thread does not terminate as expected, not that there is more than one foreground thread.

Clean Shutdown To perform a clean shutdown of a process call the `Abort` method on the thread and then call the `Join` method to wait for it to end.

In our example, the `SiteMonitor` thread accesses web sites using the `WebClient` object from the `Net` namespace. `WebClient` retrieves web pages by opening sockets, starting threads, and closing sockets. Ending this thread in the middle of some operations can cause undesirable results. It's a good idea to terminate the thread cleanly, using the `Abort` method. It also is a good idea to use the `Join` method to wait for the thread to terminate. Since our application is a Windows application, we can add an `Application Closing` event handler:

```
Private Sub WebSiteMonitorForm_Closing(...) Handles MyBase.Closing
   If Not IsNothing(SiteMonitor) Then
     SiteMonitor.Abort()
     SiteMonitor.Join(1000)
   End If
End Sub
```

The parameters are omitted for space reasons. Since the user may not click on Initialize before closing the application, we first check to see if `SiteMonitor` has been assigned. If it has, we invoke the `Abort` method and then the `Join` method. Since `Join` expects that the thread has started, we need to change the `Join` method to add defensive code that checks if the thread is alive before calling `Join`.

```
Public Sub Join(ByVal HowLong As Integer)
  If MonitorThread.IsAlive Then
    MonitorThread.Join(HowLong)
  End If
End Sub
```

This allows the application to shut down cleanly.

5.5   USING SUSPEND AND RESUME

As a child you may have played a game called "freeze tag" or "statue tag." In the game, one, and only one, of the players is It. If you're It, your goal is to freeze all of the other players by tagging them. If a player you tag is touched by a player who is not frozen, that person is thawed and can return to play. This is fairly close to how the Suspend and Resume methods work.

When a thread's Suspend method is invoked it goes into a frozen state. This state is very similar to the WaitSleepJoin state except that in order to leave that state the thread must either terminate or the Resume method must be invoked. Just as in the game of freeze tag, the thread that invokes the Suspend method is not required to be the same one that invokes the Resume method.

The Suspend and Resume methods are not a means of synchronizing threads. In the next chapter we discuss ways of having threads talk to each other without bad things happening. When the Suspend method is invoked, it causes the thread to pause its execution as soon as it reaches a point where it can do so. This means that if that thread owns a certain resource, it will continue to own that resource even though it is in a suspended state. In general Suspend and Resume should be avoided. They are covered here for completeness and so that if you ever encounter a situation where you need them you know what they are.

A multithreaded version of freeze tag is available at www.manning.com/dennis. It is simple, but demonstrates how Suspend and Resume can be used.

5.5.1   The Suspend method

We have seen how a thread can put itself to sleep for a period of time. Suppose you had two threads: Thread A and Thread B. Thread A is the main thread, meaning it is created when the application domain is created. It creates and starts Thread B. Thread B does some work, and during its work Thread B sleeps for a period of time. Thread A calls the Interrupt method on Thread B, forcing Thread B to continue its execution. Figure 5.9 is a visual representation of the flow that occurs.

The number 1 in figure 5.9 is the point where Thread A creates Thread B and calls Start. The number 2 is where Thread A calls Interrupt on Thread B. Notice that Thread B put itself to sleep. Thread B decides to go to sleep at the point that the Sleep statement is evaluated because the Sleep statement places the thread into a safe point.

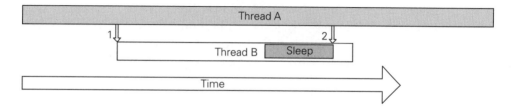

Figure 5.9   Impact of sleep and safe points

Suspend   Suspend is a method on the Thread object that allows one thread to pause the execution of another thread (including its own). The suspend request will take effect as soon as the thread being suspended reaches a safe point.

A thread cannot call Sleep on a different thread. In order for one thread to pause the execution of another, it must use the Suspend method. Unlike Sleep, Suspend doesn't necessarily cause the thread to pause immediately. The thread must enter a safe point before it can be suspended.

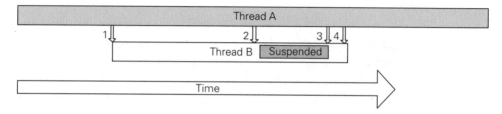

Figure 5.10   Example of Suspend

Thread A starts Thread B at point 1 in figure 5.10. Notice that at point 2 Thread A calls Suspend on Thread B. It takes a little time for Thread B to enter the Suspended state. A thread cannot cause itself to exit the Suspended state. Instead, some other thread must invoke the Resume method (point 3) to cause a thread to exit the Suspended state. Thread B terminates at point 4.

NOTE   Suspend is not a synchronization mechanism. It should not be used in place of a synchronization mechanism. It should only be used in situations where synchronization is not a concern.

In the previous chapter we discussed the ThreadState property of the Thread class. When Suspend is called on a thread the ThreadState property's Suspended bit is turned on. When Suspend is called on a thread, that has already been suspended, it has no effect. If a thread called Suspend 1,000 times on a thread, and then called Resume once, the thread would exit the Suspended state and continue execution.

There are paths from one state to another that are allowed, while other paths are not. We call these paths state transitions. An example of an allowed state transition is going from the Unstarted state to the Running state when the Start method is called. When an invalid state transition is attempted, a `ThreadStateException` is thrown. For instance, when a thread is in the `Suspended` state as a result of some other thread calling the thread's `Suspend` method, if the `Abort` method is invoked on that thread a `ThreadStateException` is thrown.

```
public void ForceAbort()
{
  try
  {
    if ((MonitorThread.ThreadState & ThreadState.Suspended)  > 0)
    {
      status = "Can't abort a suspended thread";
      MonitorThread.Resume();
    }
    MonitorThread.Abort();
  }
  catch(System.Threading.ThreadStateException ex)
  {
    status = "Abort attempted:" + ex.Message;
    System.Diagnostics.Trace.WriteLine(status);
  }
}
```

Since our application doesn't restrict what buttons the user can click, we need to provide error handling. In general, error handling is a good idea, but when dealing with threads it is very important. At the very least, it's a good idea to wrap all calls to methods that can change the state of a thread with `try catch` blocks. A more robust form of error handling would be to check the state the thread is in before attempting to change it. Spending time developing robust error handling can greatly reduce the time associated with maintenance and debugging a multithreaded application. This concept is true of developing any application, but because of the potentially high complexity of developing multithreaded applications it is imperative to provide good error logging, if not error handling.

5.5.2 The Resume method

In the previous section we covered the `Suspend` method. We saw how it allows us to interrupt the execution of a thread and place it in a `Suspended` state. To exit the `Suspended` state, we use the `Resume` method. Regardless of how many times `Suspend` was called, a single call to `Resume` allows the thread to exit the `Suspended` state.

> **Resume**   Resume is a method on the `Thread` object that allows a thread to continue execution after it has been suspended by calling the `Suspend` method.

In the last chapter we discussed several other thread states. In this chapter we have added to that list. The `Suspended` state is entered whenever a thread has its `Suspend` method invoked. In order to exit that state, we must call `Resume`. If a thread is in the `Suspended` state and some method other than `Resume` is called, it will likely result in a `ThreadStateException`.

	ThreadStateException occur when a method is called that attempts to cause a thread to move into a state that is not allowed based upon the thread's current state. An example is when a thread is in the Stopped state; it cannot be moved to the Running state by calling Start.

Thread-State-Exception

ThreadStateExceptions occur when a method is called that attempts to cause a thread to move into a state that is not allowed based upon the thread's current state. An example is when a thread is in the Stopped state; it cannot be moved to the Running state by calling Start.

For example, if a thread is in the Suspended state and Abort is called on that thread, a ThreadStateException will be raised on the calling thread. This brings us back to handling exceptions when dealing with threads. Every method that acts upon a thread should be included in a try catch block that logs any exceptions that occur. Many of the examples so far have not included error handling, primarily because it can make it difficult to see the actual concepts involved. In general, unless the purpose of the code is to demonstrate a concept, error handling should be included around every call to each method on an instance of the Thread class that could cause a state transition.

5.6   EXPLORING THREAD STATES

Threads can be in multiple states. For instance, a thread can be in the Background and WaitSleepJoin states at the same time. Other states are mutually exclusive; for instance, a thread cannot be in the Aborted and the Running state at the same time. Table 5.1 outlines the states a thread can be in concurrently.

Table 5.1   Mutually exclusive thread states: N indicates that a thread cannot be in two states at the same time, while a Y indicates it can.

State	AbortRequested	Aborted	Background	Unstarted	Suspended	Running	WaitSleepJoin	Stopped	SuspendRequested
AbortRequested									
Aborted	N								
Background	Y	Y							
Unstarted	Y	N	Y						
Suspended	Y	N	Y	N					
Running	N	N	N	N	N				
WaitSleepJoin	Y	N	Y	N	Y	N			
Stopped	N	N	Y	N	N	N	N		
SuspendRequested	Y	N	Y	N	N	N	Y	N	

It is important when dealing with threads to know what state the thread is in. Since threads can change state between the time you check and the execution of some instruction, it is imperative that error handling be in place to handle unforeseen circumstances. Traditional single-threaded development usually involves controlling what can happen based on the current state the program is in. Since state is ever-changing in multithreaded development, a more flexible approach must be taken. For instance, it might make sense to do the following:

```
if (SiteMonitor.Suspended)
{
  SiteMonitor.Resume();
}
```

The problem is that between the time that the test to see if Suspended is true and the time Resume is called, a different thread might have called Resume on the same thread. Instead, the call in the example should be contained in a try block.

Figure 5.11 contains an extended version of the state transition diagram we presented at the end of chapter 4.

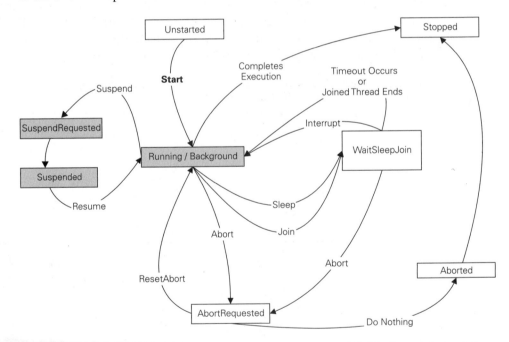

Figure 5.11 Expanded state transition diagram from chapter 4. A link indicates that a state transition can occur between those two states.

5.7   DIGGING DEEPER INTO THREAD CONTROL

It's unlikely that you will need to use the advanced topics in this section, but it's a good idea to be aware of them. If you are new to multithreaded development, you can safely skip this section. The material covered here contains concepts that are not required to develop a multithreaded application.

5.7.1   Controlling thread priority

So far our web site monitor has monitored only one site. If we add a second site to monitor, it might well be that one of the sites is more important than the other. It is possible to give each thread a different priority, and this may improve responsiveness. I say *may* because dealing with thread priority (figure 5.12) is somewhat tricky. It depends a great deal on what a thread is doing, what the machine executing the process is doing, and the configuration of the machine. If each thread is processor bound, then giving one thread a higher priority than another might result in some threads not being given a chance to do their work. Processor bound means the thread is using the CPU more than other resources. Changing priority of a thread may make no difference, it might make things much worse, or it might make things much better. We'll explore this in detail and discuss when adjusting a thread's priority is a good idea and when it is not.

When a thread is created, it inherits the priority of that process. In figure 5.12 the process has a priority of 8. Thread3 has the same priority as the process since it has a priority level of `Normal`. Priority is a relative thing. If all threads in a process have the same priority, they will be given a chance to execute roughly the same number of times. The catch here is that priority makes a difference only when a thread is available for scheduling. A thread needs to be in a state where it can do work to be scheduled.

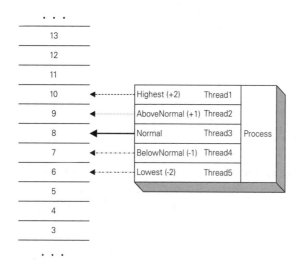

Thread Priority is relative to the priority of the process. In this example, the process has a priority of 8.

Thread1 in that process is set to the highest priority level and has a priority level of 10.

Thread5 is set to the lowest priority level and has a priority of 6.

If Thread5 and Thread1 are both available for scheduling, Thread1 will execute.

Figure 5.12   How a thread's priority is calculated

The priority system is based on a scale from 0 to 31, with 31 being the highest. To change the priority of a thread, we use the `ThreadPriority` property on the instance of the `Thread` class. For example, if we have an instance of the `Thread` class called `WorkingThread`, we can change its priority to `AboveNormal` by using the following statement:

```
WorkingThread.Priority = ThreadPriority.AboveNormal
```

From time to time the OS may temporarily increase the priority of a thread. This is called a priority boost. This is often done when the scheduler determines that a thread has some needed resource allocated, but doesn't have a high enough priority that it can complete its usage of the resource. By assigning a priority to a thread, you are giving the scheduler a hint as to how it should execute your thread. It will follow your guidance pretty closely, but it may intervene from time to time.

A process has a priority associated with it. `PriorityClass`, which is an enumeration of five values, sets the process's priority. The enumerated values, along with the corresponding base priority, are listed in table 5.2. The process priority combined with the thread's priority yields the dynamic priority of the thread. This is the value that is used by the operating system scheduler. Table 5.2 presents a simplified version of how a thread's priority is calculated.

Table 5.2 Process Class and Associated Priority

Priority Class	Base Priority
RealTime	24
AboveNormal	10
Normal	8
BelowNormal	6
Idle	4

When you're doing multithreaded development, initially it's best not to change thread priority. It is possible to mask serious issues, such as race conditions, which we will cover in the next chapter, by changing the priority of a thread. This is a short-term solution and will most likely not fix the problem. Changing thread priority is an optimization, and as with all optimizations it should be done only after careful analysis and profiling. When you're profiling, it is best to use the same type of hardware the application will be deployed on. So, if the application will be installed on a four-processor machine, it is a good idea to profile, and test, the application on a four-processor machine. Scheduling of threads is done on a per-processor basis. The behavior of an application may change when you move from a single processor to a multiprocessor machine:

	Process Base Priority
+	Thread Priority Delta
+	Priority Boost (If Any)
	Thread Current Priority

There are circumstances where changing a thread's priority is always a good idea. When a task is not critical to completion of some work and it can be delayed, it likely makes sense to lower that thread's priority. This may free up resources for other threads. If a thread has important work to do (is processor intensive), but that work isn't always present, it is probably a good idea to increase the thread's priority. Small changes in priority are typically the best. This is not an example of *if a little does a little good, a lot will do a lot of good.*

5.7.2 Setting processor affinity

Under normal situations the OS scheduler assigns the highest priority available thread to each processor in the system. This means that if a process has more than one thread, each of those threads may execute on different processors. Generally this is exactly what is wanted. An exception is when the process contains CPU-intensive activity or the server is under a high load from other sources.

By limiting what processor a process can utilize, you create situations where performance can be improved. A processor contains a certain amount of memory, called a *cache*. By keeping the same thread on the same processor, you ensure that the cache is utilized more frequently, and performance improves. The scheduler in Windows attempts to keep a thread on the same processor if possible for that very reason. This is known as soft processor affinity.

Processor Affinity   Processor affinity is a means of controlling the scheduling of a process so that a certain process's threads will execute on a set of processors.

A process can also tell the scheduler that it should run only on certain processors. This keeps the process on the processors where it is allowed to execute. This is called processor affinity. It is possible to change a process's processor affinity using the `System.Diagnostics.Process` class. Using the static/shared method on the `Process` class called `GetCurrentProcess` retrieves a reference to the current process. We can then change the `ProcessorAffinity` property to indicate the desired affinity. `ProcessorAffinity` is a pointer to a 32-bit integer. It contains a bitmask on which processors a process can execute. The low-order bit corresponds to the first processor in the machine, CPU 0. The high-order bit matches the last processor that can be installed in the machine, which under 32-bit Windows is 32. In figure 5.13 we can infer that the machine has at least three processors and that the process can execute on CPU 1 and CPU 2 but not on CPU 0.

...	0	1	1	0

Figure 5.13 Bitmask value example

The integer value returned by `ProcessorAffinity` would be 6:

$$(0*2^3) + (1*2^2) + (1*2^1) + (0*2^0)=6$$

Figure 5.14 shows the impact of changing the processes' processor affinity.

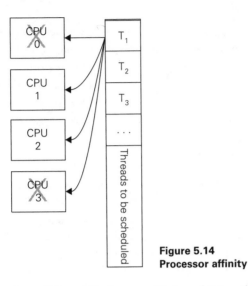

Figure 5.14
Processor affinity

Since Thread T_1 has an affinity of 6 it will not be scheduled on CPU 0 or CPU 3. It will only be scheduled on CPU 1 or CPU 2.

When a process first loads, it can determine what processors it can execute on by examining the contents of `ProcessorAffinity`. It is important to remember that even though you might set the processor affinity, it is possible that it will change during the life of the process. One way this can happen is by using Task Monitor. If you right-click on a process, on a machine with more than one processor, you can select Set Affinity. This will display the dialog box in figure 5.15.

By selecting what processor the current process can execute on, you can essentially override any settings that might have been specified by the program. Remember this

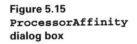

Figure 5.15
`ProcessorAffinity`
dialog box

when developing. Do not count on multiple processors. Even in situations where there are multiple processors the scheduler may choose to execute each thread of a process on the same processor. Under symmetric multiprocessing, the process has very little control of how it is scheduled. In general, it is better to let the operating system take care of it for you.

USING TASK MANAGER TO SET PROCESSOR AFFINITY

1 Open Task Manager.
2 Right-click on the process that you wish to change the processor affinity of.
3 Select Set Affinity from the context menu that pops up.
4 Update the check boxes.
5 Click OK.

One use of this type of capability would be to restrict a misbehaving multithreaded application to execute on a single processor. This may remove concurrency issues. Since each thread in the process would execute on the same processor, true concurrency would not be reached. This may reduce timing issues. This approach is not a replacement to proper design and implementation, but under extreme circumstances it is a valid short-term fix.

5.7.3   Specifying an ideal processor

Suppose that you wanted the web site monitor to utilize a certain processor. One way you could accomplish this is to set the process's processor affinity as we discussed in the last section. A less restrictive approach is to set the thread's ideal processor.

> **Ideal Processor**   An ideal processor is one that a thread would prefer to be scheduled on. The scheduler may or may not honor that preference.

This allows us to give the scheduler a hint as to what processor we think that the thread should execute on. The scheduler may or may not listen to our hint because we don't know as much about the load on the system as it does. It may be that some other process also thinks it should execute on the same processor we think we should execute on.

The motivation of setting an ideal processor is to take advantage of the CPU's cache. Since it has been working with the data our thread uses, the data is already in the CPU's cache. Loading the CPU's cache is a relatively expensive operation. Processors have caches because it is much faster to retrieve data from a cache than it is from main memory. Caching is also done at multiple levels. If the data the processor needs isn't in the first-level cache it looks in the second. If the data isn't in the second-level cache, it looks in main memory. Not all systems have a second-level cache. For those systems with only a first-level cache, if the data needed isn't in that cache it is loaded there from main memory. Processor cache sizes have grown to where relatively large first-level caches are not unusual. When a processor references data, it is generally loaded into the cache (listing 5.5).

Listing 5.5 Setting a process's ideal processor (C#)

```
. . .
Process MyProcess;
ProcessThread MyProcessThread;
. . .
private void ThreadMethod()
{
  MonitorThreadId= AppDomain.GetCurrentThreadId();
  MyProcess = Process.GetCurrentProcess();
  for (int i=0;i<MyProcess.Threads.Count;i++)
  {
    if( MyProcess.Threads[i].Id == MonitorThreadId)
    {
      MyProcessThread = MyProcess.Threads[i];
      break;
    }
  }
  if (MyProcessThread== null)
  {
    throw new Exception("Thread Not Found in Current Process");
  }
. . .
  MyProcessThread.IdealProcessor = 2;
. . .
```

Listing 5.5 shows how to set a process's ideal processor. The `Threading.Thread` object does not enable us to set a thread's ideal processor. Instead, we must use the `Diagnostics.ProcessThread` object. In order to retrieve the `ProcessThread` object that corresponds to a certain thread, we must first determine the thread's ID. This isn't exposed as a property of the `Thread` object. Instead, we need to call `App-Domain.GetCurrentThreadId` from a method that is executing on the thread we're dealing with.

The `System.Threading.Thread` class does not expose the OS thread ID because on some platforms one-for-one mapping may not exist between a managed thread and an OS thread. Certain handheld platforms may not provide OS multi-threaded support. On those platforms the .NET framework will provide the multi-threaded support itself, instead of relying on the OS. The framework provides an abstraction between the physical threading implementation and managed threading. This means that interacting with OS-level threads and processes may restrict the platforms an application can execute on.

Once we have the thread's ID, we can look for it in the current process. We retrieve the current process using the `Diagnostics.Process.GetCurrentProcess` method. Once we have the current process, we examine its `Threads` collection. We look at each `ProcessThread` object in the `Threads` collection, checking the `Id` property to see if it is the same as our current thread's ID. Once we find the matching

ProcessThread, we can set its IdealProcessor property. IdealProcessor is a write-only property. This means we can set the ideal processor but we cannot see what the current ideal processor is. Only one processor can be the ideal processor at a time. Instead of passing in a bitmask as we did in setting the process's processor affinity, we pass in a value indicating which is the ideal processor. For example, we pass in 2 to indicate that CPU 2 is our ideal processor. To undo the ideal processor setting, we use the ProcessThread's ResetIdealProcessor method. This removes the setting of the current ideal processor.

STEPS TO SET IDEAL PROCESSOR

1 Retrieve the current thread's ID using GetCurrentThreadId.
2 Retrieve the current process by calling GetCurrentProcess.
3 Look for the current thread in the current process's threads.
4 Set IdealProcessor on the ProcessThread object.

Setting the ideal processor is a way of giving the scheduler a hint as to where the thread should be executed. If we've selected a process affinity mask, the ideal processors should be one of the processor we've selected.

The concept of an ideal processor is so important that the scheduler attempts to keep threads on the same processor, if possible. Figure 5.16 shows that by keeping a thread on the same processor the contents of the processor's cache need to be refreshed less often than if a different processor was used. Under most circumstances the scheduler does a good job. Setting the ideal processor is an optimization and should be done only once. It is clear that it improves performance. Optimization should be performed after correctness has been reached, and only if it is needed.

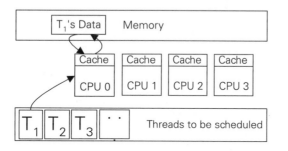

Figure 5.16 Motivation for setting an ideal processor

T_1 has selected CPU 0 as its ideal processor. By keeping T_1's most recently used data in CPU 0's cache, performance can be improved. If T_1 is then scheduled on a different CPU, the data will need to be loaded into that CPU's cache. If instead T_1 were consistently scheduled on CPU 0, the data would already be in the cache. One thing to keep in mind is that other processes can set things like ideal processor. Just as tools like Process Viewer can change thread priority, a program can change the ideal processor. To test out setting IdealProcessor you can use the ProcessThreadViewer program that is available from the publisher's web site at www.manning.com/dennis. The program allows inspection of a process and each of its threads. You can also set IdealProcessor for a particular thread. This tool is for learning purposes only and can result in system instability. Be careful playing with it.

5.8   SUMMARY

This chapter exposed you to the basic concepts and syntax of thread control. You've learned how to put a thread to Sleep and Interrupt it. You've learned that one thread can call Suspend and Resume on another thread. Most important, you've learned the rules governing the termination of an application domain with regard to background and foreground threads.

We've also covered some deeper topics in section 5.7. Don't be concerned if they seem a bit overwhelming. It's not important that you understand them until you plan to use them, at which time you can return to these sections. Now that you've learned how to control threads, we can move on to the next chapter and see how threads can communicate.

CHAPTER 6

Communicating with threads

Communication is very important. In software development a project that does not have good communication among the team members is not likely to succeed. The same is true in multithreaded development. The ability for one thread to communicate with another allows for robust solutions. Since C# and VB.NET do not allow for methods without classes, each method associated with a thread delegate is associated with the class it resides in. This means that the method has access to the data elements that are contained within its class. This provides an easy and powerful way for a thread to have access to data elements. Those data elements are encapsulated in a class and can be protected.

The first way of communicating between threads that we will cover is the use of public fields. Public fields are no more than public data elements. They can be manipulated directly from other objects. This is one of the simplest ways of communicating with threads. It has many drawbacks, all of which are related to using public fields in general. Public fields violate the concept of encapsulation. Encapsulation encourages the designer of objects to restrict knowledge of the inner workings of an object as much as possible. This means that if I'm using an object I should not need to know how it works to use it.

We then move on to the use of public properties as a means of communicating with threads. Public properties solve many of the issues of public fields. The area where public properties fall short is when communication between threads involves multiple pieces of data.

The last means of communicating with threads we cover in this chapter involves using first-in, first-out queues associated with a public method. Public methods can have multiple parameters and can be used to submit elements to the queue.

We complete the chapter by discussing race conditions and deadlocks. These are two common issues related to thread communications. We will discuss their causes and explore ways of avoiding both of these conditions.

6.1 USING DATA TO COMMUNICATE

When a thread is created using managed code, there is no way to pass information to it directly. Instead, we must take advantage of the fact that all methods in the .NET framework are associated with a class or an instance of a class. This means that if we change a value of an instance of a class, a thread associated with that instance of the class will be able to see that change. The simplest way of changing a value associated with a class is to use a public field.

6.1.1 Public fields

We will continue using the web site monitoring tool we introduced in the last chapter as our example. When a web site goes down, logging that information is only part of the goal. The more important part is letting someone know the site is down. One way of informing people is to send email messages.

The .NET framework makes it very easy to send messages using the `System.Web.Mail` namespace. The `SmtpMail` object contains a static/shared property called `SmtpServer` that identifies the name address of the SMTP server to use to send the email. The `send` method causes a message to be sent using the specified SMTP server. Listing 6.1 contains the class `SMTPNotification`.

Listing 6.1   SMTP mail notification thread (C#)

```csharp
using System;
using System.Web.Mail;
using System.Threading;
namespace PublicFields
{
  public class SMTPNotification
  {
    // Public Fields
    public bool TimeToSendNotification;
    public string To,Subject,Body,From,ServerName;
    //
    Thread SendingThread;
    public SMTPNotification()
```

```
    {
      SendingThread= new Thread(new ThreadStart(ThreadMethod));
      ServerName="mail";
      From=To="noone@nowhere.com";
      Subject="Test from code " ;
      Body = "This is the Body";
      TimeToSendNotification=false;
      SendingThread.Name="SMTPThread";
      SendingThread.Start();
    }
. . .
    private void ThreadMethod()
    {
      while(true)
      {
        try
        {
          if (TimeToSendNotification)   ❶ Controls when a
          {                                message is sent
            SmtpMail.SmtpServer = ServerName;
            SmtpMail.Send(From,To,Subject,Body);
            TimeToSendNotification=false;
          }
          Thread.Sleep(1000);
        }
        catch(Exception ex)
        {
          System.Diagnostics.Trace.WriteLine(ex.Message);
        }
      }
    }
  }
}
```

❶ Since sending an email message involves connecting to a mail server through the network, it may take a relatively long time. It is better to send the message on a different
thread than the one monitoring the web site. The notification thread is dedicated to
sending notification email messages. It sleeps the majority of the time, waking up to
check for work and then sleeping again. When the monitoring thread determines that
a web site is down and that it should notify someone, it sets a public Boolean field,
TimeToSendNotification, to true. This indicates that it is time to send a message. The notification thread sees this, and uses the From, To, Subject, and Body
public fields to send the email message.

While having one thread control the operation of another is the idea, this approach
introduces many problems. Setting the public fields must be done in the proper sequence.
Generally, performing a series of assignments in a certain order is not a good thing.

Since the fields are public, every consumer of the class has access to those data elements. This means that there is no restriction as to who can manipulate those values, and in what order. It also means that the user of the object must be familiar with how the object behaves. This violates the concept of encapsulation.

PUBLIC FIELD COMMUNICATION

One way for one thread to communicate with another is to set public fields. The issues with this approach are:

- Decreased encapsulation of information—other objects are required to know too much about the inner workings of an object.
- The lack of synchronization opportunities.
- The possibility that data changes are missed due to timing issues.

Any value can be assigned to the fields since there is no validation mechanism. The only validation that can be performed is before the message is actually sent. Ideally we would not allow the value to be assigned if it isn't valid. We will cover this in the next section on properties. In the next chapter we will discuss synchronization concepts in detail. For now, synchronization becomes an issue when multiple threads are manipulating the same data. One thread may change the value while another is accessing it. When this occurs, the results of the interaction become indeterminate. This is one of the biggest challenges of multithreaded programming and is amplified by allowing direct manipulation of data elements.

The web site monitoring thread does not stop and wait for the notification thread to finish its work (figure 6.1). There is the possibility that during the time the notification thread is sending the message the web site monitoring thread may determine that the web site is still down and that another message should be sent. The web site monitoring thread would populate the To, From, Body, and Subject fields and then set the TimeToSendNotification field to true. During this time, the TimeToSendNotification field would already be true since the notification thread is in the process of sending the message. Once that message is sent, the notification thread would set the TimeToSendNotification to false. This means that the second notification message would not be sent. If more than one web site is being monitored, the failure of one site might not be reported because of the slow notification time.

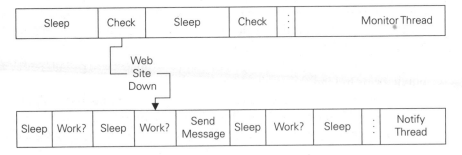

Figure 6.1   How two threads can interact

The goal is for one thread to impact the state of another. In the next section we'll cover properties. Public properties address many of the issues with using public fields as a communication mechanism.

6.1.2 Public properties

Public properties behave a lot like public fields. Properties are essentially a pair of methods. One of the methods is used to get the value while the other is used to set it. They are a powerful and convenient way of limiting access to data elements. Since access to the internal data value is limited to access by the property, the value being assigned can be inspected. The following example shows how to define a public property:

```
Public Class SMTPNotification
  Private mTimeToSendNotification As Boolean
. . .
  Public Sub New()
. . .
    mTimeToSendNotification = False
. . .
  End Sub
. . .
  Public Property TimeToSendNotification() As Boolean
    Get
      Return mTimeToSendNotification
    End Get
    Set(ByVal Value As Boolean)
      If Value = False Then
        Throw New Exception("Assigning to False is not allowed")
      End If
      If mTimeToSendNotification = True Then
        Throw New Exception("Missed notification")
      End If
      mTimeToSendNotification = Value
    End Set
  End Property
. . .
End Class
```

If the mTimeToSendNotification data element is true, we do not want to allow it to be assigned true again. This is a means of enforcing rules regarding the object. In this case, the mTimeToSendNotification is used to signal when the notification thread should send a notification email. Replacing a true value with another true value can only occur when the notification message has not been sent. In our example we throw an exception, forcing the caller to deal with the invalid state transition.

Additionally, we can ensure that only certain values are assigned. In this case, the only value that should be assigned to the TimeToSendNotification property is True. If an attempt is made to assign False to the property, an exception is thrown.

Properties Properties are a means of controlling data access that allow for robust error handling and data protection. They are implemented as a pair of methods that control the getting and setting data element values. If only the `Get` portion of the property is present, the property is read-only. If only the `Set` portion of the property is present, the property is write-only.

Properties are an important aspect of object-oriented programming. They allow the consumer of a class to interact with that class without being tied to the internal implementation. This means that the users of a class can interact with it without knowing how the class actually performs its operations (figure 6.2). The internal workings of the class may change and the consumer of that class need not change the way they are using the class. This is very closely related to the concept of an interface, which serves as a contract between the provider of some service and the consumer of that service.

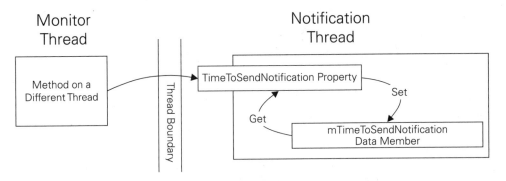

Figure 6.2 Using properties for thread communication

Our example uses properties to cross thread boundaries. This addresses several of the issues we raised with public fields in the last section. We can control when a value is changed. We can determine if the value is valid for a given situation and can even restrict certain properties to being set only once. An example of this is the `Name` property on the `Thread` class. It can be assigned only once.

You might be wondering how properties are actually implemented. Listing 6.2 shows the `Set` portion of the `TimeToSendNotification` property (MSIL).

Listing 6.2 The Set portion of the TimeToSendNotification property (MSIL)

```
.method public specialname instance void
        set_TimeToSendNotification(bool Value) cil managed
{
  // Code size        47 (0x2f)
  .maxstack  8
  IL_0000:  nop
  IL_0001:  ldarg.1
  IL_0002:  ldc.i4.0
  IL_0003:  bne.un.s    IL_0010
```

```
IL_0005:  ldstr      "Assigning to False is not allowed"
IL_000a:  newobj     instance void [mscorlib]System.Exception::.ctor(string)
IL_000f:  throw
IL_0010:  nop
IL_0011:  ldarg.0
IL_0012:  ldfld      bool PublicProperties.SMTPNotification::mTimeToSend-
Notification
IL_0017:  ldc.i4.1
IL_0018:  bne.un.s   IL_0025
IL_001a:  ldstr      "Missed notification"
IL_001f:  newobj     instance void [mscorlib]System.Exception::.ctor(string)
IL_0024:  throw
IL_0025:  nop
IL_0026:  ldarg.0
IL_0027:  ldarg.1
IL_0028:  stfld      bool PublicProperties.SMTPNotification::mTimeToSend-
Notification
IL_002d:  nop
IL_002e:  ret
} // end of method SMTPNotification::set_TimeToSendNotification
```

Notice that the method name is set_TimeToSendNotification. The compiler maps the Set portion of the property to a method named set_PropertyName, where PropertyName is the name of the property. This lets us see that properties are intended to make it easy for developers to wrap access to data elements with methods. This follows a common approach of writing a Get and Set method for each data element of a class. If a property includes a Get portion, a method named get_PropertyName is also generated. In the case of TimeToSendNotification the MSIL is shown in listing 6.3.

Listing 6.3   The Get portion of the TimeToSendNotification property (MSIL)

```
.method public specialname instance bool
        get_TimeToSendNotification() cil managed
{
  // Code size       12 (0xc)
  .maxstack  1
  .locals init ([0] bool TimeToSendNotification)
  IL_0000:  nop
  IL_0001:  ldarg.0
  IL_0002:  ldfld      bool PublicProperties.SMTPNotification::mTimeToSend-
Notification
  IL_0007:  stloc.0
  IL_0008:  br.s       IL_000a
  IL_000a:  ldloc.0
  IL_000b:  ret
} // end of method SMTPNotification::get_TimeToSendNotification
```

Notice that the return data type of the `get_TimeToSendNotification` method is `bool`, just as the data type of the single parameter to `set_TimeToSend-Notification` was also `bool`. It isn't important to understand all of the MSIL; however, by looking at it you can often learn a great deal.

In our example, the web site monitoring thread determines that the site is down. It checks to see if it has been instructed to send notification messages. If it has, it sets the various properties on the class associated with the notification thread and then sets the `TimeToSendNotification` property to true. This changes the private data element that controls when the notification thread sends email messages.

If a second assignment is made to `TimeToSendNotification` before the sending of the message is complete and the value of the internal data element is set to true, an exception is raised. We will address this particular problem with a more robust solution involving the use of queues between threads.

6.1.3 Queues and threads

People work at different speeds. Some work very quickly; others take longer to accomplish their tasks. This is true of threads as well. One thread may be able to do its work very quickly while another may take longer. Often a thread will receive a rapid succession of elements to deal with and then have long periods where it is idle. A way to handle these situations is to utilize a queue. Recall that a queue is a first-in, first-out collection. Logically, an element is added at the end of the queue and is later retrieved from the front. This works well with threading issues.

WHY USE QUEUES?
- Threads execute at different speeds and a queue can act as a buffer between them.
- Queues enable the sequential processing of entries.
- Queues allow the workload to be spread out over a longer period of time.
- Fire-and-forget situations are good uses of queues.

In the last section we saw how public properties address many of the issues with thread communication. Several issues could not be overcome using properties. The biggest issue is that properties accept a single value. This means that multiple properties need to be set in order to perform the desired task. One way of dealing with this might be to have a property that deals with an object, in our case a `MailMessage` object. `MailMessage` objects are in the `System.Web.Mail` namespace and represent an SMTP mail message. There are no technical reasons why setting a property couldn't add an instance of the `MailMessage` object to a queue; however, this is not how properties are expected to behave. Instead a public method is a more logical fit.

In listing 6.4 the `SendNotification` method accepts four parameters and assigns them to the properties of the `MailMessage` object. It then adds that object to the notification queue. The notification queue is an instance of the `Collections.Queue` class. It is instantiated in the constructor.

```csharp
using System;
using System.Web.Mail;
using System.Threading;
using System.Collections;
namespace QueuesAndThreads
{
  public class SMTPNotification
  {
    Queue NotificationQueue;
    private string mServerName;

    Thread SendingThread;
    public SMTPNotification()
    {
      NotificationQueue=new Queue();
      SendingThread= new Thread(new ThreadStart(NotificationMethod));
      mServerName="";
      SendingThread.Name="SMTPThread";
      SendingThread.Start();
    }
 . . .
    private void NotificationMethod()
    {
      while(true)
      {
        try
        {
          // While there are entries in the queue
          while (NotificationQueue.Count > 0 )           ◁── Loops while there are
          {                                                   entries in the queue
            MailMessage message =
                (MailMessage)NotificationQueue.Dequeue();  ◁── Extracts a
            SmtpMail.SmtpServer = mServerName;                MailMessage object
            SmtpMail.Send(message);                           from the queue
          }
          Thread.Sleep(1000);
        }
        catch(Exception ex)
        {
          System.Diagnostics.Trace.WriteLine(ex.Message);
        }
      }
    }

    public void SendNotification(
        string ToLine,string From,string Subject, string Body)
    {
      MailMessage Message=new MailMessage();
      Message.To=ToLine;
      Message.From=From;
```

```
        Message.Subject=Subject;
        Message.Body=Body;
        NotificationQueue.Enqueue(Message); ◁─┐  Adds a Message
    }                                          object to the
                                               notification queue
. . .
    }
}
```

You can see in figure 6.3 that the web site monitoring method that adds the entry to
the notification queue executes on the web site monitoring thread. Even though that
execution occurs on a different thread, the `Notification` object is still restricting
access to its data elements. This enforces that the only way to interact with the notification queue is via the appropriate method.

The notification thread changes from waiting for a flag to be set to looking at the size
of the notification queue. If there are no entries in the queue it sleeps for one second;
while there are entries in the queue, it retrieves and processes them. This changes the job
of the notification thread to servicing the notification queue. You can see this by looking
at `NotificationMethod` in listing 6.4. This is a very common construct. The basic
idea is to have a class that contains a queue and a method that services that queue.

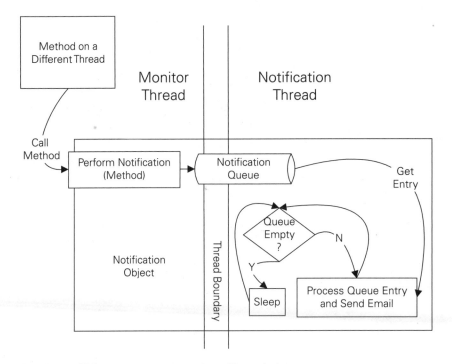

Figure 6.3   Using a queue to cross thread boundaries

1 Encapsulate data elements relating to the area in a class.
2 Create or find an object that represents a unit of work, in our case the `MailMessage` object.
3 Add a private queue data member.
4 Create a public method that adds elements representing the unit of work to the queue.
5 Create a method that retrieves elements from the queue and processes them.
6 Create a thread associating it with the queue servicing method.
7 Instantiate and start the thread in the constructor of the class.
8 Provide a means of cleaning up and terminating the thread, such as a `Dispose` method.

This approach is one that is very reusable. It solves many of the issues we've encountered so far. In the next sections we'll discuss some issues that are not solved by this approach, and in the next chapter we'll introduce solutions to those problems.

6.2 WHEN THINGS GO BADLY

In the physical world the more moving parts an object contains the higher the probability of a mechanical failure. The same is true in software development. Any time two threads interact with the same piece of data the possibility of things going wrong exists. The two most common errors are race conditions and deadlocks.

6.2.1 Race conditions

The winner of a race is generally the first person to reach the end of the course. While this may be great for athletic competition, it is not desirable in a program. A race condition occurs whenever the outcome of the event is dependent on which thread reaches a state first. To demonstrate this we'll do some addition (figure 6.4).

Suppose you had two threads, Thread A and Thread B, as seen in figure 6.4. Both threads act upon a variable named X. One thread adds 1 to the value currently in X while the second thread adds 2. In our example the initial value of X is 4. Both Thread A and Thread B read that value to their stacks. Thread A adds 1 to its copy of X and Thread B adds 2. Thread B happens to be faster than Thread A and updates X with 6. Thread A is unaware of anyone else accessing X and updates it with 5. By saving its value, Thread A undoes Thread B's work. This is an example of a race condition.

Race Condition A race condition is a situation where the result depends on the time it takes a thread to execute instructions. Since the results are not predictable these conditions are generally to be avoided.

Race conditions are considered indeterminate events, in that the outcome of the event cannot be predicted beforehand. Additionally, they are essentially random events. Under some circumstances, this is tolerable. If, however, your bank didn't guard against race conditions you'd likely find a new bank (figure 6.5).

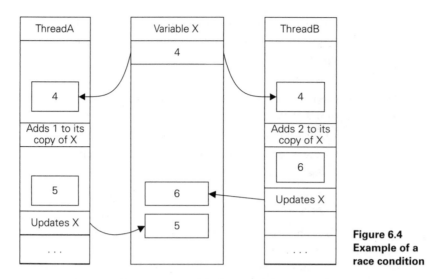

Figure 6.4
Example of a
race condition

Suppose that you have an initial balance of $20 in your checking account. You win the lottery and deposit $1,000,000 to your account. At the very instance your deposit is being processed, a $10 check you wrote to a local pizza chain is being processed. Without synchronization, your balance could be $10 or $1,000,020 instead of the correct $1,000,010. Since these conditions are not uncommon, it is unimaginable that they would be allowed to happen. Banks generally deal with this by using a transaction. Transactions are a form of synchronization management.

One way of dealing with race conditions is to restrict access to shared resources. We will discuss this in detail in the next chapter. A good design minimizes the number of shared resources. In those cases where sharing a resource is required, concurrency control must be enforced.

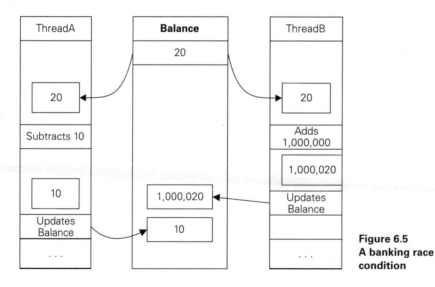

Figure 6.5
A banking race
condition

TIP   If a program works fine on a single processor but does not on a multiple processor, it is likely due to a race condition. It is important to test multi-threaded applications during development on multiprocessor machines.

Race conditions are one of the most common areas where mistakes are made when dealing with multiple threading. A symptom of this is that the program seems to work fine on the developer's machine (equipped with a single processor) but does not on the production machine (equipped with multiple processors). Race conditions can happen on multiple- or single-processor machines. It is really a matter of probability. If concurrency control isn't enforced, eventually shared resources will cause a problem.

6.2.2   Deadlock

As a child you may have found yourself in a battle of wills with another child. Suppose you wanted to color. If you have the coloring book and someone else has the crayons, unless someone is willing to yield there will be no coloring. The same thing can happen in multithreaded development. In order for deadlock to occur, more than one thread must be attempting to access two or more resources. If there is no competition for resources, there will be no deadlock. If you as a child owned multiple boxes of crayons and multiple coloring books, then you may never have faced a coloring deadlock situation. Deadlocks are another common problem in concurrent programming. Databases deal with them on a frequent basis. Figure 6.6 shows how a deadlock can occur.

The best way to deal with deadlocks in an application is to avoid entering into one. When a deadlock occurs, the completion of a task is very unlikely. In order for some task to complete, another task must release its resources. This involves being able to detect when a deadlock is occurring and then resolve it. This is moderately complex.

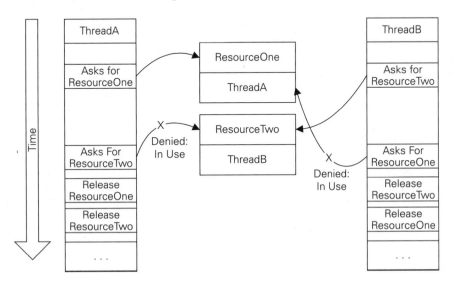

Figure 6.6   Anatomy of a deadlock

Deadlock Deadlock is a state where one thread owns one or more resources and requires one or more additional resources to complete its execution. A different thread owns the required additional resources. That thread requires one or more of the resources that the first thread owns.

Fortunately, following a few guidelines can minimize the occurrence of deadlock. The first guideline is to always acquire resources in the same order. In the example, Thread A asks for ResourceOne, then ResourceTwo while Thread B asks for ResourceTwo, then ResourceOne. This allows both threads to have ownership of a resource and to be in need of the other resource. Figure 6.7 shows the threads asking for the shared resources in the correct order. While this will not totally eliminate the possibility of deadlock, it does reduce it. It is still possible for more complex dependency chains to be formed, but the discussion is beyond the scope of this book.

Once a resource is attained and processing is complete, it is important to release the resources in the reverse order that they were acquired. This works much like a stack. In figure 6.6 we did not release the resources in the correct order.

It is also a good idea to wait before reclaiming a resource. Failure to do so may cause starvation of a thread for a particular resource. Even though a thread is releasing a resource, if the thread immediately reacquires it no other threads will have an opportunity to utilize that resource.

Resources should be acquired as late in processing as possible and be released as soon as possible. This minimizes contention for those resources and increases concurrency. This goes with acquiring only resources that you are certain you will need. A common mistake is to acquire a resource that *might* be needed. It is better to wait until you are certain you need the resource before acquiring it.

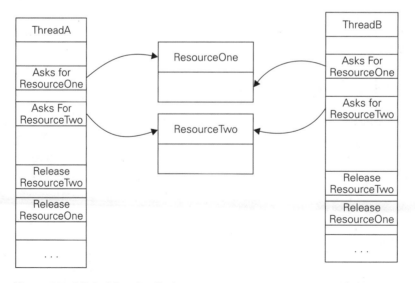

Figure 6.7 Minimizing deadlock

- Always acquire resources in the same order.
- Always release resources in the reverse order of acquisition.
- Minimize indefinite waits for resources.
- Acquire resources no sooner than needed and release as soon as possible.
- Only acquire resources when you are certain you will need them.
- If unable to acquire a resource, release all other acquired resources and try again later.
- Combine to less atomic elements, reducing the possibility of deadlock but also decreasing the overall concurrency. This is discussed in section 7.3.

Deadlock is a fairly simple thing. It requires a minimum of two threads and two resources. It also is fairly easy to avoid if the proper steps are taken. Figure 6.8 restates what a deadlock condition looks like.

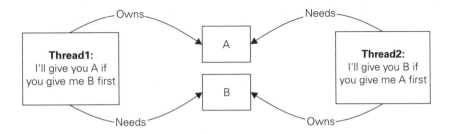

Figure 6.8 Deadlock demonstrated

Sometimes the best approach is to revisit the level of locking being performed. Chapter 7 discusses the various forms of locking. But it might be that by combining, or even breaking down, the items being locked, overall concurrency can be increased while the probability of deadlock is decreased.

6.3 SUMMARY

In this chapter we discussed how threads communicate. We looked at the two common issues associated with multithreaded development: deadlock and race conditions. The next chapter will provide more tools to help you deal with those concurrency issues.

You'll likely notice that static methods associated with threads have not been used to this point. There are times that threads using static methods make sense. The majority of the time a thread should be associated with an instance—not all instances—of a class. An example of when a static method should be used is when a thread, or a group of threads, will process all messages. This can greatly simplify termination issues and minimize the cost of creating new threads. This is essentially how the `ThreadPool` class we discuss in chapter 10 is implemented.

You've seen how threads can communicate. Now we can move on to discuss how we can restrict that communication using concurrency control mechanisms.

C H A P T E R 7

Concurrency control

Controlling thread interaction is a key element of multithreaded development. Concurrency control is making sure that only a single thread is accessing a shared resource at a single time. If multiple threads interact with a resource simultaneously, undesirable results can occur. To avoid conflicts we must address the concept of thread safety—a focus of this chapter.

Collections are a valuable construct: It is difficult to develop an application of any complexity without using a collection of some sort. In order to support multithreaded applications, collections have a static method that converts a collection to being thread-safe. Multiple threads can access a thread-safe collection without fear that data will be lost or that the program will encounter an unexpected error.

One means of being thread-safe is to use only atomic operations, referred to as interlocked in the .NET framework. Using atomic operations ensures that a unit of work will not be interrupted. This is important because if a thread is interrupted partway through an operation, the values that existed when it started that operation may change without its knowledge. This leads to race conditions.

A more powerful way of dealing with thread safety is to use synchronized regions of code. This is accomplished using the `lock` and `SyncLock` keywords or by using the `Monitor Enter` and `Exit` methods. This allows a region of code to be marked in such a way that only one thread can execute in that region at a given point in time.

The `Monitor` class provides other methods that allow for a high degree of control over multiple threads. They allow pausing execution of a thread in such a way that some other thread can signal when it is time for it to do additional work. Optionally, a timeout can be specified that results in a construct that is quite similar to placing the `Sleep` method in a loop.

C# provides the `volatile` keyword for giving the compiler a hint as to the synchronous nature of the variable. When a variable is marked as volatile, certain types of optimizations will not be performed on instructions that access that variable. This approach is useful but does not ensure thread safety.

Next, we cover the synchronization supplied by COM+. .NET makes it easy to utilize that functionality. When you use the COM+ approach, an instance of a class can be marked as requiring synchronization. This will ensure that only one thread at a time accesses the methods and properties of the object. This is a simple form of synchronization, but it does not come without a performance penalty. With the COM+ approach, performance is roughly an order of magnitude worse than with synchronous locks.

We close the chapter with a discussion of when to perform optimizations. This is a key concept to grasp. Making something faster that does not execute for very long doesn't increase overall performance significantly. Optimizations should be performed when they can produce measurable results. Optimizing an infrequently executed section of code only adds complexity, and likely bugs.

7.1   WHAT DOES THREAD-SAFE MEAN?

In the last chapter we saw how queues can be used as a means of thread communication, and we briefly discussed the issue of concurrency control. Related to concurrency control is the concept of thread safety. Thread safety implies that a method or an instance of an object can be used on multiple threads at the same time without undesirable events such as crashes, race conditions, and deadlocks occurring.

> **Thread-Safe**   A class or method is classified as thread-safe if multiple threads can interact with it simultaneously without ill effects.

Since not being thread-safe can cause such undesirable things to happen, why not make everything thread-safe? Thread safety does not come without a performance penalty. The majority of programs developed are single-threaded, meaning that the most objects and methods are called by only one thread. In that case there is no reason to make a method or object thread-safe. It would be an unnecessary and unreasonable performance penalty to make all objects thread-safe.

Thread safety ties in closely with race conditions. Race conditions are the cause of many of the problems with multithreading.

7.1.1   Race conditions in collections

To see a race condition in action, let's create three threads. Two threads are tasked with filling a queue. The third thread's job is to try to keep the same queue empty. Figure 7.1 shows the logical layout of the example.

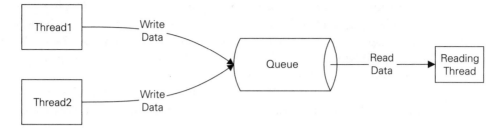

Figure 7.1 Two threads filling a queue while a third empties it

Queues contain references to objects. In this case, we'll be working with a structure named `Entry`. Listing 7.1 shows the definition of the `Entry`. Each `Entry` structure contains a thread name and a counter value. When an `Entry` is created the name of the thread is passed in, along with a counter value, to make it easy to determine where a particular `Entry` came from.

Listing 7.1 Definition of the Entry structure used to populate the queue (VB.NET)

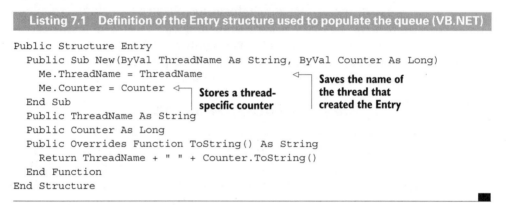

```
Public Structure Entry
  Public Sub New(ByVal ThreadName As String, ByVal Counter As Long)
    Me.ThreadName = ThreadName
    Me.Counter = Counter        ⟵  Saves the name of
  End Sub                              the thread that
  Public ThreadName As String          created the Entry
  Public Counter As Long
                              ⟵  Stores a thread-
                                 specific counter
  Public Overrides Function ToString() As String
    Return ThreadName + " " + Counter.ToString()
  End Function
End Structure
```

Structures have been in Visual Basic for some time; a major change in VB.NET is that a structure can have constructors. The `New` method is invoked when an instance of the structure is created. Listing 7.2 contains the code that creates an instance of the `Entry` and adds it to the queue.

Listing 7.2 The method executed by both writing threads (VB.NET)

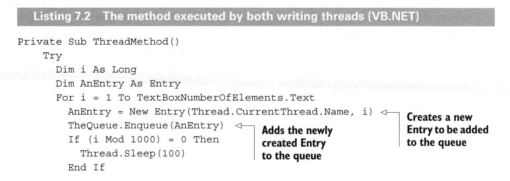

```
Private Sub ThreadMethod()
    Try
      Dim i As Long
      Dim AnEntry As Entry
      For i = 1 To TextBoxNumberOfElements.Text
        AnEntry = New Entry(Thread.CurrentThread.Name, i)  ⟵  Creates a new
        TheQueue.Enqueue(AnEntry)  ⟵                            Entry to be added
        If (i Mod 1000) = 0 Then      Adds the newly           to the queue
          Thread.Sleep(100)           created Entry
        End If                        to the queue
```

```
      Next
      Dim updateit As TextBoxUpdater
      updateit = New TextBoxUpdater(AddressOf UpdateControl)
      Dim Message As String
      Message = "Thread " + Thread.CurrentThread.Name + " Finished" + vbCrLf
      Dim args As Object() = {TextBoxOutput, Message}
      TextBoxOutput.Invoke(updateit, args)
   Catch ex As Exception
      MessageBox.Show(ex.Message)
   End Try
End Sub
```

The method repeats until the number of entries added to the queue is the same as the value contained in the `TextBoxNumberOfElements` textbox. Once the thread has added all of the entries to the queue, it writes a message to the `TextBoxOutput` textbox control, then terminates. Listing 7.3 shows how we create the two writing threads.

Listing 7.3 Code that creates the two writing threads (VB.NET)

```
. . .
    Thread1 = New Thread(AddressOf ThreadMethod)
    Thread1.Name = "1"
    Thread1.IsBackground = True
    Thread2 = New Thread(AddressOf ThreadMethod)
    Thread2.IsBackground = True
    Thread2.Name = "2"
    Thread1.Start()
    Thread2.Start()
. . .
```

Notice that both threads use the method `ThreadMethod` to populate the queue. `ThreadMethod` uses the name of the thread that's assigned when the thread is created to pass in to the constructor of the `Entry` structure. We use a third thread to keep the queue empty. That thread is created in much the same way, as listing 7.4 shows.

Listing 7.4 Creation of the reading thread (VB.NET)

```
. . .
    ThreadRead = New Thread(AddressOf ThreadReadMethod)
    ThreadRead.IsBackground = True
    ThreadRead.Name = "Reader"
    ThreadRead.Start()
. . .
```

The `ThreadReadMethod` checks to see if `TheQueue` contains any entries; if it does, it retrieves the entry. The thread sleeps for one tenth of a second between checking to see if there's an entry to remove.

Listing 7.5 The method that the reading thread executes (VB.NET)

```
Private Sub ThreadReadMethod()
  Dim AnEntry As Entry
  Try
    While True
      If TheQueue.Count > 0 Then
        AnEntry = CType(TheQueue.Dequeue(), Entry)
      End If
      Thread.Sleep(100)
    End While
  Catch ex As Exception
    MessageBox.Show(ex.Message)
  End Try
End Sub
```

When this example is executed on a machine with multiple processors, the error message shown in figure 7.2 will almost certainly happen. When the example is executed on a single-processor machine, the error will still occur but not as often.

Figure 7.2 Error message indicating a race condition

The text of this message is typical of errors associated with race conditions. The two writer threads most likely attempted to add an entry to the queue at the same time. The steps leading up to the error probably went something like this. One of the threads attempts to add an entry to the queue (figure 7.3).

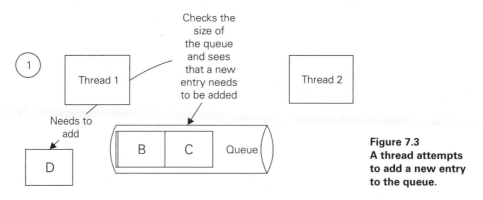

**Figure 7.3
A thread attempts
to add a new entry
to the queue.**

The queue isn't large enough to hold the new entry so it must be enlarged to make room for the entry. Queues are generally implemented on top of a more basic structure like an array. The array has a certain size available to it initially, and is grown as needed to accommodate more entries. Figure 7.4 shows a thread causing the array to be increased in size.

Thread 2 also has an entry it would like to add to the queue. It arrives just after Thread 1 and sees that there is room in the queue for its entry (figure 7.5).

Since the array is large enough for the new entry, Thread 2 can place its entry in the queue. It uses the slot that was allocated as a result of Thread 1's request (figure 7.6).

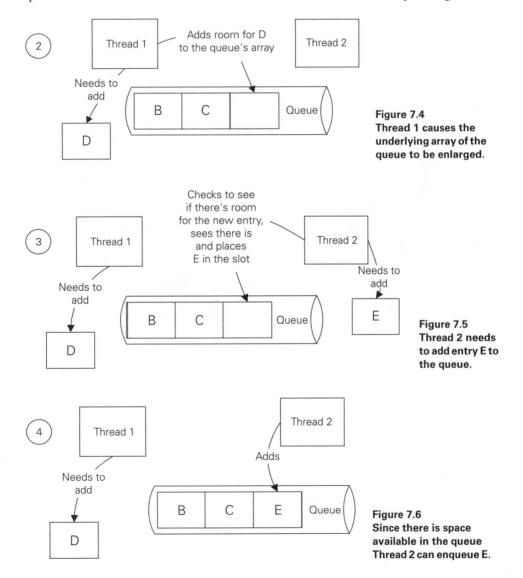

Figure 7.4
Thread 1 causes the underlying array of the queue to be enlarged.

Figure 7.5
Thread 2 needs to add entry E to the queue.

Figure 7.6
Since there is space available in the queue Thread 2 can enqueue E.

Thread 1 attempts to add D to the queue and sees that there is no room (figure 7.7). This causes the error message in figure 7.2.

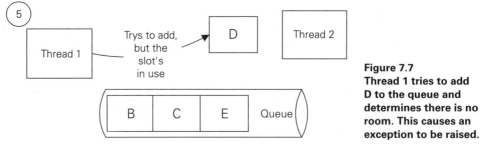

Figure 7.7
Thread 1 tries to add D to the queue and determines there is no room. This causes an exception to be raised.

Why doesn't the queue attempt to allocate space for Thread 1 again? As long as a single thread accesses the collection, there is no reason to assume that the space allocated would no longer be available. When an unforeseeable situation occurs, the best thing to do is to throw an exception. Additionally, if the Enqueue method contained retry logic, it is possible that something much worse than an exception, such as an infinite loop or thread starvation, could occur. In the next section we see how we can use collections safely in a multithreaded environment.

7.1.2 Making collections thread-safe using Synchronized

We've seen that the Queue class in the Collections namespace is not thread-safe. This is the general rule for collections, with the exceptions of the Hashtable and ArrayList classes. Hashtable is thread-safe for multiple readers and a single writer. Multiple threads can read from the same Hashtable safely as long as no more than one thread is updating it. This is most likely because a reader-writer lock guards the Hashtable's data. In the next chapter we'll discuss reader-writer locks. The ArrayList class is thread-safe for multiple readers. This means that multiple threads can be reading from the same ArrayList as long as no thread attempts to update it.

In the last section we saw how the Queue class is not thread-safe. Fortunately it is easy to make a Collection thread-safe. The static/shared Synchronized method of the Collection class returns a collection that is thread-safe.

> **Listing 7.6   Code that creates a thread-safe queue (C#)**

```
. . .
private void Form1_Load(object sender, System.EventArgs e)
{
  UnsafeQueue= new Queue();
  TheQueue = Queue.Synchronized(UnsafeQueue);
}
. . .
```

The listing shows how to convert a `Queue` that is not synchronized, and thus not thread-safe, to one that is. As a matter of practice it is better to not store the reference to the unsafe queue in a variable. So instead, the following should be used:

```
TheQueue = Queue.Synchronized(new Queue());
```

This removes the possibility of someone inadvertently using the unsafe queue. Additionally, the code is a bit smaller and easier to follow. If at a later date it is determined that the queue need not be thread-safe, it is easy to remove the call to `Queue.Synchronized` and revert to the unsafe queue.

Synchronized The `Synchronized` method is a way of making a collection thread-safe. It is a static/shared method on `Collection` classes that accepts an instance of the collection and returns a reference to a thread-safe object.

Figure 7.8 shows the logical flow of the example using a synchronized queue. Think of synchronized objects as intersections with yield signs. Only one thread at a time can go through the "intersection." If no other threads are present, there is no need to stop. The threads only need to stop when some other thread is accessing the object. When the thread is yielding, it goes to the `WaitSleepJoin` state.

When accessing collections from multiple threads, synchronized access is a must. Synchronization is not free; there is a very real performance cost. If multiple threads can manipulate a collection, it must be thread-safe. The question is simply do you want a stable program? If so, then you must make shared collections thread-safe. The alternative is to redesign the solution so that multiple threads cannot access the collection.

Figure 7.9 shows the impact of using synchronized collections. It shows that synchronized queues are at least two and a half times slower enqueuing and dequeuing elements than using the unsynchronized counterparts. This is a small price to pay for thread safety, and if the objects are accessed from multiple threads they must be synchronized.

The *X*-axis represents the number of elements that were queued and then dequeued. The *Y*-axis represents how many seconds the operation took. The unsynchronized object is consistently two times faster than the synchronized object.

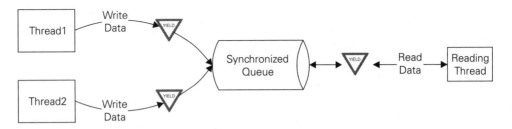

Figure 7.8   Using synchronized queues

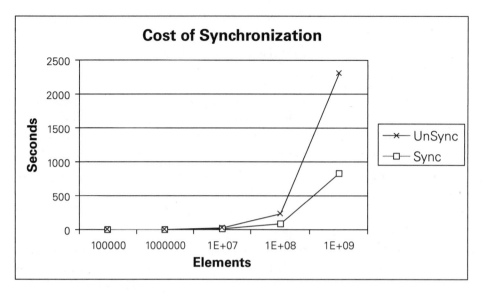

Figure 7.9   Graph of the cost of synchronization

7.1.3   Thread safety in libraries

It is important when doing multithreaded development to know what methods are and are not thread-safe. In .NET all public static methods are thread-safe. As a general rule, all others are not. Some commonly used thread-safe classes are:

System.Console	System.Diagnostics.Debug
System.Enum	System.Diagnostics.Trace
System.Text.Encoding	System.Diagnostics.PerformanceCounter

When you're developing your own libraries, it is important that a thread-safe method be accurately documented as being thread-safe. Without clear documentation the best bet is to assume that the method is not thread-safe. This means that if you are interacting with a method that is not thread-safe, you must take measures to ensure that only one thread at a time interacts with that method. We'll cover ways of accomplishing this in this chapter.

TIP   When working with an object, assume that it is not thread-safe until you can determine otherwise.

It is important to note that the `System.Windows.Form.Control` class is not thread-safe. The Win32 platform is not thread-safe. In order to interact with Windows Forms and Controls from multiple threads, you must use either the `Invoke` or `BeginInvoke` method.

Windows Forms   Windows Forms are not thread-safe. Accessing a form or control from different threads will likely cause the application to become unstable and terminate.

You may be feeling a bit overwhelmed at this point. Not to worry. By following a few guidelines, you will be able to write high-performance multithreaded applications that are scalable. The basic rule is to minimize the amount of cross-thread communication that occurs. Additionally, all access to a class's data members should be done through properties or methods. This will allow you to protect those data elements from concurrency issues and make your objects and methods thread-safe.

7.1.4 Understanding and detecting thread boundaries

When doing multithreaded development, you should know where the thread boundaries are. In figure 7.10 the thread boundary falls on the queue. A thread boundary exists at a point where two or more threads can access a common element. By keeping those boundaries in methods and properties, you minimize the total number of boundaries. This allows you to focus your attention on those places where you know interactions occur, rather than protecting an element from interaction from any number of points.

Think of it in terms of land. If a piece of property has a fence, it is much easier to secure than land that does not because the fence restricts access to the property. Fences generally have gates that allow access to the area contained within the fence. In multithreaded development, we use classes to restrict access to our data members. We generally call it encapsulation. We put a gate in here and there by using properties and methods. This allows things outside of the class to interact with things inside, but only when we allow it. By minimizing the number of places where interaction between threads can occur, we can greatly simplify multithreaded development (figure 7.10).

If the object or method is not thread-safe it is important that you know that. Many threading issues remain hidden on single-processor machines only to cause grief on a multiple-processor one. Unfortunately, this is usually in a production environment, where failure is far more obvious than during development.

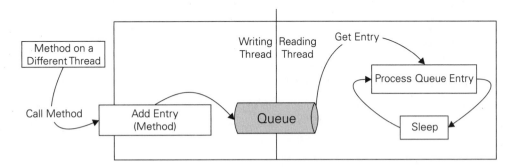

Figure 7.10   The queue lies on the thread boundary, which makes it susceptible to concurrency issues.

7.2 ATOMIC OPERATIONS

One of my earliest programming assignments was to write the pseudocode to make a peanut butter and jelly sandwich. When everyone had submitted solutions, the instructor took the class to the cafeteria and followed our pseudocode. It was quite humorous to see the results. Many of the steps were omitted or too general to be followed. The point of the exercise was to teach us to think in small units of work. Most actions are made up of many smaller actions. For example, opening the jar of peanut butter involves grasping the lid, holding it under a constant amount of pressure, and rotating the jar. In conversation, we simply tell someone to "open the jar." We understand that the operation actually is made up of many smaller operations. This is just as true in software development as it is in making a sandwich.

When one of those smaller operations is guaranteed to be completed without being interrupted, we call that operation atomic. Recall from chapter 1 that when multiple threads are executing on a processor there are many interrupts to an individual thread's execution. A thread that is executing is periodically interrupted and moved from the processor. A different thread is then given a chance to work. This is called a context switch. If a context switch can occur during an operation, that operation is not atomic. It is best to assume that operations are not atomic and that a context switch can occur during processing. In the following sections we'll cover the necessary mechanisms to protect data.

Atomic Operations	Atomic operations are statements that will always complete without interruption. This ensures that they will complete as expected without need for synchronization.

To understand what is happening we can look at the MSIL that corresponds to instructions. A detailed discussion of IL is beyond the scope of this book, but it does offer some valuable insight. Consider the following instruction:

```
X += 1
```

This produces the following MSIL:

ldloc.0	Load local variable in location zero onto the stack
ldc.i4.1	Load the value 1 into the stack
add.ovf	Add the top two elements of the stack and put the result back onto the stack
stloc.0	Save the top value in the stack to local variable in location zero

As you can see, what we think of as being a single instruction is in reality four. It is quite likely that after the MSIL is compiled to machine instructions that this will change, although it may not. The point is that an instruction that on the surface seems to be quite simple may actually be doing many things. Figure 7.11 shows how two increment operations can interact to yield incorrect results.

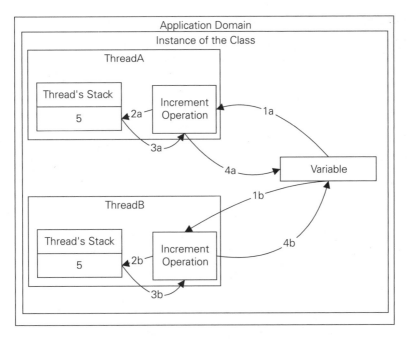

Figure 7.11 If operations are not atomic, a value can be changed on one thread without another thread's knowledge.

If steps 1a and 1b happen at the same time, or roughly the same time, a race condition will occur because the increment operation is not an atomic operation. In order for the class variable to be incremented, it must first be on the thread's stack. During the time it is on the stack of a thread, a different thread may get a copy of the value. If the operation were atomic, Thread B would not be able to access the class variable until Thread A had completed its interaction with it.

ILDASM   ILDASM is a tool for disassembling a .NET program to IL. This allows analysis of the code generated by the compiler, and can yield insight, such as what operations are likely to be thread-safe.

To view the IL of a program, use the ildasm.exe program that's located in the Framework's bin directory. It allows a compiled .NET program to be reduced to IL for analysis.

7.2.1   The Interlocked class

We saw in the last section how the += and ++ operators are not atomic and thus not thread-safe. The `Interlocked` class provides several static methods that perform atomic operations. When more than one thing is interlocked, it means that an action on one is constrained or restricted by actions on the other. For example, if two people are locked together with handcuffs and one tries to go north while the other tries to go south, there will be a constraining result.

The Increment and Decrement methods

A very common operation is to increase and decrease a value by 1. It is so common that C++ and C# include the ++ and – operators. To accomplish an atomic increment, we can use the Increment method of the Interlocked class. The method accepts a reference to an integer or a long. The variable passed in is incremented in place and its new value is the return value for the method (listing 7.7).

Listing 7.7 A method executed by a thread that increments a value NumberOfIterations (C#)

```csharp
private void ThreadMethod()
{
  try
  {
    for (long i = 0 ;i < NumberOfIterations;i++)
    {
      Interlocked.Increment(ref ActualValue);
    }
  }
  catch(Exception ex)
  {
    Trace.WriteLine(Thread.CurrentThread.Name + " " + ex.Message);
  }
}
```

In listing 7.7 if the value before the Increment method executes is 5, after it executes the ActualValue variable will contain 6 and 6 is the return value for the Increment method. In the example, the return value is not being used.

Increment   Increment is a static method of the Interlocked class that increases the value of the variable passed in by one. It is a thread-safe method since it is guaranteed to perform its operation without being interrupted.

By examining the following statement using ILDASM, we can learn how the inter-locked operation works:

```
System.Threading.Interlocked.Increment(ref a);
```

`call int32 [mscorlib]System.Thread-ing.Interlocked::Increment(int32&)`	Invokes the Interlocked method of MSCORLIB
`pop`	Removes the top element from the stack

Notice that the actual increment is a single instruction, compared to the multiple instructions in the previous section.

Decrement   Decrement is an atomic static method of the Interlocked class that decreases the value of the variable passed in by 1. It is the converse of the Increment method.

In a single-threaded environment, the following statements will result in the variable being returned to the value it was before they executed:

```
Interlocked.Increment(ref ActualValue);
Interlocked.Decrement(ref ActualValue);
```

Figure 7.12 shows how that even though each thread executes its increments and decrements with interrupts in between, the value at the end of the execution is correctly the same as it was at the beginning.

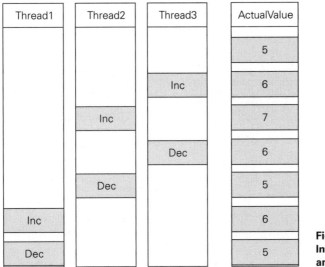

Thread1	Thread2	Thread3	ActualValue
			5
		Inc	6
	Inc		7
		Dec	6
	Dec		5
Inc			6
Dec			5

Figure 7.12
**Interlocked Increment
and Decrement**

As with the Synchronized collections, these methods are slower than the +=, ++, -=, and -- operators. That is a small price to pay for stability and reliability of an application.

Exchange and CompareExchange

Suppose you wanted to assign a unique value to each instance of a particular class. The value would serve as an ID. In our web site monitoring application the notification queue previously contained MailMessage objects. While this was convenient, it is more flexible for the queue to contain an object of our own design. By adding a NotificationEntry object, we can assign each entry a unique number.

In the last section we saw how the Interlocked.Increment method can be used to increment a variable in a thread-safe way. Another method of the Interlocked class is Exchange. Interlocked.Exchange is essentially a thread-safe assignment statement. It accepts two parameters: a reference to the variable being assigned to and the variable being assigned from. It returns the value that previously occupied the first parameter. In listing 7.8 we assign IdCounter a number based on the current date and time.

```
Shared Sub InitializeIdCounter()
  Dim BaseNumber As Integer
  DayOfIntitalization = DateTime.Now.Day
  BaseNumber = (DateTime.Now.Year - 2000) * 1000000000
  BaseNumber += DateTime.Now.Month * 10000000
  BaseNumber += DateTime.Now.Day * 100000
  BaseNumber += DateTime.Now.Hour * 1000
  BaseNumber += DateTime.Now.Minute * 10
  Interlocked.Exchange(IdCounter, BaseNumber)
End Sub
```

Unless the application starts, stops, and restarts in the same minute, the value of IdCounter will be unique for each run of the program. This approach relies on the system clock, which always carries a certain amount of risk. It is very easy to change the date and time of the machine. IntializeIDCounter is contained in the shared New method.

```
Shared Sub New()
  Trace.Assert(IdCounter = 0)
  InitializeIdCounter()
End Sub
```

This method is called the first time an instance of the class containing it, NotificationEntry, is instantiated.

New   When a subroutine is named New in VB.NET, it is treated as a constructor. Constructors are methods that are automatically called when an object is instantiated.

The public New method of a class is called after the shared New method. In the public New method, we can increment the value of IdCounter:

```
MessageId = Interlocked.Increment(IdCounter)
```

By using the Increment and Exchange methods, we can initialize and increment the shared variable IdCounter in a thread-safe way.

It's nice when unique identifiers can be related to something meaningful. In our case, it would be nice if you could determine the date the entry was generated based on the IdCounter. To do this we need to add listing 7.9 to our public New method.

Listing 7.9   Using CompareExchange (VB.NET)

```
While DayToReInitialize < 0
  Thread.Sleep(100)
End While
Dim ReturnValue As Integer
ReturnValue = Interlocked.CompareExchange(DayToReInitialize, _
    -1, DateTime.Now.Day)
```

```
If ReturnValue = -1 Then
  While (DayToReInitialize = -1)
    Thread.Sleep(100)
  End While
End If
If DayToReInitialize = -1 Then
  InitializeIdCounter()
End If
```

This code is a little tricky, so we'll go over it carefully. The key element is the Compare-Exchange instruction. It checks to see if the DayToReInitialize is equal to today. If it is, it sets DayToReInitialize to -1. It saves the value returned from CompareExchange to a variable so we can check it. If it is -1, some other thread must also have determined that it's time to reinitialize, so the current thread should sleep until the thread doing the update is finished. If a value other than -1 is returned and DayToReInitialize is -1 then the current thread should do the reinitialization (figure 7.13).

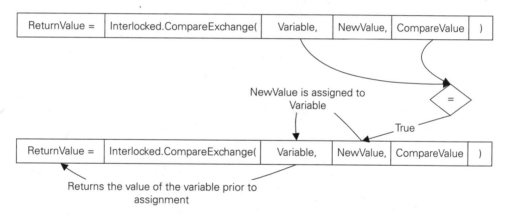

Figure 7.13   Interlocked CompareExchange checks to see if the supplied value is the same as the compare value then the new value is assigned to the variable and returned.

The CompareExchange method is relatively difficult to use. Unless the highest possible performance is needed, a different, more understandable approach should be used such as synchronous locks, which we discuss in the next section. Locks are likely the most common form of concurrency control. When most developers with multithreaded experience are asked to describe multithreaded development, they will most often speak of critical sections and locks.

7.3   THE LOCK AND SYNCLOCK KEYWORDS

Locks have become an important part of everyday life. We use locks on our houses to keep people out who do not belong. If you only had one key, and the only way to get into the house was with the key, then only one person could be in the house at a time. This is how a lock in the multithreaded world works.

Unlike the `Interlocked` mechanism, more than one line of code can be protected. This is a fairly simple solution to a complex problem.

```
SyncLock IdCounterObject
  If DayToReInitialize = DateTime.Now.Day Then
    InitializeIdCounter()
  End If
  MessageId = Interlocked.Increment(IdCounter)
End SyncLock
```

The way it works is that a thread encounters a `lock` (in C#) or `SyncLock` (in VB.NET) statement. It checks to see if the locking object (think of it as the key) is available. If it is not, the thread enters the `WaitSleepJoin` state until it can acquire the lock. If the locking object is available, the thread acquires the lock and begins executing the guarded instructions (figure 7.14). This is similar to the `Synchronized` version of collections we discussed earlier.

Locks can only be acquired using reference types. Value types, such as long and integer, cannot be used with locks directly. In order to lock on a value type, you must either use the `GetType` statement or introduce an object to serve as the locking object. While this introduces a certain amount of additional memory usage, it may reduce the complexity of the code and yield a more maintainable solution.

Critical Section   A critical section is a region of code, that is mutually exclusive. This means that while one thread is executing that region of code no other thread can. Critical sections are created using the `lock` and `SyncLock` constructs.

Locks are a means of creating a critical section. Unlike a Win32 critical section, it is not necessary to create a variable to serve as the key to the critical section. Instead, any instance of an object can be used to control entering the critical section. A common approach is to lock on the instance of the object itself using the `me`/`this` statement. Many of the examples you will see use this form of locking. This is the simplest form of synchronization control. It creates a high degree of control over access but at the expense of flexibility. Under some circumstances this is a valid solution. Other times a more granular approach is required.

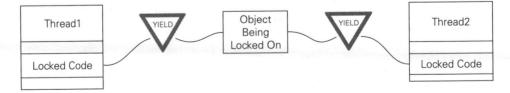

Figure 7.14   How a lock is used to coordinate two threads.

CHAPTER 7   CONCURRENCY CONTROL

SyncLock   SyncLock is a Visual Basic keyword that is used as a synchronization mechanism to create a section of code that only a single thread can access at a time. This is accomplished by acquiring a lock on an object. If the object is currently locked, the thread must wait until the lock is released.

Suppose you had a class with three data elements in it. One approach would be to restrict access based on the class as a whole. This would mean that only one of the three data elements could be changed at once. If these elements were independent, this might be too restrictive. An alternative would be to have three objects that serve as locks. In order to access one of the data elements the corresponding lock would first be acquired. Figure 7.15 graphically demonstrates this design tradeoff.

This introduces the concept of concurrency. Concurrency is a measure of how many things can happen at once. A high degree of concurrency will often produce higher performance than a low degree. The tradeoff is between concurrency and the risk of race conditions, deadlocks, and complexity.

In the previous chapter we discussed deadlocks. Deadlocks are a very real problem with SyncLocks. Using the lock/SyncLock statement there is no way to time out a request for a resource. So if a thread monopolizes a resource, all other threads requesting that resource will be in a WaitSleepJoin state until the resource becomes available. To reduce the possibility of deadlock, the lock is released whenever the thread exits the locked region. This is true if an exception is raised or processing completes normally.

The design constraints regarding deadlock should always be followed when using the lock/SyncLock statements. If used correctly, lock/SyncLock is a powerful means of controlling synchronization.

You may be wondering how lock/SyncLock works; we'll cover that in the next section.

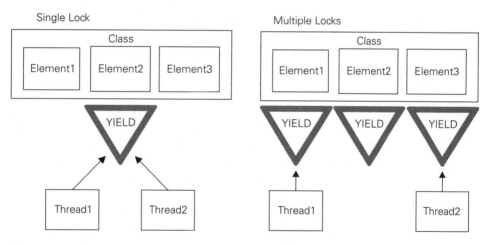

Figure 7.15   A single lock can be used to guard multiple items or a lock can be used to protect each item independently.

7.4 THE MONITOR CLASS

During grade school there were generally people tasked with the job of hall monitor. A hall monitor attempts to make sure that students and visitors are in the right places at the right time. If you walk into a strange school and start roaming the halls, you're likely to meet a hall monitor. A monitor is something that watches over something else. What the monitor watches might be the flow of students and visitors in the hall of a school or, in the case of multithreaded development, the access to resources by threads. `Monitor` is a class in the `Threading` namespace that contains methods for capturing and releasing synchronous locks.

7.4.1 The Enter and Exit methods

`Monitor.Enter` is called when a lock is requested. It blocks and doesn't return until the lock has been granted. If the thread that is calling `Enter` already has the lock it is requesting, the lock count for that object is incremented and the thread is allowed to pass. If the thread that is calling `Enter` does not have the lock and another thread does, it will wait until that other thread releases the lock by calling `Monitor.Exit`. If the lock count for the parameter passed into `Enter` is zero, the current thread is granted ownership of that lock and the lock count is incremented to one.

Compared to synchronous locks

We discussed what the `lock/SyncLock` method does in section 7.3. If you're like me, you want to know how things work. `SyncLocks` are implemented using the `Monitor.Enter` and `Monitor.Exit` methods. Table 7.1 shows two segments of code that produce almost identical MSIL.

Table 7.1 How the Lock Method Is Implemented Using the Monitor `Enter` and `Exit` Methods

CLock.cs	CEnterExit.cs	These two pieces of code
object o = new object();	object objLock = new object();	produce virtually identical MSIL.
lock(o)	object tmpObject = objLock;	The lock statement is
{	Monitor.Enter(tmpObject);	implemented using
o=123;	try	Monitor.Enter and Monitor.Exit.
}	{	
	objLock =123;	
	}	
	finally	
	{	
	Monitor.Exit(tmpObject);	
	}	

There are two things to notice about the code in table 7.1. The first is that the `Monitor.Enter` instruction is not inside the `try` block. There are two exceptions that `Enter` can throw: `ArgumentNullException` and `ArgumentException`.

`ArgumentNullException` is thrown whenever the parameter passed to the `Enter` method is null. In this case calling `Exit` would be inappropriate. `ArgumentException` is raised when the parameter to `Enter` is a value type, for instance an integer. If this were the case, then calling `Exit` on the same value would result in another exception. It is better to deal with the invalid parameter earlier than later. Another thing to notice is the introduction of the `tmpObject` variable. This is introduced to deal with the case in which the value that is being locked on changes.

If the `tmpObject` variable is left out, you have the code in listing 7.10.

Listing 7.10   The mistake of assigning a value to something being locked upon (C#)

```
public void EnterExit_NoTemp()
{
  object objLock = new object();
  Monitor.Enter(objLock);    ◄┐
  try
  {
    objLock =123;                    objLock is not the
  }                                  same in these two
  finally                            instructions
  {
    Monitor.Exit(objLock);           ◄┘
  }
}
```

When the `Monitor.Exit` statement is executed, a `SynchronizationLockException` is generated. This is because at the point the `Exit` statement is executed, the `objLock` variable has not been locked on. Note that adding a `catch` clause to the `try` block would not catch this exception since the exception is raised in the `finally` block. To capture the exception, and possibly reduce the time needed to track down the bug, enclose the entire section above in a `try` block as seen in listing 7.11.

Listing 7.11   Exception handling reduces the time to track down a problem (C#).

```
try
{
  object objLock = new object();
  Monitor.Enter(objLock);
  try
  {
    objLock=123;
  }
  finally
  {
    Monitor.Exit(objLock);    ◄┐
  }                                The exception will
}                                  be thrown in the
catch(Exception ex)                finally clause
{
  Console.WriteLine(ex.Message);   ◄┘
}
```

This will allow for earlier detection of this kind of error. The following guidelines for using `Enter` and `Exit` should be used:

- To release a lock, call `Exit` the same number of times that `Enter` has been called.
- Always place `Exit` in a `finally` clause and all code that should happen within the synchronized region inside the `try` block.
- Ensure that the object passed to `Enter` is the same one that is passed to `Exit`.
- Ensure that the object is initialized before calling `Enter`.
- Always call `Enter` before calling `Exit`.
- Avoid changing the value of an object being locked on.
- Use a variable that is dedicated to being locked upon as the locking mechanism.

These guidelines are general, but if they are followed the amount of debugging required will be greatly reduced.

Creating critical sections

The `Enter` and `Exit` methods are used to create critical sections of code. We use critical sections as a means of protecting a shared resource from interaction by multiple threads. Only one thread may be in a critical section at a time. A thread enters the critical section when it invokes the `Enter` method and is granted a lock on the locking object. A thread exits the critical section at the point it invokes the `Exit` method the same number of times that it had previously invoked the `Enter` method.

This is essentially the same way that the Win32 critical section object works. To use a Win32 critical section you must first create the critical section object using the `InitializeCriticalSection` API call. `InitializeCriticalSection` allocates an area of memory that is used by `EnterCriticalSection` and `ExitCriticalSection`. This is different than the .NET approach, which allows any non-value type object to be used as the locking mechanism.

`Exit` must be called as many times as `Enter` is called to release a lock. Unlike the synchronous lock, exiting the scope where the lock was acquired does not release the lock. Care should be taken to ensure that a thread releases any owned locks before it terminates. Because of the indeterminate nature of the .NET framework, the results of terminating a thread that is in a critical section are not predictable.

7.4.2 The TryEnter method

We've seen how `Monitor` `Enter` and `Exit` work when things go well, but what happens if one of the threads doesn't release the lock when finished with it? When any other thread calls the `Enter` method, it will be blocked indefinably. This means that if one thread fails to release a lock all threads that try to `Enter` that lock will hang (listing 7.12).

Listing 7.12   The importance of releasing locks (VB.NET)

```
Private Sub TryEnterMethod()
  Dim MyName As String
  MyName = Thread.CurrentThread.Name
  Dim Entered As Boolean
  While (True)
    TryEnterLocation = "Before TryEnter " + Now.ToString()
    Entered = Monitor.TryEnter(LockingObject, 2000)          Returns true if the
    TryEnterLocation = "After TryEnter " + Now.ToString()    lock is acquired
    If Entered Then
      SharedString = MyName + " " + Now.ToString()
      TryEnterLocation = "In Lock " + Now.ToString()
      Thread.Sleep(1000)                                      Is called if the
      Monitor.Exit(LockingObject)                             lock is acquired
      TryEnterLocation = "After Exit " + Now.ToString()      Executes if the lock
    Else                                                      was not acquired
      TryEnterLocation = "Unable to acquire lock " + Now.ToString()
      Debug.WriteLine(MyName + " : Unable to acquire lock")
    End If
    Thread.Sleep(1000)
  End While
End Sub
```

Fortunately the `TryEnter` method is available. `TryEnter` comes in three different flavors. The `TryEnter` method, in listing 7.12, attempts to acquire a synchronous lock on the supplied parameter. If it can acquire the lock, the method returns true. If some other thread has the lock, the method waits for two seconds and then returns false. This allows a thread to wait for a period of time and, if the lock doesn't become available, to move on and do other things.

Monitor.Try-   `Monitor.TryEnter` is a static method that allows a thread to request a
Enter   lock while optionally specifying a timeout.

Such timeout-based processing is very powerful. For instance, you could have a thread running that simply tried to acquire a frequently used lock on a regular interval. If unable to acquire the lock, it might signal instability of the application or system. The thread doing the checking could then log the fact that the system is unresponsive to the event log.

Variations   • `TryEnter(object)`
of TryEnter   • `TryEnter(object, TimeSpan)`
                    • `TryEnter(object, Integer)`

Another version of the `TryEnter` method accepts a `TimeSpan` as the timeout value. As we discussed in chapter 4, `TimeSpan` objects allow for greater flexibility in specifying time duration. The `TimeSpan` version of the method also returns true if the `TryEnter` method was able to acquire the lock and false if not.

The last version of the `TryEnter` method accepts only the object being locked on as the parameter. This version of the method returns immediately if it is unable to acquire the lock rather than waiting a certain amount. This is identical to calling `TryEnter` with zero as the duration in milliseconds.

Suppose that you wanted to know if a lock were available. The following creates a property that indicates the availability of the lock:

```
Public ReadOnly Property LockAvailable()
Get
  Dim bAvailable As Boolean
  bAvailable = Monitor.TryEnter(LockingObject)
  If bAvailable Then
    Monitor.Exit(LockingObject)
    Return True
  End If
  Return False
End Get
End Property
```

To tell if the lock is available you must first try to acquire it. If successful, we release it and return true. Otherwise, we return false. It is important to release the lock as soon as it is acquired. We would not want our checking the availability of the lock to make it unavailable for long periods of time.

It is important to always release a lock after it is no longer needed. The following method will acquire the lock and never release it. This will keep all other threads from using the lock:

```
Private Sub BadThreadMethod()
    Thread.Sleep(60000)
    Dim MyName As String
    MyName = Thread.CurrentThread.Name
    While (True)
      BadThreadLocation = "Before Enter " + Now.ToString()
      Monitor.Enter(LockingObject)
      BadThreadLocation = "In Lock " + Now.ToString()
      SharedString = MyName + " " + Now.ToString()
      Thread.Sleep(1000)
    End While
End Sub
```

Instead, something similar to the following should be used:

```
Private Sub GoodThreadMethod()
    Dim MyName As String
    MyName = Thread.CurrentThread.Name
    While (True)
      GoodThreadLocation = "Before Enter " + Now.ToString()
      Monitor.Enter(LockingObject)
      Try
        GoodThreadLocation = "In Lock " + Now.ToString()
        SharedString = MyName + " " + Now.ToString()
```

```
        Thread.Sleep(500)
    Finally
        Monitor.Exit(LockingObject)
    End Try
    GoodThreadLocation = "After Exit " + Now.ToString()
    Thread.Sleep(2000)
  End While
End Sub
```

Notice that the lock is released in the `Finally` clause. This ensures that if an exception occurs while the lock is held it is released.

7.4.3   Wait and Pulse

Until now our thread methods relied on `Sleep` to pause between executions. `Sleep` should not be viewed as a synchronization mechanism. Attempting to do so will likely result in race conditions and inefficient code. Suppose that you wanted to add an entry to a queue and then signal that processing should begin on that item. This can be done in a nonblocking way by using the `Wait` and `Pulse` methods. Figure 7.16 demonstrates the steps involved with using `Wait` and `Pulse`.

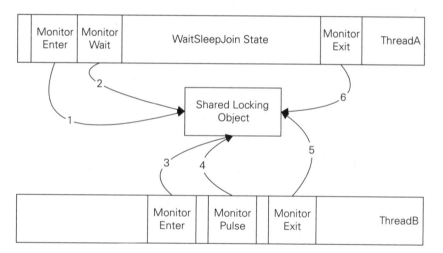

Figure 7.16   Steps involved in using `Pulse` and `Wait`

Step 1 involves Thread A acquiring a lock to the shared locking object. Once that lock is acquired, the `Wait` method of the `Monitor` class is used on the shared locking object. This places Thread A into the `WaitSleepJoin` state. Recall that in this state the thread is essentially idle. The first two lines of the following code example demonstrate steps 1 and 2. In the following example `QueueWaitLock` is the shared locking object referred to in the diagram.

```
Monitor.Enter(QueueWaitLock);
Result= Monitor.Wait(QueueWaitLock,60000);
if (Result)
```

```
{
  Debug.WriteLine("Pulsed");
}
else
{
  Debug.WriteLine("Timed out");
}
Monitor.Exit(QueueWaitLock);
```

Both `Wait` and `Pulse` must be invoked from within a region of code guarded by a synchronization block. All this means is that a `Monitor.Enter` and `Monitor.Exit` must surround the `Monitor.Wait` and `Monitor.Pulse` methods. The motivation for this is to eliminate the possibility of a race condition occurring. By ensuring that only one thread at a time can call `Wait` or `Pulse`, the chance of a race condition occurring is eliminated. Additionally, the same object that is locked on using the `Monitor.Enter` method must also be the object that is passed to the `Pulse` and `Wait` methods.

Monitor.Wait   `Monitor.Wait` is a static method that allows a thread to enter a `WaitSleepJoin` state. The thread will exit the `WaitSleepJoin` state when the object being waited on is signaled using the `Pulse` or `PulseAll` method or an optional timeout value expires.

`Pulse` signals one thread that is waiting on the synchronized object. Like `Wait`, `Pulse` must be invoked from within a synchronized section of code.

Monitor.Pulse   `Monitor.Pulse` is a static method of the `Monitor` class that allows a thread to signal one of the threads that have previously called `Wait` on a shared object.

The process begins with acquiring a lock on the object being waited on. This corresponds to step 3 in the diagram. Once acquired, the `Pulse` method is invoked (step 4). After `Pulse` the lock should be released (step 5). The following code example demonstrates steps 3–5 in the diagram at the start of this module. `TryEnter` is used in place of `Enter`.

```
Entered = Monitor.TryEnter(QueueWaitLock,1000);
if (Entered)
{
  Monitor.Pulse(QueueWaitLock);
  Monitor.Exit(QueueWaitLock);
}
else
{
  Trace.WriteLine("Unable to add entry");
}
```

Notice that we use `TryEnter` to attempt to acquire the lock. We wait for at most one second for the lock. If we are unable to acquire the lock, we log the condition and return. This prevents a thread from getting stuck waiting on another thread that may not be responding.

Once a thread invokes Pulse, it must call the Monitor.Exit method to allow those threads that are waiting on the object to continue. To be precise, if step 5 in figure 7.16 does not occur, neither will step 6. At the point Wait is invoked, the lock on the shared locking object is released automatically, allowing a different thread to acquire a lock on the shared locking object and perform a Pulse. For the thread that was in the WaitSleepJoin state to continue, Thread A in our example, it must reacquire a lock, on the shared locking object. For it to successfully reacquire the lock the Pulsing thread, Thread B, must release the lock.

STEPS TO WAIT

1 Acquire a lock on the waiting object using the Enter method.
2 Invoke Wait with an optional timeout.
3 Release the lock using the Exit method.

STEPS TO PULSE

1 Acquire a lock on the waiting object using the Enter method.
2 Invoke the Pulse method.
3 Release the lock using the Exit method.

The steps the waiting thread goes through are outlined in figure 7.17.

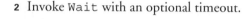
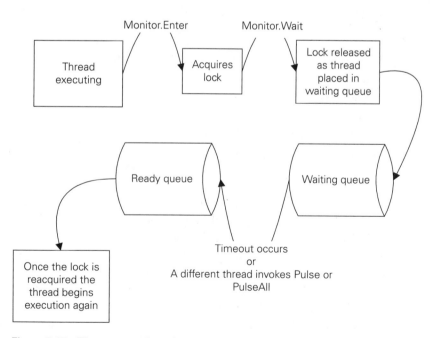

Figure 7.17   The states a thread goes through when Wait and Pulse are used

A thread goes through distinct states when `Wait` and `Pulse` are used. When the `Wait` statement is executed, the thread enters the waiting queue. The thread exits the waiting queue if it receives a `pulse`, or if a timeout occurs. Once it exits the waiting queue, it is added to the ready queue. When it can reacquire the lock, it will resume execution.

Synchronization Lock Exception A synchronization lock exception is thrown whenever an attempt is made to invoke `Pulse` or `Wait` without having first acquired a lock.

We've seen how a single thread can be controlled using `Pulse`; now we'll examine how multiple threads can respond to `PulseAll`.

7.4.4 The PulseAll method

Suppose that you receive a phone call from a client or supervisor wanting to know if all of the organization's web sites are functioning properly. Rather than wait for the next polling interval, you would like to check the sites immediately. One way to do this is to use `Thread.Interrupt`. This triggers an interrupt on the thread that it is associated with the instance of the `Thread` object on which it is invoked. Each thread would need to be interrupted.

Similarly, the `Pulse` and `Wait` approach we covered in the last chapter could be used. Instead of having a `Thread.Sleep` statement, you would have a `Monitor.Wait` statement. Unless the object that is being waited on is pulsed, `Wait` with a timeout value functions like the `Sleep` method:

```
Thread.Sleep(mSleepTime)
```

`Thread.Sleep` can be replaced with the following lines:

```
SyncLock WaitLockObject
   Monitor.Wait(WaitLockObject, mWaitTime)
End SyncLock
```

`WaitLockObject` is a shared/static object. Recall from the last section that in order to `Wait` on an object the thread must first enter a synchronized region of code. One way to do this is to use the `SyncLock` statement. This is equivalent to calling `Monitor.Enter` and `Monitor.Exit`.

Since `WaitLockObject` is shared/static, there is only one instance of it for all instances of the `WebSiteMonitor` class. To signal those threads waiting for the lock, we use the `PulseAll` method which alerts all threads waiting on a lock that the state of the object has changed and that they should resume processing. The differences between `Pulse` and `PulseAll` are shown in figure 7.18.

`PulseAll` empties the waiting queue, moving all entries into the ready queue. As soon as each of the threads in the ready queue are able to reacquire the lock, they begin executing.

`Wait`, `Pulse`, and `PulseAll` can only be called successfully if the synchronization lock around them locks on the same object that is passed in as the parameter. The following example demonstrates the incorrect way to call `PulseAll`:

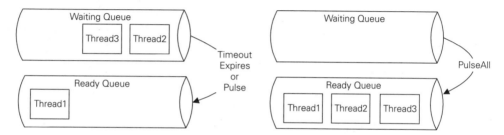

Figure 7.18 The difference between `Pulse` and `PulseAll`

```
SyncLock LockObjectOne
  Try
    Monitor.PulseAll(LockObjectTwo)
  Catch ex As Exception
    MsgBox(ex.Message)
  End Try
End SyncLock
```

Notice that the `SyncLock` is performed on `LockObjectOne` while `PulseAll` uses `LockObjectTwo`. This causes a `SynchronizationLockException` to be raised. The correct code is:

```
SyncLock LockObjectThree
  Try
    Monitor.Wait(LockObjectThree)
    MsgBox("Good Thread After Wait")
  Catch ex As Exception
    MsgBox(ex.Message)
  End Try
End SyncLock
```

7.5 DIGGING DEEPER INTO CONCURRENCY CONTROL

There is much more to currency control than the basics we've covered so far. In this section we cover those elements that are a little less frequently used.

7.5.1 C#'s volatile keyword

This topic is restricted to C#. VB.NET does not support the `volatile` keyword. Not to worry, very few situations require its use. In general it is easier to use the other synchronization mechanisms we've covered in this chapter. This topic is covered for completeness.

The Volatile Keyword   Volatile is a hint to the compiler that a value may change without its knowledge and that it should not make assumptions regarding the value during optimization.

The most important thing to know about a volatile field is that it is not thread-safe. If two threads attempt to update a `volatile` field at the same time, bad things will likely happen. By using the `volatile` statement you're telling the compiler that this variable's value may change in an unforeseen way. This keeps the compiler from optimizing instructions that access the variable.

GUIDELINES • Making a field `volatile` does not make it thread-safe.

• All fields enclosed in a `synchronization` block and accessed by multiple threads should be `volatile`.

• A `volatile` field cannot be passed as a reference. This means that an interlocked method cannot be used with a `volatile` field.

Compilers often perform optimizations to increase performance. One of the ways it optimizes is by placing frequently used variables into registers. A register is a location in the processor that can be accessed quickly. Once the value is in the register, the compiler assumes that nothing else changes the value of the variable. This means the generated code only accesses main memory when it knows it needs to retrieve the value. In the case of multithreaded applications, a different thread may change the value after the optimized code has read it in. The optimized code might not notice the change in the value. Listing 7.13 demonstrates the use `volatile`.

Listing 7.13   The use of the volatile keyword (C#)

```
private volatile int CurrentThreadCode;
. . .
System.Random rnd = new System.Random();
int RandomIndex;
int TickCount;
do
  RandomIndex= rnd.Next(NumberOfListeningThreads);
while (CurrentRandomIndex ==RandomIndex);
CurrentRandomIndex =RandomIndex;
TickCount =Environment.TickCount;
 CurrentThreadCode =
   ListeningThreads[RandomIndex].GetHashCode();
. . .
while(true)
{
  if (CurrentThreadCode == MyId)
  {
. . .
```

One form of optimization that causes multithreaded applications grief is reordering instructions. This makes most developers a little nervous. We like to think that if we do an assignment and then a test that the test instruction will always occur after the assignment. Some processors reorder instructions. Those processors are smart enough to do this in such a way that the outcome of the program is the same as if the instructions had not been reordered.

VOLATILE RESTRICTIONS

- Only fields are allowed to be `volatile`
- A `volatile` field can only be one of the following:
  - Reference type
  - Unsafe pointer
  - `sbyte`, `byte`, `short`, `ushort`, `int`, `uint`, `char`, `float`, `bool`
  - An enum type based on one of the allowed discrete value types

When a variable is marked as being `volatile`, the compiler ensures that all accesses to that variable are not reordered. Additionally, it ensures that each read of the variable comes from memory, not from a register. Marking a variable as `volatile` does not make it thread-safe. If more than one thread is writing to the value, a synchronization lock should be used. The situation where `volatile` can safely be used is when one or more threads are reading the value while only one thread is updating it. If a synchronization lock is used, there is no reason to use `volatile`.

WHEN TO USE VOLATILE

- A variable is accessed from multiple threads.
- No `Synchronization` mechanisms are being used.
- Only one thread will update the value.

Interlocked methods do not work with volatile variables. The reason is that the interlocked methods accept references to variables as their parameters. Volatile variables cannot be passed as references. The following line generates a compiler error:

```
Interlocked.Increment(ref CurrentThreadCode);
// Produces The following Error:
// Cannot pass volatile field
// 'VolatileExample.Form1.CurrentThreadCode'
// as ref or out, or take its address
```

Only certain types of variables can be volatile. Only class fields can be marked as volatile. Since a local variable is usually accessed by a single thread this is not too restrictive.

The code for this module is available from the publisher's web site. An alternative solution is presented that uses `Monitor.Wait` and `Pulse` instead of the `volatile` field. The code is simpler and easier to understand. Additionally, the listening threads notice the change in the variable more quickly than they do in the volatile version. Simple is generally good. Simple things are easy to understand and therefore easier to maintain.

7.5.2   COM+-based synchronization

COM+ is a set of runtime services, easily accessed via .NET, that facilitates developing enterprise applications. One of the services COM+ supplies is synchronization. COM+ uses the concept of a context as its means of synchronizing access to objects. To set the `Synchronization` attribute the class must be derived from the `Context-BoundObject` class, or a class derived from `ContextBoundObject`.

Context-BoundObject

`ContextBoundObject` is the base class that all objects that are bound to a particular context are inherited from.

```
Imports System.Runtime.Remoting.Contexts          Marks the entire class
                                                   for synchronization
<Synchronization()> Public Class Data
  Inherits ContextBoundObject                      Synchronized classes must be derived
  Dim x As Integer                                 from ContextBoundObject, or from
  Public Function Inc() As Integer                 a class derived from it, to utilize
    x += 1                                          context-based synchronization
    Return x
  End Function
  Public Property Count()
    Get
      Return x
    End Get
    Set(ByVal Value)
      x = Value
    End Set
  End Property
End Class
```

In our example, the class `Data` inherits directly from `ContextBoundObject`. The
`<Synchronization()>` attribute tells the compiler that all access to instances of
data must occur in a serialized way. To accomplish this a proxy is created to cross from
the default context to the context containing the instance of `Data`.

ContextBound-   All calls to objects derived from `ContextBoundObjects` go through a
Objects   proxy. This increases the time for each call to complete.
Use Proxies

For more information on this topic, the reader is encouraged to learn about COM+. An
in-depth discussion is beyond the scope of this book. The key point is that it is a simple
way to make objects thread-safe. That simplicity is not without cost. The cost of mar-
shaling values across the context boundaries is significant. Depending on the frequency
of those calls across the boundary, performance can be an order of magnitude worse
when compared to using synchronization locks. Figure 7.19 shows how COM+ performs synchronization.

When faced with the decision to make an object context bound and restricting the
process to a single processor, you should use benchmarks to aid in making the decision.
The key metric to consider is the frequency of calls to their duration. The following
simple formula can be used to determine the percentage that the overhead is contributing
to the overall execution time:

```
Percentage  = Call Overhead  / (Call Overhead + Call Duration)
```

Suppose that calling an object in a bound context takes an additional second to occur
when compared to calling an object in the same context. Suppose that the time each
call takes to complete is 60 seconds.

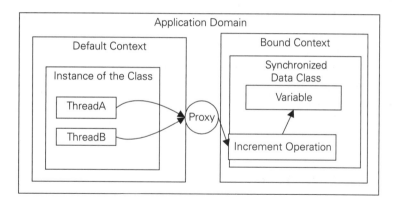

Figure 7.19 **How a synchronized context is implemented**

```
Percentage = 1 / (1 + 60) = 1.6%
```

That's less than 2 percent of the total time per call, not a bad price to pay for the simplicity. Suppose instead the call only takes five seconds to complete:

```
Percentage = 1 / (1 + 5) = 16.7%
```

The percentage changes to about 17 percent. Depending on performance needs, that may be too high of a price to pay.

7.6   SUMMARY

In this chapter we've discussed how to effectively manage thread interactions. We've seen that traditional software development concepts, such as encapsulation, can be used in multithreaded development. We've discussed the most common forms of access control, and explored some less commonly used mechanisms, such as interlocked operations. One of the most important things to get from this chapter is being able to identify where concurrency control is needed, by identifying the thread boundaries we discussed in section 7.1.4. Once you know where the moving parts contact each other, you can use one of the means we discussed to make sure that contact happens in a controlled way. In the next chapter we explore a different type of synchronization control known as a wait handle.

CHAPTER 8

WaitHandle classes

WaitHandle-derived classes provide a means of constructing powerful synchronization mechanisms. In this chapter we will cover ManualResetEvent, AutoResetEvent, and Mutex.

Just as the Monitor class allows for a thread to wait to acquire a lock on an object, the AutoResetEvent allows a thread to wait for a class derived from WaitHandle to become signaled. Each object derived from WaitHandle has two states: signaled and unsignaled. When an AutoResetEvent becomes signaled, any thread waiting for that event is released from the WaitSleepJoin state, triggering the AutoResetEvent to return to the unsignaled state.

WaitHandle-derived classes have advantages over the Monitor class. One is that it is possible to wait for multiple WaitHandle-derived classes. Using the WaitAll method, a thread can wait until all WaitHandle-derived classes in an array, or for only one, to become signaled. More important, WaitHandle-derived classes allow for interaction between managed and unmanaged code because they expose underlying OS handles.

ManualResetEvent is similar to AutoResetEvent, but it differs in its behavior when a thread is waiting. Unlike the AutoResetEvent class that returns to the unsignaled state, ManualResetEvents remain in the signaled state. The Reset method changes ManualResetEvent from signaled to unsignaled.

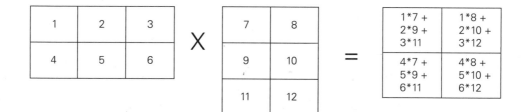

Figure 8.1 Matrix multiplication explained

The `Mutex` object is similar to the `Monitor` object in that it controls access of threads to regions of code. It differs in that it can control access to regions of code in different processes. This allows for robust synchronization at a process level, as well as a thread level.

The examples used in this chapter relate to matrix multiplication. Matrix multiplication is the process of combining two matrices to produce a third. The number of columns in the first matrix must equal the number of rows in the second. The resulting matrix will have the same number of rows that the first matrix has and the number of the columns that the second has.

Figure 8.1 shows how one matrix is multiplied by the second to produce the third. Notice that to produce the top-left cell of the result matrix, we start by multiplying the cell in the top-left in the first matrix by the top-left in the second. We then add that result to the product of the cell in the first row, second column in the first matrix times the cell in the first column, second row in the second, and so on. Matrix multiplication is being used because it is a relatively common mathematical construct used in many fields. Operations research, computer graphics, statistics, and engineering all use matrix multiplication.

8.1   THE WAITHANDLE CLASS

The `WaitHandle` class (figure 8.2) allows for a form of manual synchronization; manual in the sense that you, the developer, need to do most of the work. The previous chapter introduced automatic synchronization. This chapter focuses on more powerful, and fundamental, constructs of synchronization.

As you can see in figure 8.2 `WaitHandle` is an abstract base class and, because it is, instances of it cannot be created. To utilize the methods of `WaitHandle`, either we must use static/shared methods or an instance of a class derived from it must be instantiated.

The `WaitHandle` class is a wrapper around the Win32 synchronization handles. All classes derived from `WaitHandle` support multiple wait operations. Because these classes are closely tied to Win32 objects, they are less portable than the `Monitor` class.

WaitHandle Class `WaitHandle` is an abstract base class that allows for the creation of synchronization mechanisms. The three mechanisms that are derived from `WaitHandle` are `Mutex`, `AutoResetEvent`, and `ManualResetEvent`.

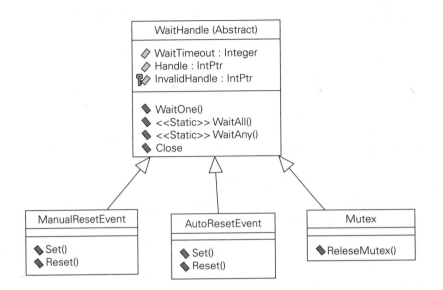

Figure 8.2 UML diagram of the `WaitHandle` class

The only property that the `WaitHandle` class exposes is `Handle`, which may be used to get or set the underlying OS handle. `WaitTimeout` is a public field that contains the value that the `WaitAny` method returns when it times out. `WaitAny`, `WaitOne`, and `WaitAll` are the most important methods in the `WaitHandle` class. We will cover each of these in detail in this chapter.

An important concept when dealing with the manual synchronization classes is object signaling. When an object is signaled, it can be thought of as being in an on state.

`ManualResetEvent` can be thought of as opening a door. Until the door is closed there is no limit on the number of people who can go through it. The `Set` and `Reset` methods are used to change the event's signaled state. We'll cover it in detail later, but for now think of it as being somewhat similar to the `Monitor.Wait` method used with the `Monitor.PulseAll` method.

`AutoResetEvent` is similar to calling `Monitor.Pulse` on an object being waited on. It allows one thread to proceed and changes its signaled state from signaled to unsignaled. It is very similar to the `ManualResetEvent` class, except that when a thread exits from the `WaitOne` method, the object is no longer signaled. It is as though a call to `Reset` is automatically made when the `WaitOne` method exits.

`Mutex` is used to create a mutually exclusive region of code. It can also be used to create mutually exclusive regions of code that exist in different processes. This sort of cross-process exclusion is a very powerful mechanism. `Mutex` is similar to `Monitor.Enter` and `Exit` except that `Mutex` can span multiple processes. To enter `Mutex` a call is made to `WaitOne`. To enter `Mutex` the object must be signaled; to exit a call is made to `ReleaseMutex`. Calling the `ReleaseMutex` method results in the instance of `Mutex` becoming signaled.

Each of these objects can be used in the static `WaitAny` and `WaitAll` methods of the `WaitHandle` class. `WaitAny` allows for waiting until one of many objects becomes signaled. An example of when this would be useful is a search algorithm. When one of the threads finds the answer, it's time to stop looking. `WaitAll` is a way of waiting for all objects in a set to be signaled before allowing processing to continue. This is useful when work is split up among multiple threads and processing cannot continue until all threads have completed their work.

This section is intended to introduce each of the `WaitHandle` classes. We will cover each in detail in the next sections. The important thing to understand is that a `WaitHandle`-derived object is either signaled or not. Think of this as a Boolean variable. It is either on or off.

These classes are less intuitive than the `Monitor` class. They provide a great deal of power over the synchronization of threads. If the `Monitor` class is not sufficient, these classes provide the capability of creating very powerful synchronization constructs.

8.2   THE AUTORESETEVENT CLASS

`AutoResetEvent` is a form of thread synchronization that alternates between a signaled state and an unsignaled one. Think of it as acting much like the toll turnstile at the subway station. To get past the turnstile someone must first deposit the correct fare. Once the fare has been deposited, only one person may enter. The turnstile switches from the state where it allows the person to enter to the state where it does not as soon as one person has entered. In this analogy, the turnstile is in a signaled state once someone deposits the fare. It switches to the unsignaled state as soon as someone passes through the turnstile.

Auto-ResetEvent   `AutoResetEvent` is a class that is derived from `WaitHandle`. It is a thread synchronization mechanism that is in one of two states. When it is signaled, any thread that calls, or has called, `WaitOne` will be allowed to proceed, automatically resetting the class to the unsignaled state.

The `AutoResetEvent` class contains the `Set` and `Reset` methods. Invoking `Set` results in the instance of the `AutoResetEvent` class becoming signaled. Invoking `Reset` can be used to change the instance of the `AutoResetEvent` class to unsignaled.

8.2.1   Using the Set method

`AutoResetEvent.Set` is the method to insert the token, so to speak. `Set` ensures that the state of the instance of the `AutoResetEvent` is signaled. If the state is signaled before `Set` is called, it will remain signaled. This toll turnstile does not give change. If more than one call to `Set` is made, the result will be the same: exactly one thread will be allowed to pass.

Set   `Set` is a method of `AutoResetEvent` that changes the state of an instance of that class to signaled. If the instance of `AutoResetEvent` is already signaled, the method has no effect.

`AutoResetEvent` will automatically switch from signaled to unsignaled as soon as a thread calls `WaitOne`, or some other wait method that we will cover later in the chapter. `WaitOne` is similar to getting in line to go through the turnstile. If `Set` is called before `WaitOne`, it is the same result as paying the fare before anyone is in line. As soon as they walk up they are allowed to proceed.

One way that `AutoResetEvent` is very different than the typical subway turnstile is that there is no orderly progression. This means that there is no way of determining the order in which multiple threads waiting for a shared `AutoResetEvent` object will be released when the `Set` method is invoked. The behavior of `AutoResetObject` on a single-processor machine is often quite different than its behavior on a multiple-processor machine. This reinforces the importance of regular testing during development on hardware that is similar to the targeted platform.

Another way `AutoResetEvent` differs from the subway turnstile is that the threads waiting do not change the state of `AutoResetEvent`. They do not deposit their own token in the turnstile. Someone else must do it for them, since they are in a `WaitSleepJoin` state while they are waiting.

Do not assume that one thread will execute before or after a different thread that is also waiting on a shared `AutoResetEvent`. When `AutoResetEvent` is signaled and one or more thread is waiting, all that is guaranteed is that a single thread will be released and that `AutoResetEvent` will return to the unsignaled state.

8.2.2   Using the Reset method

The `Reset` method changes the signaled state of `AutoResetEvent` to unsignaled. This is done automatically when a thread is released from the `WaitSleepJoin` state. There may be circumstances when no thread is waiting and it is set to signaled. Before a thread waits on that event, it may be determined that it should no longer be signaled. In that case, calling `Reset` will change the state back to unsignaled.

Reset   `Reset` is a method of the `AutoResetEvent` class that changes the state of an instance of that class to unsignaled. Calling the method is generally not required since the release of a thread from the `WaitSleepJoin` state automatically changes the state of `AutoResetEvent` to unsignaled.

The constructor of `AutoResetEvent` contains a parameter that controls the initial state of the instance of the class. If `False` is passed in, the instance of the `AutoReset-Event` class is initially unsignaled. If `True` is passed in, it is initially signaled.

Listing 8.1 demonstrates the `Set` method of the `AutoResetEvent` class.

Listing 8.1   Using WaitOne and Set to update the display (VB.NET)

```
Private UpdateUIEvent As AutoResetEvent
.  .  .
    UpdateUIEvent = New AutoResetEvent(False)
.  .  .
        Dim M1 As ClassSimpleMatrix
```

```
        Dim M2 As ClassSimpleMatrix
        Dim M1Cols, M1Rows As Long
        Dim M2Cols, M2Rows As Long
  . . .
        M1 = New ClassSimpleMatrix(M1Cols, M1Rows)
        M2 = New ClassSimpleMatrix(M2Cols, M2Rows)
        M1.Randomize(100)
        M2.Randomize(100)
        M3 = M1.Multiply(M2)         Change to
        UpdateUIEvent.Set()    ◄──┘  signaled
  . . .
    Private Sub UpdateUI()               Wait until
      While (True)                       UpdateUIEvent.Set
        UpdateUIEvent.WaitOne()  ◄──┘    is called
        If Not M3 Is Nothing Then
          If (listView1.InvokeRequired) Then
            Dim args As Object() = {listView1, M3}
            Dim updateit As ListViewUpdater
            updateit = AddressOf UpdateListViewWithMatrix
            listView1.Invoke(updateit, args)
          Else
            UpdateListViewWithMatrix(listView1, M3)
          End If
        End If
      End While
    End Sub
```

Since the `AutoResetEvent` class is derived from the `WaitHandle` class it is important to understand the methods of `WaitHandle`. Section 8.3 discusses the `WaitHandle` class in detail.

8.3   WAITHANDLE

`WaitHandle` is an abstract base class. This means that no instance of it can be created. Classes that are derived from `WaitHandle` can be created, assuming they are not abstract base classes themselves. In section 8.2 we discussed one class that is derived from `WaitHandle`, the `AutoResetEvent` class. In this section we discuss three of the methods of the `WaitHandle` class: `WaitOne`, `WaitAll`, and `WaitAny`.

8.3.1   WaitOne

`WaitOne` is used to wait for a class that's derived from `WaitHandle` to reach a signaled state. In the last section we covered one way `AutoResetEvent`, which is derived from `WaitHandle`, becomes signaled.

WaitOne   `WaitOne` is an instance method of all classes derived from `WaitHandle`. It attempts to put the instance of the object it is associated with into the `WaitSleepJoin` state. If it is successful it returns true; otherwise, it returns false. A timeout value can optionally be included.

`WaitOne` returns a Boolean value that indicates it is signaled. In the case where `WaitOne` is invoked with no parameters, it will always return true because it blocks until it becomes signaled. If it returns, it must have been signaled. So in the next example `ReceivedSignal` will always be true:

```
Bool ReceivedSignal = TheEvent.WaitOne();
```

The other versions of `WaitOne` accept two parameters. The first parameter is a timeout value, either an integer or a `TimeSpan` object. If it is an integer, the value indicates how many milliseconds to wait. If the instance of `AutoResetEvent` becomes signaled before the timeout period `WaitOne` will return true.

exitContext Parameter   The `exitContext` parameter of `WaitOne` controls how the method behaves when invoked from within a synchronized context. If `WaitOne` is invoked in a synchronized context and the `exitContext` parameter is not true, deadlock will likely occur.

The second parameter, `exitContext`, to the timed-out version of `WaitOne` is a Boolean that controls how `WaitOne` behaves when it is invoked from within a synchronized context. If the second parameter is false, `WaitOne` behaves the same as it does when it is called with no parameters, except a timeout value can be specified. If the `exitContext` parameter is true and the `WaitOne` method is invoked from within a synchronized context, the context is exited before the thread enters the `WaitSleep-Join` state. The context is then reentered when the thread exits the `WaitSleepJoin` state. Unless the COM+ approach to synchronization is being used, there is no reason to be concerned with this parameter. If the `Synchronization` attribute is being used on the class, then the value should be set to true.

Listing 8.2   Specifying if the current context should be exited before the wait begins (C#)

```
private void ThreadMethod()
    {
      try
      {
        bool ReceivedSignal;
        for (int i=0;i<10;i++)
        {
          // ExitContext is true == Deadlock
          ReceivedSignal =TheEvent.WaitOne(2000,ExitContext);   ⟵
          if (ReceivedSignal)                          Exit the context
          {                                            before the wait
            Console.WriteLine("received signal" );           begins
          }
```

```
        else
        {
          Console.WriteLine("Timed Out" );
        }
      }
    }
```

If the `Synchronization` attribute is set and the class is derived from `Context-BoundObject`, then any wait methods should have the `exitContext` flag set to true. Failure to do so results in a deadlock (figure 8.3). If the waiting thread enters the `WaitSleepJoin` state before exiting the synchronized context no other thread can enter that context until the waiting thread exits. If `WaitOne` is used, the thread will never exit and the process will need to be terminated.

If this form of synchronization is being used, ensure that the `Synchronization` attribute on the class indicates that the class should be reentrant. Waiting in a synchronized context should be avoided; in those cases where it cannot, ensure that the `exitContext` parameter is set to true.

Figure 8.3 is a simplified version of the context bound object's issue with waiting on events.

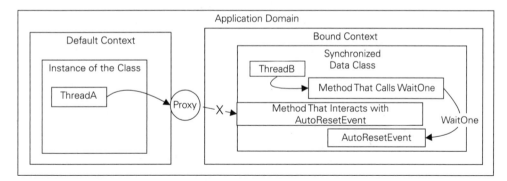

Figure 8.3 Context synchronization can result in deadlock if the correct value is not passed to `exitContext`.

The other forms of the wait methods also contain the `exitContext` parameter. The behavior is the same for each of those methods.

8.3.2   WaitAll

Suppose that you have a large amount of work to accomplish. It would be nice to split it up among multiple threads. Since there is no guarantee that the threads will end their work at the same time, it is important to have a means to wait for all of them to finish. `WaitAll` is a shared/static method on the `WaitHandle` class. It allows the caller to wait until all elements in an array of `WaitHandle`-derived classes become signaled.

WaitAll WaitAll is a shared/static method of the WaitHandle class. It has three forms, all of which accept an array of WaitHandle-derived objects. An optional timeout and exitContext parameter can also be passed.

In Listing 8.3 the call to WaitHandle.WaitAll will only return if all elements in FinishedState become signaled.

Listing 8.3 WaitAll is used to wait for all objects to become signaled. (VB.NET)

```
. . .
    Private finishedState() As AutoResetEvent        ⟵  Allocates an
. . .                                                    array to pass
  Private Sub ManagerMethod()                            to WaitAll
    Dim i As Long
    Dim signaled As Boolean
    Dim tmpObject As Object
    While True
      signaled = workAvailable.WaitOne(1000, False)
      If signaled Then
        WaitHandle.WaitAll(finishedState)              ⟵  Returns when all
        ' Wait for all threads to finish their work        elements become
        If Not notify Is Nothing Then                      signaled
          ' Gather up the results and send them back
          resultObjects = New ArrayList()
          For i = 0 To workers.Length - 1
            tmpObject = workers(i).GetResults
            While Not tmpObject Is Nothing
              resultObjects.Add(tmpObject)
              tmpObject = workers(i).GetResults
            End While
          Next
          notify(resultObjects)
          notify = Nothing
        End If
        finishedWithWork.Set()
      End If
    End While
End Sub
```

Listing 8.3 is from a class library that creates a configurable number of threads and distributes work to each. This is very similar to ThreadPool, discussed in chapter 10. The basic architecture of the component is described in figure 8.4.

The class library consists of a manager class that manages a collection of threads. This allows the complexity of thread management to be encapsulated in a single location. The manager distributes work to each thread and then waits until they all finish their work. The WaitAll method is used to wait until each thread signals their work is finished using their AutoResetEvent. When all threads have finished executing, the manager thread collects the results and invokes a delegate that returns them to the calling class.

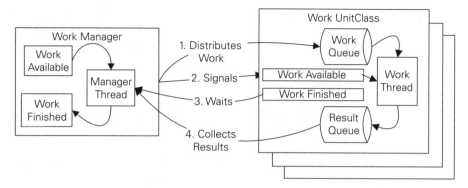

Figure 8.4 High-level architecture of a ThreadPool-like implementation.

- The number of objects that can be waited on depends on the OS. Under current Windows systems it is 64.
- Duplicate `WaitHandle` objects are not allowed.
- Null objects are not allowed in the array of `WaitHandle` objects.
- All objects in the array must be derived from `WaitHandle`, directly or indirectly.

Matrix multiplication is a good candidate for distributing work to threads. Recall that each output cell is calculated independently. Figure 8.5 shows how the highlighted cell can be calculated on a thread independent of other calculations.

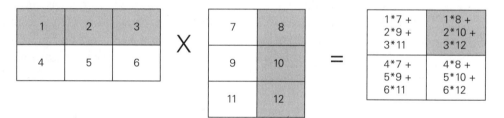
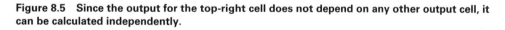

Figure 8.5 Since the output for the top-right cell does not depend on any other output cell, it can be calculated independently.

`WaitAll` allows for timed-out operation in the same way `WaitOne` does. A timeout value can be specified, either as an integer indicating the number of milliseconds or as a `TimeSpan` object. The `ExitContext` parameter is also present. Its behavior is the same as it is for `WaitOne`.

8.3.3   WaitAny

Suppose that you wanted to know when one `AutoResetEvent`, out of many, becomes signaled. The `WaitHandle.WaitAny` method accepts an array of `Wait-Handle` objects and waits until one of them becomes signaled or an optional time-out expires. If one of the elements in the array becomes signaled, the index of that element is returned. If no element becomes signaled and a timeout occurs, the constant `WaitHandle.WaitTimeout` is returned. If more than one element becomes signaled, the return value is the index of the lowest element to become signaled.

WaitAny   `WaitAny` is a static method of the `WaitHandle` class. It accepts an array of `WaitHandle` references. If one of the `WaitHandles` in the array becomes signaled, its index is returned. If a timeout is specified and no `WaitHandle` becomes signaled during the timeout period, the constant `WaitHandle.WaitTimeout` is returned.

Suppose you had an array of `WaitHandle`-derived objects that contained five elements. If elements two and four become signaled during a call to `WaitAny` on that array, the return value would be 1. The return value is the zero-based index, so the second element would correspond to a return value of 1.

WaitAny   `WaitAny` is bound by the same restrictions as `WaitAll`.
Restrictions

The example from the last section was a component that allowed for easy distribution of work among multiple threads. It relied on each worker thread having a queue to store work in. This allowed more than 64 tasks to be queued up at once. Figure 8.6 shows a different architecture.

Instead of the queue being in the worker class, it is in the manager class. This allows for more flexibility. Suppose you only wanted to process work until a solution is found. Using the manager as the means of distributing the work makes this much simpler. The way the manager works is that a collection of work items is added using the `DoWork` method. These entries are added to the manager's work queue and the manager is informed that there is work to do. It does a `WaitAny` on the workers to find one which is `ReadyForWork`. When one is found, work is assigned to it from the work queue. Once the thread has completed its work, it sends `ReadyForWork` back

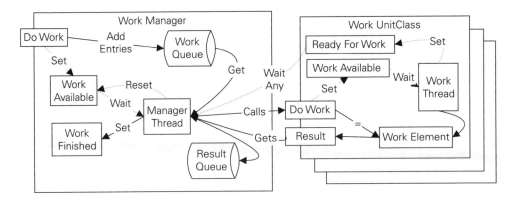

Figure 8.6   A refined manager/worker architecture

to the signaled state and the manager picks up the completed element. Listing 8.4 demonstrates the basic elements of the architecture presented in figure 8.5.

Listing 8.4   A revised work manager using queues in the manager object (C#)

```
. . .
private AutoResetEvent[] FinishedState;    ←┘   Declares an array of
                                                AutoResetEvents
. . .
FinishedState = new AutoResetEvent[HowManyWorkers];  ←┐  Allocates the array of
for (long i = 0;i<HowManyWorkers ;i++)                  │  AutoResetEvents
{
  Workers[i] = new ClassWorkUnit("Worker" + i.ToString());  ←┐  Allocates the
  FinishedState[i] = Workers[i].Finished;  ←┐                 │  worker class
}
. . .                                        Assigns the element
bool Signaled ;                              the WaitHandle array
int ThreadReadyForWork;                      an AutoResetEvent
while (true)
{                                                   Waits for one of the
  Signaled = WorkAvailable.WaitOne(100, false);     AutoResetEvents to
  if (Signaled)                                     become signaled
  {
    ThreadReadyForWork= WaitHandle.WaitAny(FinishedState,100,false); ←┘
    if (ThreadReadyForWork != WaitHandle.WaitTimeout)
    {
      Unit WorkUnit = Workers[ThreadReadyForWork].GetResults();
      if (WorkUnit  != null)
        CompletedQueue.Enqueue(WorkUnit);
      WorkUnit =null;
      if (WorkQueue.Count > 0)
      {
        WorkUnit = (Unit) WorkQueue.Dequeue();
        if (WorkUnit != null)
          Workers[ThreadReadyForWork].Work(WorkUnit);
      }
```

The basic concept is that the worker thread waits for an AutoResetEvent to become signaled saying that there is work to do. Once it completes that work, it sets Ready-ForWork to signaled. One interesting point with this approach is that ReadyForWork is created initially signaled. The following statement creates the AutoResetEvent and sets it to being initially signaled:

```
ReadyForWork = new AutoResetEvent(true);
```

As stated earlier, if more than one element in the array being waited upon becomes signaled, the lowest index corresponding to a signaled object will be returned. Figure 8.7 demonstrates this concept.

We've examined the methods of the WaitHandle class; now let's look at the ManualResetEvent and Mutex classes that are derived from WaitHandle.

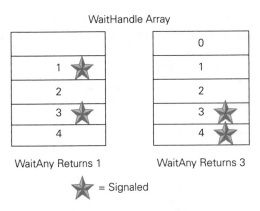

WaitHandle Array

WaitAny Returns 1   WaitAny Returns 3

★ = Signaled

Figure 8.7
The WaitAny method always returns the index of the lowest signaled element in the wait array.

8.4 *MANUALRESETEVENT*

Suppose that you want to know if an AutoResetEvent object is signaled. One way you could do this is to call WaitOne on it, passing in zero for the wait time. If the AutoResetEvent were not signaled, it would return false. If it were signaled, it would return true. The problem is that when an AutoResetEvent is signaled and a wait is performed on it, the object automatically switches to being not signaled. This means that if one thread were inspecting the state of things it would change them by observing them. To address this and similar issues, we can use ManualResetEvent. As the name indicates, the state of the event does not change when it is waited on. The behavior can be thought of as being similar to a water faucet. When turned on, it will stay on until it is turned off. This contrasts with the AutoResetEvent, which turns itself off as soon as someone notices that it is on.

**Manual-
ResetEvent**   The ManualResetEvent is a synchronization mechanism that remains in a signaled state regardless of how many times a wait method is called on it. It must be changed from the signaled state using the Reset method.

Listing 8.5 shows an example that demonstrates using a ManualResetEvent object.

Listing 8.5   The ManualResetEvent offers greater control (VB.NET).

```
Private ReadyForWork() As ManualResetEvent       ◁─┐ Declares an array of
. . .                                                ManualResetEvents
ReDim ReadyForWork(HowManyWorkers - 1)     ◁─┐
. . .                                           Resizes the array to the
  For i = 0 To HowManyWorkers - 1              number of workers
  Workers(i) = New ClassWorkUnit("Worker" + i.ToString())
  ReadyForWork(i) = Workers(i).ReadyForWork    ◁─┐ Retrieves the Worker's
  ResultsReady(i) = Workers(i).ResultsReady         instance of the
Next                                                ManualResetEvent
. . .
Public Function WorkerThreadAvailability() As Boolean()
Dim Results() As Boolean
ReDim Results(Workers.Length - 1)
```

```
Dim i As Long
For i = 0 To Workers.Length - 1
  Results(i) = ReadyForWork(i).WaitOne(0, False)  ⊲┐ Inspects the signaled
Next                                                │ state of the
Return Results                                      │ ManualResetEvent
End Function
```
■

To change an instance of the `ManualResetEvent` class from being signaled to not, we use the `Reset` method. `Reset` returns a Boolean indicating the success of the operation. As with all operations that return a value, ensure that the operation succeeds.

```
If Not ReadyForWorkEvent.Reset() Then
  Throw New Exception("Unable to reset ReadyForWorkEvent")
End If
```

Instances of the `ManualResetEvent` class provide a robust means of synchronizing activity. They provide a high degree of control and are easy to use. They can be used with the `WaitOne`, `WaitAny`, and `WaitAll` methods.

TIP The `WaitHandle.WaitTimeout` constant is currently 258.

Table 8.1 compares the results of the wait methods of `AutoResetEvent` and `ManualResetEvent`.

Table 8.1   Comparison of `AutoResetEvent` and `ManualResetEvent`

Statements	AutoResetEvent		ManualResetEvent	
	Return Code	Signaled	Return Code	Signaled
TheEvent.Set()	True	Yes	True	Yes
TheEvent.WaitOne(0, False)	True	Yes	True	Yes
TheEvent.WaitOne(0, False)	False		True	Yes
TheEvent.Reset()	True		True	
TheEvent.WaitOne(0, False)	False		False	
TheEvent.Set()	True	Yes	True	Yes
WaitHandle.WaitAny(H, 0, False)	0	Yes	0	Yes
WaitHandle.WaitAny(H, 0, False)	258		0	Yes
TheEvent.Reset()	True		True	
WaitHandle.WaitAny(H, 0, False)	258		258	
TheEvent.Set()	True	Yes	True	Yes
WaitHandle.WaitAll(H, 0, False)	True	Yes	True	Yes
WaitHandle.WaitAll(H, 0, False)	False		True	Yes
TheEvent.Reset()	True		True	
WaitHandle.WaitAll(H, 0, False)	False		False	

The Return Code column under each type of reset event indicates the value returned by the statement. The Signaled column indicates if the object is signaled. Notice that `ManualResetEvent`'s signaled state does not change except for when `Set` and `Reset` are invoked on it. The value 258 corresponds to the `WaitHandle.Wait-Timeout` constant.

TIP   If multiple threads manipulate the same `ManualResetEvent`, a synchronization block may be needed to ensure proper execution.

Both the manual and autoreset events are useful constructs. Many things can only be accomplished by using a `ManualResetEvent`. One word of warning, the following instruction is atomic.

```
TestAutoEvent.WaitOne()
```

While similar statements with a `ManualResetEvent` are not.

```
TestManualEvent.WaitOne()
TestManualEvent.Reset()
```

To ensure proper execution, enclose the preceding lines in a synchronization block.

8.5   MUTEX CLASS: WAITONE AND RELEASEMUTEX

Suppose that you wanted to use a single text file to store the output of multiple threads. We've seen how race conditions can happen. Any time a shared resource is used, there is the chance of a race condition. Since a file might be accessed not only by multiple threads but also multiple processes, the operating system provides for various file-sharing restrictions.

Listing 8.6   Using a Mutex to guard a shared text file (C#)

```
. . .
public class ClassSafeFile
{
    private string Filename;
    private Mutex TheMutex;
    public ClassSafeFile(bool UseMutex,string Filename )
    {
        if (UseMutex)
        {
            TheMutex=new Mutex(false,"Manning.Dennis.Threading.Ch8.S8");   ◁─┐
        }
        this.Filename = Filename;                                           Creates a Mutex
    }                                                                       that is not
    public void Write(string Contents)                                      initially signaled
    {
        int ByteCount = System.Text.Encoding.Unicode.GetByteCount(Contents);
        byte[] Bytes = System.Text.Encoding.Unicode.GetBytes(Contents);
```

```
         FileStream TheStream;
         bool Success = true;
         if (TheMutex != null)
         {
             Success = TheMutex.WaitOne(10000,false);    ◁─┐ Waits for up to 10
         }                                                  │ seconds trying to
                                                            │ acquire the lock
         if (Success)
         {
             try
             {
                 TheStream = File.Open(
                     Filename,
                     FileMode.
                     OpenOrCreate,
                     FileAccess.Write,
                     FileShare.Read);
                 TheStream.Seek(0,SeekOrigin.End);
                 TheStream.Write(Bytes,0,ByteCount);
                 TheStream.Close();
             }
             finally
             {
                 if (TheMutex != null)
                 {
                     TheMutex.ReleaseMutex();    ◁─┐ Releases the
                 }                                 │ acquired Mutex
             }
         }
         else
         {
             throw new Exception("Timed out waiting for File");
         }
     }
}
. . .
```

Listing 8.6 allows multiple threads to read the file but only one to write. If two threads attempt to open a file for write simultaneously, a System.IO.IOException is raised. This exception will likely be handled by waiting for a period of time and then attempting to open the file again. An alternative is to synchronize access to the file.

Mutex   A Mutex is a named synchronization object derived from WaitHandle that allows for creation of mutually exclusive regions of code.

A Mutex is a synchronization construct that allows for the creation of a mutually exclusive region of code. A Mutex serves much of the same function as Monitor.Enter and Monitor.Exit. If using Enter and Exit can solve a problem, they should be used. A Mutex takes roughly two orders of magnitude longer to acquire and release a lock than a monitor. That means that it takes roughly 100 times longer to acquire and release a `Mutex` than it does to do a `Monitor.Enter` and `Monitor.Exit`. Table 8.2 offers a comparison of the `Mutex` class to the `Monitor` class.

Table 8.2 Comparison of `Mutex` and `Monitor`

	Monitor	Mutex
High performance	Y	
Allows for object being initially owned		Y
Timed-out lock acquisition	Y	Y
Waits for one of many locks		Y
Waits for all of many locks		Y
Cross-process support		Y
Can lock on any object	Y	
Tests for signaled	Y	Y
Support for COM+ synchronization		Y
Named		Y
The number of releases must match the number acquires	Y	Y

`Mutex` offers several benefits over `Monitor`. The biggest is that it is derived from `WaitHandle` and can be used with `WaitOne`, `WaitAny`, and `WaitAll`. This means that a thread can use the `WaitAll` method and wait until it acquires all of the `Mutex` in an array. This would be very difficult to do using `Monitor`.

`Mutex` is signaled when no thread owns it. When ownership of `Mutex` is acquired using one of the wait methods, it is set to unsignaled. `Mutex` can be created in the unsignaled state. This means the thread that creates `Mutex` acquires ownership of it. To create `Mutex` that is initially owned, pass in true for the `initiallyOwned` parameter of the constructor. When `ReleaseMutex` is called, `Mutex` is no longer owned and becomes signaled. Additionally, if a thread that owns `Mutex` terminates normally, the `Mutex` is released and becomes signaled.

When `Mutex` is created, it is assigned a name, which should be unique. If `Mutex` with the supplied name exists, it is returned; otherwise, a new `Mutex` is created. As long as a thread retains a reference to the `Mutex`, it will continue to exist. At the point the last thread with a reference to a `Mutex` terminates, the `Mutex` is destroyed. Additionally, a thread can call the `Close` method on the `Mutex` class to release the `Mutex`. Once a `Mutex` has been released, it cannot be used.

Since a `Mutex` has a name, it can be used across processes. In listing 8.6 only one thread of one process can access the file at a point in time. The other threads will wait, for at most ten seconds, to acquire the file. This approach can be used with any shared resource.

The cost of using `Mutex` is very high compared to using `Monitor`. The reason for the difference in performance is that `Mutex` is a kernel object. `Mutex` is a very powerful construct. Because of its performance it should only be used when a faster synchronization mechanism will not suffice.

8.6 SUMMARY

In this chapter we've covered manual synchronization constructs. As with most things, the manual classes offer higher flexibility at the cost of ease of use and in some cases performance. Understanding when to use each of the synchronization classes is an important lesson and one that will come with time. A guiding principle should be to use the highest performance, least complex solution. There will be requirements that dictate which sort of synchronization to use; for example, if cross-process synchronization is required, then the `Mutex` class is a likely candidate for the solution. Likewise, if a single process is involved and the highest level of performance is required, likely a `Monitor` implementation will be required.

The next chapter deals with a reader/writer lock. Reader/writer locks can be created from synchronization primitives. They offer a solution to a very specific problem. By being familiar with the various tools at your disposal, you'll be able to better choose which tool to use in a given situation.

CHAPTER 9

Reader/Writer lock

ReaderWriterLock is a synchronization mechanism allowing access to data. It allows multiple threads to read the data simultaneously, but only one thread at a time to update it. While a thread is updating, no other thread can read the data. The name is misleading. It may cause you to think there are two locks; in reality there is a single lock that restricts both reading and writing.

Think of how a conversation in a group generally goes. One person talks while the others listen. Think of how inefficient a conversation would be if only one person could talk to one person in a group at a given time. This is the very reason that conference calls are used. In business, it is often beneficial to have a single conference call, involving all of the parties at once, rather than have multiple person-to-person calls. A ReaderWriterLock allows multiple threads to read data at the same time. The only restriction is that a thread cannot modify the data while someone is reading it.

The majority of data accesses are reads, but occasionally a thread needs to change a value. This is problematic in that one thread may modify a data element while another one is accessing it. To combat this, the choices are to protect the element with a synchronization lock, such as lock and SyncLock, or to use ReaderWriterLock.

This chapter uses a simulated auction to demonstrate this concept. To test our synchronization system we can utilize multiple threads. Each thread will have a list of items it is instructed to acquire, along with an allotment of bidding points. Since an auction involves many reads to data and a few writes, it is ideal for demonstrating the concepts of a reader/writer lock.

The .NET implementation of `ReaderWriterLock` is efficient enough for highly granular use. In our example, each auction item has its own `ReaderWriterLock`, allowing for a higher level concurrency and ensuring fairness in lock allocation between threads. When a thread requests a write lock, no other threads will be granted a read lock until the write lock request is satisfied.

The `ReaderWriterLock` is a very useful construct. Most environments force developers to write their own or purchase a third-party tool, but the .NET platform makes this construct available for general use. `ReaderWriterLocks` are a powerful tool for selectively guarding data.

9.1 ACQUIRING A READ LOCK FROM A READERWRITERLOCK

The read portion of the `ReaderWriterLock` is the means that a thread uses to indicate that it is reading the protected data. This is needed because the determination of whether a thread can write to the protected data is based on the presence of one or more threads reading it. It doesn't make much sense for a read lock to be used without a write lock. If no thread is changing the data, there isn't much need in restricting access to it, since the data must be constant in nature. Figure 9.1 presents the logical structure of a `ReaderWriterLock`.

Remember that all access to a data element must be restricted to effectively protect the data. If there are ten ways to examine and three ways to update a data element, but only nine of the possible reading paths are protected, the concurrency issues that the `ReaderWriterLock` is supposed to be avoiding will still occur.

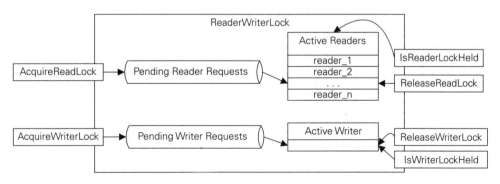

Figure 9.1 Logical structure of the ReaderWriterLock

9.1.1 Acquiring and releasing a reader lock

Suppose that you wanted to control access to data elements so that multiple consumers of that data could read it concurrently without data corruption. One way to do this is to use a `ReaderWriterLock`.

Reader-WriterLock   A `ReaderWriterLock` is a synchronization mechanism that allows concurrent data reading but restricts data writing to occur only when no readers are present.

A `ReaderWriterLock` selectively allows access to data. It allows multiple threads to acquire a reader lock, which is acquired when the thread will be performing only read operations. Nothing keeps an errant thread from acquiring a reader lock and performing write operations. Care should be taken to ensure that only read operations occur in a region guarded by a read lock.

The power of a `ReaderWriterLock` is that it allows read operations to be logically separated from write operations. Since multiple read operations do not result in data corruption, there is no reason that multiple threads cannot simultaneously read a variable without ill effects.

To acquire a read lock, we invoke the `AcquireReadLock` method on the instance of the lock we wish to acquire. `AcquireReadLock` accepts a timeout value as its only parameter. As with many other synchronization methods, the timeout can either be an integer specifying the number of milliseconds to wait or an instance of the `TimeSpan` class.

In listing 9.1, we pass in the constant `Timeout.Infinite` to indicate we wish to wait indefinitely until we are able to acquire a read lock. We are assured that when the method returns we have acquired a read lock. As a general rule, using `Timeout.Infinite` is a bad idea. A better approach is to supply a timeout value because it removes the possibility of a `ReaderWriterLock`-related deadlock. To keep this chapter's examples simple, we use `Timeout.Infinite`.

Once a thread has acquired a read lock, it can perform any reads that are required, and once those reads are complete it should release the lock using the `ReleaseReadLock` method. The number of calls to `ReleaseReadLock` must match the number of calls to `AcquireReadLock`. If a thread fails to release the lock the same number of times it acquires the lock a write lock will not be granted to other threads. This will lead to deadlock if `Timeout.Infinite` is being used, as well as stopping the granting of any write locks.

TIP   When the number of releases is greater than the number of acquires, a `System.ApplicationException` is thrown.

If a thread attempts to release a lock that it does not own, an exception is generated with the message "Attempt to release mutex not owned by caller." This might make you think that the `ReaderWriterLock` is implemented using the `Mutex` synchronization primitive we covered in section 8.5; however, it is not. This is a case of a somewhat misleading error message. If this exception is encountered, it indicates that the number of releases is greater than the number of acquires.

```
Private ItemLock As ReaderWriterLock                         Declares the
. . .                                                        ReaderWriterLock
Public ReadOnly Property CurrentPrice() As Decimal
Get
  ItemLock.AcquireReaderLock(Timeout.Infinite)              Waits indefinitely
  Try                                                        for a reader lock
    Return TheCurrentPrice
  Finally
    ItemLock.ReleaseReaderLock()          Releases the
  End Try                                  reader lock
End Get
End Property
```

In Listing 9.1 notice that the `ReleaseReadLock` is located in a `Finally` statement. This ensures that if an exception is generated while the thread owns the read lock it will correctly be released. This is a good example of how `Finally` clauses should be used with exception handling. Figure 9.2 shows how multiple threads can access shared data using a `ReaderWriterLock`. Note that the shared data is not actually contained within the `ReaderWriterLock` but is guarded by it.

Each thread acquires the lock, accesses the data, and releases the lock. Since both threads are reading the data, there is no restriction on when the threads can access the data.

In this section we waited indefinitely to acquire the read lock. In the next section we'll discuss how to wait for a predetermined period of time. Once that time has expired, we need a means of determining if we have acquired the lock. Since `Acquire-ReaderLock` does not return a value, we must use the `IsReaderLockHeld` property that we discuss in the next section.

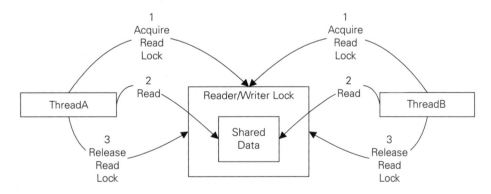

Figure 9.2   Two threads can read the shared data using the `ReaderWriterLock` to protect its value.

9.1.2 IsReaderLockHeld

Suppose you wanted to wait a certain amount of time for a lock to be acquired. The parameter to the `AcquireReaderLock` method specifies how long to wait for a reader lock to become available. As we saw in the previous section, it can either be an integer specifying the number of milliseconds to wait or a `TimeSpan` object. If the lock is not acquired in the specified time, an `ApplicationException` is raised. Listing 9.2 demonstrates one way of acquiring a reader lock and utilizing a timeout.

Listing 9.2   An improved way of acquiring a read lock (C#)

```csharp
. . .
public decimal CurrentPrice
{
  get
  {
    do
    {
      try
      {
        ItemLock.AcquireReaderLock(1000);          // Attempts to acquire
      }                                            //   a reader lock
      catch(System.ApplicationException ex)
      {
        System.Diagnostics.Debug.WriteLine(ex.Message);
      }
    } while (!ItemLock.IsReaderLockHeld);          // Determines if the
    try                                            //   lock was acquired
    {
      return TheCurrentPrice;
    }
    finally
    {
      ItemLock.ReleaseReaderLock();                // Releases
    }                                              //   the lock
  }
}
. . .
```

The code loops until it acquires the reader lock; if it takes more than one second to acquire the lock, an `ApplicationException` is raised. The property `IsReader-LockHeld` returns a Boolean value true if the current thread has a reader lock to the data, false if it does not.

IsReader-LockHeld   `IsReaderLockHeld` is a property of the `ReaderWriterLock` class that indicates if the thread on which the executing code inspects the property currently owns a reader lock.

Another use for the `IsReaderLockHeld` property is to determine if invoking the `ReleaseReaderLock` method results in the lock being freed:

```
try
{
  return TheCurrentPrice;
}
finally
{
  ItemLock.ReleaseReaderLock();
  if (ItemLock.IsReaderLockHeld)
  {
    throw new Exception("Reader Lock still held after release");
  }
}
```

This can help detect situations where the number of releases is less than the number of acquires. The closer the error-detecting code is to the error, the easier it is to detect the error. If the error were not detected here, the mistake would likely manifest itself by having no other thread able to access the read lock. This would make the program hang. These sorts of issues are much more difficult to resolve without error-detecting instructions.

> **TIP**   Use the `IsReaderLockHeld` property to determine if a lock is held before `AcquireReaderLock` and after `ReleaseReaderLock`. This helps track down the number of acquires not matching the number of releases. Since there is a performance penalty, this sort of checking should only be performed during development. Release builds should not include this check.

When faced with an inconsistent or undesirable outcome, the first step should be to include robust error-detecting and -handling code. This is an area where exceptions and assertions can play a key role. Additionally, it is a good idea to determine if a thread already has a reader lock before the acquire method is called. The following code demonstrates a more defensive way of dealing with the acquire method:

```
. . .
if (ItemLock.IsReaderLockHeld)
{
  throw new Exception("Reader Lock held before acquire");
}
do
{
  try
{
  ItemLock.AcquireReaderLock(1000);
. . .
```

The concept here is to make sure that the conditions of a thread are in the state you think they are. If not, throw an exception to help track down the error.

9.2 ACQUIRING A WRITER LOCK FROM A READERWRITERLOCK

In the previous section we discussed the reader portion of `ReaderWriterLock`. Now we turn to the write portion. The purpose of a write lock is to ensure that no threads are reading data while it is being updated.

9.2.1 Acquire, release, and IsLockHeld

The goal of a write lock is to enable multiple threads to read shared date while restricting write access in a way that ensures data corruption does not occur. We have already covered the read lock. Multiple threads can safely read data at the same time. Only one thread can be modifying data at one time. While a thread is modifying the shared data, no other thread can access the data without the risk of data corruption. In terms of our simulated auction, a write lock allows a new bid to be accepted. Listing 9.3 demonstrates the bidding process.

Listing 9.3   A bid must be higher than the current price (VB.NET).

```
Public Sub Bid(ByVal Amount As Decimal, ByVal BiddersName As String)
  If ItemLock.IsWriterLockHeld Then                          ◁─┐ If a write lock
    Throw New Exception("Writer lock held before acquire")     │ is held, throw
  End If                                                        │ an exception
  Try
    Do
      Try
        ItemLock.AcquireWriterLock(TimeoutValue)          ◁─┐ Try to acquire
      Catch Ex As System.ApplicationException               │ the lock
        System.Diagnostics.Debug.WriteLine(Ex.Message)
      End Try
    Loop While Not ItemLock.IsWriterLockHeld         ◁─┐ Loop until the
    If AuctionComplete Then                            │ writer lock is
      Throw New Exception("Auction has ended")         │ acquired
    End If
    If (Amount > TheCurrentPrice) Then
      TheCurrentPrice = Amount
      TheBiddersName = BiddersName
    Else
      Throw New Exception("Bid not higher than current price")
    End If                            ┌ Once the update is
  Finally                             │ complete, release
    ItemLock.ReleaseWriterLock()   ◁─┘ the writer lock
    If (ItemLock.IsWriterLockHeld) Then
      Throw New Exception("Writer Lock still held after release")
    End If
  End Try
End Sub
```

As you can see in listing 9.3, it is similar to `AcquireReadLock` in that it accepts a timeout parameter. The `AcquireWriteLock` method is, obviously, used to acquire a write lock.

Acquire-
WriterLock   `AcquireWriterLock` is a method on the `ReaderWriterLock` class that allows a thread to request ownership of a write lock. It accepts a timeout parameter and throws an `ApplicationException` if the lock cannot be acquired in the specified time period.

If the write lock cannot be acquired within the specified duration, an exception is raised. Figure 9.3 shows the relationship between a read lock and a write lock.

At any given point a thread cannot have a write lock and some other thread have a read lock on the same instance of the `ReaderWriterLock` class. When a thread wishes to acquire a write lock, it calls `AcquireWriteLock`. It then must wait until all threads that currently have read locks release them. Once all threads have released the read locks, the requesting thread is granted its write lock. While that thread has a write lock, no other threads will be able to acquire a read or write lock.

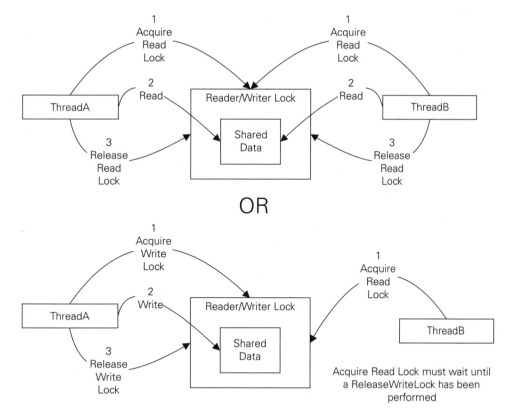

Figure 9.3   When a write lock has been granted, no thread will be granted a read or write lock until it is released.

`IsWriterLockHeld` is a property of the `ReaderWriterLock` class that allows a thread to determine if it has acquired a write lock on an instance of the `ReaderWriterLock` class. If the thread currently owns a write lock, true is returned.

To release a write lock, a thread uses the `ReleaseWriterLock` method of the `ReaderWriterLock` class. If the thread does not own the lock, an `Application-Exception` is raised with the message "Attempt to release mutex not owned by caller." Once the thread has released its write lock, other threads are able to acquire their desired locks. This ensures that the data a thread is viewing doesn't change while it is looking at it. Care should be taken to ensure that a thread does not modify shared data unless it currently owns a write lock.

9.2.2 UpgradeToWriterLock

There are times when it's unclear if the lock required will be a reader or a writer. For example, in the auction simulation, in order to determine if a new bid is higher than the existing bid we must first look at what the current bid is (listing 9.4). Once we've examined the current bid, we can see if the new bid is higher.

Listing 9.4   Checks to see if the new bid is higher than the existing (C#)

```csharp
public void Bid(decimal Amount, string BiddersName)
{
  if (ItemLock.IsWriterLockHeld)
  {
    throw new Exception("Writer Lock held before acquire");
  }
  if (ItemLock.IsReaderLockHeld)
  {
    throw new Exception("Reader Lock held before acquire");
  }
  ItemLock.AcquireReaderLock(Timeout.Infinite);      // Initially acquire
  try                                                //   a reader lock
  {
    if (DateTime.Now > TheAuctionEnds)
    {
      throw new Exception("Auction has ended");
    }
    if (Amount > TheCurrentPrice)                    // See if we need to
    {                                                //   acquire a writer lock
      ItemLock.UpgradeToWriterLock(60000);           // Upgrade to
      if (!ItemLock.IsWriterLockHeld)                //   a writer lock
      {
        throw new Exception("Writer Lock not held after upgrade");
      }
      if (Amount > TheCurrentPrice)                  // Check to see if
      {                                              //   we're still the
        TheCurrentPrice = Amount;                    //   highest bidder
        TheBiddersName=BiddersName;
```

```
        }
        else
        {
          throw new Exception("Bid not higher than current price");
        }
      }
      else
      {
        throw new Exception("Bid not higher than current price");
      }
    }
    finally                                     ReleaseReaderLock
    {                                           releases both
      ItemLock.ReleaseReaderLock();  ◁───┘     Reader and Writer
      if (ItemLock.IsWriterLockHeld)
      {
        throw new Exception("Writer Lock still held after release");
      }
      if (ItemLock.IsReaderLockHeld)
      {
        throw new Exception("Reader Lock still held after release");
      }
    }
}
```

In listing 9.4, it's unclear if a writer lock is needed until the bid amount is compared to the current price. In the last section, we dealt with this by acquiring a write lock. A more optimal solution is to acquire a read lock and determine if a write lock is required. If it is, we call `UpgradeToWriterLock`.

The advantage is that we only require a write lock when it is needed. Since write locks keep all reader locks from accessing data, using them unnecessarily results in reduced performance. Be careful when upgrading from a read to a write lock. There is a relatively small chance that during the transition from read to write some other pending write request may change the value. Figure 9.4 presents a graphical version of the logic involved.

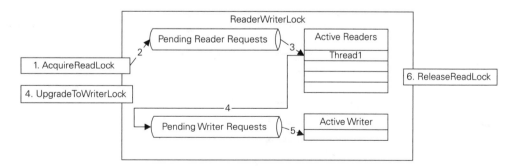

Figure 9.4   Acquiring a read lock

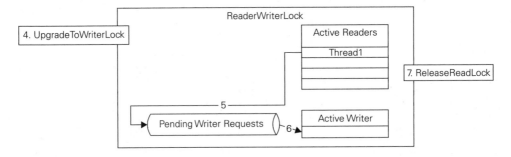

Figure 9.5   The steps involved in an UpgradeToWriterLock

The process begins by the calling thread requesting a read lock (step 1). This causes an entry to be added to the pending reader requests queue (step 2). Once that lock is granted (step 3), the calling thread can then request the upgrade to the writer lock. Figure 9.5 shows the steps involved in the upgrade.

When the calling thread calls `UpgradeToWriterLock` (step 4), the thread is removed from the list of active readers and placed in the pending writer requests queue (step 5). If a request from a different thread is already in the pending writer requests queue, it will be allowed to gain a write lock before the thread that requested the upgrade. The reason is the write lock requests are serviced in the order they are received, without any sort of priority associated with them. Once the requesting thread has been granted the write lock, it is moved to the active writer location (step 6). Listing 9.5 contains a class that can be used to see how a value can change during `UpgradeToWriterLock`.

Listing 9.5   A value can change during an UpgradeToWriterLock

```
Imports System.Threading
Public Class SimpleExample
  Dim rwLock As ReaderWriterLock
  Dim protectedValue As String
  Dim pauseThreadTwo As ManualResetEvent
  Dim ThreadOne As Thread
  Dim ThreadTwo As Thread

  Public Sub New()
    protectedValue = "Initial Value"
    rwLock = New ReaderWriterLock()
    pauseThreadTwo = New ManualResetEvent(False)
  End Sub

  Public Sub Test()
    ThreadOne = New Thread(AddressOf MethodOne)
    ThreadOne.Start()

    ThreadTwo = New Thread(AddressOf MethodTwo)
    ThreadTwo.Start()
  End Sub
```

```
Private Sub MethodOne()
  rwLock.AcquireReaderLock(1000)
  Dim seqNum As Integer = rwLock.WriterSeqNum
  Dim readValue As String = protectedValue
  pauseThreadTwo.Set()
  Thread.Sleep(1000)
  rwLock.UpgradeToWriterLock(10000)
  If (protectedValue <> readValue) Then
    Dim feedback As String
    feedback = "Value Changed:"""
    feedback += readValue
    feedback += """ != """
    feedback += protectedValue + """"
    Console.WriteLine(feedback)
  End If
  rwLock.ReleaseReaderLock()
End Sub

Private Sub MethodTwo()
  pauseThreadTwo.WaitOne()
  rwLock.AcquireWriterLock(10000)
  protectedValue = "Set in Method Two"
  rwLock.ReleaseWriterLock()
End Sub

Public Sub WaitForFinished()
  ThreadOne.Join()
  ThreadTwo.Join()
End Sub

End Class
```

The output produced by listing 9.5 is:

```
Value Changed:"Initial Value" != "Set in Method Two"
```

Why not just acquire the write lock while holding the read lock? Consider the example in listing 9.6.

Listing 9.6   ReaderWriterLock Deadlock example (C#)

```
ReaderWriterLock RWLock=new ReaderWriterLock();
RWLock.AcquireReaderLock(Timeout.Infinite);
// Read some value
RWLock.AcquireWriterLock(Timeout.Infinite);
// The above instruction will not return
// Write some value
RWLock.ReleaseWriterLock();
RWLock.ReleaseReaderLock();
```

The problem is `AcquireWriteLock` will not return until it has successfully acquired a write lock and a write lock will not be granted until all read locks are released. Since the current thread has a read lock, it will never be able to acquire a write lock. This is a form of deadlock. It is unusual in that only one thread is required to form this deadlock.

Acquiring a Writer Lock   To acquire a writer lock, all threads with a reader lock, including the thread requesting the write lock, must release them. `UpgradeToWriterLock` is an alternative to releasing the reader lock.

Since `AcquireWriterLock` does not consider which thread owns any outstanding reader locks, the same thread that is attempting to gain a write lock owns a read lock and will not be able to acquire the write lock.

Upgrade-ToWriter-Lock   `UpgradeToWriterLock` is a method on the `ReaderWriterLock` class that allows a thread that has a read lock to convert it to a write lock, without first releasing the read lock.

An alternative might be to release the read lock before attempting to acquire the write lock. Listing 9.7 shows how this might be done.

Listing 9.7   Releasing the read lock and then acquiring a write lock (C#)

```
ReaderWriterLock RWLock=new ReaderWriterLock();
RWLock.AcquireReaderLock(Timeout.Infinite);
// Read some value
RWLock.ReleaseReaderLock();
// A different thread may change what was
// previously read during the read lock, this
// will likely result in a race condition.
RWLock.AcquireWriterLock(Timeout.Infinite);
// Change some value
RWLock.ReleaseWriterLock();
```

When `ReleaseReaderLock` is called, the read lock is released. There is no way to regain that lock; instead, a new lock will need to be acquired. The next section discusses a way of going from a read lock, to a write lock, and then back to a read lock.

9.2.3   DowngradeFromWriterLock

We know how to convert from a read to a write lock. Suppose we want to do the opposite? `UpgradeToWriterLock` returns `LockCookie`, which can be used with the `DowngradeFromWriterLock` method to change from a writer lock to a reader lock. There is no possibility of change between the time `DowngradeFromWriterLock` is called and the read lock is granted because when moving from a writer to a reader there is no chance that some other thread is already a reader, or can become one.

This is not true when moving from a reader to a writer. In order to handle possible race conditions, `UpgradeToWriterLock` uses the writer request queue. If a thread requests a write lock, it is given the same priority as a thread that is converting from a reader lock. If the reader request queue was a priority queue, the threads that had obtained a read lock could potentially starve the threads that attempted a write lock request directly.

Listing 9.8 demonstrates downgrading from a writer to a reader lock. Note that this can only be performed if the thread originally obtained a read lock and used the Upgrade-ToWriterLock method. The cookie returned by UpgradeToWriterLock can only be used with DowngradeFromWriterLock.

Listing 9.8   Using the DowngradeFromWriterLock method

```
using System;
using System.Threading;
namespace Manning.Dennis
{
  public class DataUD:ThreadedTesterBase
  {
    ManualResetEvent[] interactEvents;
    public DataUD(ref Data pd,string n,string v)
      :base(ref pd,n,v)
    {
      interactEvents =new ManualResetEvent[4];
      for (int i=0;i< interactEvents .Length;i++)
      {
        interactEvents[i]=new ManualResetEvent(false);
      }
    }

    public void Interact(ActionsEnum index)
    {
      interactEvents[(int)index].Set();
      // Give the associated thread time to do its thing
      Thread.Sleep(1000);
    }
    public enum ActionsEnum
    {
      UpgradeToWrite=0,
      DowngradeToRead=1,
      ReleaseRead=2
    }
    protected override void ThreadMethod()
    {
      LockCookie cookie;
      Message("Enter");
      acquireEvent.WaitOne();
      Message("Starting Wait for Read Lock");
      protectedData.rwLock.AcquireReaderLock(Timeout.Infinite);

      Message("+++ UD- Acquired Read Lock");
      string s = protectedData.Value;
```

```
        interactEvents[(int)ActionsEnum.UpgradeToWrite].WaitOne();
        Message("^^^ UD- Upgrading Read Lock");
        cookie=protectedData.rwLock.UpgradeToWriterLock(Timeout.Infinite); ◁─┐
        protectedData.Value= valueToWrite;
                                                             Convert the read
                                                            lock to a write lock
        interactEvents[(int)ActionsEnum.DowngradeToRead].WaitOne();
        Message("vvv UD- Downgrading Read Lock");
        protectedData.rwLock.DowngradeFromWriterLock(ref cookie);      ◁─┐
        string s2 = protectedData.Value;
                                                             Change back
                                                            to a read lock
        interactEvents[(int)ActionsEnum.ReleaseRead].WaitOne();
        Message("??? UD- Releasing Read Lock");
        protectedData.rwLock.ReleaseReaderLock();
        Message("---Released Read Lock");
      }
    }
  }
}
```

One of the biggest advantages of the `DowngradeFromWriterLock` method is
that it will not block. This means that it will immediately return granting the thread
a read lock because there cannot possibly be a read lock at the point a write lock has
been granted. Additionally, at the point the write lock is released, all pending read
locks will also be released.

Listing 9.8 uses a base class that reduces the complexity of the `DataUD` class. Other
classes use this base class. Listing 9.9 contains the base class code.

Listing 9.9   The base class that listing 9.8 relies on

```
using System;
using System.Threading;
namespace Manning.Dennis
{
  public abstract class ThreadedTesterBase
  {
    protected string valueToWrite;

    protected bool acquireCalled;
    protected bool interactCalled;
    protected ManualResetEvent acquireEvent;
    protected ManualResetEvent interactEvent;
    protected Data  protectedData;
    protected Thread workerThread;
    protected string name;
    protected void Message(string msg)
    {
      protectedData.Message(msg);
    }
    public void Acquire()
    {
      acquireCalled = true;
      acquireEvent.Set();
```

```
      // Give the associated thread time to do its thing
      Thread.Sleep(1000);
    }
    public void Interact()
    {
      if (!acquireCalled)
      {
        throw new Exception("Call Acquire first");
      }
      interactCalled = true;
      interactEvent.Set();
      // Give the associated thread time to do its thing
      Thread.Sleep(1000);
    }
    protected ThreadedTesterBase(ref Data pd,string name,string valueToWrite)
    {
      this.valueToWrite = valueToWrite;
      acquireCalled = false;
      interactCalled = false;
      acquireEvent = new ManualResetEvent(false);
      interactEvent = new ManualResetEvent(false);
      this.protectedData = pd;
      workerThread = new Thread(new ThreadStart(ThreadMethod));
      workerThread.Name = name;
      this.name = name;

      workerThread.Start();
    }
    protected abstract void ThreadMethod();

    public void WaitForFinish()
    {
      workerThread.Join();
      // Give the associated thread time to do its thing
      Thread.Sleep(0);
    }
  }
}
```

This base class simplifies the creation of threads used during the testing process. Listing 9.10 contains code that drives the example.

Listing 9.10 Code that demonstrates that a DowngradeFromWriterLock does not block

```
public void UpgradeDowngradeExample()
{
  Data pdata = new Data();
  DataWriter w1;
  DataWriter w2;
  DataUD ud1;
```

```
            ud1= new DataUD    (ref pdata,"Upgrader1:  {0}","Upgrader1");
            w1= new DataWriter(ref pdata,"Writer_1 : {0}","writer_1");
            w2= new DataWriter(ref pdata,"Writer_2 : {0}","writer_2");
            Thread.Sleep(1000);
            w1.Acquire(); // acquire write lock
            ud1.Acquire();
            ud1.Interact(DataUD.ActionsEnum.UpgradeToWrite);
            w1.Interact();   // set value and release lock
            w2.Acquire();   // acquire write lock
            w2.Interact();   // set value and release lock
            ud1.Interact(DataUD.ActionsEnum.DowngradeToRead);
            ud1.Interact(DataUD.ActionsEnum.ReleaseRead);
            w1.WaitForFinish();
            Console.WriteLine("Enter to exit");
            Console.ReadLine();
    }
```

The `DataWriter` class is contained in listing 9.11.

Listing 9.11   DataWriter class

```
using System;
using System.Threading;
namespace Manning.Dennis
{
  public class DataWriter :ThreadedTesterBase
  {
    public DataWriter(ref Data protectedData,string name,string valueToWrite)
      :base(ref protectedData,name,valueToWrite)
    {
    }
    protected override void ThreadMethod()
    {
      Message("Enter");
      acquireEvent.WaitOne();
      Message("Starting Wait for Write Lock");
      protectedData.rwLock.AcquireWriterLock(Timeout.Infinite);
      Message("+++Acquired Writer Lock");
      interactEvent.WaitOne();
      Message("Setting value");
      protectedData.Value=valueToWrite;
      Message("???Releasing Writer Lock");
      protectedData.rwLock.ReleaseWriterLock();
      Message("---Released Writer Lock");
    }
  }
}
```

A caution regarding upgrading and downgrading reader locks: A lock should be short-lived. This will increase concurrency and decrease contention for locks. If a thread goes from being a reader to a writer and back to a reader, and stays in that state for an extended period of time, other threads will not be able to acquire a write lock. In general, locks should not be held the vast majority of the time, and only acquired when needed. The general rule of acquiring late and releasing early applies.

9.2.4   WriterSeqNum and AnyWritersSince

Suppose you wanted to know if any changes had occurred since you acquired and released a reader lock. One way to determine this is to use the `WriterSeqNum` property of the `ReaderWriterLock` object. This property returns a value that can be used with the `AnyWritersSince` method to determine if any writer locks have been released since `WriterSeqNum` was acquired.

Listing 9.12   WriterSeqNum can be used to see if data has changed (VB.NET).

```
Public Sub Bid(ByVal Amount As Decimal, ByVal BiddersName As String)
  Dim WriterSeqNum As Integer
. . .
   ItemLock.AcquireReaderLock(Timeout.Infinite)
. . .
    If (Amount > TheCurrentPrice) Then              Retrieve the writer
      WriterSeqNum = ItemLock.WriterSeqNum    ⊲─┘  sequence number
      ItemLock.ReleaseReaderLock()                  and save it
      Thread.Sleep(1000) ' Make the changes more obvious
      ItemLock.AcquireWriterLock(Timeout.Infinite)
      If (ItemLock.AnyWritersSince(WriterSeqNum)) Then  ⊲─┐ Look for
        If (Amount > TheCurrentPrice) Then                │ new writers
          TheCurrentPrice = Amount
          TheBiddersName = BiddersName
        Else
          Throw New Exception("Bid not higher than current price ")
        End If
      Else
        TheCurrentPrice = Amount
        TheBiddersName = BiddersName
      End If
    Else
      Throw New Exception("Bid not higher than current price")
    End If
```

In listing 9.12 we first acquire a reader lock. To simplify the code we wait indefinitely for the lock. Once the reader lock is acquired we retrieve the writer sequence number—the number of nonnested times a write lock has been acquired and released. It starts at 1 and increases by 1 each time `ReleaseWriterLock` is invoked by a thread that results in that thread no longer owning the write lock.

Writer-SeqNum	WriterSeqNum is a property of the ReaderWriterLock class that returns an integer that indicates the current number of write locks acquired.			

Table 9.1 demonstrates how various statements impact the values of WriterSeqNum along with the return value of the AnyWritersSince method.

Table 9.1   How Statements Impact WriteSeqNum Values

Statements	Any Writers Since	Writer Sequence Number	Is Read Lock Held	Is Write Lock Held
Dim WSN As Integer	N/A	N/A	N/A	N/A
Dim RW As ReaderWriterLock = New ReaderWriterLock()	N/A	1	F	F
RW.AcquireReaderLock(Timeout.Infinite)	N/A	1	T	F
WSN = RW.WriterSeqNum	F	1	T	F
RW.ReleaseReaderLock()	F	1	F	F
RW.AcquireWriterLock(Timeout.Infinite)	F	2	F	T
RW.AcquireWriterLock(Timeout.Infinite)	F	2	F	T
RW.ReleaseWriterLock()	F	2	F	T
RW.ReleaseWriterLock()	T	2	F	F
RW.AcquireReaderLock(Timeout.Infinite)	T	2	T	F
WSN = RW.WriterSeqNum	F	2	T	F
RW.ReleaseReaderLock()	F	2	F	F
RW.AcquireWriterLock(Timeout.Infinite)	F	3	F	T
RW.AcquireWriterLock(Timeout.Infinite)	F	3	F	T
RW.ReleaseWriterLock()	F	3	F	T
RW.ReleaseWriterLock()	T	3	F	F

Notice that initially the WriterSeqNum is one. At the point AcquireWriterLock executes, the value changes to 2. The method AnyWritersSince returns false until the second ReleaseWriterLock executes. This is due to the nesting of the write locks. Notice that there are two calls to AcquireWriterLock and two calls to ReleaseWriterLock. The second ReleaseWriterLock actually releases the lock and indicates that there has been a writer since the sequence number was acquired.

USAGE	AnyWritersSince and WriterSeqNum allow for an easy way to determine if a value might have changed. It allows for a thread to cache values and increase performance. AnyWritersSince changes when IsWriterLockHeld changes from true to false. WriterSeqNum increases when IsWriterLockHeld changes from false to true.

The value of `WriterSeqNum` changes when a thread acquires a write lock for the first time while the return value for `AnyWritersSince` changes when a thread releases the write lock for the last time. Notice the correlation between the change in the return value of `AnyWritersSince` and `IsWriterLockHeld`.

9.3 RELEASELOCK AND RESTORELOCK

When reading a book it's nice to be able to stop, save your place, and resume. Often a bookmark is used to keep track of the current location. Similarly, the `ReaderWriter-Lock` class allows a thread to release its locks and later restore them. `ReleaseLock` is a method on the `ReaderWriterLock` class that allows a thread to release all locks, regardless of the nesting depth, and save the state to a lock cookie. Once the state is stored in the lock cookie, the `RestoreLock` method can be used to put the lock back to the same state it was in before `ReleaseLock` was called. Listing 9.13 demonstrates the use of `ReleaseLock` and `RestoreLock`.

Listing 9.13   The use of ReleaseLock and RestoreLock (C#)

```
static void TestSimpleReleaseLock()
{

  RW.AcquireWriterLock(Timeout.Infinite);
  LockCookie Lock = RW.ReleaseLock();     ← Saves the current
  . . .                                     lock state
  RW.RestoreLock(ref Lock );              ← Restores the state
  RW.ReleaseWriterLock();                   of the locks
}
. . .
```

It is possible that some other thread has acquired a lock during the period between `ReleaseLock` and the call to `RestoreLock`. To handle this situation the `Restore-Lock` method blocks until it can acquire the required locks. Unlike the other `Reader-WriterLock` methods that acquire locks, there is no means to specify a timeout value.

ReleaseLock   `ReleaseLock` is a method on the `ReaderWriterLock` that releases all currently held locks and stores the state information to a `LockCookie` structure for later restoration using the `RestoreLock` method.

The value that `ReleaseLock` has over releasing the locks using `ReleaseReader-Lock` or `ReleaseWriterLock` is that it can release all locks, regardless of the nesting level, in a single call. If, for instance, a thread determined that it should die, it could call `ReleaseLock`. The alternative would be to know what sort of lock is currently held and the number of times acquire has been called.

RestoreLock   `RestoreLock` is a method of the `ReaderWriterLock` class that accepts a reference to a `LockCookie` as its only parameter. `RestoreLock` blocks until it can acquire the required locks.

The following instruction releases all locks that the current thread has on the RW instance of `ReaderWriterLock`:

```
RW.ReleaseLock();
```

Instead of using the `ReleaseLock` method, the following instructions perform roughly the same function:

```
while(RW.IsReaderLockHeld)
{
  RW.ReleaseReaderLock();
}
while (RW.IsWriterLockHeld)
{
  RW.ReleaseWriterLock();
}
```

Since `ReleaseLock` returns a `LockCookie` structure we can save the current lock state for future use. During the period between `ReleaseLock` and `RestoreLock`, other threads have access to the values. This means that the values that are being protected by the `ReaderWriterLock` may have changed before `RestoreLock` is called. To handle this situation we can use the `AnyWritersSince` method we discussed in the previous section.

RestoreLock   `RestoreLock` is a method of the `ReaderWriterLock` class that accepts a reference to `LockCookie` as its only parameter. `RestoreLock` blocks until it can acquire the required locks.

Listing 9.14 checks to see if some other thread has acquired a write lock since the `ReleaseLock` statement was executed.

Listing 9.14   The safe way to use ReleaseLock and RestoreLock (C#)

```
RW.AcquireWriterLock(Timeout.Infinite);  ←— Acquire a write lock
int SeqNum = RW.WriterSeqNum;                           ←┐ Save the current
LockCookie Lock = RW.ReleaseLock();                      │ WriterSeqNum

. . .

RW.RestoreLock(ref Lock );       ←— Restore the write lock
if (RW.AnyWritersSince(SeqNum ))                        ←┐ Look for
{                                                        │ new writers
  Trace.WriteLine("A thread has written to the data");
}
else
{
  // Data has not changed since ReleaseLock
}
RW.ReleaseWriterLock();
```

This is the safest way to use the release and restore lock methods. Failure to use the `AnyWritersSince` method may result in data values changing without the knowledge of the thread that uses `RestoreLock`. If the functionality of release and restore lock is required, use care to ensure that the `ReaderWriterLock` is not bypassed.

9.4 SUMMARY

We've seen how a `ReaderWriterLock` can be used to allow multiple threads read access to a data element while preserving the integrity of the data. `ReaderWriter-Locks` are a powerful construct that fit certain synchronization needs. When the situation is right, using a `ReaderWriterLock` can result in a marked performance increase.

In the next chapter we examine the `ThreadPool` class. `ThreadPools` are collections of threads that are reused to perform some short-lived task. `ThreadPools`, like `ReaderWriterLocks`, can solve certain problems very well.

C H A P T E R   1 0

The ThreadPool class

A thread pool is a collection of threads tasked with units of work that exist for the life of the thread pool. It allows easy distribution of work among multiple threads and is an ideal construct for dealing with multiple short-lived tasks that can be performed in parallel. In this chapter we explore the powerful features of the .NET thread pool.

For the examples in this chapter we revisit the matrix multiplication problem we discussed in chapter 8. The WorkManager class from chapter 8 was a simplified thread pool system. In the first section we will replace the thread control logic with a thread pool.

10.1 THREADPOOL CLASS AND QUEUEUSERWORKITEM

In chapter 8 we constructed a simplistic thread pool implementation; not surprisingly the result was somewhat complex. A thread pool allows for a simple means of performing multiple tasks on different threads. The thread pool manages its threads: It controls their number, lifetime, priority, and activities. The example in listing 10.1 demonstrates adding items for the ThreadPool to process using the QueueUserWorkItem method.

Listing 10.1   ThreadPool example (C#)

```
private void ThreadMethod(object O )        ThreadMethod
{                                           is invoked by
  Unit Work;                                the thread pool
  Work = (Unit)O;
  Work.DoWork();
  ResultObjects.Add(Work);
  Interlocked.Decrement(ref ExpectedCompleteElements);
  if (ExpectedCompleteElements ==0)
  {
    FinishedWithWork.Set();
  }
}

public void DoWork(Unit[] Work, WorkFinished Finished )
{
  ResultObjects.Clear();
  Notify = Finished;
  ExpectedCompleteElements=Work.Length ;
  WaitCallback callback = new WaitCallback(ThreadMethod);
  for (long i = 0;i <Work.Length ;i++)
  {
    ThreadPool.QueueUserWorkItem(callback, Work[i]);    QueueUserWorkItem
  }                                                     adds work elements
}                                                       to the thread pool
```

There are several restrictions on thread pools. There can be only one thread pool per process. This means that if multiple tasks are being performed using thread pools in the same process, they will share the same thread pool. If one of the tasks takes a disproportionate share of the processing time, the other tasks will suffer. The reason that there is only one thread pool per process is that the method `QueueUserWorkItem` on the `ThreadPool` class is a static/shared method. The likely reason that the designers made this choice is to maximize performance.

ThreadPool   A `ThreadPool` is a class in the `Threading` namespace that allows concurrent work to be performed in a simple way.

One of the most expensive operations when dealing with threads is the creation of threads. Recall that the main purpose of a thread pool is to manage a set of threads so that new ones do not need to be created to perform a task. Instead, one of the existing idle threads is assigned a task to complete. Once that task is completed, the thread becomes available for other work; under normal circumstances it does not terminate.

Since the `WorkManager` class now uses the .NET thread pool, the design becomes much simpler (figure 10.1).

The tradeoffs between using a thread pool and managing threads in a custom way are shown in table 10.1. Thread pools are ideal for short-lived, independent tasks that are not in conflict.

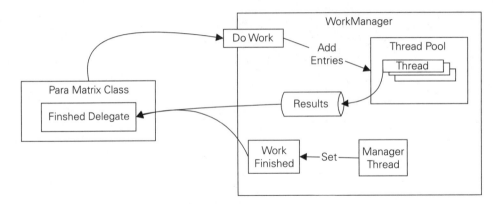

Figure 10.1   WorkManager using the ThreadPool class

Since the tasks are executing on multiple threads, any shared data must be protected using some form of synchronization mechanism, such as ReaderWriterLock, Monitor, or a synchronization lock. Care should be taken to ensure that deadlock does not occur since the control provided to a thread in a thread pool is limited.

Table 10.1   Comparison of ThreadPool and Generic Thread Management

	ThreadPool	Generic Thread
Ideal for short running tasks	Y	N
Control thread name	N	Y
Control thread priority	N	Y
Control life of thread	N	Y
Highly flexible	N	Y
Thread synchronization recommended (Sleep, Wait, Suspend)	N	Y

10.2   *THE REGISTERWAITFORSINGLEOBJECT METHOD*

A common use of threads is to wait for some event to occur. The ThreadPool class provides built-in support for waiting for a WaitHandle-derived object to become signaled. At the point the WaitHandle object becomes signaled, the WaitOrTimer-Callback delegate is invoked. WaitOrTimerCallback accepts two parameters. The first is an object that contains state information used by the callback to perform any needed processing. The second parameter indicates why the method is being invoked. If the second parameter is true, the method is being invoked because the WaitHandle-derived object became signaled. If the parameter's value is false, the WaitHandle-derived object did not become signaled during the specified timeout. Listing 10.1 demonstrates using the ThreadPool class's RegisterWaitFor-SingleObject.

Listing 10.2 RegisterWaitForSingleObject Example (VB.NET)

```
Public Class ClassWorkManager
  Private ExpectedCompleteElements As Integer
  Public Delegate Sub WorkFinished(ByVal Results As ArrayList)
  Public Delegate Function WorkToDo(ByVal Param As Object) As Object
  Private Notify As WorkFinished
  Private FinishedWithWork As AutoResetEvent
  Private ResultObjects As ArrayList
. . .
  Public Sub DoWork(ByVal Work() As Unit, ByVal Finished As WorkFinished)
    ResultObjects.Clear()
    Dim i As Long
    Notify = Finished
    ExpectedCompleteElements = Work.Length
    For i = 0 To Work.Length - 1
      ThreadPool.QueueUserWorkItem( _
        New WaitCallback(AddressOf ThreadMethod), _
        Work(i))
    Next
    Dim SignaledCallback As WaitOrTimerCallback
    SignaledCallback = New WaitOrTimerCallback(AddressOf ManagerMethod)

    ThreadPool.RegisterWaitForSingleObject(FinishedWithWork, _
      SignaledCallback, ResultObjects, Timeout.Infinite, True)
  End Sub
```
Register the WaitHandle-derived object
```
  Public Sub ThreadMethod(ByVal O As Object)
    Dim Work As Unit
    Work = O
    Work.DoWork()
    ResultObjects.Add(Work)
    Interlocked.Decrement(ExpectedCompleteElements)
    If ExpectedCompleteElements = 0 Then

      ' Cause the WaitHandle derived class to become signaled.
      FinishedWithWork.Set()
    End If
  End Sub

  Private Sub ManagerMethod(ByVal O As Object, ByVal signaled As Boolean)
    ' This method is invoked when the WaitHandle derived class
    ' becomes signaled.
    Notify(ResultObjects)
  End Sub
. . .
End Class
```

The state object is passed to the RegisterWaitForSingleObject method. When
the WaitHandle-derived class becomes signaled, that state information is passed to the
WaitOrTimerCallback delegate. The next-to-last parameter of RegisterWait-
ForSingleObject is a timeout value. This is the time the thread in the pool waits

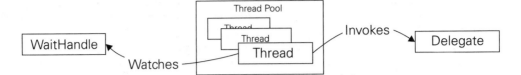

Figure 10.2 `RegisterWaitForSingleObject` logical overview

for the `WaitHandle`-derived object to become signaled. If the timeout occurs, the last parameter to `WaitOrTimerCallback` will be false. If the object becomes signaled before the timeout, it will be true.

Register-WaitFor-SingleObject
`RegisterWaitForSingleObject` is a shared/static method of the `ThreadPool` class. It allows a delegate to be associated with a `WaitHandle`-derived object, such as an `AutoResetEvent`. When the `WaitHandle`-derived object becomes signaled, or a timeout occurs, the passed-in delegate is invoked.

The last parameter of `RegisterWaitForSingleObject` controls if the wait occurs only once or if it repeats (figure 10.2). If this value is true, the delegate will wait only once for the `WaitHandle`-derived object to become signaled. If the parameter is false, the delegate will be invoked repeatedly. The frequency of invocation depends on whether or not a timeout is specified, along with how often the `WaitHandle`-derived object becomes signaled.

One way to understand the `RegisterWaitForSingleObject` method is to attempt to implement a simplified version of it. The `RegisterWaitForSingle-Object` method in listing 10.3 responds much the same way as the "real" `Register-WaitForSingleObject` method.

Listing 10.3   A simplified RegisterWaitForSingleObject method (VB.NET)

```
Public Class MyWaitForEvent
  Private Shared MyThread As Thread
. . .
Public Shared Sub RegisterWaitForSingleObject( _
  ByVal EventOfInterest As WaitHandle, _
  ByVal WhatToInvoke As WaitOrTimerCallback, _
  ByVal state As Object, ByVal Timeout As Integer, _
  ByVal OnlyOnce As Boolean)
    MyStateObject = state
    MyEventOfInterest = EventOfInterest
    MyOnlyOnce = OnlyOnce
    MyWhatToInvoke = WhatToInvoke
    MyTimeout = Timeout
    MyThread = New Thread(AddressOf ThreadMethod)
    MyThread.IsBackground = True
    MyThread.Name = "MyWaitForEventThread"
    MyThread.Start()
End Sub
```

```
Private Shared Sub ThreadMethod()
  Dim timedOut As Boolean
  Do
    timedOut = Not MyEventOfInterest.WaitOne(MyTimeout, False)
    MyWhatToInvoke(MyStateObject, timedOut)
  Loop While Not MyOnlyOnce
End Sub
. . .
```

This method creates a thread that is started when the shared/static method that performs the same function as `RegisterWaitForSingleObject` is invoked. This simplified version of the method does not execute in a thread pool, but it conveys the key elements of what the `ThreadPool` method does. `RegisterWaitForSingleObject` is a powerful way of monitoring a `WaitHandle`-derived object, such as an `AutoResetEvent` and invoking a delegate when it becomes signaled.

10.3   *INFORMATIONAL METHODS AND PROPERTIES*

One of the most powerful advantages that the .NET framework offers over previous Microsoft development platforms is the amount of diagnostic information available. This section introduces three `ThreadPool`-related informational methods and properties.

10.3.1   GetMaxThreads and GetAvailableThreads

Suppose you wanted to know how many threads the `ThreadPool` class might use, and how many it was using. This can give insight into the nature of your application. The `ThreadPool` class does intelligent assignment of tasks to threads. If a large number of threads are being used, the tasks are likely I/O bound. The `GetMaxThreads` method of the `ThreadPool` class is used to determine the largest number of threads `ThreadPool` will use. The `GetMaxThreads` method returns two `out` parameters. The first is the maximum number of worker threads the thread pool will use; the second is the maximum number of threads associated with servicing completion ports. Listing 10.4 shows `GetMaxThreads` and `GetAvailableThreads` in use.

Listing 10.4   GetMaxThreads and GetAvailableThreads example (C#)

```csharp
private void timer1_Tick(object sender, System.EventArgs e)
{
  int NumberOfWorkerThreads;
  int NumberOfCompletionPortThreads;
  int MaxNumberOfWorkerThreads;
  int MaxNumberOfCompletionPortThreads;

  // Return the maximum number of threads that can be
  // active in the thread pool.
  ThreadPool.GetMaxThreads(
    out MaxNumberOfWorkerThreads,
    out MaxNumberOfCompletionPortThreads);
```

```
ThreadPool.GetAvailableThreads(
    out NumberOfWorkerThreads,
    out NumberOfCompletionPortThreads);
label7.Text = NumberOfWorkerThreads.ToString();
label9.Text = MaxNumberOfWorkerThreads.ToString();
label10.Text = MaxNumberOfCompletionPortThreads.ToString();
label12.Text = NumberOfCompletionPortThreads.ToString();
}
```

The number of available threads

The numbers returned by `GetMaxThreads` indicate the number of threads that can be allocated for `ThreadPool`. To determine how many threads are available for work in `ThreadPool`, we use the `GetAvailableThreads` method. It also returns two values: the number of worker threads available and the number of threads available for servicing completion ports.

GetMax- `GetMaxThreads` is a static/shared method of the `ThreadPool` class that
Threads returns the maximum number of worker and completion port threads that will be used.

If the number of available threads is zero, the `ThreadPool` class must wait until a thread becomes available. During this time any work items added will simply increase the size of the work queue in the `ThreadPool` object. The number of elements that can be queued is limited only by the amount of available memory.

GetAvailable- `GetAvailableThreads` returns the number of worker and completion
Threads port threads available to service requests.

The number of threads available does not necessarily correlate to the number of threads in the process. Until a thread is needed, it is not created. Once a thread is created it will exist as long as the `ThreadPool` object feels it is needed. The number of threads in use is a helpful measure. It is determined by subtracting the number of available threads from the maximum number of threads, giving an indication of load. If a task is processor bound, the number of threads in use will likely stay close to the number of processors in the computer. If a task is I/O bound, the number of threads in use will increase, likely to the maximum number of threads allowed. The `sleep` statement for a thread can be used to simulate an I/O bound task:

```
object WorkUnit(object param )
{
  MultParam  tmpParm = (MultParam)param;
  Thread.Sleep(10000);
  return ClassParaMatrix.MultRowColumn(
    tmpParm.M1,
    tmpParm.M2,
    tmpParm.Column,
    tmpParm.Row);
}
```

When the change in the example is made to the WorkUnit method in the Class-ParaMatrix class, the thread pool will exhaust the number of available threads. This increases the processing time; however, the tasks do successfully complete.

- The number of available threads will always be the same or less than the maximum number of threads.

- A process that exhausts the available threads is either I/O bound or contains long-running tasks that possibly should not be performed in a thread pool.

- ThreadPool will only create a managed thread when it determines that one is needed.

- ThreadPool manages the life of its threads.

- The maximum number of threads is determined by multiplying the number of processors by 25.

As of this writing, the algorithm used to determine the maximum number of allowed threads allows 25 threads per processor. So if you have a quadprocessor machine, the values returned by GetMaxThreads will be 100. If a series of tasks consistently exhausts the number of threads available, it may be an indication that the tasks may not be suited for use in a thread pool.

10.3.2   The IsThreadPoolThread property

In chapter 5 we saw that the Thread class supports a Name property. The Name property cannot be set on threads that are being used by ThreadPool. To determine if a given thread is part of ThreadPool, we can use the IsThreadPoolThread property of the Thread class. Listing 10.5 shows how we can determine if a thread pool is managing a thread.

Listing 10.5   Inspects the IsThreadPoolThread property of the Thread class (C#)

```
private void buttonInspectMainThread_Click(object sender, System.EventArgs e)
{
  MessageBox.Show(Thread.CurrentThread.IsThreadPoolThread.ToString());
}
private void ThreadPoolThreadMethod(object o)
{
  MessageBox.Show(Thread.CurrentThread.IsThreadPoolThread.ToString());
}

private void buttonTThreadPoolThread_Click(object sender, System.EventArgs e)
{
  WaitCallback myCallback;
  myCallback=new WaitCallback(ThreadPoolThreadMethod);
  ThreadPool.QueueUserWorkItem(myCallback);
}
```

The `IsThreadPoolThread` property is a read-only property. This means that it can only be inspected, never assigned. This makes sense. If it could be changed, it would be possible to take a thread that was part of a pool and change the value of `IsThreadPoolThread` to indicate it was not.

10.4 TWO UNSAFE METHODS

There are times that performance is the only concern. In cases when the highest performance is the goal and the `ThreadPool` class is involved, the unsafe methods should be used. `UnsafeQueueUserWorkItem` performs the same function as `QueueUserWorkItem` except that it does not ensure the same level of security (listing 10.6). The same is true of `UnsafeRegisterWaitForSingleObject`. The unsafe methods are faster because they are doing slightly less than their safe counterparts. First we will review security in .NET, in particular the evidence approach of determining the level of trust for code.

Listing 10.6 The use of the UnsafeQueueUserWorkItem method (VB.NET)

```
Dim i As Long
Dim HowManyTimes As Integer
Try
   HowManyTimes = Convert.ToInt32(TextBoxHowMany.Text)
   NumberRemaining = HowManyTimes
Catch ex As Exception
   MessageBox.Show(ex.Message)
   Exit Sub
End Try
Dim callback As WaitCallback
callback = New WaitCallback(AddressOf NoOp)
StartTime = Now
For i = 1 To HowManyTimes
   ThreadPool.UnsafeQueueUserWorkItem(callback, Nothing)   <──┐ Adds a work item
Next                                                              without examining
                                                                 the stack
```

Security is a huge topic and what we cover here is just scratching the surface. An entire book could, and likely will, be written on security. Our focus is on how it pertains to threading: to protect users from malicious code. While I hope that no one reading this writes malicious code, there are plenty of people who do. To combat this, numerous approaches have been invented. Most revolve around who is executing the code. .NET introduces the concept of evidence and assigning a level of trust to code itself rather than its user. Regardless of my security level, if the code I attempt to execute is from an untrusted source it should not be executed unconditionally.

Unsafe-QueueUser-WorkItem `UnsafeQueueUserWorkItem` is a method on the `ThreadPool` class that enters a work item for the thread pool to service. It is faster than `QueueUserWorkItem` because it does not transfer the caller's stack information to the thread in the thread pool that services the request. This reduces security but improves performance.

The way that .NET determines what should be allowed to execute involves gathering evidence, such as the URL where the code originated, whether the code is signed, and, if so, by whom. The call stack is also inspected.

Evidence Evidence refers to the collection of data elements that are applied to a security policy to make a determination if code should be executed.

The call stack is inspected because it is possible that an assembly is trusted but the code calling it is not. An example of this would be if a financial institution released code to access your financial records that are stored in a secure proprietary format. While it is acceptable, and expected, that the financial institution would call that assembly, it is not desirable for malicious code to use that assembly to access and disseminate your financial information (figure 10.3).

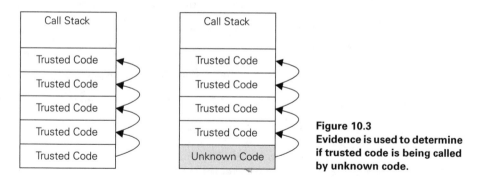

Figure 10.3
Evidence is used to determine if trusted code is being called by unknown code.

Figure 10.3 refers to trusted code. For our discussion here, code that is trusted is code with sufficient positive evidence to allow it to be executed by the .NET runtime after comparison to the security policy. Since an unknown piece of code is executing code in the right-hand box, that code should not be allowed to execute with the same level of trust as if it were executed by trusted code.

TYPES OF EVIDENCE

- Location of the assembly
- Source URL of the assembly
- Internet zone from which the assembly was retrieved
- Signed code
- Strong name

The performance gains resulting from using the unsafe methods are marginal. Care should be taken to be sure that the time to add the entries to the thread pool is the bottleneck before using the unsafe methods. Most likely greater return can be gained by optimizing the code that performs the work relating to the work entry. Once the security restrictions are relaxed, it is possible that some undesirable outcome may occur. The capability is there, but it should be used with care and only when truly needed. It should be viewed as a last resort, and should not be done without careful analysis.

10.5 THE USE OF THREADPOOLS IN .NET

The ThreadPool class provides considerable functionality to the .NET platform. Server-based timers, asynchronous execution of delegates, asynchronous file I/O, and network socket connections all rely on the system thread pool to perform their operations. By providing a robust set of classes to perform relatively complex operations, the .NET framework allows for a new level of efficiency in programming.

SELECTED FEATURES OF .NET THAT USE THREADPOOL

- Location of the assembly
- Source URL of the assembly
- Internet zone from which the assembly was retrieved
- Signed code
- Strong name

Listing 10.7 demonstrates asynchronous execution of delegates.

Listing 10.7   Asynchronous delegate execution (C#)

```
delegate void TheDelegate();
private void TheMethod()
{
  System.Diagnostics.Trace.WriteLine("The Method");
  Thread.Sleep(1000);
}
private void ASyncCallbackMethod(IAsyncResult ar )
{
  System.Diagnostics.Trace.WriteLine("ASyncCallbackMethod");
}
private void buttonBeginInvoke(object sender, System.EventArgs e)
{
  TheDelegate MyDelegate = new TheDelegate(TheMethod);
    AsyncCallback MyAsyncCallback = new
      AsyncCallback(ASyncCallbackMethod) ;
  MyDelegate.BeginInvoke(MyAsyncCallback, null);
}
```

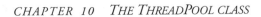

To accomplish something similar without using a thread pool would take considerable effort. The easiest solution would be to create a thread for each `BeginInvoke`. The problem with this approach is that as the number of invocations increases the quantity of resources required to process those invocations also increases.

Network operations greatly benefit from the use of thread pools. The `WebClient` object uses the thread pool to retrieve web pages. The following code retrieves a web page and places the results in a string:

```
Results = "";
WebClient client =new WebClient();
Byte[] Bytes;
Bytes = client.DownloadData((string)State);
Results = System.Text.Encoding.UTF8.GetString(Bytes);
client.Dispose();
```

The caller of the `DownloadData` method is unaware that `DownloadData` performs its processing using threads. In general, hiding complexity from the caller of a method is desirable.

Another .NET construct that uses the thread pool are server-based timers. Server-based timers should not be confused with Windows Forms timers. The difference between the two is significant. Windows Forms timers simply post a message to the message queue at the specified interval. All processing of the messages happens on the same thread. This means that if some operation that takes considerable time is invoked from the message queue processing thread, the application will hang until that message is processed. We discuss timers in detail in chapter 14.

Server-based timers are thread pool based. A delegate is invoked at the specified interval. The following example shows the usage of a server-based timer:

```
. . .
private System.Threading.Timer timer2;
. . .
System.Threading.TimerCallback callback;
callback=new System.Threading.TimerCallback(timer2_Elapsed);
timer2 = new System.Threading.Timer(callback,null,100,100) ;
. . .
```

Server-based timers allow for longer running processing to occur without the user interface being affected. Without thread pools, server-based timers wouldn't be feasible.

10.6   SUMMARY

In this chapter we've examined the `ThreadPool` class. We've seen that it is an easy way to distribute small units of work among multiple threads. We've also seen that the .NET framework itself relies on the `ThreadPool` class for much of its asynchronous processing such as server-based timers and network communication. The next chapter introduces the concept of `ThreadStatic` data and thread local storage.

C H A P T E R   1 1

ThreadStatic and thread local storage

Sharing data is a primary concern in multithreaded programming. One way to minimize development effort is to restrict access to data elements to a single thread. Thread local storage (figure 11.1) is a way to create a variable that can store values associated with each thread. This allows the code of each thread to reference what appears to be the same data element but is instead associated with the referencing thread.

Stack-based variables are inherently local to a thread. Additionally, if an instance of a class contains a single thread, the instance variables of that class are also local to the thread. In cases where static/shared variables must be used, or multiple threads are associated with a class, some means must be taken to ensure that concurrency issues are addressed. One way to do this is by using the ThreadStatic attribute. Additionally, more primitive thread local storage mechanisms are introduced.

Thread local storage is a powerful construct. In situations where a class cannot be restricted to containing a single thread, it is an alternative to using synchronization constructs on a shared data element. If a data element is associated with one, and only one, thread then using thread local storage may be an ideal solution.

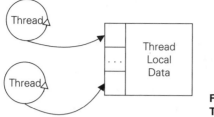

Figure 11.1
Thread local storage

11.1 USING THREADSTATIC VARIABLES

Unrestricted data sharing between threads is a risky thing to do. In previous chapters we've seen that synchronization objects, such as the Monitor class, can be used to restrict access to data by multiple threads. If a variable is not a communication mechanism, there generally is no reason for it to be shared among threads.

One way that a variable is not shared is by declaring it local to a method. When a local variable is declared in a method, it is created on the stack of the thread that executed the statement. We declare a variable in a method and rightly assume that no other thread will manipulate it. The following instructions create a thread stack based variable named x. The variable x is local to the StackBasedVariable method:

```
Private Sub StackBasedVariable()
  Dim x As Integer
End Sub
```

Alternatively, variables can be declared as instance variables of a class. In the next example, ClassVariable is an instance variable. This means that its value can differ between each instance of ClassTestStatic.

```
Public Class ClassTestStatic
  Private ClassVariable As Integer
  <ThreadStatic()> Private Shared ThreadStaticVariable As Integer
  Private Shared StaticVariable As Integer
  Private Sub StackBasedVariable()
    Dim x As Integer
  End Sub
End Class
```

StaticVariable is a shared variable. Some languages refer to shared/static variables as class variables. The value in StaticVariable is the same across all instances of ClassTestStatic. The term *shared* implies that the variable is shared among all instances of the class. This is correct. However, static/shared variables do not require an instance of the class to exist. The following is perfectly legal and sometimes desired:

```
Private Sub Test()
  ClassTestStatic.StaticVariable = 1
  ClassTestStatic.ThreadStaticVariable = 1
End Sub
```

The variable `ThreadStaticVariable` is a different sort of shared/static variable. In a single-threaded application it behaves the same as `StaticVariable`. The difference is that when more than one thread accesses the variable its value will be determined based on the thread that is accessing it. The best way to think of it is that there is an array of `ThreadStaticVariables`. The element of the array that is accessed is determined by the thread accessing it. This isn't exactly how it's implemented, but it would be possible to implement thread local storage that way.

ThreadStatic `ThreadStatic` is an attribute that is added to the declaration of a variable in a class. It informs the compiler that if the variable is accessed from different threads each thread should have a distinct static variable. This is a simple way to make a variable local to a thread and create thread local storage. `Thread-Static` is the managed equivalent of the C++'s `__declspec(thread)`.

`ThreadStatic` variables behave like thread stack based variables in that their value depends on the thread. However, they are accessible to the thread in the same way a static/shared variable is. `ThreadStatic` variables are a convenient way of making data stored in a class accessible to a thread without synchronizing access or passing values as parameters. Not all designs need utilize `ThreadStatic` variables. For example, if an approach of one thread per class was taken, then thread static variables make no sense. If more than one thread can access data elements in a class, and the value is meaningful only to that thread, then thread static variables should be considered.

Listing 11.1 demonstrates the use of thread static variables.

Listing 11.1 Thread static example (VB.NET)

```vbnet
Public Class ClassThreadStatic_Test
  <ThreadStatic()> Shared ThreadStatic_Data As String = "Initial"      ◁── Makes a variable
  Private TheForm As FormTestThreadStatic                                   unique per thread
  Public Sub New(ByVal TheForm As FormTestThreadStatic)
    Me.TheForm = TheForm
  End Sub
  Public Sub Test()
    Dim callback As New WaitCallback(AddressOf CallbackMethod)
    ThreadPool.QueueUserWorkItem(callback, "1")
    ThreadPool.QueueUserWorkItem(callback, "2")
    ThreadPool.QueueUserWorkItem(callback, "3")
    ThreadPool.QueueUserWorkItem(callback, "4")
  End Sub
  Private Sub CallbackMethod(ByVal state As Object)
    Dim sLine As String
    sLine = "Before Assign ThreadStatic_Data = "
    sLine += ThreadStatic_Data + " "
    sLine += Thread.CurrentThread.GetHashCode().ToString()
    TheForm.AddFeedbackLine(sLine)
    ThreadStatic_Data = state                         ◁── Assigns the thread's copy
    Thread.Sleep(5000)                                    of the ThreadStatic_Data
    sLine = "After Assign ThreadStatic_Data = "
```

```
      sLine += ThreadStatic_Data + " "
      sLine += Thread.CurrentThread.GetHashCode().ToString()
      sLine += " " + ThreadStatic_Data.GetHashCode().ToString()
      TheForm.AddFeedbackLine(sLine)
   End Sub
End Class
```

Thread static variables are one way of having data associated with a particular thread. In the next section we discuss an alternative method of storing data on a per-thread basis. The data elements are stored in locations that may or may not have names. These locations are called slots. In the next section we discuss unnamed data slots.

11.2   USING UNNAMED DATA SLOTS

In the previous section we saw how the `ThreadStatic` attribute can be used to create data elements that are accessed by multiple threads. `ThreadStatic` instructs the compiler that a particular variable should be viewed as local to a thread. A more involved way of accomplishing thread local data storage is to use unnamed data slots. An unnamed data slot is a storage location that is local to a thread. The slot is allocated using the `AllocateDataSlot` method of the `Thread` class. Once allocated, when multiple threads access the data slot they are given their own area of storage.

Unnamed Data Slot   An unnamed data slot is a region of memory associated with a thread that does not have a name. Unnamed data slots are created using the `Allocate-DataSlot` method.

`AllocateDataSlot` is not, and should not, be called by each thread. It is executed once, setting up the data slot for all threads. `AllocateDataSlot` returns a `Local-DataStoreSlot` which is used by each thread to access its local data store. Since .NET provides garbage collection, there is no method that frees an unnamed data slot.

Allocate-DataSlot   `AllocateDataSlot` is a method of the `Thread` class that creates an unnamed storage location that is relative to the thread accessing it.

In listing 11.2, `TheSlot` is a class variable contained in the same class as `CallbackMethod`. `CallbackMethod` is passed as a parameter to the constructor of the `WaitCallback` delegate for use with the `ThreadPool` object.

Listing 11.2   Unnamed data slot example (C#)

```
public class ClassTLS_UnnamedSlot_Test
{                                                    Declare a variable to
    System.LocalDataStoreSlot TheSlot;  ⟵───┘       access the data slot

    private FormTestThreadStatic TheForm ;
    public ClassTLS_UnnamedSlot_Test(FormTestThreadStatic TheForm)
    {
```

```
        TheSlot = Thread.AllocateDataSlot();     ◁─┐ Allocate a thread
        this.TheForm  = TheForm ;                    │ local data slot
    }
    public void Test()
    {
        WaitCallback callback = new WaitCallback(CallbackMethod);
        ThreadPool.QueueUserWorkItem(callback, "1");
        ThreadPool.QueueUserWorkItem(callback, "2");
        ThreadPool.QueueUserWorkItem(callback, "3");
        ThreadPool.QueueUserWorkItem(callback, "4");
    }

    private void CallbackMethod(object state)
    {
        string sLine;
        sLine= "Before Assign TLS = ";               Retrieve any data
                                                      that is in the slot
        string sData= (string)Thread.GetData(TheSlot);  ◁─┘ before assignment
        sLine += sData;
        sLine += " Hash Code=" + Thread.CurrentThread.GetHashCode().ToString();
        TheForm.AddFeedbackLine(sLine);       Store thread-specific
                                              data in the thread
        Thread.SetData(TheSlot,state);   ◁─┘ local data slot
        Thread.Sleep(5000);                           Retrieve the thread-
        sLine= "After Assign TLS = ";                 specific data from
        sData= (string)Thread.GetData(TheSlot);  ◁─┘ the data slot
        sLine += sData;
        sLine += " Hash Code=" + Thread.CurrentThread.GetHashCode().ToString();
        TheForm.AddFeedbackLine(sLine);
    }
}
```

The ThreadPool class is an easy way to create multiple threads and demonstrate thread local storage. Listing 11.2 demonstrates how four entries are added to the ThreadPool. Each entry is associated with CallbackMethod, differing only by the supplied parameter. Because CallbackMethod contains a Sleep statement that pauses the ThreadPool thread for 5 seconds, we are certain that the threads involved will differ. If the method did not contain the Sleep statement, it is possible that the same thread would service each entry.

When the Test method is invoked, the following output is produced:

```
Before Assign TLS =  Hash Code=43
Before Assign TLS =  Hash Code=48
Before Assign TLS =  Hash Code=49
Before Assign TLS =  Hash Code=50
After Assign TLS = 1 Hash Code=43
After Assign TLS = 2 Hash Code=48
After Assign TLS = 3 Hash Code=49
After Assign TLS = 4 Hash Code=50
```

Notice that even though each thread is accessing data using `TheSlot` with `GetData` and `SetData`, the values are unique to each thread. `SetData` and `GetData` allow for saving and retrieving a value stored in an object.

GetData and SetData   `GetData` is a method of the `Thread` class that retrieves thread local values from a data slot, while `SetData` is used to store a reference to an object in thread local storage.

Thread local storage is a relatively scarce resource, and should only be used when needed. Creating data slots is relatively expensive, and should be performed only once. If the static nature of data can be determined in advance, then the `ThreadStatic` attribute should be used instead. Unnamed data slots offer a very secure means of storing values specific to a particular thread. In the next section we discuss named data slots that offer a more convenient way of storing thread local values if a lesser level of security is tolerable.

11.3   USING NAMED DATA SLOTS

There are times when it is easier to keep track of a value by using a name rather than by passing a variable. `GetNamedDataSlot` allows a thread local storage slot to be retrieved using a name. In listing 11.3 `TheSlot` is allocated in the class constructor, `Public Sub New`, using the `AllocateNamedDataSlot` method of the `Thread` class.

AllocateNamed-DataSlot   `AllocateNamedDataSlot` is a method on the `Thread` class that allocates thread local storage and associates it with a supplied name.

If a slot has not been created using the `AllocateNamedDataSlot` method before `GetNamedDataSlot` is called, the slot will then be allocated. This means that calling `AllocateNamedDataSlot` is optional. As a good coding practice, if it can be determined that a thread local data slot will be required then allocation should be performed before accessing the slot.

GetNamed-DataSlot   `GetNamedDataSlot` is a method of the `Thread` class that retrieves thread local storage based upon a supplied name. If the slot does not exist before `GetNamedDataSlot` is invoked, it will be created.

If a slot exists when `AllocateNamedDataSlot` is called, `ArgumentException` is raised. Consider the following example:

```
Try
  TheNamedSlot = Thread.AllocateNamedDataSlot("TheSlot")
  TheNamedSlot = Thread.AllocateNamedDataSlot("TheSlot")
Catch ex As Exception
  System.Diagnostics.Trace.WriteLine(ex.Message)
  System.Diagnostics.Trace.WriteLine(ex.ToString())
End Try
```

The first `AllocateNamedDataSlot` will succeed. The second will generate the following output:

```
Item has already been added.  Key in dictionary: "TheSlot"  Key being added:
"TheSlot" System.ArgumentException: Item has already been added.  Key in
dictionary: "TheSlot"  Key being added: "TheSlot"
    at System.Collections.Hashtable.Insert(
       Object key, Object nvalue, Boolean add)
    at System.Collections.Hashtable.Add(Object key, Object value)
    at System.LocalDataStoreMgr.AllocateNamedDataSlot(String name)
    at System.Threading.Thread.AllocateNamedDataSlot(String name)
    at TLS_NamedSlot_TestApp.ClassTLS_NamedSlot_Test..ctor(
       FormTestThreadStatic TheForm) in D:\My Documents\books\
       threading\chapter11\projects\VB\11.4\TLS_NamedSlot_TestApp\
       TLS_NamedSlot_Test.vb:line 10
```

This offers some insight into how named data slots are implemented in .NET. We can
see that the exception was raised because an entry already existed in a `Hashtable`.
This means that `Hashtable` is used to associate the named data slot with its name.

Named slots offer an alternative to keeping a variable with the originally allocated
slot, as must be done when using an unnamed data slot. They are more convenient than
using an unnamed data slot, but are not as convenient as using the `ThreadStatic`
attribute. If more flexibility is required, then one of the data slot methods should be used.

Listing 11.3 shows how to allocate a slot, store data, and then retrieve data from it
in a thread local way.

Listing 11.3 Named slot example (VB.NET)

```
Public Class ClassTLS_NamedSlot_Test                        Create a named
  Dim TheNamedSlot As System.LocalDataStoreSlot  ⦧──┘ data slot
  Private TheForm As FormTestThreadStatic
  Public Sub New(ByVal TheForm As FormTestThreadStatic)
    TheNamedSlot = Thread.AllocateNamedDataSlot("TheSlot")
    Try
      TheNamedSlot = Thread.AllocateNamedDataSlot("TheSlot")
    Catch ex As Exception
      System.Diagnostics.Trace.WriteLine(ex.Message + " " + ex.ToString())
    End Try
    Me.TheForm = TheForm
  End Sub
  Public Sub Test()
    Dim callback As New WaitCallback(AddressOf CallbackMethod)
    ThreadPool.QueueUserWorkItem(callback, "1")
    ThreadPool.QueueUserWorkItem(callback, "2")
    ThreadPool.QueueUserWorkItem(callback, "3")
    ThreadPool.QueueUserWorkItem(callback, "4")
  End Sub
  Private Sub CallbackMethod(ByVal state As Object)
    SetDataMethod(state)
    Thread.Sleep(5000)
    GetDataMethod()
  End Sub
  Private Sub SetDataMethod(ByVal TheData As Object)
```

```
      Dim TheSlot As System.LocalDataStoreSlot
      TheSlot = Thread.GetNamedDataSlot("TheSlot")      ◁── Retrieve the named
      Thread.SetData(TheSlot, TheData)                         slot for use with the
    End Sub                                                    SetData method
  Private Sub GetDataMethod()
    Dim sData As String
    Dim sLine As String
    Dim TheSlot As System.LocalDataStoreSlot
    TheSlot = Thread.GetNamedDataSlot("TheSlot")        ◁── Retrieve the named
    sLine = "After Assign TLS = "                            slot for use with the
    sData = Thread.GetData(TheSlot)                          GetData method
    sLine += sData
    sLine += " Hash Code=" + Thread.CurrentThread.GetHashCode().ToString()
    TheForm.AddFeedbackLine(sLine)
  End Sub
End Class                                                                    ∎
```

We have seen how to create and access a named data slot in this section. Unlike unnamed data slots, named data slots can be freed. In the next section we will discuss the impact of freeing a data slot.

11.4   FREEING NAMED DATA SLOTS

There are times when we wish to stop using one variable and start using another. The FreeNamedDataSlot method of the Thread class is used to change which data slot is associated with a name. Since .NET is a nondeterministic environment, calling FreeNamedDataSlot does not actually free the object contained in the slot. Instead, it is similar to calling the Remove method of a Hashtable. Listing 11.4 shows the impact of using FreeNamedDataSlot.

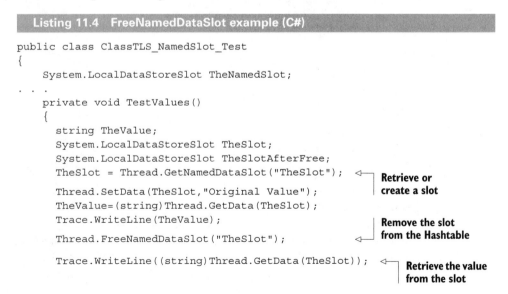

Listing 11.4   FreeNamedDataSlot example (C#)

```
public class ClassTLS_NamedSlot_Test
{
    System.LocalDataStoreSlot TheNamedSlot;
. . .
    private void TestValues()
    {
      string TheValue;
      System.LocalDataStoreSlot TheSlot;
      System.LocalDataStoreSlot TheSlotAfterFree;
      TheSlot = Thread.GetNamedDataSlot("TheSlot");        ◁── Retrieve or
      Thread.SetData(TheSlot,"Original Value");                create a slot
      TheValue=(string)Thread.GetData(TheSlot);
      Trace.WriteLine(TheValue);                             Remove the slot
      Thread.FreeNamedDataSlot("TheSlot");              ◁── from the Hashtable

      Trace.WriteLine((string)Thread.GetData(TheSlot));  ◁── Retrieve the value
                                                             from the slot
```

```
      TheSlotAfterFree = Thread.GetNamedDataSlot("TheSlot");  ◁──┐
      TheValue=(string)Thread.GetData(TheSlotAfterFree);           │
      if (TheValue == null)                                        │
      {                                   Associate "TheSlot"      │
         Trace.WriteLine("No Data");       with a different        │
      }                                        data slot           │
   }
 . . .
}
```

At the point `FreeNamedDataSlot` is invoked on "TheSlot", the value of the variable `TheSlot` is unaffected. The output from the above code follows:

```
Original Value
Original Value
No Data
```

Notice that the second line output contains "Original Value." The `GetData` statement immediately after the call to the `FreeNamedDataSlot` method generates this line. This is proof that `FreeNamedDataSlot` does not destroy the contents of the slot.

To see what is going on in the `FreeNamedDataSlot` we can pass in a null value for the name of the slot:

```
private void TestRemoveNull()
{
  try
  {
    Thread.FreeNamedDataSlot(null);
  }
  catch (Exception ex)
  {
    Trace.WriteLine(ex.ToString());
  }
}
```

This produces the following output:

```
System.ArgumentNullException: Key cannot be null.
Parameter name: key
   at System.Collections.Hashtable.Remove(Object key)
   at System.LocalDataStoreMgr.FreeNamedDataSlot(String name)
   at System.Threading.Thread.FreeNamedDataSlot(String name)
```

Without `FreeNamedDataSlot` there would be no way to change what data slot a name was associated with. Since `AllocateNamedDataSlot` throws an exception when the name is already associated with a slot, we must have some way of making a name available for reuse. That is exactly what `FreeNamedDataSlot` does.

It is important to understand how `FreeNamedDataSlot` behaves when multiple threads are involved. If a thread calls `FreeNamedDataSlot`, then any calls to `Get-NamedDataSlot` by it or a different thread will result in a different data slot being returned. Unless the threads have a variable with a `LocalDataStoreSlot` value stored in it, their values will be lost. It may be that is what is desired, but since there is the possibility of data disappearing while a thread is accessing it, care should be taken when using `FreeNamedDataSlot`.

FreeNamed-
DataSlot
`FreeNamedDataSlot` is a static method on the `Thread` class that removes an association between a name and a thread local data slot. It allows a name to be associated with a different set of thread local slots.

One reason that you might want to use it is if the threads are working on a solution and one of the threads finds the answer. One thread could easily signal all other threads to stop their work. Under general circumstances data slots are allocated and used for the life of the program, or at least the life of the threads accessing them.

11.5 SUMMARY

In this chapter we've discussed ways of associating data with a particular thread. Using the `ThreadLocal` attribute is the simplest, and least flexible, way of making data values dependent on which thread accesses them. If a more robust mechanism is needed, then named data slots should be used. If the highest degree of control is required, then an unnamed data slot should be used and managed using some sort of collection. Not every application will require the use of thread local storage. It should only be used in cases where it is a good fit.

The next chapter discusses delegates to a higher degree of detail than we have thus far. Delegates are one of the most exciting aspects of the .NET framework.

Delegates

Delegates are a powerful means of associating methods and instances of objects. They are one of the largest areas of innovation of the .NET platform. Delegates are intertwined throughout not only multithreaded development in .NET, but also general development. This chapter covers the delegates associated with multithreaded development.

Additionally, it covers asynchronous execution of delegates. Asynchronous delegates are those invoked using the `BeginInvoke` method. An important aspect of any asynchronous development is determining when a task has completed, and gathering any results. This is accomplished using the `EndInvoke` method. The `AsyncCallback` delegate allows a method to be invoked when an asynchronous task completes.

The chapter concludes with a discussion of dynamic delegates. This is a form of late binding, where the method and object associated with it are determined at runtime.

12.1   DELEGATES REVISITED

A common need in programming is to be notified when something happens. There are two basic ways to deal with this need: polling and notification.

One way to know if something happens is to frequently check to see if what is being watched meets some criteria. This is generally referred to as polling. The problem with polling is that the interval between checks is constant, while the occurrence of the phenomenon being monitored likely is not. This means that if the interval of checking is one hour, it may be that the phenomenon occurs and goes unnoticed for 59 minutes. Additionally, if more than one occurrence of the phenomenon occurs during the interval, only one instance is captured.

Polling   Polling is the process of repeatedly checking the status of some decision criteria to determine if predefined criteria have been met. The duration between the time the criteria are met and the time they are detected can be referred to as latency.

Think of polling as the time-old question that almost every child asks—often more than once—during a trip. "Are we there yet?" The child is polling to determine if the phenomenon he or she is concerned with has occurred. The general response from parents is "Not yet, I'll tell you when we get there." This brings us to the other common way of checking to see if something happens: notification.

Notification requires some means of communication between the entity being notified and the entity doing the notification. In the .NET framework this is accomplished by using a delegate. The history behind delegates can be traced back to function pointers in C/C++.

Delegate   A delegate is a type-safe, object-oriented means of referencing, and eventually invoking, a method as though it were any other variable. They are often referred to as type-safe function pointers.

A delegate is an object that associates a method with an optional instance of another object. This allows a delegate to be invoked on an instance of a class, not only on static methods. This is a major improvement over function pointers that required the method that was having its address taken be static. Figure 12.1 demonstrates using a delegate.

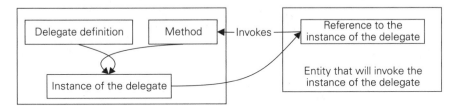

Figure 12.1 Using a delegate

First, there must be a delegate declaration. This tells the compiler what the methods that will be associated with the delegate must look like, in terms of parameters and return value. An example of a declaration of a delegate is:

```
delegate void SimpleDelegate();
```

This delegate can only be used with methods that do not accept parameters and do not return a value. Attempting to associate the delegate with some other type of method will produce a compile error. This is a powerful feature of delegates. This means that delegates can be used without fear that the method does not match the delegate's definition, since this will result in a compile-time error.

Use of Delegates Delegates are a powerful way of allowing one class to notify another when a condition is met. This allows one instance of a class to inform an instance of a different (or the same) class that something happened that it cares about. Delegates are widely used in the .NET framework.

Once the delegate is defined, an instance of it can be created. This is very similar to creating a user-defined data type. The delegate usage looks much like any other object:

```
SimpleDelegate MyDelegate;
MyDelegate = new SimpleDelegate(MethodToPointTo);
```

This creates an instance of the `SimpleDelegate` and associates it with the `MethodToPointTo`. Once the instance of the delegate is created, the next step is to invoke the delegate. This causes the method associated with the delegate to be executed. Invoking a delegate is identical to executing a method:

```
DoSomethingAndCallBack(MyDelegate);
```

This causes the method `MethodToPointTo` to be executed. Listing 12.1 shows the elements involved in entirety.

Listing 12.1 Using delegates (C#)

```
public class FormDelegates_Revisited : System.Windows.Forms.Form
{
. . .
    delegate void SimpleDelegate();        Define the signature
    void MethodToPointTo()                 of SimpleDelegate
    {
      MessageBox.Show("In the Method to point to");
    }

    private void DoSomethingAndCallBack(SimpleDelegate TheDelegate)
    {
      Trace.WriteLine(TheDelegate.Target.ToString());
      TheDelegate();        Invoke the
    }                       delegate
    private void buttonTest_Click(object sender, System.EventArgs e)
    {                              Define an instance          Instantiate the
      SimpleDelegate MyDelegate;   of the delegate             instance of the
      MyDelegate = new SimpleDelegate(MethodToPointTo);        delegate
      DoSomethingAndCallBack(MyDelegate);   Pass the instance of the
    }                                       delegate as a parameter
```

Now that we have seen how delegates are used, let us move on to how they relate to multithreading.

12.2 THE THREADSTART DELEGATE

In previous chapters we briefly discussed the `ThreadStart` delegate. The only way to create a thread using managed code is to use a `ThreadStart` delegate. Visual Basic.NET developers might be confused by the following example:

```
Private TestThread As Thread
  Private Sub ThreadMethod()
  End Sub
  Public Sub Test()
    TestThread = New Thread(AddressOf ThreadMethod)
  End Sub
```

The use of the `ThreadStart` delegate is not obvious: Nowhere in the code is it declared. However, if we look at the MSIL for the `Test` method in table 12.1 we can see that `ThreadStart` is being used. This is an example of the convenient things that Visual Basic does for developers.

Table 12.1   MSIL Generated by Visual Basic

IL_000a	newobj	instance void [mscorlib]System.Threading.ThreadStart::.ctor(object, native int)

Listing 12.2 shows the usage of the `ThreadStart` delegate.

Listing 12.2   Using the ThreadStart delegate (VB.NET)

```
Imports System.Threading
Public Class FormTestThreadStart
  Inherits System.Windows.Forms.Form
. . .

Private TestThread As Thread
  Private Sub TestMethod()
    MessageBox.Show("In Test Method on Thread " + Thread.CurrentThread.Name)
  End Sub
. . .
  Private Sub CreateTestThread()
    Dim TestThreadStart As ThreadStart
    ' Create a new instance of the ThreadStart delegate,
    ' associating it with TestMethod
    TestThreadStart = New ThreadStart(AddressOf TestMethod)

    ' Creates a new thread that will execute
    ' the TestSharedThreadStart ThreadStart delegate.
    TestThread = New Thread(TestThreadStart)

    TestThread.Name = "TheTestThread"
    TestThread.Start()
    TestThread.Join()
. . .
```

The `ThreadStart` delegate provides a standardized way of passing a reference to a method to the `Thread` class constructor. This is accomplished by passing in a reference to a method. In Visual Basic this involves the `AddressOf` operator. In C# the name of the method suffices. Once the instance of the delegate is created, the only properties available are `Target` and `Method`. Both are inherited from the delegate base class.

ThreadStart Delegate The `ThreadStart` delegate is a class derived indirectly from the `Delegate` class. It allows a thread to be associated with an instance of a class and a method.

The `Method` property is of type `System.Reflection.MethodInfo` and this is how the thread knows what to invoke. One of the methods of the `RuntimeMethodInfo` class is `Invoke`, which is how the method associated with the delegate is executed.

One of the most powerful advances of delegates over function pointers is the ability to associate a delegate with a particular instance of a class. The `Target` property is how this is accomplished. In cases where there is no instance of a class to be associated with, the `Target` property is `Nothing/null`. When the method associated with a delegate is `Shared/static` there is no instance with which to be associated. The `Target` property is of type `object`.

In the example code at the beginning of this section we declare a `ThreadStart` delegate called `TestThreadStart`. When the `Thread` starts it does something similar to the following:

```
TestThreadStart.Method.Invoke(TestThreadStart.Target, Nothing)
```

Since the method passed to the `ThreadStart` delegate cannot have any parameters, we pass in `Nothing` in the last parameter. This parameter is used to pass values to the method associated with the delegate.

Unless there is a specific need, there is no reason to retain a reference to the `ThreadStart` delegate. If development is being done in Visual Basic .NET, there is little reason to create a `ThreadStart` delegate. If development is being done in C#, `ThreadMethod` can be created in-line:

```
TestThread = new Thread(new ThreadStart( TestMethod));
```

Another form of asynchronous execution involves callbacks. Callbacks are essentially delegates that are invoked when some condition is satisfied.

12.3 CALLBACKS

Callbacks are a way of notifying a consumer when some event occurs. Think of it in practical terms. If you call a coworker and he or she is busy, he or she may offer to call you back. This is the idea behind a callback. A caller invokes a method on an object, passing a delegate that can be used to signal some event. The object stores the reference to the delegate until it is needed.

We will discuss several multithreading-related callbacks in this section.

12.3.1   TimerCallback

Often there is a need for actions to be performed at set intervals. Earlier we discussed the differences between polling and notification. One way to implement polling is to use a timer. Windows developers naturally think of the Windows message timer. The message timer enters a `WM_TIMER` message in a window's message queue at regular intervals. Visual Basic exposes this functionally using its `Timer` control. For certain types of operations the message timer is adequate. A key issue with the message timer is that it relies on a single-threaded message pump to process the messages. If the task associated with the timer takes a long time, the message queue is blocked until it completes its work. This explains why poorly written applications freeze when doing long-running operations.

A more flexible approach is to use a thread-based timer. In chapter 10 we discussed the `ThreadPool` class. One use of the class is to create a thread-based timer. For user interface intensive operations it is better to use a message timer since the calls back to the user interface will need to be passed to the user interface thread using the `Invoke` mechanism. For operations that are not tied extensively to the user interface, the thread-based timer is an excellent choice.

TimerCallback   `TimerCallback` is a delegate that is used with the `System.Threading.Timer` class to create a thread-based timer. `TimerCallback` is invoked when the timer interval expires.

The following example code shows how `Timer` is created. First we must create `TimerCallback`, passing in a method to be invoked:

```
. . .
System.Threading.Timer myTimer;
void CallbackMethod(object state)
{
  Trace.Write(state);
  Trace.WriteLine(DateTime.Now.ToString());
}
private void StartTimer(long First,long Each, object state)
{
  TimerCallback myCallback;
  myCallback= new TimerCallback(CallbackMethod);
  myTimer=new System.Threading.Timer(myCallback,state,First ,Each );
}
. . .
```

The `Timer` constructor accepts four parameters:

- `TimerCallback`. This lets `Timer` know what method to invoke when it's time to invoke a method.

- An object to transmit state information. This is the same mechanism that the `ThreadPool` class uses to communicate with its worker threads.

- The time to wait before the timer executes the first time. It can be zero, indicating the timers should start immediately, or `Timeout.Infinite`, indicating the timer should not start at this time.
- The time to wait between invoking `TimerCallback`. It also can be zero, `Timeout.Infinite`, or the number of milliseconds to wait.

If the duration of the method associated with `TimerCallback` is greater than the interval to wait, each instance will be executing on a different thread. This means that if more than one instance of the method associated with `TimerCallback` is executing at the same time, the operation will be performed in parallel. Since the thread-based timer uses `ThreadPool`, there is a limit on how many threads can be executing at once. When that limit is reached, no new threads will be created and those items waiting to execute will be entered into a queue. Care should be taken in the methods associated with `TimerCallback` to ensure they are thread-safe.

Combine   The += operator is a shortcut for the shared/static `Combine` method. In Visual Basic the `Combine` method must be used.

A powerful feature of delegates is the ability to associate multiple methods with a single delegate. This is called a multicast delegate. In C# this is accomplished using the += operator. The following code example associates three methods with the same delegate:

```
ClassTwo AClass = new ClassTwo();
TimerCallback myCallbackInfo;
myCallbackInfo= new TimerCallback(InfoCallbackMethod);
myCallbackInfo += new TimerCallback(AClass.InfoCallbackMethod);
myCallbackInfo += new TimerCallback(AddLineCallback);
myCallbackInfo("test");
```

Each method associated with the delegate will be invoked. The order of invocation is the same as the order the methods were added to the delegate. In this case `Info-CallbackMethod` will execute, and once it has completed, `Aclass.InfoCall-backMethod`, and then `AddLineCallback`. This allows for a series of methods to occur in a certain order.

The `ThreadStart` delegate can be used in a multicasting way. This means that when one method exits, another begins. This is a way to isolate cleanup code that should execute after the main logic has completed.

12.3.2   WaitCallback

In chapter 10 we discussed the `ThreadPool` class in detail. The following examples show how a work item is created and added to `ThreadPool` for processing:

```
. . .
  Private Sub WorkMethod(ByVal state As Object)
    Trace.Write(Thread.CurrentThread.GetHashCode.ToString())
    Trace.Write(" ")
    Trace.WriteLine(state.ToString())
  End Sub
```

```
Private Sub AddWorkItem()
  Trace.WriteLine(Thread.CurrentThread.GetHashCode.ToString())
  Dim WorkItem As WaitCallback
  WorkItem = New WaitCallback(AddressOf WorkMethod)
  ThreadPool.QueueUserWorkItem(WorkItem, DateTime.Now)
End Sub
. . .
```

The `WaitCallback` delegate is how a method and a state parameter are associated with an entry in the thread pool's user work item queue.

> **WaitCallback** `WaitCallback` is a delegate used to associate a work item in `ThreadPool` with a method to invoke.

The `WaitCallback` class, along with all system delegates in the .NET framework, is derived from the `MulticastDelegate` class. Multicast delegates allow a series of methods to be associated with a single delegate, letting a chain of execution occur. The following code selectively adds two methods to the `WorkItem` callback.

```
Dim TempCallback As WaitCallback
Dim WorkItem As WaitCallback
WorkItem = Nothing
If CheckBoxTime.Checked Then
  TempCallback = New WaitCallback(AddressOf WorkMethodTime)
  WorkItem = WaitCallback.Combine(WorkItem, TempCallback)
End If

If CheckBoxSleep.Checked Then
  TempCallback = New WaitCallback(AddressOf WorkMethodSleep)
  WorkItem = WaitCallback.Combine(WorkItem, TempCallback)
End If
```

If `WorkItem` is `Nothing`/null when passed to `WaitCallback`, the result is the same as a simple assignment.

Since a delegate can reference multiple methods, we must use `GetInvocationList` of `MulticastDelegate` to determine what methods are associated with a delegate.

> **GetInvocation-** `GetInvocationList` is a method of the `MulticastDelegate` class
> **List**   that returns a collection of `Delegates` associated with the current instance of `MulticastDelegate`.

The following example demonstrates how to determine what methods will be invoked, along with any targets:

```
Private Sub DisplayDelegateInfo(ByVal D As MulticastDelegate)
  Dim TheDelegate As System.Delegate
  Trace.WriteLine("====")
  Trace.WriteLine(D.ToString())
  For Each TheDelegate In D.GetInvocationList()
    Trace.WriteLine("*****")
    With TheDelegate.Method
      Trace.WriteLine("Method: " + .Name)
```

```
        Trace.WriteLine("FullName: " + .DeclaringType.FullName)
      End With
      If (TheDelegate.Target Is Nothing) Then
        Trace.WriteLine("Target: Null")
      Else
        With TheDelegate.Target
          Trace.WriteLine("Target Type:" + .GetType().FullName)
          Trace.WriteLine("Target: " + .ToString())
        End With
      End If
    Next
End Sub
```

The Target object is a reference to the instance of a class associated with the method. In the case of a Shared/static method, the target will be Nothing/null.

The Method property returns an instance of MethodInfo which provides a means of examining the method in detail. In the example, DeclaringType refers to the class that contains the method declaration. The Name property of the MethodInfo class returns the name of the method.

12.3.3 WaitOrTimerCallback

There are times that waiting until a timer's interval has passed is not desirable. In those situations ThreadPool's RegisterWaitForSingleObject allows for timer-like functionality. We covered RegisterWaitForSingleObject in chapter 10. Listing 12.3 shows how to use RegisterWaitForSingleObject.

Listing 12.3 Using RegisterWaitForSingleObject (C#)

```
. . .
private AutoResetEvent AutoReset;
. . .
private void Test()
{
  AutoReset = new AutoResetEvent(false);
  Delegate Callback;
  Delegate TempCallback;

  Callback = new WaitOrTimerCallback(FirstCallbackMethod);

  TempCallback= new WaitOrTimerCallback(SecondCallbackMethod);
  Callback = MulticastDelegate.Combine(Callback ,TempCallback);

  TempCallback= new WaitOrTimerCallback(ThirdCallbackMethod);
  Callback = MulticastDelegate.Combine(Callback ,TempCallback);

  TempCallback= new WaitOrTimerCallback(FourthCallbackMethod);
  Callback = MulticastDelegate.Combine(Callback ,TempCallback);

  ThreadPool.RegisterWaitForSingleObject(AutoReset,
    (WaitOrTimerCallback) Callback, null, 10000, false);
}
. . .
```

To associate a `WaitHandle`-derived class with a method we must use `WaitOrTimer-Callback`. `WaitOrTimerCallback` requires that the method to be associated with it have two parameters: (1) an object used to pass state information and (2) a Boolean used to indicate why the method is being invoked. If it is true, the method is being invoked because the `WaitHandle`-derived object did not become signaled in the time span specified by the timeout value passed to `RegisterWaitForSingle-Object`. If the value is false, the method is being invoked because the `WaitHandle`-derived object became signaled before a timeout could occur.

In listing 12.3 we created a chain of four methods that will be executed each time the delegate is invoked. `FirstCallbackMethod` is one of those methods. It checks to see a value has been set for the `SharedData` data slot. If it has, a trace message is written out to that effect. It then sets the `SharedData` slot to First:.

```
private void FirstCallbackMethod(object state, bool timedOut)
{
  LocalDataStoreSlot Slot;
  Slot =Thread.GetNamedDataSlot("SharedData");
  string Data;
  Data = (string)Thread.GetData(Slot);
  if (Data != null && Data.Length > 0)
  {
    Trace.WriteLine(Data + " was left from a previous call");
  }
  Data = "First:";
  Thread.SetData(Slot,Data);
}
```

There are times that the methods in an invocation list need to communicate with each other. This allows a chained form of processing, similar to a pipeline architecture. In the previous code a named data slot called `SharedData` is used to share information between the different methods in the invocation list.

Using Multicast Delegates   One means of communication between methods that are part of the same invocation list is to use thread local storage.

Remember, when using thread local storage with a thread pool the threads are reused. This means that the contents of a data slot might contain information from a previous work item.

TIP   In `ThreadPool`, when using thread local storage, care must be taken to ensure that a previous thread's activities do not affect the current activity.

The alternative to using thread local storage is to utilize the state object that is passed in. If this approach is taken, it is best to use a collection of some sort, such as `Hashtable`. This way an element can be set in the collection without changing the actual state object:

```
System.Collections.Hashtable StateInfo;
StateInfo= new System.Collections.Hashtable();
```

```
ThreadPool.RegisterWaitForSingleObject(AutoReset,
        (WaitOrTimerCallback) Callback, StateInfo, 10000, false);
```

In each method we can then set an entry in the table:

```
if (state != null)
{
  System.Collections.Hashtable StateInfo;
  StateInfo = (System.Collections.Hashtable )state;
  StateInfo["SharedData"] = Data;
}
```

12.4 *HANDLING THREAD EXCEPTIONS IN WINDOWS FORMS*

In an ideal world, all thread-related exceptions would be dealt with using the appropriate try/catch mechanisms. To handle those cases where some execution is not handled, we can use ThreadExceptionEventHandler. This section applies to Windows Forms development only because the event handler is associated with the Application object. The following code shows how ThreadException can be used:

```
. . .
Public Sub New()
  MyBase.New()
  AddHandler Application.ThreadException, AddressOf Handler
  Thread.CurrentThread.Name = "Main"
  InitializeComponent()
End Sub
. . .
Private Sub Handler(ByVal s As Object, ByVal e As ThreadExceptionEventArgs)
  MessageBox.Show(e.ToString() + vbCrLf + e.Exception.Message)
End Sub
. . .
```

If you use the Application.ThreadException event any unhandled thread exceptions, except for ThreadAbortException, that are generated on the main thread of the application will be captured. Recall that ThreadAbortException is raised when Abort is called on the thread. If the Application's ThreadException handler handled the ThreadAbortException it would be impossible to call Abort on a thread and have the thread terminate.

Thread-Exception ThreadException is an event of the Application class that allows for handling any unhandled thread exception. It uses the ThreadException-EventHandler delegate. Only thread exceptions raised on the main thread of the application, that is, the thread that installs the handler, will be handled.

When the following statement is executed, the exception handler will catch the exception and display a dialog box:

```
Throw New System.Threading.ThreadStateException("My Exception")
```

When the exception is raised, a dialog box containing the following is displayed:

```
System.Threading.ThreadExceptionEventArgs
My Exception
```

In a production application a more robust error-handling mechanism would be used. Instead of displaying a dialog box, most likely an entry would be logged to the event log indicating that the exception occurred. This should not be seen as a way of not having to deal with exceptions; instead, it should be viewed as a safety net.

Thread-Exception-EventArgs   `ThreadExceptionEventArgs` is a class that is passed as the second parameter of the `ThreadExceptionEventHandler` delegate. It contains a reference to the exception that caused the handler to be invoked. This information is available via the `Exception` property.

There may be confusion about events and delegates. Events are implemented using delegates. For example, the `ThreadException` event uses `ThreadException-EventHandler` to handle any thread exceptions. To see this, we can examine the MSIL for the `New` method at the beginning of this section:

```
newobj instance void[System]
 System.Threading.ThreadExceptionEventHandler::.ctor( object,
 native int)
```

The exception handler must have two parameters: an object and an int. The first is the sender object, a reference to the thread that raised the exception. This will always be the thread that added the thread exception handler. If some other thread causes an unhandled thread exception to be raised, the `Application` thread exception handler will not catch the exception.

TIP   The thread exception handler will only catch thread exceptions that are raised on the main thread of the application. If an unhandled thread exception is raised on some other thread, the thread will terminate. This underscores the importance of using `try`/`catch` statements.

The following code example creates a thread that attempts to call `Resume` on `myThread`. If the thread is in any other state than suspended, this will cause an exception to be generated.

```
Private Sub NewThreadMethod()
  myThread.Resume()
End Sub
Private Sub CreateThreadToResume()
  Dim NewThread As New Thread(AddressOf NewThreadMethod)
  NewThread.Name = "NewThread"
  NewThread.Start()
End Sub
```

In the case where `MyThread` is not in the suspended state, the following is generated:

```
Unhandled Exception: The thread 'NewThread' (0x1050) has exited with code 0
(0x0).
System.Threading.ThreadStateException: Thread is not user-suspended; it can
not be resumed.
```

The fact that the ThreadException event does not handle all exceptions that occur in an application domain reinforces the need for robust error handling using try/catch blocks.

12.5 ASYNCHRONOUS DELEGATES

Suppose that you wanted to write a method that might be executed synchronously or asynchronously, depending on what was required at the time. In the following example AMethod may be executed directly, synchronously, or asynchronously using a delegate:

```
. . .
delegate void ADelegate();
private void AMethod()
{
  int Worker,Complete;
  ThreadPool.GetAvailableThreads(out Worker,out Complete);
  string Line;
  if (Thread.CurrentThread.Name == null)
  {
    Line = "{null}";
  }
  else
  {
    Line = Thread.CurrentThread.Name;
  }
  Line += " ";
  Line += Thread.CurrentThread.GetHashCode().ToString();
  Line += " ";
  Line += Worker.ToString();
  MessageBox.Show(Line);
}
private void Test()
{
  AMethod();
  ADelegate MyDelegate = new ADelegate(AMethod);

  MyDelegate();

  MyDelegate.BeginInvoke(null,null);
}
. . .
```

Both the Visual Basic .NET and C# compilers produce methods to support asynchronous execution of delegates. Consider the following example:

```
public class SimpleDelegate
{
  public delegate void ASimpleDelegate();
}
```

This declares a delegate that accepts no parameters and does not return a value. Figure 12.2 shows the disassembled view of the `SimpleDelegate` class. Notice that `BeginInvoke`, `EndInvoke`, and `Invoke` are added to `ASimpleDelegate`.

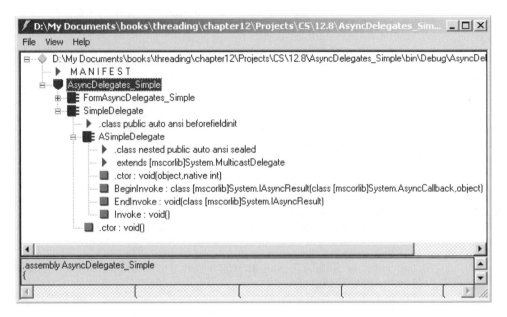

Figure 12.2 Disassembled view of the `SimpleDelegate` class

Also notice the signature of the `BeginInvoke` method. In our example at the beginning of this section we pass in `Nothing`/`null` for the two parameters. In the next section we will discuss `IAsyncResult` and `AsyncCallback`.

BeginInvoke   `BeginInvoke` is a compiler-generated method that allows a delegate to be executed asynchronously. This is accomplished using the `ThreadPool` class.

One major difference between direct invocation of a delegate and using `BeginInvoke` is that `BeginInvoke` cannot be used when multiple targets are involved. This means that multiple methods cannot be associated with a delegate that will be executed asynchronously. The following example causes an exception to be raised:

```
ADelegate MyDelegate = new ADelegate(AMethod);
MyDelegate += new ADelegate(ADifferentMethod);
MyDelegate.BeginInvoke(null,null);
```

12.5.1   EndInvoke

There are many times that a method needs to return a value or provide output parameters. This is a little more complex when dealing with asynchronous execution. To retrieve the results we must use the `EndInvoke` method. The compiler generates `EndInvoke`, just as it generates `BeginInvoke`.

EndInvoke   EndInvoke is a compiler-generated method that is used to retrieve the return value and/or any output parameters of an asynchronous delegate.

This means that the signature of the EndInvoke method depends on the signature of the delegate it is associated with. In the following example the EndInvoke method accepts two parameters and returns a string:

```
. . .
Delegate Function TestDelegate(ByRef state As Object) As String

Private Function TestMethod(ByRef state As Object) As String
  Dim ThreadHashCode As String
  ThreadHashCode = Thread.CurrentThread.GetHashCode().ToString()
  state = " State: Testmethod " + ThreadHashCode
  Return "ReturnValue: Returned From TestMethod "
End Function
Private Sub Test()
  Dim MyDelegate As TestDelegate
  MyDelegate = New TestDelegate(AddressOf TestMethod)
  Dim state As New Object()
  Dim AsyncResults As IAsyncResult
  AsyncResults = MyDelegate.BeginInvoke(state, Nothing, Nothing)
  Dim ReturnValue As String
  ReturnValue = MyDelegate.EndInvoke(state, AsyncResults)
  Trace.Write(ReturnValue)
  Trace.WriteLine(state.ToString())
End Sub
. . .
```

EndInvoke will always accept one more parameter than the delegate it is associated with and have the same return value as that delegate. The additional parameter is an object that supports IAsyncResult.

> **TIP**   If the compiler tells you that "No overload for method 'EndInvoke' takes 'X' arguments" where *X* is the number of arguments you are attempting to use, it is likely because the parameters of the delegate are not declared as byref or ref. The compiler rightly assumes that it does not have to deal with values being returned if the parameter is not marked as a reference.

BeginInvoke returns an instance of an object that supports IAsyncResult. That return value should be passed to EndInvoke to retrieve any out parameters and to determine the return value.

EndInvoke is a blocking call. That means that it will not return until the delegate instance it is associated with completes execution. The thread that calls EndInvoke will stop executing until EndInvoke returns. An alternative is to use AsyncCallback.

12.5.2   AsyncCallback

AsyncCallback is a means of associating a delegate with the asynchronous delegate. When the asynchronous delegate completes its execution, the method associated with AsyncCallback is invoked. That method can then call EndInvoke and retrieve output values or the return code. In the following code example, we start execution of MyDelegate in the TestCallback method. When we call BeginInvoke we pass in CompleteCb as the second parameter. The method associated with CompleteCb, Complete, is executed as soon as TestMethod completes its execution.

```
Private Sub TestCallback()
  Dim state As Object = ""
  Dim TheAsyncResult As IAsyncResult
  Dim MyDelegate As TestDelegate
  MyDelegate = New TestDelegate(AddressOf TestMethod)
  Dim CompleteCb As AsyncCallback
  CompleteCb = New AsyncCallback(AddressOf Complete)
  TheAsyncResult = MyDelegate.BeginInvoke(state, CompleteCb, Nothing)
  Trace.WriteLine("Exiting TestCallback")
End Sub

Private Sub Complete (ByVal TheAsyncResult As IAsyncResult)
  Dim TheResults As AsyncResult = CType(TheAsyncResult, AsyncResult)
  Dim ReturnValue As String
  Dim state As Object = ""
  Dim MyDelegate As TestDelegate
  MyDelegate = CType(TheResults.AsyncDelegate, TestDelegate)
  ReturnValue = MyDelegate.EndInvoke(state, TheAsyncResult)
  Trace.Write(ReturnValue)
  Trace.WriteLine(CType(state, String))
End Sub
```

Complete is invoked as soon as the asynchronous execution is complete. It calls EndInvoke and retrieves both the output parameters and the return value of TestMethod.

The last parameter in the BeginInvoke method is an object that is passed through to the IAsyncResult object. It is available from the AsyncResult object by accessing the AsyncState property.

12.6 CREATING AND INVOKING DYNAMIC DELEGATES

Suppose you know that at some point you need to execute one of five delegates. One way to do that would be to create a large case statement and create each of the delegates. Another alternative is to use the CreateDelegate method of the Delegate class. CreateDelegate allows for late binding. It allows a developer to determine at runtime what method is associated with a particular delegate, along with an optional target. The target is the same as the target from the previous sections in this chapter; it is an instance of a class that the method belongs to. In the following example the target is the current class, referenced by the this keyword:

```
. . .
void TestMethod4()
{
 StackTrace MyTrace=new StackTrace ();
 Trace.WriteLine(MyTrace.GetFrame(0).GetMethod().Name);
}
delegate void TestDelegate();
private void buttonTest_Click(object sender, System.EventArgs e)
{
 Delegate MyDelegate;
 string[] Methods = { "TestMethod0", "TestMethod1" , "TestMethod2",
"TestMethod3","TestMethod4"};
 Random Rnd=new Random(Environment.TickCount);
 string MethodToUse = Methods[Rnd.Next(Methods.Length)];
 MyDelegate = Delegate.CreateDelegate(typeof(TestDelegate),this,MethodToUse
);
 MyDelegate.DynamicInvoke(null);
}
. . .
```

Once the delegate has been created we need some means of invoking it. The `Dynamic-Invoke` method allows for invocation of delegates that are created using the `Create-Delegate` method. It accepts an array of objects as its only parameter. These objects are the parameters, if any, that the method associated with the delegate expects.

CreateDelegate `CreateDelegate` is a static method of the delegate class. It creates a delegate of a specified type and associates it with a target object and a method to invoke.

The late binding referred to in this section refers to binding a method, and option object, to a delegate. It should not be confused with other forms of late binding.

DynamicInvoke `DynamicInvoke` is a method of the delegate class. It allows delegates created using `CreateDelegate` to be invoked. It accepts a single parameter, which is an array of objects that should correspond to the arguments of the method associated with the delegate.

There are many situations where late binding is a good idea. There are things that must be accounted for when doing late binding. One situation that can arise is that the target method referenced does not exist. In that case the following exception is raised:

```
An unhandled exception of type 'System.ArgumentException' occurred in
mscorlib.dll

Additional information: Error binding to target method.
```

The alternative to using `CreateDelegate` and `DynamicInvoke` is to use a large case statement:

```
private void UseCaseStatement()
{
  TestDelegate MyDelegate=null;
  string[] Methods ={"TestMethod0","TestMethod1"};
```

```
Random Rnd=new Random(Environment.TickCount);
string MethodToUse = Methods[Rnd.Next(Methods.Length)];
switch(MethodToUse)
{
  case "TestMethod0":
    MyDelegate = new TestDelegate(TestMethod0);
    break;
  case "TestMethod1":
    MyDelegate = new TestDelegate(TestMethod1);
    break;
}
if (MyDelegate != null)
  MyDelegate();
}
```

One of the biggest advantages of using this approach is that if references to nonexistent methods exist they will be caught at compile time rather than runtime. As with all things there are tradeoffs to both approaches and the situation will dictate which is the better approach.

12.7   SUMMARY

In this chapter we discussed various forms of delegates. Delegates allow for a high degree of flexibility. They allow a reference to a method to be treated like any other variable, without the risks of using function pointers in C++. Delegates are a key part of any asynchronous development in the .NET platform. By understanding delegates in general, you'll find that multithreaded development becomes much simpler.

CHAPTER 13

Exceptions

Exceptions are a flexible and powerful way of handling alternative outcomes. Exceptions are particularly important in multithreaded development. This chapter revisits the concepts behind exceptions and then examines the exceptions that are associated with threads. The chapter ends by examining `UnhandledException` of the application domain object.

Exceptions provide a way to force a condition to be dealt with. Traditional error handling relies on the caller of the method or function checking to see if an error happened. If the caller does not check, the error goes unnoticed. Exceptions force a caller to deal with an unexpected condition. If the caller does not handle the exception, the call stack is searched for an appropriate handler. If none is found, the exception becomes an unhandled exception. When an unhandled exception occurs on a thread, it is terminated.

Appropriate exception handling is an important part of good multithreaded development practices. Time spent adding exception handlers will be more than returned during the debugging and stabilization phases of development.

13.1 EXCEPTIONS REVISITED

Exceptions are a powerful way of handling exception conditions in programs. They have many advantages over other forms of error handling. One area where an exception is very robust is in giving information about the location of the condition that caused the exception to be raised. This can be augmented by chaining exceptions together, essentially re-throwing the exception after adding additional information:

```
Private Sub TestMethod2()
  Try
    TestMethod3()
  Catch ex As Exception
    Dim NewException As Exception
    NewException = New Exception("TestMethod2", ex)
    Throw NewException
  End Try
End Sub
```

In the example, when an exception is caught by a method it creates an exception, adding its own information along with a reference to the original exception. Once the new exception is created, it is thrown.

One of the biggest shortcomings of traditional error handling is the reliance on return values. A typical usage has a function return some value to indicate success and some other value to indicate an error occurred. One variation of this is to have a parameter that returns error code. The following code is typical of that sort of error handling:

```
Private Function OldFashionedFunction() As Boolean
  Dim SomethingBadHappened As Boolean
  SomethingBadHappened = False
  If SomethingBadHappened Then
    Return False
  Else
    Return True
  End If
End Function
```

The caller of this function must check the return value to see if an error occurred. One acceptable form of usage is:

```
  Private Sub OldFashionedCaller()
  If Not OldFashionedFunction() Then
    ' Handle the error
  Else
    ' Things went well
  End If
End Sub
```

One major problem with this approach is that it trusts that the caller will check the return value. All too often the return value, and the possible error, is ignored:

```
Private Sub NotCheckingReturnCode()
  OldFashionedFunction()
End Sub
```

One of the biggest advantages of an exception is that it forces a method to deal with an error or lose control of execution. Additionally, the error-handling routines can be separated from the main code of the method, allowing for more maintainable code:

```
Private Sub ExceptionBasedFunction()
  Dim SomethingBadHappened As Boolean
  SomethingBadHappened = False
  If SomethingBadHappened Then
    Throw New Exception("Something bad happened")
  End If
End Sub
```

13.2 THREAD-RELATED EXCEPTIONS

Now we turn our attention to the exceptions most commonly encountered when doing multithreaded development. Since exceptions are going to occur, it is important that a program handle them in an appropriate way.

13.2.1 The ThreadAbortException class

ThreadAbortException is different from most exceptions in that when the exception is handled, unless ResetAbort is called, exiting the try/catch block causes the method to also exit. Recall from section 4.3.2 that ResetAbort allows Thread-AbortException to behave like other exceptions. ThreadAbortException is raised whenever an instance of the Thread class has the Abort method invoked. It allows a thread method opportunity to perform any needed exit processing.

Most exceptions behave as follows:

```
private void TypicalException()
{
  try
  {
    throw new Exception("Test");
  }
  catch (Exception ex)
  {
    Trace.WriteLine("In Catch");
  }
  finally
  {
    Trace.WriteLine("In Finally");
  }
  Trace.WriteLine("After Try");
}
```

When the exception is generated in the try block, control transfers to the catch clause. After the catch clause has executed, control transfers to the finally block.

After the `finally` block executes, control transfers to the next instruction, in this case a `Trace` statement.

ThreadAbort-Exception   `ThreadAbortException` is raised on a thread whenever `Abort` is called on the instance of the `Thread` class associated with the thread. It allows for a graceful exit.

In the case of `ThreadAbortException` at the point the `try` block exits, the method containing the `try` block also exits. This allows the thread's method to be informed that the thread is in the process of exiting, and alternatively call `ResetAbort`. Listing 13.1 shows the typical flow that occurs when a `ThreadAbortException` is raised.

Listing 13.1   Typical ThreadAbortException flow (C#)

```csharp
public class FormThreadAbortException : System.Windows.Forms.Form
{
. . .
  private Thread TheThread;
  private void ButtonStart_Click(object sender, System.EventArgs e)
  {
    StartTheThread();
  }
  private void StartTheThread()
  {
    TheThread = new Thread(new ThreadStart(ThreadMethod));    ◁──┐ An instance of
    TheThread.IsBackground = true;                                 the Thread class
    TheThread.Name = "TheThread";                                  is created
    TheThread.Start();         ◁──┐ The new thread
  }                                  starts
  private void ThreadMethod()
  {
    try
    {
      while (true)
      {
        Trace.Write("*");
        Thread.Sleep(1000);
      }
    }
    catch (ThreadAbortException ex)
    {

      Trace.WriteLine(ex.ToString());    ◁──┐ A ThreadAbortException
    }                                           occurs
    finally
    {
      Trace.WriteLine("Finally!");
    }
    Trace.WriteLine("This will not be reached");    ◁──┐ This instruction will
  }                                                        not be reached
```

```
    private void ButtonAbortThread_Click(object sender, System.EventArgs e)
    {
      //
      TheThread.Abort();   ◁─┐ A ThreadAbortException
    }                        │ is raised on the thread
. . .
```

If the thread's method calls ResetAbort, ThreadAbortException behaves like
any other exception. An important note: ResetAbort must be called in the catch
clause. If it is called in the finally clause it will have no effect:

```
. . .
catch (ThreadAbortException ex)
{
  Thread.ResetAbort();
  Trace.WriteLine(ex.ToString());
}
finally
{
  Trace.WriteLine("Finally!");
}
Trace.WriteLine("This will be reached");
. . .
```

One version of the Abort method allows an object containing state information to be
passed in. This is passed to the exception listed in the catch clause. The object is available by accessing the ExceptionState property of ThreadAbortException.

13.2.2   The ThreadInterruptedException class

Threads go through many states during their lives. When a thread is sleeping, it enters
WaitSleepJoin. Once in that state, it can leave it several ways; one way is that a
timeout on a sleep statement expires. That is what will happen in listing 13.2.

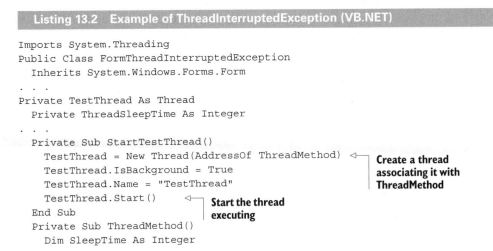

Listing 13.2   Example of ThreadInterruptedException (VB.NET)

```
Imports System.Threading
Public Class FormThreadInterruptedException
  Inherits System.Windows.Forms.Form
. . .
Private TestThread As Thread
  Private ThreadSleepTime As Integer
. . .
  Private Sub StartTestThread()
    TestThread = New Thread(AddressOf ThreadMethod)   ◁─┐ Create a thread
    TestThread.IsBackground = True                       │ associating it with
    TestThread.Name = "TestThread"                       │ ThreadMethod
    TestThread.Start()   ◁─┐ Start the thread
  End Sub                   │ executing
  Private Sub ThreadMethod()
    Dim SleepTime As Integer
```

```
    Try
        While True
            Try
                SyncLock Me
                    SleepTime = ThreadSleepTime
                End SyncLock
                ' Do processing here
                Thread.Sleep(SleepTime)
            Catch ex As System.Threading.ThreadInterruptedException
                Debug.WriteLine(ex.ToString(), "ThreadExceptions")  ⟵
            End Try                                          Catch
        End While                              ThreadInterruptedException
    Catch ex As ThreadAbortException
        Debug.WriteLine(ex.ToString(), "ThreadExceptions")
    Catch ex As Exception
        Debug.WriteLine(ex.ToString(), "ThreadExceptions")
        EventLog.WriteEntry(Application.ProductName, ex.ToString())
    End Try
End Sub
 . . .

Private Sub ButtonInterrupt_Click(. . .) Handles ButtonInterrupt.Click
    TestThread.Interrupt()  ⟵   Signal the thread to
End Sub                          exit the WaitSleepJoin
 . . .                           state
```

Another way that a thread can exit `WaitSleepJoin` is that some resource that is being waited upon becomes available. If some other thread had a lock on the current instance of the object, `Me/this` in listing 13.2, the thread would enter the `WaitSleepJoin` state when it encountered the `SyncLock` statement. Once the other thread released the lock on the current instance, the thread executing `ThreadMethod` would exit the `WaitSleepJoin` state.

The `Join` method is used to wait for a thread to terminate. The thread that calls `Join` on some other thread's object enters `WaitSleepJoin` until a timeout expires or the joined thread terminates.

A more direct way that a thread can leave the `WaitSleepJoin` state is by using the `Interrupt` method. `Interrupt` is a way of forcing a thread to exit the `Wait-SleepJoin` state. This is accomplished by using `Exception`. When a thread has `Interrupt` called on it, if the thread is currently in the `WaitSleepJoin` state, `ThreadInterruptedException` is raised on that thread. If the thread is not in the `WaitSleepJoin` state, as soon as it enters the state `ThreadInterruptedException` will be raised.

Thread-Interrupted-Exception   `ThreadInterruptedException` is raised when a thread is in the `Wait-SleepJoin` state and some other thread calls `Interrupt`, or a thread has previously had `Interrupt` called on it and it enters `WaitSleepJoin`. `ThreadInterruptedException` allows a thread to be awakened so that it can resume its processing.

A thread can call `Interrupt` on itself, causing `ThreadInterruptedException` to be raised as soon as the thread enters a `WaitSleepJoin` state. If `Interrupt` is called numerous times before the thread enters `WaitSleepJoin`, it will only cause the thread to exit the state once. Think of it as a Boolean flag. When that flag is set to true, the thread will exit the `WaitSleepJoin` state and reset the flag to false. Continuing with the flag metaphor, calling `Interrupt` sets the flag to true.

> **TIP** A thread can have `Interrupt` called at all times. The thread must either be unstarted or currently executing for calling `Interrupt` to have any effect. Calling `Interrupt` on a thread that has exited does not generate an error.

In listing 13.2 the only action we take when `ThreadInterruptedException` is raised is to write out a debug statement. Generally speaking, there is no reason to log an event to the event log, or take some other error-tracking steps, for things such as thread interruptions. They are not an error; at most they may be a symptom of a problem. Suppose that logic exists that keeps track of the last time an action was taken. If that action did not happen in a timely manner, the watching thread could call `Interrupt` on the tardy thread. Doing so should be logged as an informational message for later analysis. It may well be that the tardy thread is hanging on some errant logic.

In the example code, we also catch only `ThreadInterruptedException` at the innermost level of the thread's method. Other exceptions will propagate up to the outer exception handler. This is a powerful feature of exception handling. Exception handlers can choose which exceptions they will deal with, and allow another one to deal with all other exceptions.

13.2.3 The ThreadStateException class

Threads transition from one state to another. As we saw in chapters 4 and 5, not all state transitions are allowed. In table 13.1, *Yes* indicates that, if a thread is in the state in the first column and a method or property along the top is called, a `ThreadState-Exception` is raised.

Table 13.1 States and Methods/Properties That Raise the ThreadStateException

State	Start	Abort	Suspend	Resume	Interrupt	Priority	IsBackground
Unstarted			Yes	Yes			
Running	Yes			Yes			
WaitSleepJoin	Yes			Yes			
Suspended	Yes						
Stopped	Yes	Yes	Yes	Yes		Yes	Yes

Notice that `Abort` and `Interrupt` do not cause `ThreadStateException` to be raised regardless of the state of the thread. Other methods, such as `Resume`, cause an exception to be raised unless they are called when the thread is in a certain state.

The reason that some methods can be called without raising an exception and others cannot revolves around race conditions.

ThreadState-Exception `ThreadStateException` is a thread-related exception that is raised whenever an illegal state transition is attempted.

Consider what would happen if `Abort` could not be called on a thread in the `Stopped` state without `ThreadStateException` being raised. Before `Abort` could be called, the thread state would need to be inspected to determine if the thread were in `Stopped`. If it was not, `Abort` could be called. The race condition occurs when the state of the thread changes after the test has been performed.

`Interrupt` can be called at any time. Again, if `Interrupt` were restricted so that it could only be called when a thread was in the `WaitSleepJoin` state, the likelihood of a race condition would be very high. Instead, calling `Interrupt` causes a thread to exit `WaitSleepJoin` if it enters it. If the thread never enters the state, calling `Interrupt` has no effect.

Why do some methods seem to care what state the thread is in and others do not? If the thread can exit a state without the method of interest being called, `ThreadStateException` will not be raised. For example, if a thread is in the `Unstarted` state, the only way it can leave that state is if `Start` is called. Therefore, if the thread is not in that state and `Start` is invoked, it is safe to assume an invalid state transition is being attempted and the runtime raises an exception.

Impact of Race Conditions Methods that rely on a thread being in a certain state raise `ThreadStateException` only if there is no way that the thread can exit the restricted state. For example, a thread that is the `Suspended` state can only exit when `Resume` is called. Thus, any time a thread is not in the `Suspended` state and `Resume` is called it is an invalid state transition.

A counter example is if a thread is in the `WaitSleepJoin` state it is possible, and very likely, that the thread will exit without `Interrupt` being called. With that knowledge, it is reasonable that `Interrupt` cannot require the thread be in the `WaitSleepJoin` state when it is called.

The terminal state for a thread is `Stopped`. When a thread is in the `Stopped` state, only `Abort` and `Interrupt` can be called without raising `ThreadStateException`. This makes a good deal of sense because you wouldn't want to manipulate a thread that is in the `Stopped` state. Since `Abort` generally causes a thread to enter the `Stopped` state, it would be too restrictive to raise an exception when `Abort` is called on a thread in the `Stopped` state.

A `ThreadStateException` can be raised when:

- The thread is in the terminal state, `Stopped`.
- The thread is in a state that can only be exited by calling a method on the thread object, such as `Suspended` and `Unstarted`.

A thread can enter the Suspended state only if Resume is called.

ThreadStateExceptions are not raised when the thread is in a state that it can exit without a method, such as WaitSleepJoin, being called on the thread object. When a method is invoked that has no perceivable effect, such as calling Abort on a thread in the Stopped state, it doesn't make sense to raise an exception.

Care should be taken to handle possible ThreadStateExceptions. Thread-ExceptionEventHandler, covered in section 12.4, is an ideal way of dealing with ThreadStateExceptions if the application involved is a Windows Form.

In general, every interaction with a thread object should be wrapped with a try/catch block. Multiple catch clauses can be used to differentiate between the serious exceptions and the less important ones. Something similar to the following can be used to separate the catching of ThreadStateException and other Exceptions:

```
catch(ThreadStateException ex)
{
. . .
}
catch (Exception ex)
{
. . .
}
```

13.2.4 The SynchronizationLockException class

We saw in chapter 7 how to acquire a lock using the Monitor.Enter method. We also discussed the SynchronizationLockException class. Synchronization-LockException is raised when a method that is intended to be invoked from within a synchronized region is invoked from a region of code that is not synchronized. This means that all methods except for Enter and TryEnter of the Monitor class will generate SynchronizationLockException if invoked from a region of code that is not synchronized.

> **Synchro-nization-LockException** SynchronizationLockException is an exception raised when a Monitor method, other than Enter and TryEnter, is invoked from code that is not in a synchronization block.

An interesting aspect of the following code involves performance counters. Performance counters are an easy way to expose metrics of the actions a program is taking.

```
Imports System.Diagnostics
. . .
Dim PerfCounter As PerformanceCounter
. . .
PerfCounter = New PerformanceCounter("Dennis - Multithreading", "Lock-Count", False)
. . .
Private Sub EnterWaitExit()
  Monitor.Enter(LockObject)
```

```
    PerfCounter.Increment()
    Monitor.Wait(LockObject)
    Monitor.Exit(LockObject)
    PerfCounter.Decrement()
End Sub
```

In this case we increase the counter when `Enter` is called and decrease it when `Exit` is called. If the resulting value is greater than zero, it indicates that `Enter` was called more than `Exit`. This means that a lock on the object is still in force.

> **TIP**   Performance counters are a good way to keep track of the number of times a lock count has been incremented.

As with all methods that can raise exceptions, the `Monitor` methods should be contained within a `try/catch` block. Failure to do so will likely result in an unhandled exception, which causes the thread on which it was raised to be terminated.

> **Behavior of Exit**   Because of non-deterministic finalization in .NET, there may be times that you can call `Exit` more times than `Enter`. You will be able to call `Exit` until the garbage collector collects the garbage. After the collection has occurred, calls to `Exit` will cause `SynchronizationLockException` to be raised. `Pulse`, `PulseAll`, and `Wait` always raise an exception if invoked from an unsynchronized block of code.

To avoid race conditions, no attempt should be made to determine if a lock is currently held. A more robust approach is to call `TryEnter`. If the lock is acquired, a synchronized method can then be invoked, such as `Pulse`. Since calls to `TryEnter` and `Enter` are allowed when the current thread holds the lock, no harm will come from attempting to acquire a lock.

When a lock is no longer required, the number of calls to `Exit` should equal the total of the number of calls to `Enter` and `TryEnter`. Calling `Exit` more times than `Enter` after the lock has been collected will cause `SynchronizationLockException` to be raised. This should be viewed as a logic error.

> **TIP**   `Exit` should be called as soon as possible after `Pulse` and `PulseAll` because in order for a thread to exit the `WaitSleepJoin` state it must reacquire a lock on the object that it was waiting on. If the thread that calls `Pulse` does not release that lock, the thread will not be allowed to exit the `Wait-SleepJoin` state.

The example program for this section allows a user to interact with the `Monitor` locking mechanism to see the effects of invoking methods that require synchronization without having first acquired the lock. The overall flow is described in figure 13.1.

When the user clicks a button (e.g., Wait), a string by the same name is added to a queue that is an instruction for the thread that services that queue. A thread is running with the sole purpose of keeping its instruction queue empty. When it sees an instruction is in the queue, it dequeues it and attempts to process it. This is accomplished by

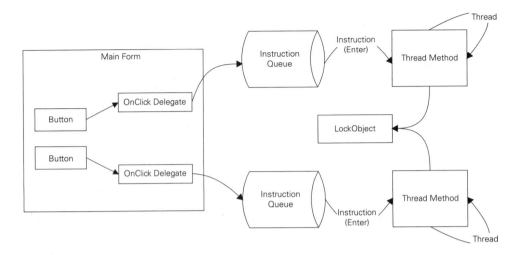

Figure 13.1 The logical flow of the synchronization exception example

using a large switch statement, containing all of the instructions that the thread knows how to process. In this case the thread executes the following statement:

```
Case "Wait"
  Monitor.Wait(LockObject)
```

Multiple threads are required because some methods of the `Monitor` class, such as `Enter`, may not return. If a call were made to `Wait` on the main thread of the application, it would be impossible to call `Pulse`, since the thread would be blocked by the `Wait`. A queue is introduced because the thread servicing the queue may be blocked by an instruction.

13.3 THE APPDOMAIN UNHANDLEDEXCEPTION EVENT

One of the most difficult things to track down is an unhandled exception in a production system. The `AppDomain` object provides an `Event` that is invoked when an unhandled exception is encountered. Invoking the event does not handle the exception; it merely allows the information to be stored to help in diagnosing the problem later. If an unhandled exception occurs on a thread other than the main thread, the user is likely not going to notice. It might be possible to have the application create another thread after having logged that a thread died in an unexpected way. If the main thread encounters an unhandled exception, the application will terminate. It would be appropriate to display a meaningful message to the user as well as log the information to help the support staff diagnose the issue.

Unhandled- `UnhandledException` is an event that allows a delegate of the application
Exception domain object to be invoked when an unhandled exception occurs.

The following code example adds a handler to the UnhandledException event that logs the exception to the event log. This is a good start, but likely a more robust logging mechanism would be needed in a production system.

```
. . .
private void AddUnhandledExceptionHandler()
{
  UnhandledExceptionEventHandler MyHandler;
  MyHandler = new UnhandledExceptionEventHandler(MyExceptionHandler);

  // Add a handler to the UnhandledException event.
  System.AppDomain.CurrentDomain.UnhandledException += MyHandler;
}
private void MyExceptionHandler(object sender , UnhandledExceptionEventArgs e)
{
  Exception TheException;
  TheException = (Exception)e.ExceptionObject;
  if (!EventLog.Exists(Application.ProductName))
  {
    EventLog.CreateEventSource(Application.ProductName, "Application");
  }
  EventLog.WriteEntry(Application.ProductName, "Unhandled Exception: " +
    TheException.ToString(), EventLogEntryType.Error);
}
. . .
```

Once a handler is in place it can be removed using the -= operator in C# and the RemoveHandler statement in VB.NET.

It is important to understand what the user will likely see when an unhandled exception occurs. The best you can hope for is shown in figure 13.2.

While developers find this information very useful, typical business users will not. They likely will not click the Details button and will instead click Continue. After they have clicked the Continue button, they will probably call the support personnel and

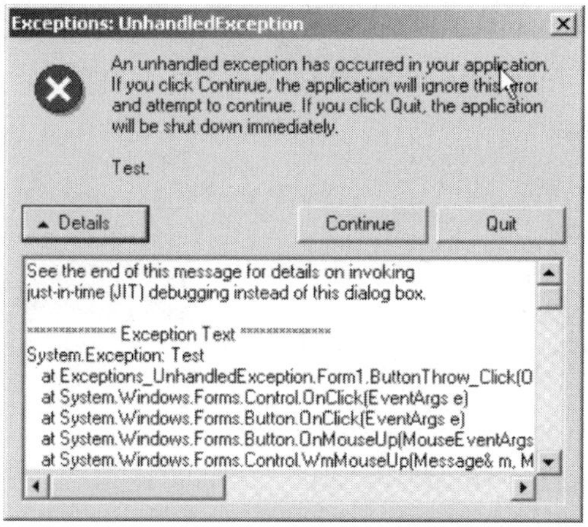

**Figure 13.2
A typical UnhandledException
dialog box**

inform them that they just encountered an error. They will not be able to send anything to the support staff to resolve the issue.

TIP   Use the `UnhandledException` event as a means of logging unhandled exceptions to the event log.

Think about support issues during development. By planning for failure, you can produce a higher quality product. When an issue is encountered, a mechanism will be in place to make resolving those issues much easier. In an ideal world there is no need for error handling and logging, but we do not live in an ideal world. Software often encounters environments that developers never imagined could exist. The software must be prepared to record these events so that issues can be resolved.

13.4   SUMMARY

Exceptions provide a robust way of dealing with error conditions. Since an unhandled exception terminates a thread, it is imperative that complete and thorough error handling be in place. At the very least, an `UnhandledException` handler should be put in place to record the occurrence of an unhandled exception. If time is spent during the early stages of development adding error handling, the overall quality of the product will be much higher. Additionally, as errors are encountered it will be much easier to correct them. The return on investment for adding error handling is very high.

Timers

Timers, a reoccurring event that has a predefined interval, are a common construct, and most Visual Basic programmers have used a timer at some point. Timers meet a common need of performing an operation after a ceratin amount of time has passed. This chapter focuses on timers available in the .NET framework.

14.1 USING WINDOWS FORMS TIMERS

Windows Forms timers are one of the most common kinds of timers. They are simple to use, and for Visual Basic developers the only viable way of seeming to do multiple things at once. This section explores Windows Forms timers, first by examining their background and then how they are implemented in the .NET framework.

14.1.1 How Windows Forms timers are implemented

Most Windows developers are familiar with Windows Forms timers. In Visual Basic version 6.0, and previous versions, the timer was added to a form using a stopwatch icon. The Visual Basic timer has a `Name` property, along with an `Enabled` property that controls if the timer's `Timer` method is invoked at the intervals specified in the `Interval` property.

The Visual Basic timer is implemented using the Win32 API call `SetTimer`. The `SetTimer` API call causes a `WM_TIMER` message to be posted to the associated window's message queue at the interval specified. This is an important characteristic of all

Windows Forms-based timers; they utilize the window's message queue to indicate when the timer's method should be invoked. This means that all timer methods occur on the same thread as the message queue processing method.

Without getting into too much detail of Windows API programming, each Windows application that supports a user interface has a loop in it whose sole purpose is to process messages. This is generally called the message loop. Communication is based on a message being added to a queue that this loop services. When a message is processed, an appropriate method is invoked. All of this is occurring on a single thread. That is why Visual Basic applications that do not use the DoEvents method often stop updating the screen during long-running operations. This emphasizes the single-threaded nature of Visual Basic applications.

Windows Forms Timers A Windows Forms timer is a mechanism for performing operations at regular intervals. It is based on entering a message in the window's message queue.

DoEvents is essentially a recursive call back to the message loop. Once the message queue has been serviced, DoEvents returns to the method that calls it. This brings us to an issue with DoEvents: If a message is processed during the DoEvents call that is long-running, it too will cause the application to become unresponsive. The key point here is that Windows Forms timers are an ideal way of performing operations of short duration that are related to the user interface. Any other use will eventually result in a responsiveness issue.

To see that Windows Forms timers use the message queue, we can add a message filter to our form that looks for the WM_TIMER message. Message filters are a way of restricting, or monitoring, messages. If you wanted to keep an application from responding to an event, one way to do so is to use a message filter. For our needs we simply want to know that a particular message is about to be processed.

Message Filters A message filter is a class that implements the IMessageFilter interface. The filters allow for detection and selective removal of the messages that the loop processes.

To add a message filter, you must first create a class that supports IMessageFilter. This class must provide a Boolean function named PreFilterMessage that accepts a reference to a message. The return value of PreFilterMessage determines if a message is processed or filtered. When the return value is true, the message will not be processed; if it returns false, the message will be processed. To add a message filter we simply pass an instance of the class that supports IMessageFilter to the Application object's AddMessageFilter method, as seen in the following example code:

```
Filter = new ClassTimerMessageFilter(textBoxFeedback);
Application.AddMessageFilter(Filter);
```

ClassTimerMessageFilter supports IMessageFilter. The constructor accepts an instance of a control object, and we use that instance to add a line to the textbox indicating that a WM_TIMER message is about to be processed.

When a `WM_TIMER` message is processed, the Windows Forms timer invokes the `Tick` delegate. This is a multicast delegate that can cause multiple methods to be executed. To add a delegate, use the += operator in C# and the `AddHandler` statement in Visual Basic .NET. The following example adds an event handler:

```
timer1.Tick += new EventHandler(TickHandler);
```

Since Visual Basic .NET does not currently support operator overloading, it cannot use the += operator to add a handler.

14.1.2   Controlling Windows Forms timers

Creating a Windows Forms-based timer is very easy. The toolbox in Visual Studio includes an easy-to-use `Timer` control. Figure 14.1 shows the location of the Windows Forms timer in the toolbox.

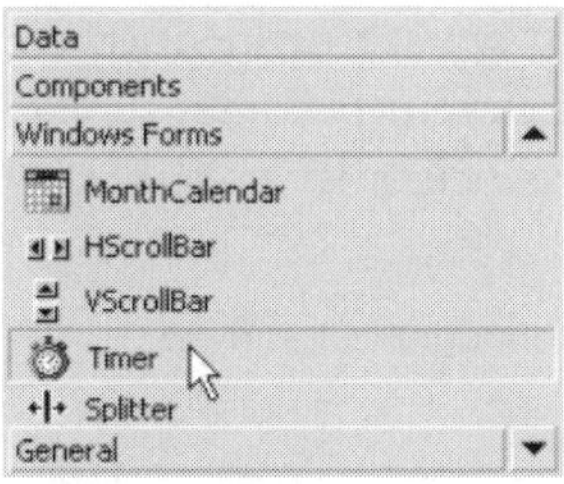

Figure 14.1
Selecting the Windows Forms timer from the toolbox

Using the timer control from the toolbox is the easiest way to add a timer to the form. This is basically the same as adding a timer in Visual Basic 6.

Dragging and dropping the timer icon onto a form will create the first two lines of the code that follows:

```
. . .
Friend WithEvents Timer1 As System.Windows.Forms.Timer
. . .
Me.Timer1 = New System.Windows.Forms.Timer(Me.components)
. . .
Private Sub Timer1_Tick(ByVal sender As System.Object,
   ByVal e As System.EventArgs) _
     Handles Timer1.Tick
. . .
```

Once a timer is added to a form we need to interact with it. A timer is a simple device. It contains a switch that indicates whether or not it is active. This is exposed as a property called `Enabled`. To turn on the timer, simply set `Enabled` to `True`:

```
Timer1.Enabled = True
```

The frequency of the timer is important. A timer's interval should be set to be frequent enough so that an event of interest does not pass unnoticed, but it should not be set so small as to flood the message queue with `WM_TIMER` messages. To control the frequency of a timer, we use the `Interval` property, which accepts an integer value that indicates the number of milliseconds to pause between raising the `Tick` event.

Interval   Interval is an integer property of the Timer class that controls the amount of time, in milliseconds, before the raising of the Tick event.

The Tick event is how the timer makes its presence known. In the previous example the method Timer1_Tick is executed every time the Tick event is raised on the Timer1 instance of the timer class. Event handlers can be added and removed as needed. To add a handler, you must first add a method with the same signature as Timer1_Tick in the example. That method will be invoked every time the Tick event is raised. Since Tick is a multicast delegate, multiple methods can be associated with it. The same method can be associated and removed multiple times.

Tick   The Tick event is raised whenever the timer object is enabled and the specified interval expires. Multiple event handlers can be associated with the same Tick event.

To add a Tick event handler, declare an object of type EventHandler and pass in the address of the method to be invoked when the event becomes signaled. In Visual Basic .NET use the AddHandler keyword to associate EventHandler with the event it is to handle:

```
Dim Handler As New EventHandler(AddressOf MessageBoxHandler)
AddHandler Timer1.Tick, Handler
```

To disassociate a method from an event, use the RemoveHandler keyword:

```
Dim Handler As New EventHandler(AddressOf MessageBoxHandler)
RemoveHandler Timer1.Tick, Handler
```

The Enabled property can be used to control if the Tick event is raised. Two methods can alternatively be used to control the Enabled state of the timer object. The Start method causes the Enabled property to be set to True. The Stop method causes the Enabled property to be set to False. The following code demonstrates using the Start method:

```
Timer1.Start()
Trace.Assert(Timer1.Enabled = True)
```

Calling Start or setting Enabled to True when the timer is already in the Enabled state has no effect. It does not cause the timer to start over. If the timer is switched from enabled to disabled and then back to being enabled, the interval will start over.

Start   Start is a method of the Timer class that ensures that the Enabled property has a value of True.

This brings us to an important topic. Windows Forms-based timers should not be viewed as high-precision timers. Just because the interval is in milliseconds, it is not safe to assume that the precision of the timer is also in milliseconds. Since the timer is based on entering a message into the message queue, the time for that message to be processed may not be predictable. If some other message monopolizes the queue, the time between the processing of the WM_TIMER message will not be the same as the interval.

Stop   Stop is a method of the Timer class that ensures that the Enabled property has a value of False.

Windows Forms-based timers are an easy way to update the user interface. Since they are message-based, the updates to the user interface are on the same thread as the controls. This means the topics discussed in the next chapter, such as InvokeRequired and Invoke, are not necessary. If the task involved is about displaying information to the user, then a Windows Forms-based timer is likely a good fit.

14.2   SYSTEM. TIMERS. TIMER

The System.Timers.Timer class, often referred to as a server-based timer, is similar to the Windows Forms-based timer. Server timers offer all of the features that message-based timers offer, along with features not available when using message-based timers. While the two types of timers are very close in function, there are a few differences in how they are used. When a server-based timer becomes signaled, it raises the Elapsed event. Methods are associated with the event using an ElapsedEvent-Handler object. Figure 14.2 shows how to select a server-based timer.

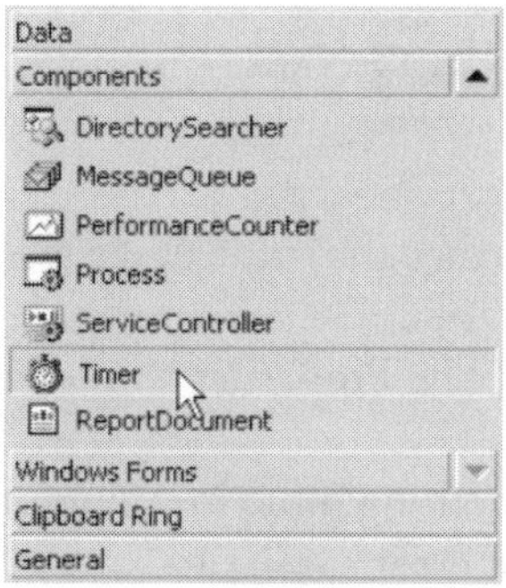

Figure 14.2
Selecting the server-based timer from the toolbox

Server-based timers are added in the same way message-based timers are. Instead of selecting the Windows Forms section of the toolbox, select the Components section.

14.2.1   Using System.Timers.Timer in Windows Forms

One major difference between a server-based and a message-based timer is the SynchronizingObject property. SynchronizingObject is used to automatically handle thread-safety issues associated with Windows Forms. Recall that Windows Forms are not thread-safe. This means that interacting with a control on a form must occur on the same thread that created it.

If an object that implements ISynchronizeInvoke is associated with SynchronizingObject then the Invoke method of the object is used. The end result is that the delegate is invoked on the SynchronizingObject's thread. This removes any concern about thread-safety, but also means that the method associated with ElapsedEventHandler executes on the form's main thread. Other messages will not be processed while the method is being executed. This may result in poor application performance. When a server-based timer is associated with `SynchronizingObject`, it suffers from the same shortcomings a message-based timer suffers from. The power of server-based timers becomes evident when they are not associated with a synchronization object.

14.2.2 System.Timers.Timer in Windows system services

One use of a server timer is in a system service, and .NET makes it very easy to create system services. While this book is not focused on enterprise application development, we will briefly go over the steps involved in creating a system service (figure 14.3), mainly because services and threads are often closely related.

When creating a project, simply select Windows Service from the list of templates.

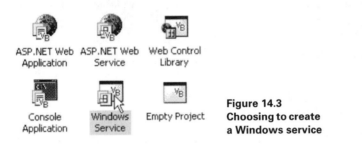

ASP.NET Web Application ASP.NET Web Service Web Control Library

Console Application Windows Service Empty Project

Figure 14.3
Choosing to create
a Windows service

This will create a shell of a system service. Next, change the name of the service to something other than the default Service1. To do this, double-click on the file Service1.vb or Service1.cs in the Solution Explorer window. The Properties window should now contain something that looks like figure 14.4.

After changing the name of the service to something more meaningful, attempt to recompile the solution. Often you will receive an error similar to "Sub Main was not found in TimerWebMonitorService.Service1." This error indicates that the startup object no longer exists in the project; to correct the error, right-click on the project in the Solution Explorer window and select Properties. That should bring up a dialog box that looks similar to the one shown in figure 14.5. Select the correct startup object, in this case `TimerWebMonitorService`.

Configurations	
⊞ (DynamicProperties)	
Design	
(Name)	**TimerWebMonitorService**
Misc	
AutoLog	True
CanHandlePowerEvent	False
CanPauseAndContinue	**True**
CanShutdown	False
CanStop	True
ServiceName	**TimerWebMonitorService**

Figure 14.4
Service configuration screen

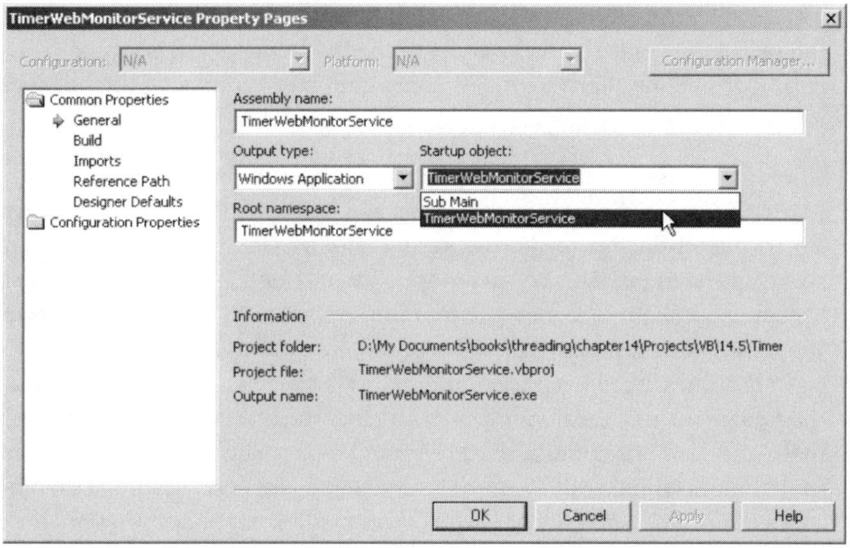

Figure 14.5   Visual Basic project Property page

You should then be able to compile the solution. If you receive an error, such as "Type Service1 is not defined," double-click the error message and change the incorrect line, replacing `Service1` with the name of the class that contains the service. This is generally located at the top of the file that contains the error. In this case, replacing `Service1` with `TimerWebMonitorService` corrects the error.

Once the solution compiles, the next step is to add an installer, which makes it possible to install the service. The installer works with `InstallUtil.exe`, located in the Microsoft.NET directory under the Windows directory. The following command will help in locating `InstallUtil.exe`:

```
cd %windir%\Microsoft.NET\Framework
```

To add an installer, right-click on the design view of the service and select Add Installer. Adding an installer adds a ProjectInstaller.vb or ProjectInstaller.cs to the solution. Once the ProjectInstaller file has been added, it needs to be modified. The following code modification must be made to indicate the type of account the service should use to log in:

```
'
'ServiceProcessInstaller1
'
Me.ServiceProcessInstaller1.Password = Nothing
Me.ServiceProcessInstaller1.Username = Nothing
' Added to indicate that the service should use the local system account
ServiceProcessInstaller1.Account =
    ServiceProcess.ServiceAccount.LocalSystem
```

This lets the installer know that the service should use the local system account. Once the installer is added and the changes made, the service is ready to be compiled and installed. The installation process uses a command similar to the following:

```
c:installutil TimerWebMonitorService.exe
```

The command will vary based upon the location of the InstallUtil.exe program.

At this point the service can be installed, although it doesn't do anything useful. To add functionality to the service, we modify `OnStart`, `OnStop`, and any other virtual/Overridable methods of interest in the `ServiceBase` class.

Let us return to the web site monitor example we discussed in previous chapters. Recall that the purpose of the web site monitor was to detect when a web server was in an unhealthy state. This is accomplished by retrieving the contents of a dynamic page that represents the health of the web server at the time when the page was produced. If that page does not contain some expected string, such as OK, it is an indication that something is wrong with the web server and that support personnel should be involved.

In our earlier examples we used a Windows Forms application to monitor a web site. A system service is a much better vehicle for a monitoring application. Since system services can be set to start as soon as the computer starts up, and can be configured to execute under various types of accounts, they are a better way of containing a monitoring application.

System services provide a process in which code can execute. To perform something meaningful, the service must either respond to requests or have a thread of timers that performs the desired actions. In our case we use the `Timer`, an instance of the `System.Timers.Timer` class.

```
Private MyTimer As System.Timers.Timer
```

The `MyTimer` member needs to be initialized and configured. This is best performed in the `InitializeComponent` method. Along with creating an instance of the timer, we also need to create an instance of the web monitoring class. This class contains all logic relating to retrieving information from a web server.

```
WSM = New WebSiteMonitor()
MyTimer = New Timer()
AddHandler MyTimer.Elapsed, New ElapsedEventHandler(AddressOf Check)
```

The OnStart method is invoked when the system service starts. This is where configuration settings are read and the timer started.

```
Protected Overrides Sub OnStart(ByVal args() As String)
  Try
    'Read Configuration Settings
    . . .
    MyTimer.Interval = WaitTimeInMinutes * 60000
    MyTimer.Start()
  Catch ex As Exception
    EventLog.WriteEntry(ex.Message, EventLogEntryType.Error)
  End Try
End Sub
```

The `OnStop` method is invoked when the service is being stopped. Since our service is timer-based, the only operation we must perform is to stop the timer.

```
Protected Overrides Sub OnStop()
    MyTimer.Stop()
End Sub
```

Additionally, `OnPause` and `OnContinue` can be overridden to allow the service to be paused and restarted at a later time.

```
Protected Overrides Sub OnPause()
  MyTimer.Stop()
End Sub

Protected Overrides Sub OnContinue()
  MyTimer.Start()
End Sub
```

To support the `OnPause` and `OnContinue` functionally, ensure that the service's properties have `CanPauseAndContinue` set to true.

14.3   SYSTEM. THREADING. TIMER

The `Threading` namespace also contains a `Timer` object. This timer is `Thread-Pool`-based. A thread in the `ThreadPool` invokes a supplied delegate at regular intervals. In some ways it is less flexible than some of the other timers we have discussed in this chapter. Once the delegate associated with the timer is set, it cannot be changed. The time period, or interval, of the timer is set during construction of the timer, and can be changed later using the `Change` method. One feature the threading timer offers that other timers do not is the differentiation between the first time period and all subsequent ones. When creating the timer object, keep in mind that the constructor accepts four parameters:

- The delegate to invoke when the time period expires
- An object to pass to the delegate on each invocation
- A parameter to control the time span from instantiation to the first execution of the delegate
- A parameter to control the time between the first execution of the delegate and the second execution, and so on

To create `Threading Timer`, first add a variable to be the instance of the timer:

```
static System.Threading.Timer ThreadingTimer;
```

Next add the logic to create an instance of the timer and associate it with the method to be invoked during each interval:

```
[STAThread]
static void Main(string[] args)
{
  int FirstTime = 1000;
  int TimeBetween = 4000;
  TimerCallback TheCallback;
  TheCallback= new TimerCallback(callback);
  ThreadingTimer = new Timer(TheCallback,null,FirstTime,TimeBetween);
  Thread.Sleep(System.Threading.Timeout.Infinite);
}
```

Next add the method that is associated with the callback delegate:

```
static void callback(object stateInfo)
{
  int Worker,Complete;
  ThreadPool.GetAvailableThreads(out Worker,out Complete);
  Console.Write(DateTime.Now.ToString());
  Console.Write( " " );
  Console.Write(Worker.ToString());
  Console.Write( " " );
  Console.WriteLine(Complete.ToString());
}
```

The Threading.Timer class does not contain a Stop or Start method. Nor does it contain an Enabled property. To control the stopping and starting of the timer, you must use the Change method. For example, calling Change with Timeout.Infinite as a value for both parameters has the same effect as calling Stop on one of the other timers. To resume the timer, call Change with a value other than Timeout.Infinite.

14.4   SUMMARY

Timers are an easy way of having an event occur at regular intervals. Choosing the right timer for a given situation is important. In general, if the timer is to update a user interface, the Windows Forms-based timer is likely the easiest and most familiar to deal with. If the timer is not being used in a Windows Form, one of the server-based timers must be used. Care should be taken to ensure that the work being performed is not greater than the interval associated with the timer. If that is the case, and a server-based timer is being used, multiple instances of the method associated with the timer will be executing.

C H A P T E R   1 5

Windows Forms and multiple threads

Windows Forms provide for a rich user experience. They provide the next step in Win32 application development. Unlike previous environments, .NET makes it relatively easy to produce high-quality applications. One way that a Windows Forms application can be enriched is through the use of multiple threads.

15.1 MULTITHREADED-RELATED ISSUES

The code wizards in Visual Studio do the majority of the work in creating the shell of a Windows Form application. It is important to understand what they do and why they do it. In this section we analyze the code that the wizard produces.

15.1.1 Introduction to the STAThread attribute

Listing 15.1 shows the essential parts of a simple Windows application. This application doesn't do much; it just displays a popup dialog box showing the apartment (discussed in-depth in chapter 16) state of the main thread.

Listing 15.1   Windows Forms execute in an STA (C#)

```
/// <summary>
/// The main entry point for the application.
/// </summary>
[STAThread]                    ❶ Creates a single-threaded
static void Main()                apartment
{
  Application.Run(new Form1());
}

private void Form1_Load(object sender, System.EventArgs e)
{
  string sAptState;
  ApartmentState MyState;
  MyState=Thread.CurrentThread.ApartmentState;    ❷ Returns the
  sAptState=MyState.ToString();                      ApartmentState of
  MessageBox.Show(sAptState);                        the current thread
}
```

❶ Notice the [STAThread] attribute. This ensures that the main thread uses a single-threaded apartment (STA). The reason is that the controls that a Windows Forms application uses require an apartment to restrict access. Chapter 16 discusses apartments in detail; for now think of an apartment as a synchronization mechanism. When one is marked as being an STA, access to things contained within that apartment are serialized using a message queue.

❷ We can determine what sort of apartment a thread is executing in by using the ApartmentState property which gets and sets a value of type System.Threading.ApartmentState. The ApartmentState enumeration contains three values: MTA, STA, and Unknown. If the value has not been set, using either the ApartmentState property or one of the apartment state attributes, the value defaults to Unknown. When the message box in listing 15.1 is displayed, it will look something like the image in figure 15.1.

While the output of the program isn't very interesting there's a lot to be learned here. When a Windows Forms project is created, the [STAThread] attribute is automatically included because many of the controls used on a Windows

Figure 15.1
The dialog box that is displayed when the code example in listing 15.1 executes

Form are COM objects. When a Component Object Model (COM) object is used in the .NET platform, the system takes care of the integration for you. However, since they are COM objects and require an STA to execute correctly, the template of the Windows Form application sets the apartment of the main thread to be an STA. We'll discuss COM integration in detail in chapter 16.

VB.NET doesn't include the STAThread attribute in the code, yet another example of how VB.NET does many things for the developer behind the scenes. Listing 15.2 contains the VB.NET code that also displays a dialog box very similar to that in figure 15.1.

```
Private Sub Form1_Load(ByVal sender As System.Object,
                       ByVal e As System.EventArgs) Handles MyBase.Load
  Dim sAptState As String
  Dim MyState As ApartmentState
  MyState = Thread.CurrentThread.ApartmentState
  sAptState = MyState.ToString()
  MessageBox.Show(sAptState)
End Sub
```

When you look at the project, you'll notice there is no Main method, as there is in listing 15.1. However, if we open the produced executable with the MSIL disassembler (listing 15.3) we'll see that one is produced.

```
.method public hidebysig static void  Main() cil managed
{
  .entrypoint
  .custom instance void [mscorlib]System.STAThreadAttribute::.ctor() = (
    01 00 00 00 )
  // Code size       14 (0xe)
  .maxstack  8
  IL_0000:  nop
  IL_0001:  newobj     instance void WindowsFormsShellProgram.Form1::.ctor()
  IL_0006:  call       void [
    System.Windows.Forms]System.Windows.Forms.Application::Run(class [
    System.Windows.Forms]System.Windows.Forms.Form)
  IL_000b:  nop
  IL_000c:  nop
  IL_000d:  ret
} // end of method Form1::Main
```

The MSIL call to the
STAThreadAttribute
constructor

The code in listing 15.3 is essentially the same MSIL that's produced by the Main method of the C# program in listing 15.1. It's not important that you understand all of the MSIL in listing 15.3; the main thing to take away from this is that the main thread of managed Windows applications developed using the .NET framework uses an STA to control interaction with their controls.

15.1.2 Threading-related issues

To see how these issues relate to using multiple threads with a Windows Form we'll use a simple example. The high-level flow is presented in figure 15.2. The example consists of a user-controllable number of threads adding a selected number of elements to a common list box. While those items are being added, a different thread is deleting items.

Figure 15.2   High-level flow of the list box example

A situation where this might occur would be having threads inform the user of their action. The alternative would be to have a single thread tasked with monitoring the status of the other threads. Figure 15.3 shows our example application.

The form contains several checkboxes, two numeric up/down controls, a Start button, a status bar, and a single list box. The Invoke checkbox controls if the list box's `Invoke` method is used to pass messages to the control. The Keep Trying checkbox tells the application to repeatedly invoke the method associated with the Start button. The Add At Top checkbox controls the location where new items are inserted into the list box control. The Delete At Top checkbox controls the location they are deleted from. The numeric up/down controls control how many elements are inserted in the list box. Each of these controls is discussed in greater detail in the following sections.

Delete-related elements

When the form loads, a single thread is created that is tasked with deleting entries from the list box. Listing 15.4 shows the delete-related code elements.

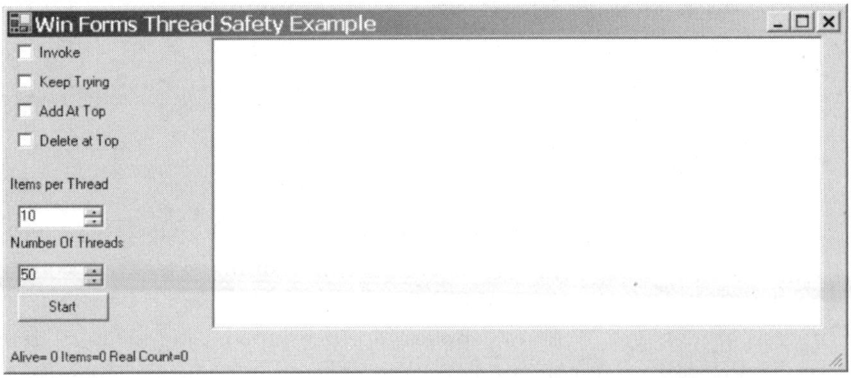

Figure 15.3   Our example application. The region on the right is a list box.

Listing 15.4   Delete-related methods and delegate (VB.NET)

```
Private Sub Form1_Load( . . .) Handles MyBase.Load
    Thread.CurrentThread.Name = "Main"
    Timer1.Enabled = True
    Timer1.Interval = 1000
    DeleteThread = New Thread(AddressOf DelThM)
    DeleteThread.Name = "Delete Thread"
    DeleteThread.IsBackground = True
    DeleteThread.Start()
End Sub
```
❶ DeleteThread is created and started

```
Private Delegate Sub DelEleDeleg()
```
❸ The delete delegate is created and invoked

```
Private Sub DelThM()
  While True
    If ListBox1.Items.Count = 0 Then
      Thread.Sleep(10)
    End If
    If ListBox1.Items.Count > 0 Then
      If checkBoxInvoke.Checked Then
        Dim myDelegate As DelEleDeleg
        myDelegate = New DelEleDeleg(AddressOf DelEle)
        ListBox1.Invoke(myDelegate)
      Else
        DelEle()
      End If
    End If
  End While
End Sub
```
❷ DelThM is the main method of DeleteThread

❸ The delete delegate is created and invoked

❹ The DelEle method is called directly

```
Private Sub DelEle()
  Dim rnd As New Random(System.Environment.TickCount)
  Dim ItemToDelete As Integer = -1
  Dim ItemCountAtDelete As Integer = -1
  If ListBox1.Items.Count > 0 Then
    If checkBoxDeleteAtTop.Checked Then
      ItemToDelete = 0
    Else
      ItemCountAtDelete = ListBox1.Items.Count
      ItemToDelete = rnd.Next(ItemCountAtDelete)
    End If
    If (ItemToDelete >= 0) Then
      ListBox1.Items.RemoveAt(ItemToDelete)
    End If
  End If
End Sub
```
❺ An element from ListBoxl is deleted

❶ To ensure there is always one, and only one, delete thread running at any given time, we create the instance of DeleteThread when the form first loads. We begin by creating a new instance of the Thread class, associating it with DelThM. We then set the thread to be a background thread and invoke its `Start` method. To help us keep track of our threads, we set the main thread's name to Main.

❷ `DelThM` serves as the main method for the delete thread. It is similar to most thread methods we've used in that it contains a loop. Each iteration of the loop starts with a check to see if there are any items in the `ListBox1`'s `Item` collection. If there aren't, the thread sleeps for 10 milliseconds. Next another check is performed to see if there are items in the `Items` collection, if there are, an element is deleted from the list box.

❸ If the Invoke checkbox is checked an instance of the `DelEleDeleg` delegate is created and associated with the `DelEle` method. This instance of the delegate is then passed to `ListBox1`'s `Invoke` method. This ensures that the delegate is executed on the same thread as the thread that created `ListBox1`.

❹ If the Invoke checkbox is not checked the `DelEle` method is invoked directly. This means that the deletion will occur on the `DeleteThread` rather than on the thread on which `ListBox1` was originally created.

❺ The `DelEle` method deletes one element from `ListBox1`. If the Delete At Top checkbox is checked, the first element in the list box will be deleted. Otherwise, a random element will be deleted from the list box. By selecting Delete At Top and Add At Top, you create a hot spot of activity.

Insert-related elements

Along with the deleting thread there are a user-controllable number of adding threads. When the user clicks the Start button on the form the number of threads created is based on the value in the Number Of Threads numeric up/down control. In figure 15.3 the number of threads is set to 50. Each thread in turn adds the number of items specified in the Items Per Thread numeric up/down control. In figure 15.3 the value is 10 items. This means that 500 (50 times 10) items will be added to the list box. Listing 15.5 contains the example code related to adding elements to the list box.

Listing 15.5   List box adding related code elements (VB.NET)

```
Private Sub Button1_Click(. . .) Handles Button1.Click    ❶
  If (CountOfDifferences > 0) Then
    StatusBar1.Text = "Differences Exist!"
    Exit Sub
  End If
  Dim NumThreads As Integer
  NumThreads = numericUpDownNumThreads.Value
  ReDim Threads(NumThreads - 1)
  Dim i As Integer
  For i = 0 To Threads.Length - 1
    Threads(i) = New Thread(AddressOf ThreadMethod)
    Threads(i).Name = "Add Thread " + i.ToString()
    Threads(i).IsBackground = True
```

❶ **Defines the method that is invoked when the user clicks Start**

❷ **Changes the size of the threads array**

❸ **Sets each element of the threads array**

```
      Next
      For i = 0 To Threads.Length - 1    ❹  Starts all inserting
        Threads(i).Start()                    threads
      Next
      Thread.Sleep(1000)
      StatusBar1.Text = "Started"
    End Sub
                                          ❺  Defines the Main method
    Private Sub ThreadMethod()                of the insert threads
      Dim i As Integer
      Dim rnd As New Random(System.Environment.TickCount)
      Thread.Sleep(rnd.Next(5000))
      Dim NumItems As Integer = numericUpDownItemsPerThread.Value
      For i = 0 To NumItems - 1
        If checkBoxInvoke.Checked Then
          Dim myDelegate As AddEleDel
          myDelegate = New AddEleDel(AddressOf AddElement)    ❻  Uses a
          Dim Parms As Object()                                  delegate
          Parms = New Object() {i, Thread.CurrentThread.Name}
          ListBox1.Invoke(myDelegate, Parms)
        Else
          AddElement(i, Thread.CurrentThread.Name)  ❼  Otherwise calls
        End If                                          AddElement directly
      Next
    End Sub

    Delegate Sub AddEleDel(ByVal i As Integer, ByVal s As String)  ❻  Uses a
    Private Sub AddElement(ByVal i As Integer, ByVal s As String)      delegate
      Dim TmpString As String
      TmpString = s
      TmpString += " " + Thread.CurrentThread.Name
      TmpString += " " + i.ToString()
      If checkBoxInsertAtTop.Checked Then
        ListBox1.Items.Insert(0, TmpString)
      Else
        ListBox1.Items.Add(TmpString)
      End If
    End Sub
```

❶ When the user clicks the Start button the Button1_Click method is invoked. The
parameters have been removed for readability's sake. The method first examines the
value of CountOfDifferences. If the value is greater than zero the method exits.
We discuss CountOfDifferences in the next section.

❷ The Threads variable is an array of System.Threading.Thread objects. It is
resized based on the value in the Number Of Threads numeric up/down control. This
allows the user to control the number of threads that are created. An alternative would
have been to use the ThreadPool class. The advantage of this approach is that the
user has a greater amount of control. The disadvantage is that the threads are created
and destroyed during each test.

❸ Once the `Threads` array is resized to the desired size, each element of the array is assigned an instance of the `Thread` class. Each instance of the `Thread` class is associated with the `ThreadMethod` method. The instance is assigned a name to make it easier to keep track of the thread, and the `IsBackground` property is set to true.

❹ After all of the instances of the `Thread` class have been created, each thread is then started. Recall that the `Start` method is a request to start the thread. The actual starting of the thread may happen at a later point. After all of the requests to start the threads have been made, the main thread pauses for one second.

❺ All threads share the same method, `ThreadMethod`. It follows the typical structure of thread methods in that it contains a loop. Inside the loop is where the processing occurs.

❻ If the user has checked Invoke before clicking Start, an instance of the `AddEleDel` delegate is created and associated with the `AddElement` method. The instance of the delegate is then invoked using `ListBox1`'s `Invoke` method. This ensures that the method associated with the delegate is executed on the thread that instantiated the `ListBox1` control.

❼ If the user has not checked Invoke, the `AddElement` method is invoked directly. This means that the method executes on the thread that calls it. In this example that thread is not the same thread that instantiated the control.

At this point we have two groups of threads. One group contains those threads that are populating the list box, the other contains a single thread that is attempting to keep that same list box empty. In the next section we discuss the information- and diagnostic-related elements of the example.

Information- and diagnostic-related elements

To detect the state of the list box and threads, the form contains a timer with an interval of one second. Listing 15.6 contains the code elements that relate to the gathering of information about the state of the threads as well as detecting the data integrity issues that we will discuss in the next section.

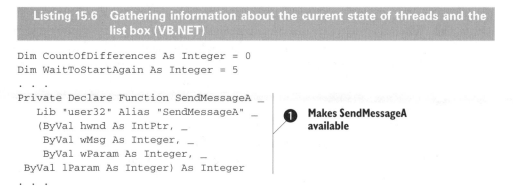

> **Listing 15.6   Gathering information about the current state of threads and the list box (VB.NET)**

```
Dim CountOfDifferences As Integer = 0
Dim WaitToStartAgain As Integer = 5
. . .
Private Declare Function SendMessageA _
    Lib "user32" Alias "SendMessageA" _         ❶ Makes SendMessageA
    (ByVal hwnd As IntPtr, _                        available
     ByVal wMsg As Integer, _
     ByVal wParam As Integer, _
  ByVal lParam As Integer) As Integer
. . .
```

```
Private Sub Timer1_Tick(. . .) Handles Timer1.Tick
    Const LB_GETCOUNT = 395                    ❷  Retrieves the number
    Dim AliveCount As Integer = 0                  of elements
    Dim i As Integer                                     Retrieves the number  ❷
    Dim RealCount As Long                                      of elements
    RealCount = SendMessageA(ListBox1.Handle, LB_GETCOUNT, 0, 0) ◁
    StatusBar1.Text = "Alive= " + AliveCount.ToString()
    StatusBar1.Text += " Items=" + ListBox1.Items.Count.ToString()
    StatusBar1.Text += " Real Count=" + RealCount.ToString()
    If (RealCount <> ListBox1.Items.Count) Then
      CountOfDifferences += 1                        ❸  Sees if the ListBoxl
      Return                                             Items collection is
    Else                                                 correct
      CountOfDifferences = 0
    End If

    If Not Threads Is Nothing Then
      For i = 0 To Threads.Length - 1
        If Threads(i).IsAlive Then              ❹  Counts the number
          AliveCount += 1                           of threads that are
        End If                                       still alive
      Next
    End If
    If AliveCount = 0 Then
      WaitToStartAgain -= 1
    End If

    If CountOfDifferences > 5 Then
      checkBoxKeepTrying.Checked = False        Invokes Buttonl_Click  ❺
    End If                                                    method
    If checkBoxKeepTrying.Checked And WaitToStartAgain <= 0 Then
      WaitToStartAgain = 5
      Button1_Click(sender, e)
    End If
End Sub
```

❶ The `Declare` keyword is used to access functions that are contained in external DLLs, such as user32. User32 contains functions relating to timers, message handling, windows management, and menus. The method we're concerned with is `SendMessageA` which is used to enter a message in the message pump associated with a window.

❷ The message we enter is `LB_GETCOUNT`, which returns the count of elements contained within a list box. For more information on the `SendMessageA` method and the `LB_GETCOUNT` constant, consult the Microsoft Windows Platform SDK. The important thing to take away from this is that the value returned from `SendMessageA` contains that number of elements actually contained within the list box.

❸ Once we've determined the number of elements contained within the list box, we compare that value to the number of items contained within `ListBox1`'s `Items` collection. These numbers should be the same. The `Items` collection is added to the

.NET framework to make it easier to determine what elements are contained within a list box. It does this by adding and removing items for the collection when methods are invoked on the instance of the list box class that causes an element to be added or removed from the list box. We'll talk about this more in the next section. For now, if the number of elements in the `Items` collection is not the same as the number of items actually being displayed, we can infer that there is a chance that a data integrity issue has arisen.

❹ Next we count the number for threads that are still alive. We then check to see if at least one thread is still alive; if not, we decrement the `WaitToStartAgain` data element.

❺ When `WaitToStartAgain` reaches zero and the Keep Trying checkbox is checked, we invoke the `Button1_Click` method. This allows us to keep invoking `Button1_Click` until the user removes the check from the Keep Trying checkbox, or until a data integrity error is encountered.

The idea is that an error will eventually happen and we will keep trying until it does. This allows us to detect race condition-related issues such as data inconsistency and stability. These issues will occur at some point if multiple threads are present in a Windows Form-based application without preventative steps being taken. It's a matter of probability, and how often they will occur rather than if they will occur.

15.1.3 Race conditions

We discussed race conditions in detail in section 6.2.1. Windows Forms are also susceptible to race conditions. There are two basic kinds of issues relating to threads and Windows Forms: data inconsistency and stability.

Data inconsistency

Any time that data is not what it is expected to be, it is a serious situation. An example of a data consistency issue that happens with Windows Forms and multiple threads revolves around the collections that are associated with controls. For example, the `ListBox` control contains an `Items` collection. This allows the control to keep track of what items are in the list without posting a message to the message queue.

Since all access to the list box control is through the `ListBox` object, it is reasonable to assume that it should know the contents of the control without having to ask Windows. The problem is that the data structure used to contain the items is not thread-safe. In section 7.1 we saw that objects in the `Collection` namespace are not thread-safe unless their `Synchronized` method is used. There is no way to tell a `ListBox` object that it should use synchronized access to its items.

To see an example of data inconsistency, in our example check the Keep Trying checkbox. Eventually the form will enter a state similar to that of figure 15.4.

The Win32 portion of the list box contains one element. The `Items` collection does not contain that element. The status bar at the bottom of the dialog box is populated by the following code:

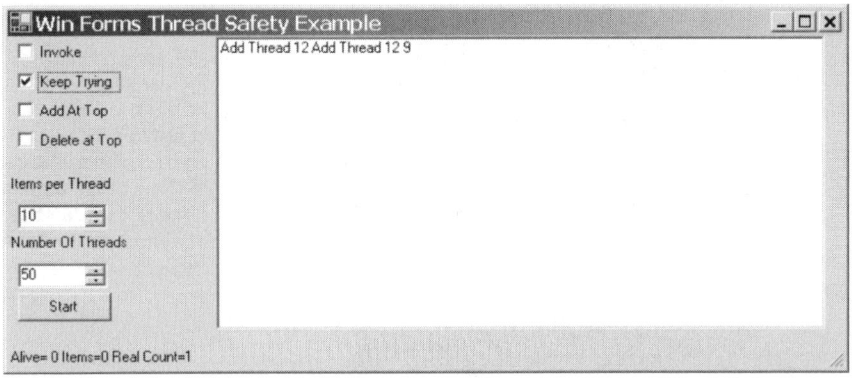

Figure 15.4   Notice that Real Count is one and the Items count is zero. The list box contains one real entry that is not present in the Items collection.

```
Dim RealCount As Long
RealCount = SendMessageA(ListBox1.Handle, LB_GETCOUNT, 0, 0)
StatusBar1.Text = "Alive= " + AliveCount.ToString()
StatusBar1.Text += " Items=" + ListBox1.Items.Count.ToString()
StatusBar1.Text += " Real Count=" + RealCount.ToString()
```

RealCount contains the actual number of elements in the list box. The Count property of the Items collection returns zero, indicating a data inconsistency has occurred. This is a serious condition because conflicting results are being returned. In section 15.1.5 we discuss how to make this not happen.

To understand what's happening here consider figure 15.5. Normally there's a one-for-one correlation between the elements in the .NET ListBox object's Items collection and the items contained within the list box.

When data inconsistency occurs, the object contains a different number of items than the Win32 list box control. Figure 15.6 shows a Win32 list box with one element and a .NET ListBox object with no elements in the Items collection.

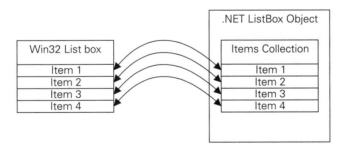

Figure 15.5   Under normal circumstances there is an object in the ListBox Items collection for every entry in the matching Win32 list box.

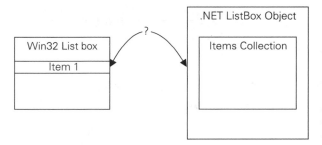

Figure 15.6
When the `ListBox` object is not in sync with the Win32 control, the number of items in the `Items` collection does not match the number of elements in the Win32 control.

This demonstrates that the .NET Windows Forms code is on top of the Win32 system, which makes sense because the .NET Windows Forms applications are native Win32 applications. They must interact with the native Win32 controls. They do this by exposing objects that correspond to those native controls, and provide extensions to make development easier and more flexible. One example of this is that the `Items` collection of the `ListBox` object allows you to determine if an element is in the collection.

Stability

Stability of an application is very important. Any time multiple threads are used with Windows Forms without using the proper mechanisms, instability can be introduced. Eventually the application will terminate unexpectedly. The stability issues will be more pronounced on a multiple-processor machine. Instability will happen on a single-processor machine, but much less frequently because of concurrency issues and having multiple threads executing at exactly the same moment.

Related to the stability and inconsistency issues is the possibility of an event-related deadlock occurring.

15.1.4 Event-related deadlocks

Deadlocks, discussed in detail in section 6.2.2, are one of the more difficult errors to track down. Deadlocks can also happen in multithreaded Windows Forms applications. Listing 15.7 demonstrates how a deadlock can occur in a Windows Forms application.

Listing 15.7 Deadlock occurs when the Moving Thread moves textBox1 (C#).

```csharp
private void Form1_Load(object sender, System.EventArgs e)
{
  Thread.CurrentThread.Name="Main";
}

private void button1_Click(object sender, System.EventArgs e)
{
  Thread movingThread = new Thread(new ThreadStart(ThreadMethod));
  movingThread.Name="Moving Thread";
  movingThread.Start();
}
```

```
private void ThreadMethod()
{
  lock(textBox1)       ❶ Acquires a lock
  {                       on the text box
    Point newLocation= new Point(
      textBox1.Location.X+1,textBox1.Location.Y+1);  Moves the text box  ❷
    Trace.WriteLine(                                   to the new location
      "Before Location Assign : " + Thread.CurrentThread.Name);
    textBox1.Location= newLocation;
    Trace.WriteLine("After Location Assign : " + Thread.CurrentThread.Name);
  }
}
private void textBox1_LocationChanged(object sender, System.EventArgs e)
{
  Trace.WriteLine("LocationChanged's lock:" + Thread.CurrentThread.Name);
  lock(textBox1)       ❸ Attempts to acquire
  {                       a lock on textBox1
    Trace.WriteLine("Will not be reached : " + Thread.CurrentThread.Name);
    textBox1.Text=Thread.CurrentThread.Name;
  }
}
```

❶ This example uses a single textbox and a button. When the button is pressed, a thread is created that acquires a lock on `textBox1`. As with all deadlocks, the acquisition of a lock is the primary cause of the deadlock. This isn't to say that locks shouldn't be used; instead, care should be taken any time a lock is used to ensure that deadlock does not occur.

❷ The thread named Moving Thread next moves the textbox to the left and down one pixel. At the point the assignment is made, the `LocationChanged` event is raised. The important element here is that the `LocationChanged` event occurs before Moving Thread releases its lock on `textBox1`.

❸ The `textBox1_LocationChanged` method is invoked when the textbox is moved. This invocation occurs, at the point the assignment is made to the `Location` property. The `Trace` output is as follows:

```
Before Location Assign: Moving Thread
LocationChanged's lock: Main
```

Notice that After Location Assign is not present in the output. Also notice that the instructions that cause the output are executed on different threads.

At the point the deadlock occurs, the application freezes. To be precise, it blocks on the lock statement in the `textBox1_LocationChanged` method. In the next section we discuss how to resolve this issue using the `Invoke` method.

15.1.5 Making Windows Forms thread-safe

Because Windows Forms use native Win32 controls, the thread that creates those controls should be the thread that communicates with them. This may seem a bit restrictive, but with the Invoke method it is very easy to ensure that the correct thread communicates with the thread.

The Invoke method

The Invoke method ensures that a delegate is executed on the thread that created the control. We'll start by correcting the event deadlock example from the previous section. Listing 15.8 contains the updated Visual Basic .NET source code.

Listing 15.8   Using the Invoke method avoids event-related deadlocks (VB.NET)

```
Private Sub Form1_Load(. . .) Handles MyBase.Load
  Thread.CurrentThread.Name = "Main"
End Sub

Private Sub Button1_Click(. . .) Handles Button1.Click
  Dim movingThread As New Thread(AddressOf ThreadMethod)
  movingThread.Name = "Moving Thread"
  movingThread.Start()                        Used to execute on  ❶
End Sub                                       a different thread

Delegate Sub locationDelegate(ByVal newLocation As Point)
Private Sub changeLocationMethod(ByVal newLocation As Point) ❷  Expects a single
  SyncLock TextBox1                                              Point parameter
    Trace.WriteLine("Before Location Assign: " + Thread.CurrentThread.Name)
    TextBox1.Location = newLocation
    Trace.WriteLine("After Location Assign: " + Thread.CurrentThread.Name)
  End SyncLock
End Sub

Private Sub ThreadMethod()                    Used to execute on  ❶
  Dim newLocation As Point                    a different thread
  newLocation = New Point(TextBox1.Location.X + 1, TextBox1.Location.Y + 1)
  Dim myLocationDelegate As locationDelegate
  myLocationDelegate = New locationDelegate(AddressOf changeLocationMethod)
  TextBox1.Invoke(myLocationDelegate, New Object() {newLocation})
End Sub                                        Expects a single  ❷
                                               Point parameter
Private Sub TextBox1_LocationChanged(. . .) Handles TextBox1.LocationChanged
  Trace.WriteLine("LocationChanged's lock: " + Thread.CurrentThread.Name)
  SyncLock TextBox1
    Trace.WriteLine("Is now reached: " + Thread.CurrentThread.Name)
    TextBox1.Text = Thread.CurrentThread.Name
  End SyncLock
End Sub
```

❶ The most noticeable change in the example is the addition of locationDelegate. This delegate allows us to associate a method with the delegate that is passed to the textbox control's Invoke method.

❷ When the `Invoke` method of `TextBox1` is executed, the method associated with `locationDelegate` is executed on the thread that initially created `TextBox1`. Since `SyncLock` is then acquired on the Main thread, it can be reacquired in `TextBox1_LocationChanged` because both methods now execute on the same thread. Here's the output of the `Trace` statements:

```
Before Location Assign: Main
LocationChanged's lock: Main
Is now reached: Main
After Location Assign: Main
```

Notice that all of the `Trace` statements occur on the `Main` thread. The application no longer freezes. The `Invoke` method also solves the stability and consistency issues we discussed in section 15.1.3. You'll notice that in figure 15.4 there is an `Invoke` checkbox. By checking it, you ensure that the `Invoke` method of the list box will be used. You will notice that the consistency and stability issues no longer occur when `Invoke` is checked.

The InvokeRequired property

The `InvokeRequired` property indicates if the `Invoke` method should be used when dealing with a control. If a control's `InvokeRequired` property is true then the `Invoke` method should be used. Listing 15.9 contains an updated `Thread-Method` that uses the `InvokeRequired` property.

> **Listing 15.9 InvokeRequired indicates if the Invoke method of a control should be used (C#).**

```csharp
private void ThreadMethod()
{
  Point newLocation= new Point(textBox1.Location.X+1,textBox1.Location.Y+1);
  locationDelegate myLocationDelegate;
  myLocationDelegate = new locationDelegate(changeLocationMethod);
  if (textBox1.InvokeRequired)
  {
    textBox1.Invoke(myLocationDelegate, new object[] {newLocation});
  }
  else
  {
    changeLocationMethod(newLocation);
  }
}
```

Listing 15.9 shows how the `InvokeRequired` property can be used to determine if `Invoke` should be used. If `InvokeRequired` is true, an instance of the `location-Delegate` is passed to the `Invoke` method of the `textBox1` control. Otherwise, `changeLocationMethod` is executed directly. Direct execution will be faster than delegate invocation, but if `InvokeRequired` is true a delegate should be used.

15.2 USING THE GRAPHICS OBJECT WITH THREADS

Dealing with graphics is relatively complex. This section is not intended to be a complete survey of graphics programming in .NET but rather an introduction to using the `Graphics` object with multiple threads. The `Graphics` object is thread-safe, enabling multiple threads to interact with it without ill effects.

15.2.1 Introduction to the Graphics object

The `Graphics` class is used to render objects onto a graphics display. Windows Forms are one of the most commonly used graphics displays used with the `Graphics` class. The `Graphics` class is contained in the `System.Drawing` namespace. It exposes the GDI+ capabilities.

15.2.2 Acquiring by overriding the OnPaint method

The first issue you'll face when doing graphics programming is acquiring an instance of the `Graphics` object. A common single-threaded way to do this is to overload the `OnPaint` method. Listing 15.10 contains an example of an overridden `OnPaint` method.

Listing 15.10   Invoked when a form detects it needs to repaint itself (VB.NET)

```
Protected Overrides Sub OnPaint(ByVal e As PaintEventArgs)
  Dim g As Graphics
  g = e.Graphics                          ❶ Contains a reference to the
  Dim stringToDraw As String                form's graphics context
  stringToDraw = "OnPaint " + Now.ToLongTimeString()
  stringToDraw += " " + Thread.CurrentThread.Name
  Dim fontToDrawWith As Font
  Dim brushToDrawWith As Brush
  fontToDrawWith = New Font("times New Roman", 12)   Renders the string ❷
  brushToDrawWith = New SolidBrush(Color.Blue)            onto the form
  g.DrawString(stringToDraw, fontToDrawWith, brushToDrawWith, 40, 40) ◁
  brushToDrawWith.Dispose()
  fontToDrawWith.Dispose()      ❸ Sees if the ListBoxl
  g.Dispose()                      Items collection is
End Sub                            correct
```

---

❶ When `OnPaint` is called, it is passed a reference to a `PaintEventArgs` object that contains a reference to a `Graphics` object. All graphics operations require a reference to the object.

❷ Once we have a `Graphics` object we can use the `DrawString` method to render a string onto the device. The `DrawString` method accepts a reference to a `Font` object, a reference to a `Brush` object, and the location to render the string. The `Font` object tells the `DrawString` method what font face should be used to render the string. Likewise the `Brush` object tells the `DrawString` method how the font should be rendered.

❸ After we have completed our drawing operations, it is important to release our graphics-related objects. All drawing objects should be viewed as a scarce resource. As soon as you have finished with them, you should release them using the `Dispose` method. One exception is if you use an existing object, such as `Brush` from the `Brushes` collection. When determining whether or not you should call `Dispose` consider if you allocated the object, using the `new` keyword. If you allocated the object, you should `Dispose` of it.

15.2.3 Acquiring by using the FromHwnd method

There are several ways to acquire a `Graphics` object. When you're doing multithreaded Windows Forms development, the static `FromHwnd` method of the `Graphics` object is a good choice. Listing 15.11 contains the method for a thread that draws the time on the form.

Listing 15.11 Using the FromHwnd method to retrieve a Graphics object (C#)

```csharp
private void DrawTimeMethod()
{
  Graphics g;
  string stringToDraw ;
  stringToDraw = "";
  Font fontToDrawWith ;
  Brush brushToDrawWith ;
  while (true)
  {
    g = Graphics.FromHwnd(this.Handle);  ❶  Graphics object associated with the current form
    stringToDraw = "OnPaint " + DateTime.Now.ToLongTimeString();
    stringToDraw += " " + Thread.CurrentThread.Name;
    fontToDrawWith = new Font("times New Roman", 12);
    brushToDrawWith = new SolidBrush(Color.Blue);
    g.DrawString(stringToDraw, fontToDrawWith, brushToDrawWith, 40, 80);
    brushToDrawWith.Dispose();
    fontToDrawWith.Dispose();
    g.Dispose();        ❷  Method that releases the Graphics object
    Thread.Sleep(1000);
  }
}
```

❶ The `FromHwnd` method returns a reference to a newly created `Graphics` object associated with the handle to the window passed in. `Hwnd` is a handle to a window. A discussion on window handles is beyond the scope of this book. All that you really need to know is that `Hwnd` uniquely identifies a window.

❷ Since the `FromHwnd` method causes a `Graphics` object to be created, we should release that reference using the `Dispose` method. By calling `Dispose` as soon as you have finished with a resource, you make that resource available for some other thread or process. If `Dispose` isn't called, the resource will be freed when the garbage collector frees the unused references. Since you know when you have finished with a resource, it is much better to decide when it is `Disposed` than having the garbage collector do it after you've finished.

Notice in this example that the current time is simply written over the previous time. Figure 15.7 is typical of the output you will see.

Figure 15.7
When `Graphics` operations are performed without using `OnPaint`, care must be taken to erase what was previously painted.

This is something that must be dealt with when doing `Graphics` programming. Listing 15.12 contains code that draws a progress bar using a filled rectangle. The brush used is a gradient.

Listing 15.12   Filling a rectangle using a gradient brush to produce a progress bar (VB.NET)

```
Private Sub DrawBarThreadMethod()
  Dim barHeight As Long
  Dim barWidth As Long
  Dim currentUnit As Integer
  Dim lastUnit As Integer
  Dim counter As Integer
  Dim bgBrush As SolidBrush
  bgBrush = New SolidBrush(Form.DefaultBackColor)
  Dim g As Graphics
  Dim x, y As Long
  Dim units As Integer
  units = 100
  Dim pixelsPerUnit As Integer
  Dim point1, point2 As Point
  Dim widthToDraw As Integer
  Dim c1, c2 As Color
  c1 = Color.Black
  c2 = Color.White
  x = 0
  barHeight = 20
  counter = 0
  Dim fillBrush As LinearGradientBrush
```

```
    Try
      While True
        counter += 1
        If counter > units Then
          counter = 1
        End If
        y = Me.Height - 50
        barWidth = Me.Width
        point1 = New Point(x, y)
        point2 = New Point(x + barWidth, y + barHeight)
        fillBrush = New LinearGradientBrush(point1, point2, c1, c2)
        pixelsPerUnit = barWidth / units
        currentUnit = counter
        g = Graphics.FromHwnd(Handle)                    ❶  Ensure the rectangle
        If (currentUnit < lastUnit) Then                     is visible
          widthToDraw = lastUnit * pixelsPerUnit - 1
          g.FillRectangle(bgBrush, x + 1, y + 1, widthToDraw, barHeight - 1)
        End If
        widthToDraw = (currentUnit * pixelsPerUnit) - 1
        g.FillRectangle(fillBrush, x + 1, y + 1, widthToDraw, barHeight - 1)
        fillBrush.Dispose()
        g.Dispose()
        lastUnit = currentUnit
        Thread.Sleep(20)
      End While
    Catch ex As Exception
      System.Diagnostics.Trace.WriteLine(ex.ToString())
    End Try
End Sub
```

❶ When the bar reaches the right side of the dialog box, it starts over at the left. At that point the area is filled with a rectangle that is the same color as the background of the form.

When the method in listing 15.12 is associated with a thread, it produces output similar to that in figure 15.8.

Figure 15.8
The gradient bar at the bottom of the dialog box is produced by the code in listing 15.12.

The association of the method in listing 15.12 to a thread should be very familiar by now. The following code associates the method with an instance of the `Thread` class:

```
barThread = New Thread(AddressOf DrawBarThreadMethod)
barThread.IsBackground = True
barThread.Name = "barThread"
barThread.Start()
```

Notice that we name the thread `barThread` so that we can keep track of it.

In the next section we'll complete our discussion on multithreaded Windows Forms development by examining the thread-related aspects of the `Application` object.

15.3 *THREAD-RELATED APPLICATION EVENTS AND PROPERTIES*

Windows Forms applications have numerous events and properites. We're primarily concerned with those events and properties that relate to multithreading.

15.3.1 The ThreadException event

The `ThreadException` event of the `Application` object is very similar to AppDomain's `UnhandledException` event. Recall from chapter 13 that AppDomain's `UnhandledException` event is raised any time an unhandled exception occurs on any thread in the application domain. Listing 15.13 sets up handlers for AppDomain's `UnhandledException` event as well as the `Application` object's `ThreadException` event.

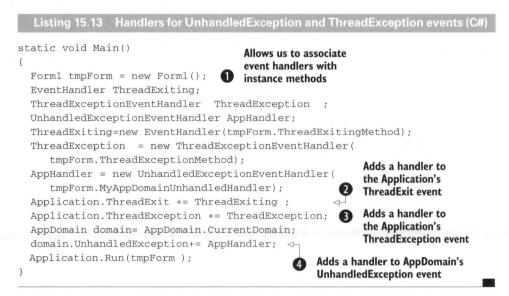

Listing 15.13 Handlers for UnhandledException and ThreadException events (C#)

```
static void Main()
{
    Form1 tmpForm = new Form1();                     Allows us to associate
    EventHandler ThreadExiting;                      event handlers with
    ThreadExceptionEventHandler  ThreadException  ;  ❶ instance methods
    UnhandledExceptionEventHandler AppHandler;
    ThreadExiting=new EventHandler(tmpForm.ThreadExitingMethod);
    ThreadException  = new ThreadExceptionEventHandler(
        tmpForm.ThreadExceptionMethod);
    AppHandler = new UnhandledExceptionEventHandler(     Adds a handler to
        tmpForm.MyAppDomainUnhandledHandler);           the Application's
    Application.ThreadExit += ThreadExiting ;        ❷  ThreadExit event
    Application.ThreadException += ThreadException;   ❸  Adds a handler to
    AppDomain domain= AppDomain.CurrentDomain;           the Application's
    domain.UnhandledException+= AppHandler;              ThreadException event
    Application.Run(tmpForm );                        ❹  Adds a handler to AppDomain's
}                                                        UnhandledException event
```

❶ In order to associate the event handlers with instance methods, rather than static methods, we must first create an instance of the `Form1` class. We pass this instance to the `Application.Run` method at the end of the static `Main` method.

❷ We first add a handler for the `ThreadExit` event. We discuss the `ThreadExit` event in the next section.

❸ After we've added the handler for the `ThreadExit` event, we add a handler for the `Application` object's `ThreadException` event. This event is invoked only when the exception occurs on the main thread. If a thread is created that causes an unhandled exception to be raised, this event will not be notified.

❹ We add an `UnhandledException` event handler to the current domain. This event handler will be invoked when any thread in the current domain experiences an unhandled exception. If a `ThreadException` event handler has been added to the `Application` object, it will handle any exceptions that occur on the main thread. This means that `AppDomain`'s `UnhandledException` will not be invoked.

Each of these event handlers do slightly different handling. The `AppDomain` handler is a bit more flexible in that it catches all exceptions that occur. These events should not be used in place of proper exception handling. Exceptions and exception handling were discussed in-depth in chapter 13.

15.3.2 The ThreadExit event

The `ThreadExit` event is similar to the `ThreadException` event in that it only applies to the main thread. If a thread other than the main thread exits, this event will not be raised. This event is raised when an application is terminating. The `ThreadExit` event is invoked after the `Form Closing` and `Closed` events are invoked.

The `ApplicationExit` event is invoked after the `ThreadExit` event. The order of events during application termination is as follows: `Closing`, `Closed`, `ThreadExit`, `ApplicationExit`.

15.3.3 The MessageLoop property

Early in this chapter we briefly discussed the concept of message pumps, also known as message queues or message loops. The application object's `MessageLoop` property allows us to determine if a thread contains a message loop. The following instruction prints out true or false depending on whether the thread it is executed on contains a message loop:

```
System.Diagnostics.Debug.WriteLine(Application.MessageLoop.ToString());
```

This is useful in determining how a thread will behave. For example, if the thread does not contain a message loop, message-based timers will not work. In that circumstance, one of the other timers will be required.

15.4 SUMMARY

In this chapter we've covered some of the issues related to multithreaded development in Windows Forms applications. Combining Windows Forms with multiple threads can lead to powerful applications. We discussed the problems relating to multithreaded development and also covered the use of `Invoke` to resolve those issues. We introduced the `Graphics` object and saw how it can be used to render objects onto a form. Finally, we discussed thread-related events and properties of the `Application` object.

C H A P T E R   1 6

Unmanaged code and managed threads

Apartments are COM constructs used to resolve concurrency control issues. Rather than forcing COM developers to use synchronization primitives, Microsoft introduced the apartment concept. This allowed for easy development of reusable components with minimal concern about concurrency control. This chapter is not intended to be a primer on COM programming. Instead, it examines the interaction of .NET with COM from a multithreaded perspective. An important thing to understand is that .NET does not use apartments for concurrency control. However, they are used when interacting with COM objects. Interaction with COM from .NET is generally referred to as interop, short for interoperability.

16.1 WHAT IS AN APARTMENT?

Many developers' introduction to multithreaded development involved the concept of an apartment. An apartment is based on a building metaphor. The process is comparable to a building that has one or more apartments. Restriction to an apartment is based on the type of apartment it is. The most common apartments are single and multithreaded.

16.1.1   Single-threaded apartment model (STA)

The majority of COM objects produced are designed to execute inside an STA. The primary reason for this is that most COM objects have been developed using Visual Basic. Visual Basic produces COM objects that execute in an STA. In this text we will refer to objects that are designed and marked to execute in an STA as an STA object. Visual Basic makes it incredibly easy to produce COM objects and is partly responsible for the wide acceptance of COM.

When an object is marked as an object that executes in an STA, it means that only one thread can access that object. Additionally, when that object is executing in an STA, if that object is accessed more than once, the same thread must access it each time. This allows the developers of STA objects to make use of thread local storage as a means of persisting state. Additionally, because only one thread is accessing the objects, concurrency control is no longer a concern. Since these STA objects are relatively simple, they are much easier to write than an object that executes in a multi-threaded apartment (MTA).

To make things a little more complex, several names for the same thing are often used. STA objects are often referred to as apartment threaded. This is somewhat misleading since every object in COM executes in an apartment. The question is how many threads can interact with an object contained within a certain apartment. If the answer is one, the apartment is STA.

16.1.2   MTA

When an apartment allows more than one thread to interact with the objects contained within it that apartment is known as an MTA. Just as STA is sometimes referred to as apartment threaded, MTA is sometimes referred to as free threaded. Objects that are marked as being free threaded will execute in an MTA. Additionally, objects can be marked as "Both," meaning that they can execute in both an STA and an MTA. A process will contain at most one MTA. This means that all MTA objects within the process will execute in a shared MTA.

16.2   *COM INTEROPERABILITY*

Organizations have invested large sums of money developing COM objects. When Microsoft developed .NET, its engineers were aware of this and built .NET in such a way that it can coexist with COM objects. It is very easy to work with COM using the .NET framework. To access a COM object from .NET, simply add a reference. One way to do this is to select Add Reference from the Project menu to bring up a dialog box similar to that in figure 16.1.

The COM tab displays COM objects that are registered. Once the desired component is located, click Select, then OK. This will add a reference to the COM object to the project.

Figure 16.2 shows the Solution Explorer window after the reference was added. Notice that DENNISATLOBJECTLib is listed in the References section.

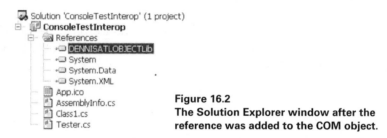

Figure 16.1 The Add Reference dialog box allows a reference to a COM object to be added, making the COM object available for use.

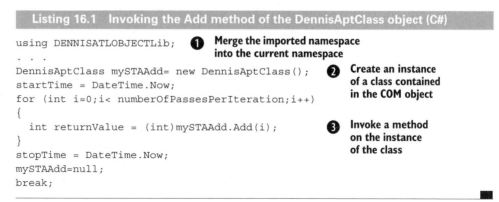

Figure 16.2
The Solution Explorer window after the reference was added to the COM object.

Just like when other references are added, the objects contained within the COM are now available for use in the project. Listing 16.1 contains an example of using a method contained in the DENNISATLOBJECTLib.

Listing 16.1   Invoking the Add method of the DennisAptClass object (C#)

```
using DENNISATLOBJECTLib;          ❶ Merge the imported namespace
                                      into the current namespace
. . .
DennisAptClass mySTAAdd= new DennisAptClass();   ❷ Create an instance
startTime = DateTime.Now;                           of a class contained
for (int i=0;i< numberOfPassesPerIteration;i++)     in the COM object
{
   int returnValue = (int)mySTAAdd.Add(i);        ❸ Invoke a method
}                                                    on the instance
stopTime = DateTime.Now;                             of the class
mySTAAdd=null;
break;
```

❶ To increase the readability of the code we use the `using` keyword so that we don't have to include `DENNISATLOBJECTLib` in each access to objects contained in that namespace. There is sometimes confusion as to what the `using` keyword does. The `using` keyword allows elements contained in the specified namespace to be accessed without being fully qualified. This can greatly reduce the size of the source code, as well as increase readability.

❷ We must now declare an instance of an object contained within the COM object. In this example we create an instance of `DennisAptClass`. Notice that the syntax is the same as creating any other object. This simplifies development since the developers don't need to determine which way an object should be created.

❸ Once the object has been created we can invoke its `Add` method. The invocation is essentially the same as other invocations.

Interacting with COM is so simple that it can be referred to as COM integration rather than interoperation. We've seen how to interact with COM in the simple case; now we'll examine potential performance issues.

16.2.1   The ApartmentState property

COM objects are marked to indicate their threading model. .NET does not use apartments when interacting solely with .NET elements. When .NET is interacting with COM, it creates an apartment for the COM object. The `ApartmentState` property of the `Thread` class is used to determine if the apartment is an STA or an MTA. Listing 16.2 contains an example of setting a thread's `ApartmentState`.

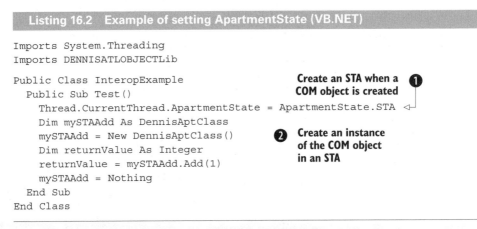

Listing 16.2   Example of setting ApartmentState (VB.NET)

```
Imports System.Threading
Imports DENNISATLOBJECTLib

Public Class InteropExample                    Create an STA when a  ❶
  Public Sub Test()                            COM object is created
    Thread.CurrentThread.ApartmentState = ApartmentState.STA
    Dim mySTAAdd As DennisAptClass
    mySTAAdd = New DennisAptClass()            ❷  Create an instance
    Dim returnValue As Integer                    of the COM object
    returnValue = mySTAAdd.Add(1)                 in an STA
    mySTAAdd = Nothing
  End Sub
End Class
```

❶ By setting the current thread's apartment state we are telling the runtime that only one thread should be allowed to access COM objects created on the current thread. Setting `ApartmentState` doesn't have an impact unless a COM object is created. Once `ApartmentState` has been set, it cannot be changed. Attempting to reassign `ApartmentState` does not result in an error; instead, the value simply does not change.

ApartmentState is set using the ApartmentState enumeration. The values for the enumeration are STA, MTA and Unknown. The default value for a thread's ApartmentState is Unknown. Under the current implementation Unknown is the same as MTA. This means that if no value is assigned to ApartmentState COM objects created on that thread, it would execute in an MTA.

In the previous chapter we discussed the STAThread attribute. It can be used to set ApartmentState. Additionally the MTAThread attribute can be used to indicate that an MTA is desired. This attribute must be set on the Main thread of the application to have an effect. The advantage of the attribute approach is that it occurs before execution of any code contained within the method. Attempting to set ApartmentState after a COM object has been created will have no effect.

❷ At the point a COM object is created, the ApartmentState property becomes important. In the next section we'll discuss the performance impact of apartment conflicts.

16.2.2 Apartment conflicts

The choice of ApartmentState has a direct impact on performance. When a COM object is created in an apartment that conflicts with the threading model of the object, there is a substantial penalty in performance. This is caused by the need to create a thread to serve as a proxy between the COM object and the calling .NET program. Figure 16.3 shows the impact of apartment conflicts.

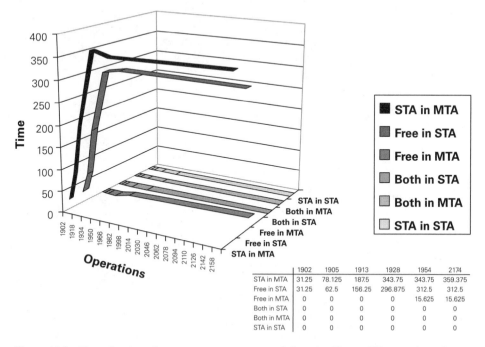

	1902	1905	1913	1928	1954	2174
STA in MTA	31.25	78.125	187.5	343.75	343.75	359.375
Free in STA	31.25	62.5	156.25	296.875	312.5	312.5
Free in MTA	0	0	0	0	15.625	15.625
Both in STA	0	0	0	0	0	0
Both in MTA	0	0	0	0	0	0
STA in STA	0	0	0	0	0	0

Figure 16.3 The selection of apartment state can result in a significant difference in performance.

Notice that the difference between a STA object executing in an MTA and an STA object executing in an STA is significant. When there are not apartment conflicts the time required to perform the operation is essentially zero. This is because the COM method can be invoked directly, rather than passing through a stub and proxy mechanism.

16.2.3   Discussion of the example

You may be wondering where the numbers in figure 16.3 came from. The process started by creating an Active Template Library (ATL)-based COM object. Listing 16.3 contains a sampling of the code involved.

Listing 16.3   Implementation of the Add method of the COM objects (C++)

```
STDMETHODIMP CDennisAdd::Add(int nValue,int * nOut)
{
     *nOut = nValue+1;
     return S_OK;
}
```

Listing 16.3 contains an example of the Add method contained in each of the COM objects benchmarked. This method demonstrates the case where the frequency of method invocation is high compared to the duration of method execution.

The threading model the COM object requires is controlled by its entry in the Registry. Listing 16.4 contains the .rgs entries associated with the object in listing 16.3.

Listing 16.4   Registry entries associated with the dual-threaded COM object (Registry file)

```
HKCR
{
  DennisATLObject.DennisAdd.1 = s 'DennisAdd Class'
  {
    CLSID = s '{405592A3-B5A3-4784-8497-B5719D5D1C58}'
  }
  DennisATLObject.DennisAdd = s 'DennisAdd Class'
  {
    CLSID = s '{405592A3-B5A3-4784-8497-B5719D5D1C58}'
    CurVer = s 'DennisATLObject.DennisAdd.1'
  }
  NoRemove CLSID
  {
    ForceRemove {405592A3-B5A3-4784-8497-B5719D5D1C58} = s 'DennisAdd Class'
    {
      ProgID = s 'DennisATLObject.DennisAdd.1'
      VersionIndependentProgID = s 'DennisATLObject.DennisAdd'
      ForceRemove 'Programmable'
      InprocServer32 = s '%MODULE%'
```

```
        {
            val ThreadingModel = s 'Both'    ❶    Indicates that object can
        }                                           execute in both STA and MTA
        'TypeLib' = s '{C56DCEBC-FB08-40BB-A79B-18159013CACE}'
    }
  }
}
```

❶ The `ThreadingModel` assignment designates the type of apartment the COM object
requires. The remainder of the .rgs file adds the appropriate entries to the Registry to
make the COM object available for consumption. Listing 16.5 contains the .NET code.

Listing 16.5   Code to test the threading model of COM objects (C#)

```
. . .
ObjectThreadingModel whatToTest;
. . .
private double OneIteration()
{
  GC.Collect();
  DateTime startTime,stopTime;
  TimeSpan howLong;
  switch(whatToTest)
  {
    case ObjectThreadingModel.STA:
      DennisAptClass mySTAAdd= new DennisAptClass();
      startTime = DateTime.Now;
      for (int i=0;i< numberOfPassesPerIteration;i++)
      {
        int returnValue = (int)mySTAAdd.Add(i);
      }
      stopTime = DateTime.Now;
      mySTAAdd=null;
      break;
    case ObjectThreadingModel.Both:                            ❶ Test the Both
      DennisAddClass myBothAdd= new DennisAddClass();             COM object
      startTime = DateTime.Now;
      for (int i=0;i< numberOfPassesPerIteration;i++)
      {
        int returnValue = (int)myBothAdd.Add(i);               ❷ Invoke the
      }                                                          Add method
      stopTime = DateTime.Now;
      myBothAdd=null;
      break;
    case ObjectThreadingModel.Free:
      DennisFreeClass myFreeAdd= new DennisFreeClass();
      startTime = DateTime.Now;
```

```
        for (int i=0;i< numberOfPassesPerIteration;i++)
        {
          int returnValue = (int)myFreeAdd.Add(i);
        }
        stopTime = DateTime.Now;
        myFreeAdd=null;
        break;
    }
    howLong = stopTime.Subtract(startTime);

    return howLong.TotalMilliseconds;
}
```

❶ If whatToTest contains the value ObjectThreadingModel.Both, then test the object in listings 16.3 and 16.4. We then create an instance of the COM object. The start time is recorded so we can determine how long the operations took to complete.

❷ We then invoke the Add method of the object. If you're faced with a real-life situation such as this, a solution would be to move the loop inside the COM object. This would decrease the number of times the call would cross the apartment boundary.

16.3 SUMMARY

When you're dealing with COM objects it's important to match the threading model of the object. If that isn't possible be prepared for the performance penalty that's associated with incompatible apartments. There are several ways to resolve the apartment conflict. One of the best ways may be to rewrite the COM object as a .NET class library. Often a rewrite isn't possible; in those cases the COM object may need to be modified to be more efficient. If the COM object can't be changed, an additional COM object may be required to wrap the original COM object.

The fact that .NET does not require the use of apartments is a compelling reason to use it. Instead of restricting entry to objects, it allows you to write efficient code that manages access to shared resources using synchronization primitives such as locks, monitors, and reader/writer locks.

CHAPTER 17

Designing with threads

Multithreaded development provides a way to develop powerful applications. This chapter focuses on how to use threads effectively to produce robust applications and reusable class libraries. One of the major advantages of containing the logic involved with multithreaded development into a class library is that the consumers of that library can use them without having to understand the internal workings of the object. This allows experienced developers to produce libraries that less experienced developers can use.

In this chapter we'll cover the asynchronous design pattern. It provides a uniform way of dealing with objects to perform asynchronous execution. To better demonstrate the concepts we'll implement a class library that performs asynchronous file sorting following the asynchronous design pattern.

17.1   USING THE ASYNCHRONOUS DESIGN PATTERN

Consistency is a good thing. One area where Microsoft has made tremendous gains is consistency in the .NET framework, and one way this was accomplished was by using design patterns. Design patterns are beyond the scope of this book, but if you view them as a recipe for producing objects that behave similarly, that will suffice for our purposes. The design pattern we're concerned with here is asynchronous. It is intended to give a standard way of interacting with asynchronous operations. For example, if you want to do an asynchronous read of a file, you use the `BeginRead` method. If you want to invoke a delegate in an asynchronous way, you use the `BeginInvoke` method. These names start with the word "begin" and indicate the nature of the operation that is being performed asynchronously.

This means that if a new method is introduced that follows the asynchronous design pattern you'll have a good idea of how to use it. This knowledge reuse is incredibly valuable. In the next section we'll go over the asynchronous design pattern by implementing a class that follows it. We'll then move on to a more generic solution where a class encapsulates a thread that performs some operation. We'll highlight the differences between this solution and the asynchronous design pattern.

17.1.1   A file-sorting example

There are times that the contents of a directory need to be arranged, moving them to different subdirectories based on their name. Figure 17.1 shows an example of a directory containing two sets of files that need to be separated. One set of files contains the word "Data" while the other contains the word "Log."

Name	Size	Type
1 of 10 Data File	1 KB	File
1 of 10 Log File	1 KB	File
10 of 10 Data File	1 KB	File
10 of 10 Log File	1 KB	File
2 of 10 Data File	1 KB	File
2 of 10 Log File	1 KB	File
3 of 10 Data File	1 KB	File
3 of 10 Log File	1 KB	File
4 of 10 Data File	1 KB	File
4 of 10 Log File	1 KB	File
5 of 10 Data File	1 KB	File
5 of 10 Log File	1 KB	File
6 of 10 Data File	1 KB	File
6 of 10 Log File	1 KB	File
7 of 10 Data File	1 KB	File
7 of 10 Log File	1 KB	File
8 of 10 Data File	1 KB	File
8 of 10 Log File	1 KB	File
9 of 10 Data File	1 KB	File
9 of 10 Log File	1 KB	File

Figure 17.1   A directory containing two sets of files

```
C:\Temp\data>tree /f
Folder PATH listing
Volume serial number is 000
C:.
├───ofdatafile
│       1 of 10 Data File
│       10 of 10 Data File
│       2 of 10 Data File
│       3 of 10 Data File
│       4 of 10 Data File
│       5 of 10 Data File
│       6 of 10 Data File
│       7 of 10 Data File
│       8 of 10 Data File
│       9 of 10 Data File
│
└───oflogfile
        1 of 10 Log File
        10 of 10 Log File
        2 of 10 Log File
        3 of 10 Log File
        4 of 10 Log File
        5 of 10 Log File
        6 of 10 Log File
        7 of 10 Log File
        8 of 10 Log File
        9 of 10 Log File
```

Figure 17.2   Sorted output of the contents of the directory from Figure 17.1

Once our program finishes executing, the output will resemble that in Figure 17.2.

To make the sorting application more interactive we'll make it a Windows Forms application. The actual sorting of the files will be performed using a class library, encouraging reuse and also allowing the use of the `Friend` and `internal` modifiers. As a review, `Friend` is a Visual Basic .NET keyword that indicates that a variable or method can be accessed by classes contained within the same assembly. This allows all elements in a class library access to certain elements, while restricting access to those elements from the outside. The idea is that classes contained within the class library understand the inner workings of the `Friend` elements and can manipulate them in a safe way. C#'s `internal` is roughly equivalent to Visual Basic .NET's `Friend`.

In the next section we discuss the class library that performs the file sorting.

17.1.2 The Sorter class library

The `Sorter` class library contains the code that performs the sorting and classification of files in a directory. It contains several events that allow the consumer of the class to be informed as to its processing. We'll start by examining an internal class that controls the processing of a directory.

The WorkUnit class

The `WorkUnit` class contains the instance-specific data values. It is used to provide instruction to the `Sorter` class regarding the source, destination, and manipulation of the files to process. Listing 17.1 contains the `WorkUnit` class.

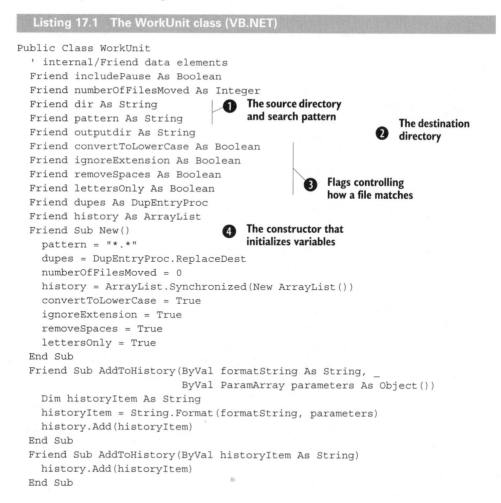

Listing 17.1   The WorkUnit class (VB.NET)

```
Public Class WorkUnit
  ' internal/Friend data elements
  Friend includePause As Boolean
  Friend numberOfFilesMoved As Integer
  Friend dir As String                    ❶ The source directory
  Friend pattern As String                   and search pattern
  Friend outputdir As String              ❷ The destination
  Friend convertToLowerCase As Boolean       directory
  Friend ignoreExtension As Boolean
  Friend removeSpaces As Boolean
  Friend lettersOnly As Boolean           ❸ Flags controlling
  Friend dupes As DupEntryProc               how a file matches
  Friend history As ArrayList
  Friend Sub New()                        ❹ The constructor that
    pattern = "*.*"                          initializes variables
    dupes = DupEntryProc.ReplaceDest
    numberOfFilesMoved = 0
    history = ArrayList.Synchronized(New ArrayList())
    convertToLowerCase = True
    ignoreExtension = True
    removeSpaces = True
    lettersOnly = True
  End Sub
  Friend Sub AddToHistory(ByVal formatString As String, _
                      ByVal ParamArray parameters As Object())
    Dim historyItem As String
    historyItem = String.Format(formatString, parameters)
    history.Add(historyItem)
  End Sub
  Friend Sub AddToHistory(ByVal historyItem As String)
    history.Add(historyItem)
  End Sub
```

```
    'public enums
    Public Enum DupEntryProc
      ReplaceDest
      RemoveSource
      DoNothing
    End Enum
    'public properties
    Public ReadOnly Property FilesMoved() As Integer
      Get
         Return numberOfFilesMoved
      End Get
    End Property
    Public ReadOnly Property Directory() As String
      Get
         Return dir
      End Get
    End Property
    Public ReadOnly Property ProcessingHistory() As ArrayList
      Get
         Return CType(history.Clone(), ArrayList)
      End Get
    End Property
End Class
```

❶ One of the most important values when sorting files is the directory to sort. This information is stored in the `dir` member of the `WorkUnit` class. The `pattern` member of the `WorkUnit` class allows us to specify filter criteria to determine what files are processed. In the example in figure 17.1 we could specify a `pattern` of "*FILE.*" to match only those files whose primary name ends in FILE. The `WorkUnit` class contains the state information required for processing. This allows the processing to be similar to message-processing systems.

❷ Knowing where to put the sorted files is as important as knowing the source directory. The `outputdir` member of the `WorkUnit` class contains the root destination path. Under the directory specified in `outputdir` subdirectories will be created based on set flags that govern processing.

❸ To make the file sorting class more flexible, processing is controlled by four Boolean values. When the `convertToLowerCase` Boolean is true, the directory that a file will be moved into will be made up of lowercase letters. The original file name is not modified. The Boolean `ignoreExtension` determines if the directory created will contain the extension of the input file(s). If `removeSpaces` is true, all spaces contained in the file name are not considered when determining the name of the directory to move a file to. The `lettersOnly` Boolean determines if the target directory should contain numbers or only letters from the input file. For the example in Figure 17.1 this is one of the most important values since the numbers are the only variation in the file names within one group. Table 17.1 outlines the impact of each of these flags.

Table 17.1   Processing Flags and Their Impact

Source File Name: 1 of 10 Data File.dat	Resulting Directory Name
convertToLowerCase = true	1 of 10 data file.dat
IgnoreExtension = true	1 of 10 Data File
removeSpaces = true	1of10DataFile.dat
lettersOnly	ofDataFile.dat
All flags true	ofdatafile

❹ In previous chapters we've discussed Visual Basic .NET's New method. Recall that it is how VB.NET implements constructors. One thing that makes New a little different is the Friend keyword. In section 17.1.1 we discussed the Friend/internal keywords. When Friend is applied to a constructor it has the result of creating a class that can be accessed external to the assembly but cannot be created. This is similar to setting the Instancing property in Visual Basic to PublicNotCreatable when creating COM objects. The New method ensures that the class is in a known state before processing begins. It sets reasonable defaults for properties and ensures that any needed objects are created.

The Sorter class

The Sorter class performs sorting of files. It examines the value in an instance of the WorkUnit class to determine what manipulation should be performed in determining which directory to move the files from the input directory to. Listing 17.2 contains the general class declaration and the events and delegates.

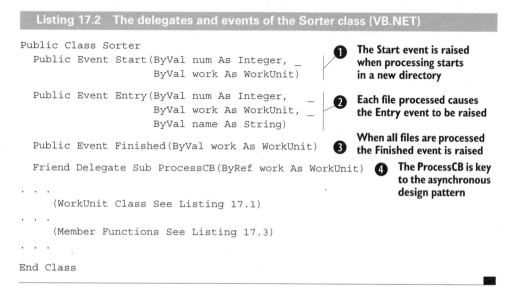

```
Public Class Sorter
   Public Event Start(ByVal num As Integer, _
                ByVal work As WorkUnit)

   Public Event Entry(ByVal num As Integer, _
                ByVal work As WorkUnit, _
                ByVal name As String)

   Public Event Finished(ByVal work As WorkUnit)

   Friend Delegate Sub ProcessCB(ByRef work As WorkUnit)
. . .
   (WorkUnit Class See Listing 17.1)
. . .
   (Member Functions See Listing 17.3)
. . .
End Class
```

❶ The Start event is raised when processing starts in a new directory

❷ Each file processed causes the Entry event to be raised

❸ When all files are processed the Finished event is raised

❹ The ProcessCB is key to the asynchronous design pattern

❶ The `Sorter` class performs the sorting of a directory. To keep the user informed about the progress of the sorting, we utilize three events. `Start` is raised when a directory is about to be sorted. It passes back the number of elements in the directory, the `num` parameter, along with a reference to the related `WorkUnit` object. This allows the client to set up any status indicating facilities, such as progress bars, to give an indication of percentage complete.

❷ `Entry` is raised when a file is processed. The `num` parameter indicates the index in the current directory. This allows for a determination of the percentage complete. A reference to the related `WorkUnit` object is passed back along with the `name` of the file being processed.

❸ `Finished` is raised when all files in the directory are processed. This allows the progress indication mechanism to indicate completion. The only parameter passed is a reference to the related `WorkUnit` object.

❹ The `ProcessCB` is an internal delegate that is used to perform the asynchronous processing. We'll discuss `ProcessCB` in more detail in the next section.

The heart of the Sorter class

So far we've discussed the supporting elements of the `Sorter` class. Now we'll take a look at the methods that perform the majority of the work. The asynchronous design pattern is based on having a method that is named `Begin` followed by the operation it performs. In our case we have a `BeginSort` method that starts the asynchronous sorting operation. Listing 17.3 contains the `BeginSort` and `EndSort` methods.

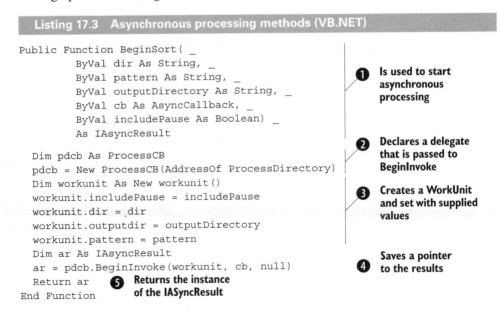

Listing 17.3 Asynchronous processing methods (VB.NET)

```
Public Function BeginSort( _
        ByVal dir As String, _
        ByVal pattern As String, _
        ByVal outputDirectory As String, _
        ByVal cb As AsyncCallback, _
        ByVal includePause As Boolean) _
        As IAsyncResult

    Dim pdcb As ProcessCB
    pdcb = New ProcessCB(AddressOf ProcessDirectory)
    Dim workunit As New workunit()
    workunit.includePause = includePause
    workunit.dir = dir
    workunit.outputdir = outputDirectory
    workunit.pattern = pattern
    Dim ar As IAsyncResult
    ar = pdcb.BeginInvoke(workunit, cb, null)
    Return ar
End Function
```

❶ Is used to start asynchronous processing

❷ Declares a delegate that is passed to BeginInvoke

❸ Creates a WorkUnit and set with supplied values

❹ Saves a pointer to the results

❺ Returns the instance of the IASyncResult

```
Public Sub EndSort( _
        ByVal ar As IAsyncResult, _
        ByRef work As WorkUnit)
  Dim pdcb As ProcessCB
  Dim arr As AsyncResult
  arr = CType(ar, AsyncResult)
  pdcb = CType(arr.AsyncDelegate(), ProcessCB)
  pdcb.EndInvoke(work, ar)
End Sub
```

6 Retrieves values from the completed processing

7 Blocks until the associated delegate completes execution

1 `BeginSort` is called to start the file-sorting process. It accepts several parameters and returns an instance of an object that implements the `IAsyncResult` interface. The object that implements `IAsyncResult` will be passed to the `EndSort` method to retrieve any information produced by the asynchronous execution.

2 In listing 17.2 we discussed the `ProcessCB` delegate. We create an instance of the `ProcessCB` delegate and call it `pdcb`. This delegate is associated with the `Process-Directory` method, which we cover in listing 17.4.

3 We discussed the `WorkUnit` object earlier. It is used to pass processing information to the `ProcessDirectory` method. The parameters passed into the `BeginSort` method are transferred to the instance of the `WorkUnit` object.

4 The `BeginInvoke` method of the `pdcb` delegate is used to begin the asynchronous delegate execution. It returns an instance of an object that supports `IAsyncResult`. We covered asynchronous execution of delegates in section 12.5. Notice that we pass in an instance of the `AsyncCallback` object, `cb`, as the second parameter to `Begin-Invoke`. If `cb` is set to an instance of the `AsyncCallback` it will be invoked when the asynchronous operation completes.

5 We then return the instance of the object that supports `IAsyncResult` to the calling method.

6 `EndSort` is invoked to retrieve the instance of the `WorkUnit` class after processing is complete. The `WorkUnit` class could be used to store information regarding which files it sorted, where it put them, how long the operations took, and so on. Notice that we pass in an instance of an object that supports `IAsyncResult` to the `EndSort` method. This object serves as a token for retrieving the correct results.

7 In order to invoke the `EndInvoke` method of the asynchronously executed delegate, we must first cast the instance of the object supporting `IAsyncResult` to an instance of the `AsyncResult` object. This is accomplished using VB.NET's `CType` method. Once we've converted `ar` to `arr`, we can retrieve the `ProcessCB` delegate and invoke the `EndInvoke` method. This populates the work variable with a reference to the work variable passed into the `BeginInvoke` method earlier.

There are times that we don't need to perform asynchronous processing. Listing 17.4 contains the `Sort` method. `Sort`, unlike `BeginSort`, blocks until it completes.

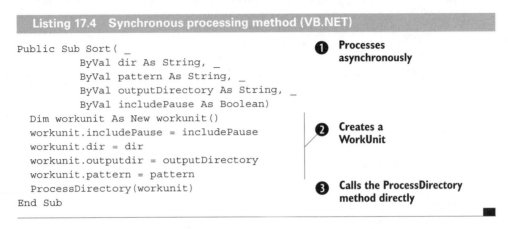

Listing 17.4   Synchronous processing method (VB.NET)

```
Public Sub Sort( _
        ByVal dir As String, _
        ByVal pattern As String, _
        ByVal outputDirectory As String, _
        ByVal includePause As Boolean)
  Dim workunit As New workunit()
  workunit.includePause = includePause
  workunit.dir = dir
  workunit.outputdir = outputDirectory
  workunit.pattern = pattern
  ProcessDirectory(workunit)
End Sub
```

❶ Processes asynchronously

❷ Creates a WorkUnit

❸ Calls the ProcessDirectory method directly

❶ Notice that the `Sort` method is considerably simpler than `BeginSort` and `EndSort`. The signature of the method is very similar. Since invocation is synchronous there is no reason to pass in a delegate to invoke when the method completes.

❷ We need to create an instance of the `WorkUnit` class in which to store the supplied parameters. These are the same steps from listing 17.3.

❸ Since `Sort` is a synchronous method we can call the `ProcessDirectory` method directly. This differs from the asynchronous approach that requires the creation of a delegate. The `ProcessDirectory` method is contained in listing 17.5.

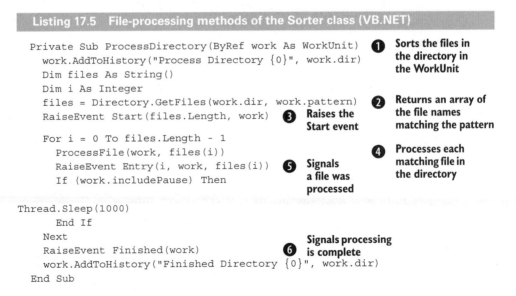

Listing 17.5   File-processing methods of the Sorter class (VB.NET)

```
Private Sub ProcessDirectory(ByRef work As WorkUnit)
  work.AddToHistory("Process Directory {0}", work.dir)
  Dim files As String()
  Dim i As Integer
  files = Directory.GetFiles(work.dir, work.pattern)
  RaiseEvent Start(files.Length, work)

  For i = 0 To files.Length - 1
    ProcessFile(work, files(i))
    RaiseEvent Entry(i, work, files(i))
    If (work.includePause) Then
      Thread.Sleep(1000)
    End If
  Next
  RaiseEvent Finished(work)
  work.AddToHistory("Finished Directory {0}", work.dir)
End Sub
```

❶ Sorts the files in the directory in the WorkUnit

❷ Returns an array of the file names matching the pattern

❸ Raises the Start event

❹ Processes each matching file in the directory

❺ Signals a file was processed

❻ Signals processing is complete

CHAPTER 17 DESIGNING WITH THREADS

```
Private Sub ProcessFile( _
        ByVal work As WorkUnit, _
        ByVal filename As String)
  work.AddToHistory("Process {0}", filename)
  Dim outputDirectory As String = work.outputdir
  Dim directoryToSort As String = work.dir
  Dim name, currentFileName As String
  currentFileName = filename
  name = filename
  name = DetermineCompareName(work, name)
  Dim newDirectory As String
  newDirectory = Path.Combine(outputDirectory, name)
  If Not Directory.Exists(newDirectory) Then
    Directory.CreateDirectory(newDirectory)
  End If
  Dim newPath As String
  Dim tmpName As String
  tmpName = Path.GetFileName(currentFileName)
  newPath = Path.Combine(newDirectory, tmpName)
  If File.Exists(newPath) Then
    Select Case work.dupes
      Case WorkUnit.DupEntryProc.ReplaceDest
        File.Delete(newPath)
        File.Move(currentFileName, newPath)
        work.AddToHistory("Moved {0} to {1}", currentFileName, newPath)
        work.numberOfFilesMoved += 1
      Case WorkUnit.DupEntryProc.RemoveSource
        work.AddToHistory("Deleted {0}", currentFileName)
        File.Delete(currentFileName)
      Case WorkUnit.DupEntryProc.DoNothing
        ' Do nothing
    End Select
  Else
    File.Move(currentFileName, newPath)
    work.AddToHistory("Moved {0} to {1}", currentFileName, newPath)
    work.numberOfFilesMoved += 1
  End If
End Sub


Private Function DetermineCompareName(ByVal work As WorkUnit, _
                                      ByVal inname As String) _
                                      As String
  Dim name As String = inname
  If (work.ignoreExtension) Then
    name = Path.GetFileNameWithoutExtension(name)
  Else
    name = Path.GetFileName(name)
  End If
  If work.removeSpaces Then
    name = name.Replace(" ", "")
  End If
```

❼ Determines what directory a file should be in

❽ Calculates the directory that a file should be moved to

```
    If work.convertToLowerCase Then
      name = name.ToLower()
    End If
    If (work.lettersOnly) Then
      Dim curC As Integer
      Dim c As Char

      Dim nameChars As Char() = name.ToCharArray()
      Dim tmpStringBuilder As New StringBuilder()
      For curC = 0 To nameChars.Length - 1
        c = nameChars(curC)
        If Char.IsLetter(c) Then
          tmpStringBuilder.Append(nameChars(curC))
        End If
      Next
      name = tmpStringBuilder.ToString()
    End If
    Return name
  End Function
```

❶ `ProcessDirectory` accepts an instance of the `WorkUnit` class as its only parameter. This is the starting point for the actual file sorting. So far we've talked about the elements in the `Sorter` class that support the asynchronous design pattern. The `ProcessDirectory` method performs the actual work.

❷ One of the first things `ProcessDirectory` does is retrieve the files from the directory named in the instance of the `WorkUnit` class into an array of strings. In order for a file name to be included in this array, it must match the pattern specified in the instance of the `WorkUnit`.

❸ To inform the user of the class that processing of the directory is beginning, the `Start` event is raised. The number of files matching the pattern in the specified directory along with a reference to the instance of the `WorkUnit` is passed back to any `Start` event handlers. This allows the user of the class to set up any feedback mechanisms, such as progress bars, with a maximum value.

❹ `ProcessFile` is then invoked on each file name in the array of files. `ProcessFile` is passed a reference to `WorkUnit` along with the name of the file to process. The `WorkUnit` reference is needed since it contains the destination directory, along with the Boolean values governing the processing of the file name to produce the corresponding directory name.

❺ After the file is processed, the `Entry` event is raised, signaling the user of the class that a file has been processed. The index of the file in the file list array, along with its name, and a reference to the `WorkUnit` item are passed to any `Entry` event handlers. This allows the user of the class to update a progress indicator.

❻ After all files are processed the `Finished` event is raised. This allows the user of the class to indicate that processing has completed.

⑦ `ProcessFile` calls `DetermineCompareName` to determine the name of the directory a file should be placed in. It then checks to see if that directory exists; if it does not, it is created. Next it checks to see if a file exists in that directory with the same name as the current file. If it does, the `dupes` data member of the `WorkUnit` object is inspected to see how processing should proceed. If there is no file name collision, the current file is moved to the specified directory.

⑧ The `DetermineCompareName` method applies the Boolean values governing directory name to the specified file name to produce the name of the directory the file should be moved to. This method contains common name manipulation methods such as removing spaces, nonletter characters, and file extensions.

17.1.3   Using the Sorter class library

So far we've covered the `Sorter` class in isolation. In this section we'll see how another class can use it. We'll start by examining the synchronous use of the `Sorter` class. We'll then explore the event handlers required. We'll finish by exploring asynchronous execution.

Synchronous execution of Sort

The simplest way to use the `Sorter` class is to use the `Sort` method. `Sort` does not return until processing of the directory has completed. Listing 17.6 contains an example of using the `Sort` method of the `Sorter` class.

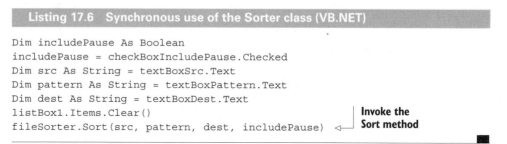

Listing 17.6   Synchronous use of the Sorter class (VB.NET)

```
Dim includePause As Boolean
includePause = checkBoxIncludePause.Checked
Dim src As String = textBoxSrc.Text
Dim pattern As String = textBoxPattern.Text
Dim dest As String = textBoxDest.Text
listBox1.Items.Clear()                                          Invoke the
fileSorter.Sort(src, pattern, dest, includePause)   ◁─┘        Sort method
```

The `Sort` method accepts four parameters:

- A string that specifies the directory to be sorted.
- A string that contains a pattern used to determine which files in the source directory are sorted.
- A string containing the destination folder. All folders that are created will be placed under the destination folder.
- A Boolean that determines if there is a one-second pause between processing each file. This helps demonstrate the need for asynchronous processing without requiring a large number of files. This would only be used during testing.

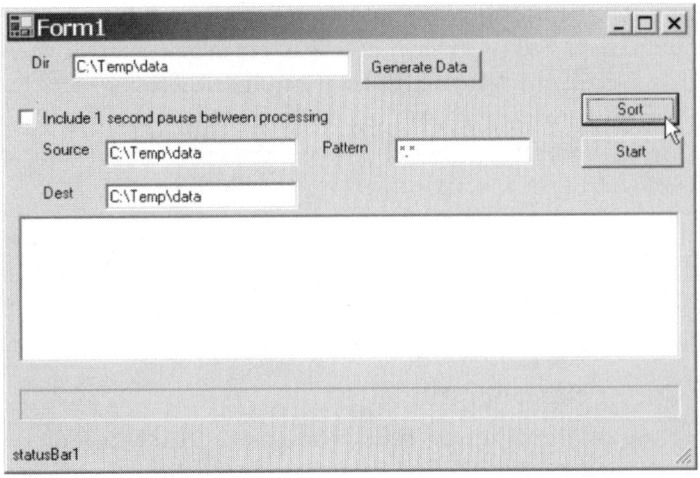

Figure 17.3
The Windows Forms application that allows synchronous and asynchronous sorting

Figure 17.3 shows the Windows Forms application that is used to call the `Sort` method of the `Sorter` class. The code in listing 17.6 is executed when the user clicks Sort.

The form will not respond to user interaction when the synchronous sort is executing. For example, if you attempt to resize the form the action will not occur until after the sorting has completed. This is because the `Sort` is occurring on the main thread of the application, the same thread that is processing messages.

While the form sort is occurring the user interface will be updated with feedback information. Figure 17.4 shows the program approximately 30 percent completed.

The next section discusses the event handlers that handle the events that are raised in listing 17.5.

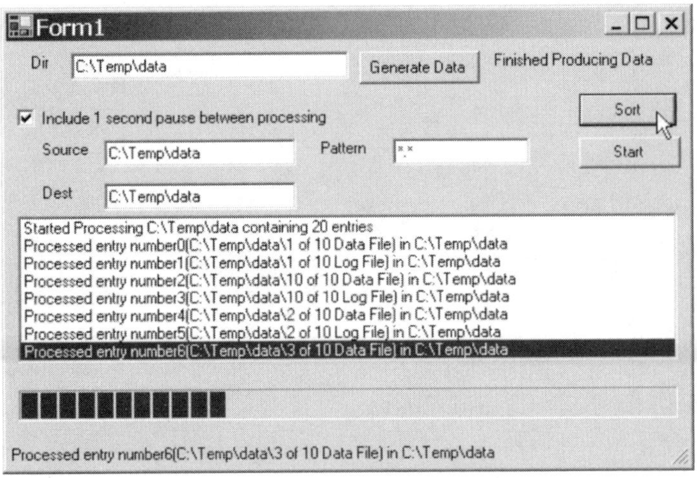

Figure 17.4
Feedback indicating the program has sorted approximately 30 percent of the files in the directory

CHAPTER 17 DESIGNING WITH THREADS

Event handlers

During processing three events are raised. The first event is the `Start` event. `Start` is raised when a directory is starting to be processed. The next event is the `Entry` event. The `Entry` event is raised every time a file in the source directory is processed. The final event raised is the `Finished` event. Listing 17.7 contains example handlers for each of these events.

Listing 17.7   Event handlers for Sorter events (VB.NET)

```vb
Sub ProcessingStarted(ByVal numberEntries As Integer, _          ❶ Handles the
                ByVal work As Sorter.WorkUnit) _                    Start event
        Handles fileSorter.Start
  Dim s As String
  s = "Started Processing "
  s += work.Directory + " containing "
  s += numberEntries.ToString()
  s += " entries"
  Dim i As Integer
  i = listBox1.Items.Add(s)
  listBox1.SelectedIndex = i
  statusBar1.Text = "Processing " + work.Directory
  progressBar1.Maximum = numberEntries
  progressBar1.Minimum = 0
  progressBar1.Value = 0
End Sub

Sub ProcessedEntry(ByVal index As Integer, _                     ❷ Handles the
                ByVal work As Sorter.WorkUnit, _                    Entry event
                ByVal name As String) _
        Handles fileSorter.Entry
  Dim s As String
  s = "Processed entry number"
  s += index.ToString()
  s += "(" + name + ") in "
  s += work.Directory
  Dim i As Integer
  i = listBox1.Items.Add(s)
  statusBar1.Text = s
  listBox1.SelectedIndex = i
  progressBar1.Value = index
End Sub
                                                                 ❸ Handles the
Private Sub Finished(ByVal work As Sorter.WorkUnit) _              Finished event
        Handles fileSorter.Finished
  statusBar1.Text = ""
  progressBar1.Value = 0
  Dim history As ArrayList = work.ProcessingHistory
End Sub
```

❶ Visual Basic .NET makes it very easy to consume events. The keyword `Handles` indicates which events the method consumes. The signature of the event handler should match the signature of the event. The `ProcessingStarted` method initializes the progress bar and adds a line to the feedback list box.

❷ When each file matching the pattern is processed, the `Entry` event is raised. The `ProcessedEntry` method handles the `Entry` event. It sets the value of the progress bar to the index of the processed file, and adds a line to the feedback list box indicating the file was processed.

❸ The `Finished` event is raised after all processing is complete. The `Finished` method sets the progress bar's value to zero, indicating that processing is complete.

One way to improve the responsiveness of the application would be to add calls to the `Application.DoEvents` method in the event handlers. However, the responsiveness would still be very jerky if the processing between events is significant. The next section discusses the use of asynchronous execution of the `Sort` method, using `BeginSort`. This results in a highly usable interface.

Asynchronous execution of Sort

Listing 17.8 shows the code that is executing when Start in figure 17.4 is clicked. The code is very similar to that in listing 17.6 with the one notable exception of the `AsyncCallback` and the invocation of the `BeginSort` method.

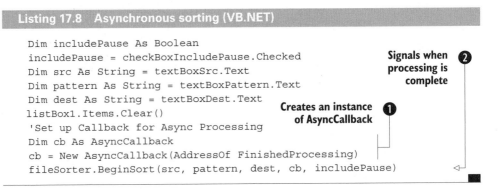

Listing 17.8   Asynchronous sorting (VB.NET)

```
Dim includePause As Boolean
includePause = checkBoxIncludePause.Checked
Dim src As String = textBoxSrc.Text
Dim pattern As String = textBoxPattern.Text
Dim dest As String = textBoxDest.Text
listBox1.Items.Clear()
'Set up Callback for Async Processing
Dim cb As AsyncCallback
cb = New AsyncCallback(AddressOf FinishedProcessing)
fileSorter.BeginSort(src, pattern, dest, cb, includePause)
```

Signals when processing is complete **❷**

Creates an instance of AsyncCallback **❶**

❶ Notice the declaration and creation of an instance of `AsyncCallback`. `AsyncCallback` allows the `FinishedProcessing` method to be invoked when the asynchronous execution is complete. This is different from the `Finished` event, which is raised in the `ProcessDirectory` method. See listing 17.5 for more on `ProcessDirectory`.

❷ `BeginSort` has the same parameters as `Sort`, with the addition of the reference to instance of `AsyncCallback`. This callback is passed to the `BeginInvoke` method, and is invoked when the delegate that `BeginInvoke` is invoked on completes execution. Listing 17.3 contains the code where `BeginInvoke` is called.

Once all asynchronous processing has completed, the `FinishedProcessing` method (listing 17.9) is invoked.

```
Private Sub FinishedProcessing(ByVal ar As IAsyncResult)
  Dim work As Sorter.WorkUnit = Nothing       EndSort allows for the
  fileSorter.EndSort(ar, work)              ❶ retrieval of results
  MessageBox.Show("Moved " + work.FilesMoved.ToString() + " files")
End Sub
```

 When asynchronous processing completes, we often want to retrieve a resulting value. Methods that are associated with `AsyncCallback` must accept a single parameter. That parameter is an object that implements `IAsyncResult`. That object can then be passed to the `EndInvoke` method on the original delegate. Listing 17.3 contains the code of `EndSort`, which simply passes the object that implements `IAsyncResult` to the `EndInvoke` method. When the `EndSort` method returns, the work variable contains the `WorkUnit` object that was originally passed into the `BeginSort` method. This allows for easy retrieval of results, in this case the number of files that were moved.

17.1.4   Steps to implement the asynchronous design pattern

To implement the asynchronous design pattern, the following steps should be followed:

1 Create a method to be invoked, marking any parameters that should be returned by the `EndInvoke` method as being `ByRef` in Visual Basic .NET, `ref` in C#. This method should perform all of the processing that will be required, or call other methods to perform the processing.

2 Define a delegate that matches the signature of the method that performs the top-level work.

3 Create a method named Begin<action>, such as `BeginSort`, which accepts any required parameters, along with a reference to an `AsyncCallback`. This method will create an instance of the delegate associating it with the work method and call `BeginInvoke`. The results of `BeginInvoke` should be returned to the caller.

4 Create a method named End<action>, such as `EndSort`, which accepts an object that implements `IAsyncResult` along with any needed reference parameters. The signature of this method will look like the delegate defined earlier, with the addition of the `IAsyncResult` object before any parameters. The return value may differ, if a single result value can be returned.

5 For completeness create a method that invokes an instance of the delegate directly, providing for synchronous processing. This method should be named <action>, such as `Sort`.

Following these steps produces an object that follows the asynchronous design pattern. There are two choices in how to interact with the object in an asynchronous way. One involves passing a callback to the Begin<action> method that is invoked when execution completes.

The alternative is to call End<action>. Calling it causes execution on that thread to block until the asynchronous execution completes. This allows the caller to start processing, continue executing some other task, and then call End<action> to wait for the asynchronous operation.

The examples in this section have been presented in Visual Basic .NET. The C# version of the examples are available from the publisher's web site.

17.2   MESSAGE QUEUE EXAMPLE

Microsoft Message Queue (MSMQ) is a messaging system that ensures delivery of messages and provides security, routing, and priority. In this section we'll examine .NET's support for MSMQ and an implementation of the asynchronous design pattern.

MSMQ can be viewed as a consumer/producer model. The idea is that messages are added to a queue and processed at some later point. MSMQ ensures that the message will not be lost along the way. This simplifies development considerably, removing a large amount of "plumbing" from application development. In this section we'll examine a very simple MSMQ application.

17.2.1   The message producer

To demonstrate .NET's asynchronous implementation of receiving a message we must first have a message to receive. Figure 17.5 shows of a program that produces a very simple message.

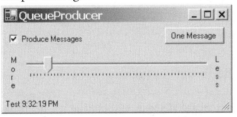

Figure 17.5   The message producer

The slider can be moved from right to left to change the frequency of message generation. The status bar displays the text of the last message generated. The One Message button produces a single message. The Produce Messages checkbox controls if messages are produced at a regular interval. Listing 17.10 contains the most important element of the message-producing application.

Listing 17.10   The AddMessage method adds a single message to the message queue (C#).

```
void AddMessage()
{
  try
  {
    string message;
```

```
      message = "Test " + DateTime.Now.ToLongTimeString();
      this.messageQueue1.Send(message );                        Adds an entry to
      this.statusBar1.Text = message;                               the message queue
    }
    catch(Exception ex)
    {
      MessageBox.Show(ex.ToString());
    }
}
```

 The Send method of the MessageQueue class is used to enter a new message into a queue. Since entering a message in a queue is not a time-consuming activity, it is performed synchronously. There are several different versions of the Send method. The one we are using here is the simplest; it accepts a single object that becomes the body of the message.

In order to execute this example you must have MSMQ installed. When the form loads initially, it attempts to create a message queue named.\Private$\ManningThreads. This is a local queue and should work on most installations. The following code creates the message queue if it does not exist:

```
if (!MessageQueue.Exists(queueName))
{
  MessageQueue.Create(queueName );
}
```

17.2.2   The message consumer

Now that we have a producer of messages, we need something to consume them. There are several ways that messages can be consumed using the MessageQueue object.

Synchronous receive

The simplest way to consume a message is to use the MessageQueue's synchronous Receive method. Receive blocks the calling thread until a message can be received. If no messages are in the queue, the method waits until either a message arrives, or, if a timeout is specified, the timeout expires. Listing 17.11 shows the Receive method being used with no specified timeout.

Listing 17.11   The Receive method used with no timeout specified (C#)

```
System.Messaging.Message msg = messageQueue1.Receive();    Blocks until a
string s="(null)";                                          message is received
if (msg != null & msg.Body != null)
{
  s = msg.Body.ToString();
}
UpdateMessageDisplay(s);
```

In the case of a Windows Forms application, while the main thread of the application is waiting on `Receive` to return it is unable to process any Win32 messages. This causes the application to hang and be unresponsive. When a message is received, the application will resume processing the messages.

Asynchronous processing using BeginReceive

A more desirable way of interacting with a message queue is to use the asynchronous processing support built into the `MessageQueue` object. Listing 17.12 shows the use of `BeginReceive` and `ReceiveCompletedEventHandler`.

Listing 17.12 BeginReceive returns before a message is received (C#)

```
private void button1_Click(object sender, System.EventArgs e)
{
  try
  {
    messageQueue1.BeginReceive();          ❶ BeginReceive returns
  }                                           before the message is
  catch(Exception ex)                         received
  {
    UpdateMessageDisplay(ex.ToString());
  }
}
private void messageQueue1_ReceiveCompleted(  ❷ ReceivedCompleted
  object sender,                                 event is raised
  ReceiveCompletedEventArgs e)
{
  string s="(null)";
  if (e.Message != null & e.Message.Body != null)
  {
    s=e.Message.Body.ToString();
  }
  UpdateMessageDisplay(s);
}
```

❶ The `MessageQueue` object follows the asynchronous design pattern. The `Begin-Receive` method returns instantly, allowing the calling thread to continue processing. In the case of a Windows Forms application, this processing is servicing the Win32 message pump. Using `BeginReceive` allows the application to respond to user interaction while it is waiting for an MSMQ message to arrive.

❷ Once a message arrives, the `messageQueue1_ReceiveCompleted` method is invoked. This is because the method is associated with the `ReceiveCompleted` event. It is important to understand that the `messageQueue1_ReceiveCompleted` method will execute on the main thread.

The `messageQueue1_ReceiveCompleted` method is associated with the `ReceiveCompleted` event during the application initialization. The following associates the method with the event:

```
ReceiveCompletedEventHandler handler;
handler=new ReceiveCompletedEventHandler(messageQueue1_ReceiveCompleted);
messageQueue1.ReceiveCompleted += handler;
```

The handler variable is introduced to improve readability. The key element is the `+=` operator being applied to the `ReceiveCompleted` event. When a `BeginReceive` operation completes, and no callback has been passed to `BeginReceive`, the `ReceiveCompleted` event will be raised.

Using BeginReceive with a callback

Another way of receiving messages asynchronously is to pass a callback to `Begin-Receive`. Listing 17.13 contains an example showing the use of a callback with the `BeginReceive` method.

Listing 17.13   The method callbackMethod is invoked when a message is received (C#).

```
private void button3_Click(object sender, System.EventArgs e)
{
  AsyncCallback callback = new AsyncCallback(callbackMethod);
  messageQueue1.BeginReceive(MessageQueue.InfiniteTimeout,null,callback);
}
private void callbackMethod(IAsyncResult ar)
{
  System.Messaging.Message msg;
  msg = messageQueue1.EndReceive(ar);
  string s="(null)";
  if (msg != null & msg.Body != null)
  {
    s = msg.Body.ToString();
  }
  UpdateMessageDisplay(s);
}
```

❶ The callback object is passed to BeginReceive

❷ EndReceive is used to retrieve the received message

❶ `BeginReceive` can accept an instance of the `AsyncCallback` class. The method associated with the callback is invoked when a message is received. In this case `call-backMethod` is invoked when a message is received and `BeginReceive` has been previously executed. At most one message will be received.

❷ `EndReceive` accepts an instance of an object that supports `IAsyncResult` as its only parameter. It returns the message that was received and triggered the invocation of the callback. The message we received in this case is a very simple one; it contains a single string.

A variation on this approach is to have the callback method begin the next read. This allows for a lightweight way of keeping a message queue empty. Listing 17.14 contains a modified callback method.

```csharp
private void callbackMethodQueueClean(IAsyncResult ar)
{
  System.Messaging.Message msg;
  msg= messageQueue1.EndReceive(ar);
  string s="(null)";
  if (msg != null & msg.Body != null)
  {
    s = msg.Body.ToString();
  }
  UpdateMessageDisplay(s);

  AsyncCallback callback = new AsyncCallback(callbackMethodQueueClean);
  messageQueue1.BeginReceive(MessageQueue.InfiniteTimeout,null,callback);
}
```

In this section we've examined the MessageQueue object and its support for asynchronous processing. By emulating this and other objects in the .NET framework, you can develop an easy-to-reuse object. This is one of the biggest benefits of using design patterns: They allow users of an object to have a baseline level of understanding once they know which pattern an object follows.

17.3   ONE CLASS ONE THREAD

There are times that we want to perform asynchronous execution without caring about the results. An example is error logging. When an error occurs, often one of the first things needed is to record that error for later analysis. Once the request to record the information is made, the next order of business is recovering from the error. Since future processing is not dependent upon the outcome of the error logging routine, it can continue while the error is being recorded. To demonstrate a different approach to asynchronous design this section discusses a multithreaded logging class. Figure 17.6 shows the test harness for the logging class.

We'll start by examining the code that executes when Initialize Logger button is clicked. Listing 17.15 contains the relevant code.

```vbnet
Try

    If Not log Is Nothing Then        ❶ Clean up any previous
      log.Shutdown()                     instances of the logger
    End If
    log = New Logger()
```

```
        log.LogFile = textBoxLogFilename.Text
        log.MessageQueuePath = textBoxMQPath.Text
        log.EventLogSource = textBoxEventLogSource.Text
        log.URL = textBoxURL.Text
        log.SQLConnectionString = textBoxConnect.Text
        log.SQLCommandTextFormat = textBoxCommand.Text
        Dim tmpWhere As Logger.WhereToLog
        tmpWhere = 0
        If checkBoxDatabase.Checked Then
          tmpWhere = tmpWhere Or Logger.WhereToLog.Database
        End If
        If checkBoxEventLog.Checked Then
          tmpWhere = tmpWhere Or Logger.WhereToLog.EventLog
        End If
        If (checkBoxMQ.Checked) Then
          tmpWhere = tmpWhere Or Logger.WhereToLog.MessageQueue
        End If
        If (checkBoxTextFile.Checked) Then
          tmpWhere = tmpWhere Or Logger.WhereToLog.File
        End If
        If (checkBoxTrace.Checked) Then
          tmpWhere = tmpWhere Or Logger.WhereToLog.Trace
        End If
        If (checkBoxWeb.Checked) Then
          tmpWhere = tmpWhere Or Logger.WhereToLog.WebPage
        End If

       log.LogTo = tmpWhere
Catch ex As Exception
   MessageBox.Show(ex.Message)
End Try
```

2 Set the logging destination parameters

3 Set the logging destination flag

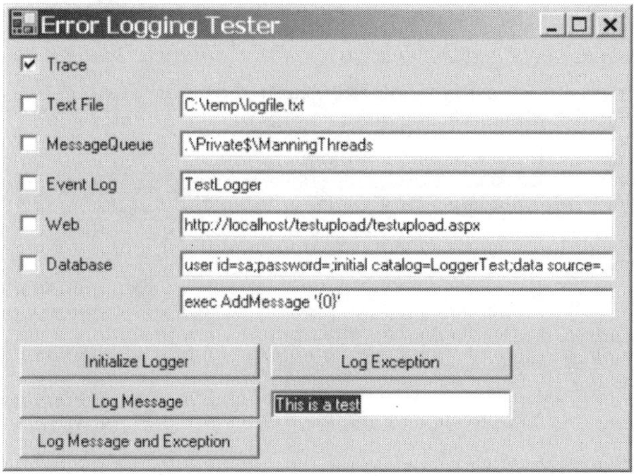

Figure 17.6
Logging class test harness

❶ First we check to see if an instance of the `Logger` class has been previously created. If it has, the `Shutdown` method is called, cleaning up the background thread. Next an instance of the `Logger` class is created and assigned to the log member variable.

❷ Depending on the destination we select, there are several values that are required. For instance, if we select that we want the logging to go to a text file we must supply a file name.

❸ The logging destination is a product of using binary on an enumeration. The `Where-ToLog` enumeration is assigned powers of two. This allows a single value to determine if content is sent to multiple locations. The following is the definition of the enumeration:

```
Public Enum WhereToLog
    Trace = 1
    File = 2
    WebPage = 4
    EventLog = 8
    MessageQueue = 16
    Database = 32
End Enum
```

As you can see the `Logger` class provides support, albeit limited, for logging to text files, web pages, the Windows NT event log, and MSMQ. The idea here is to demonstrate the concept, not produce an enterprise-quality logging component.

When the Log Message button is clicked the string that is contained in the textbox beside it is sent to the logging component. The following instructions execute:

```
If log Is Nothing Then
  MessageBox.Show("Log not initialized")
Else
  log.LogMessage(textBoxMessage.Text)
End If
```

At this point we've discussed the test program enough to dive into the actual `Logging` class. Listing 17.16 contains the most relevant code elements. The attempt here is to focus on the more interesting aspects of the class. The full source for this, and all examples, is available from the publisher's web site.

Listing 17.16   Key elements of the Logger class (VB.NET)

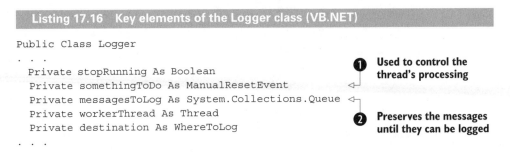

```
Public Class Logger
. . .
  Private stopRunning As Boolean
  Private somethingToDo As ManualResetEvent          ❶ Used to control the
  Private messagesToLog As System.Collections.Queue     thread's processing
  Private workerThread As Thread
  Private destination As WhereToLog                  ❷ Preserves the messages
. . .                                                    until they can be logged
```

```vbnet
Public Sub New()
  stopRunning = False
  somethingToDo = New ManualResetEvent(False)
  messagesToLog = System.Collections.Queue.Synchronized(
    New System.Collections.Queue())
  filename = ""
  destination = WhereToLog.Trace Or WhereToLog.EventLog
  workerThread = New Thread(AddressOf ThreadMethod)
  workerThread.Name = "Logging worker thread"
  workerThread.IsBackground = True
  workerThread.Start()
End Sub
Public Sub Shutdown()
  stopRunning = True
  somethingToDo.Set()
End Sub

Public Sub LogMessage(ByVal message As String)
  messagesToLog.Enqueue(message)
  somethingToDo.Set()
End Sub
. . .
Private Sub LogToFile(ByVal message As String)
  If (filename.Length = 0) Then
    Throw New Exception("Filename not set and File is target to log to")
  End If
  Dim stream As FileStream
  stream = File.Open(
    filename,FileMode.Append, FileAccess.Write, FileShare.Read)
  stream.Seek(0, SeekOrigin.End)
  Dim contents() As Byte
  contents = System.Text.Encoding.ASCII.GetBytes(message)
  stream.Write(contents, 0, contents.Length)
  stream.Close()
End Sub
. . .
Private Sub LogString(ByVal message As String)
  If ((destination And WhereToLog.Trace) > 0) Then
    Trace.WriteLine(message)
  End If
  If ((destination And WhereToLog.File) > 0) Then
    LogToFile(message + "\r\n")
  End If
  If ((destination And WhereToLog.WebPage) > 0) Then
    LogToWebPage(message)
  End If
  If ((destination And WhereToLog.MessageQueue) > 0) Then
    LogToMQ(message)
  End If
  If ((destination And WhereToLog.EventLog) > 0) Then
    LogToEventLog(message)
  End If
```

③ Creates an instance of the Thread class

④ Terminates the working thread

⑤ Returns before the message has been processed

```
      If ((destination And WhereToLog.Database) > 0) Then
        LogToDB(message)
      End If
    End Sub
    Private Sub ThreadMethod()
      While (Not stopRunning)
        While (messagesToLog.Count > 0)
          Try
            Dim message As String
            message = CType(messagesToLog.Dequeue(), String)
            LogString(message)
          Catch ex As Exception
            System.Diagnostics.Trace.WriteLine(ex.ToString())
          End Try
        End While
        somethingToDo.Reset()
        somethingToDo.WaitOne(1000, False)
      End While
    End Sub
End Class
```

⑥ Removes entries from the queue and processes them

❶ The majority of the time the logging component will not be processing any messages; that is, assuming that it's running with relatively high-quality code. So it doesn't consume unneeded resources, we use a `ManualResetEvent` to signal the thread that there's something to do.

❷ As we've done in past examples we use a queue to act as the connection point between the calling threads and the worker thread. To ensure that there are no concurrency issues, we use the `Shared/static Synchronized` method of the `Queue` class to convert the `Queue` to a thread-safe queue.

❸ The next step is to create an instance of the `Thread` class to be associated with the thread's method. This should look very familiar. The last step in the `New/constructor` is to start the newly created thread.

❹ The `Shutdown` method terminates the thread. This is accomplished by setting the `stopRunning` data member to true. The thread's method contains a main loop that checks the value of `stopRunning`. If this code was going into a production environment, `stopRunning` should be protected with a synchronization lock. Any time a class data member can be manipulated by different threads it should be protected with a synchronization lock or be thread-safe. The frequency of `Shutdown` execution should be very low, if at all.

❺ `LogMessage` enters a string into the queue that the thread processes and sets the `ManualResetEvent` to being signaled. This has the effect of waking up the thread and starting the processing.

CHAPTER 17 DESIGNING WITH THREADS

❻ The thread's job is to keep the queue empty. To ensure a message doesn't get "stuck" in the queue, we set a one-second timeout on the `WaitOne` method of `ManualReset-Event`. This will ensure that the thread will check the queue for work once a second or when it is signaled.

This example demonstrates a class that is multithreaded and does not require the code that uses the class to know anything about the multithreaded implementation. If processing is not dependent on the outcome of a task, asynchronous execution should be considered.

17.4 PERFORMANCE ISSUES

When designing multithreaded applications, you must to consider the performance implications of each design decision. A common mistake when learning a new technology is to apply it to every problem. This is a natural tendency, but should be restrained as much as possible. Instead, take the new concepts and apply them to situations where they provide value. Otherwise, the result will be solutions that are difficult to maintain and cumbersome to use.

In this section we'll briefly cover the cost of multithreaded development, the concept of concurrency, and the implication of multiple processors in a system.

17.4.1 Multithreading overhead

Threads aren't free. This is a simple statement, but it should be in the back of your mind at all times when designing a multithreaded solution. The creation of threads is relatively inexpensive, compared to creation of a process under Windows OS. This doesn't mean that large numbers of threads should be created, but rather that the cost of using a thread is not as high as some of the alternatives.

Thread pools take much of the difficulty out of multithreaded development. If a task is short in duration, and relatively frequently occurring, it is a likely candidate for a thread pool. If a task is longer lived it may require the creation of a thread.

A key element with multithreaded design is balancing the need for independent components that are self-contained with the minimization of the number of threads required. Any time there is the possibility that a large number of threads can be created, such as servicing a large number of requests, the architecture should be revisited and most likely redesigned.

17.4.2 Increasing concurrency

Concurrency is a measure of the number of activities that occur at roughly the same time. If high performance is a design goal then general concurrency should be maximized. Concurrency must be balanced against creating a large number of threads. This isn't an exact science, but rather a skill that is developed over time.

One approach is to develop a working, low-concurrency solution initially and increase concurrency to meet throughput requirements. This approach allows for optimization in areas that are known to be performance bottlenecks. It is much easier to improve on working code than it is to attempt to predict where the improvements will add value.

The nature of the work being performed will influence the design. As with all designs the tasks being performed will impact the decisions made. There is no magic formula for multithreaded applications. There are design patterns than can be followed that work for a certain class of problems, but there is no general solution. Experience, benchmarking, and patience are the best tools for becoming a seasoned multithreaded developer.

17.4.3   Implications of multiple processors

Multiple processors allow multiple threads to execute simultaneously. This is a tremendous benefit for high-performance systems. The cost of the parallelism comes in the form of shared memory. Anytime values must be shared between threads there is a considerable performance penalty if multiple processors are involved. The basic problem is that all involved threads must reach a state when the value is certain to be correct. The impact of shared values among threads should motivate designers to minimize sharing of data as much as possible.

As mentioned earlier, testing should always be done on a system that is similar to production. There are concurrency issues that will not occur, or occur very infrequently, on a single-processor system that will occur with a high degree of regularity on a multiple-processor system. The result of this sort of situation is generally reflected in a developer saying "It works on my machine," which does little to solve the production issue.

17.5   SUMMARY

This chapter has revisited the design considerations that have been covered throughout this book. The most important concept to take away from this chapter is that there is no single correct way of using multiple threads. As with many things, there are wrong ways of solving the problem, but there is no magical algorithm that will solve all design issues.

We have covered the asynchronous design pattern and seen how it is implemented in various .NET objects. The asynchronous design pattern is an ideal approach to use for many situations. One of the key advantages it has over other approaches is that developers will become very familiar with it as they do .NET development. By creating custom libraries that follow this pattern, developers will have a pretty good idea of how to use your library without having it explained to them.

We also covered the concept of associating a class with a single working thread. This generally involves a queue, and the thread's job is to keep that queue empty. A one-class one-thread approach works well for situations where the caller of a method does not care about the result of the processing of that method. Additionally, classes that contain multiple threads appear to the users of those classes as though they were any other class. An example of such a class in the .NET framework is `WebClient`. It is multithreaded, but the users of the class aren't required to know that fact to use it.

It is important when dealing with a new topic to not forget the lessons learned with previous technologies. All too often when faced with an unfamiliar task we forget the discipline, structure, and procedures that have served us well in the past.

C H A P T E R   1 8

Multithreading in J#

J# is very similar to Microsoft J++ and Java programming language. It is intended to provide a way for developers familiar with Java to utilize the .NET platform.

18.1 J#'S THREAD CLASS

J# contains a `Thread` class that is very similar to the `System.Threading.Thread` class. One fundamental difference is that the .NET `System.Threading.Thread` class is sealed. This means that it cannot be inherited from. In J# it's possible, and often desirable, to subclass the `Thread` class.

18.1.1 Extending the Thread class

One way that J# allows for threads to be created is by inheriting from the `Thread` class. In C# and VB.NET the `Thread` class is a sealed class. It contains methods and properties relating to threads and their creation. J# takes an older approach where a class can be created that contains an overridden method named `run` that is the entry point for the new thread. Listing 18.1 contains a class that was created by subclassing `Thread`.

Listing 18.1   ThreadedClass is derived from the Thread class (J#).

```
package SubclassingThread;
public class ThreadedClass extends Thread
{
    public void run()
    {
        for (int i=0;i< 100;i++)
        {
            try
            {
                String s;
                s =System.Convert.ToString(i);
                System.Diagnostics.Debug.WriteLine(s);
                this.sleep(1000);
            }
            catch(InterruptedException ex)
            {
                // Someone called interupt
                System.Diagnostics.Debug.WriteLine(ex.toString());
            }
        }
    }
}
```

Notice the only method contained in the `ThreadedClass` is `run`. This example prints out 0 to 99, pausing one second between each iteration. The following is an example of using the `ThreadedClass`:

```
ThreadedClass c;
c = new ThreadedClass();
c.start();
```

Notice that we don't call `run` directly but instead call the `start` method. The `start` method invokes `run` on a different thread. The `stop` method is used to halt a thread's execution. This is similar to the `Abort` method used in C# and VB.NET. The following causes the thread to stop executing:

```
c.stop();
```

The J# Thread class is similar to the `System.Threading.Thread` class. In the next section we compare and contrast the two classes.

18.1.2   Comparing the Thread class to System.Threading.Thread

The `Thread` class and the `System.Threading.Thread` class are similar in many ways.

Setting a thread's name

We've discussed the advantages of assigning a name to a thread. J# uses functions to manipulate a thread's name instead of properties. Listing 18.2 contains the J# version of listing 5.2.

Listing 18.2   Setting a thread's name in J# using the setName function (J#)

```
package ThreadName;                                    The setName function is used to
public class WebSiteMonitorConsole                      assign a new name to a thread
{
    /** @attribute System.STAThread() */
    public static void main(String[] args)             The getName function returns
    {                                                    the name of the thread
        System.Console.WriteLine(Thread.currentThread().getName());
        Thread.currentThread().setName("Main");
        System.Console.WriteLine(Thread.currentThread().getName());
        WebSiteMonitor SiteMonitor;
        SiteMonitor = new WebSiteMonitor("http://localhost/test.htm", 1000);
        SiteMonitor.Start();
        try
        {
            Thread.currentThread().sleep(15000);
        }
        catch(InterruptedException ex)
        {
            System.Console.WriteLine(ex.getMessage());
        }
        SiteMonitor.Abort();
        SiteMonitor.Join();
    }
}
```

Notice the addition of the initial `WriteLine` to the console. It displays the name of the main thread before the call to `setName` is made. In J# the main thread's name is set to main when the thread is created. Additionally, the name of the thread can be changed any number of times. This is different from the `System.Threading.Thread` class, which does not allow the name of a thread to be changed once it has been set.

Listing 18.2 uses the `WebSiteMonitor` class. Listing 18.3 contains the J# version of that class.

Listing 18.3   The J# version of the WebSiteMonitor class from chapter 5 (J#)

```
package ThreadName;                                    ❶ Utilizes the
public class WebSiteMonitor extends Thread  ❶             Thread class
{
    String URL;
    long startMs;
    long stopMs;
```

```
long lastRequestHowLong;
long sleepTime;

public WebSiteMonitor(String URL, int sleepTime)
{
    this.sleepTime=sleepTime;
    this.URL = URL;
}
public void Start()
{
    this.setName("WebSiteMonitor");          ❷ Controls the name
    this.start();          ❶ Utilizes the           of the thread
}                              Thread class
public void Abort()
{
    this.stop();           ❶ Utilizes the
}                              Thread class
public void Join()
{
    try
    {
        this.join();       ❶ Utilizes the
    }                          Thread class
    catch (InterruptedException e)
    {
    }
}

public void run()          ❶ Utilizes the
{                              Thread class
    System.Console.WriteLine(Thread.currentThread().getName());
    boolean notify ;
    while (true)
    {
        notify = false;
        System.Net.WebClient client;          ❸ Uses the
        client= new System.Net.WebClient();        framework's
        ubyte[] data ;                             WebClient class
        startMs= System.currentTimeMillis();
        data = client.DownloadData(URL);
        stopMs= System.currentTimeMillis();

        lastRequestHowLong =  stopMs - startMs;
        String results ;
        results = System.Text.Encoding.get_ASCII().GetString(data);
        if (results.indexOf("OK") < 0)
        {
            notify = true;
        }

        if (notify)
        {
            // Let someone know
        }
```

CHAPTER 18   MULTITHREADING IN J#

```
            try
            {
                Thread.currentThread().sleep(sleepTime);
            }
            catch(InterruptedException e)
            {
            }

        }
    }
}
```

❶ Notice that WebSiteMonitor inherits from the Thread class. When you're extending the Thread class it is necessary to include an overridden version of the run method. The run method replaces the ThreadMethod of chapter 5. Notice that the class utilizes the start, stop, and join methods. These methods are inherited from the Thread class. We'll discuss these methods in the next section.

❷ J# uses a function approach to setting values of a class. The setName function performs the same operation as the set portion of the Name property of the framework's Thread class. As mentioned earlier, the setName function is less restrictive than the Name property in that it allows multiple assignments.

❸ One reason that people use J# is to have access to the .NET framework. Notice that we're using the framework's WebClient class. This sort of migration is a powerful tool for developers coming from the Java platform because it allows them to use the language they are familiar with while taking advantage of the extensive library support that .NET offers.

Starting, stopping, and joining a thread

In chapter 4 we spent a great deal of time discussing the creation, termination, and coordination of threads. Since .NET has many of its roots in the Java world, it's not surprising that J# contains very similar methods. Other than the obvious capitalization changes the most major difference is the absence of an Abort method. Instead, J# uses a stop method. Recall from chapter 4 that the Abort method causes ThreadAbortException to be raised on the thread. This allows the thread the alternative of calling ResetAbort and ignoring the termination request. In J# the stop method causes the thread to terminate without allowing the thread the opportunity to decline the request.

The stop method is deprecated, which means that it may be removed in future releases of J#. Rather than using the stop method it's recommended to have a Boolean control the thread's execution. Generally threads contain a main loop, which should test the value of a Boolean that indicates when it's time to terminate.

The start and join methods behave as we'd expect. Listing 18.4 contains a simple class that extends the J# Thread class.

```
package StartJoin;
import System.Console;
public class Other extends Thread
{
    public void run()
    {
        Console.WriteLine("Starting other thread");
        for (int i=0;i<4;i++)
        {
            Console.WriteLine("*");
            try
            {
                Thread.sleep(1000);
            }
            catch (InterruptedException ex)
            {
            }
        }
        Console.WriteLine("Exiting other thread");
    }
}
```

The Other class is derived from the J# Thread class. It contains a single overridden version of the run method. This method is the entry point for the thread. The console application that creates an instance of this class and starts it is included in listing 18.5.

```
package StartJoin;
import System.Console;
public class ClassMain
{
    /** @attribute System.STAThread() */
    public static void main(String[] args)
    {
        Console.WriteLine("Starting main thread");
        Other otherThread;                          Causes the
        otherThread=new Other();                    other thread to
        otherThread.start();              ❶         begin executing            ❷  Releases the
        Thread.yield();                                                            remainder of
        Console.WriteLine("Joining other thread");                                 the time slice
        try                               Pauses until the
        {                                 other thread
            otherThread.join();   ❸       terminates
```

```
        }
        catch (InterruptedException ex)
        {
        }
        Console.WriteLine("Joined other thread");
        Console.WriteLine("Exiting main thread");
    }
}
```

❶ The `start` method causes `otherThread` to begin executing the `run` method on a different thread. This is identical to the framework version of the `run` method.

❷ The `yield` method causes the current thread to surrender the remainder of its time to the OS. This allows other threads the chance to run. It is used here to allow the other thread time to start before signaling the main thread to `join`. This isn't required, but it makes the output look more logical.

❸ The J# `join` method causes the current thread to wait until the thread associated with the instance of the J# `Thread` class terminates. This is the same behavior that we saw with the `System.Threading.Thread Join` method.

The following output is generated when the code from listings 18.4 and 18.5 executes:

```
Starting main thread
Starting other thread
*
Joining other thread
*
*
*
Exiting other thread
Joined other thread
Exiting main thread
```

Notice that the main thread starts and then the other thread starts. Next the main thread `join`s to the other thread, waiting for its termination. When the other thread terminates the main thread resumes processing, displaying the "Joined other thread" message and then terminating.

Controlling thread priority

In chapter 5 we discussed changing a thread's priority. Recall that a thread was assigned a priority from the `ThreadPriority` enumeration. J# takes a different approach. A thread is assigned a priority from between the `MIN_PRIORITY` and `MAX_PRIORITY` constants. Under the current implementation of J#, these map to 1 and 10 respectively. You'll notice that produces ten possible priority settings compared to the five enumeration values in the `ThreadPriority` class: `Lowest`, `BelowNormal`, `Normal`, `AboveNormal`, and `Highest`. Listing 18.6 helps us map J#'s ten values to each of the `ThreadPriority` values.

Listing 18.6 J#'s priorities range from MIN_PRIORITY to MAX_PRIORITY (J#).

```
Thread jsThread;
jsThread = Thread.currentThread();

System.Threading.Thread frameworkThread;
frameworkThread =System.Threading.Thread.get_CurrentThread();

for (int i= Thread.MIN_PRIORITY; i <= Thread.MAX_PRIORITY;i++)
{
  Console.Write(i);
  Console.Write("\t");
  jsThread.setPriority(i);
  Console.WriteLine(frameworkThread.get_Priority());
}
```

Listing 18.6 produces the following output:

```
1       Lowest
2       Lowest
3       BelowNormal
4       BelowNormal
5       Normal
6       Normal
7       AboveNormal
8       AboveNormal
9       Highest
10      Highest
```

The first column is the J# thread priority while the second column is the corresponding `ThreadPriority` enumeration value. The reason for the ten values is compatibility with other implementations of Java. Under the Windows OS there are only five priority values that a thread can be assigned. By mapping two J# values to one `ThreadPriority` enumeration value an even distribution is achieved.

Inspecting a thread's state

The .NET framework allows for exhaustive inspection of a thread's state. J# provides limited facilities for determining a thread's state. The two methods available in J# are `isAlive` and `isInterrupted`. The `isAlive` method is functionally equivalent to the framework thread's `IsAlive` property. There isn't a method in the framework `Thread` class that is comparable to the `isInterrupted` function. Initially, `isInterrupted` returns false. After the `interrupt` method is called on a J# thread the function returns true until the thread enters a sleep state. An example that demonstrates this behavior will help shine a little light on the concept. Listing 18.7 contains a class that extends the J# `Thread` class.

Listing 18.7 A thread that loops printing out asterisks (J#)

```
package ThreadState;
import System.Console;
public class OtherThread extends Thread
{
    private int iterations=0;

    public OtherThread(int iterations)
    {
        this.iterations=iterations;
    }
    public void run()
    {
        for (int i=0;i<iterations;i++)
        {
            try
            {
                Console.WriteLine("*");
                Thread.sleep(1000);
            }
            catch(InterruptedException ex)
            {
                Console.WriteLine("!");
            }
        }
    }
}
```

The thread in listing 18.7 doesn't do much. The thread loops for a configurable number of times, printing an asterisk to the console. When some other thread causes an interrupt to occur, an exclamation mark is displayed. The main portion of this example is contained in listing 18.8.

Listing 18.8 The main class of the console application (J#)

```
package ThreadState;
public class ClassMain
{
    private static void displayStatus(OtherThread t, String message)
    {
        String status = message + " ";
        status += t.isAlive() + "   ";
        status += t.isInterrupted() + "   ";
        System.Console.WriteLine(status);
    }
    /** @attribute System.STAThread() */
    public static void main(String[] args) throws Exception
    {
        System.Console.WriteLine("Message        isAlive  isInterrupted");
```

```
        OtherThread t;
        t=new OtherThread(5);
        displayStatus(t,"Before Start     ");
        t.start();
        Thread.sleep(1000) ;
        displayStatus(t,"After Start      ");
        t.interrupt();
        displayStatus(t,"After Interrupt ");
        for (int i=0;i< 6 ;i++)
        {
            Thread.sleep(1000) ;
            displayStatus(t,"                      ");
        }
        System.Console.Read();
    }
}
```

The main function starts off by writing a header to the console. Next it creates an instance of the `OtherThread` class from listing 18.7. The main function calls `displayStatus`, which calls both `isAlive` and `isInterrupted` on the supplied instance of `OtherThread` and displays their return values on the console. Next the main thread sleeps for a second to give the instance of the `OtherThread` time to start. Next display status is called again. To see the behavior of the `isInterrupted` function we call `interrupt` on the instance of the `OtherThread`. This forces the thread to exit the sleep state and resume processing. The code in listing 18.8 produces the following output:

```
Message          isAlive   isInterrupted
Before Start     false     false
*
After Start      true      false
After Interrupt  true      true
!
*
                 true      false
*
                 true      false
*
                 true      false
*
                 true      false
                 false     false
                 false     false
```

Notice that the `isInterrupted` value switches from false to true and then back to false. When the instance of `OtherThread` invokes the `sleep` function, it clears the `isInterrupted` flag. After the instance of `OtherThread` has completed execution, you can see the value for `isAlive` switch from true to false.

Background threads

In chapter 5 we discussed foreground and background threads. Recall that all background threads are terminated at the point all foreground threads exit. J# refers to background threads as daemon threads. The word *daemon* as used here is from ancient Greek. Often it is confused with *demon* from Judaism and Christianity, which refers to an unclean spirit. As used here it refers to an entity that keeps watch on things, something background threads are often tasked with.

To control if a thread is a background thread in J# we use the `setDaemon` method. The `isDaemon` method returns a Boolean that indicates if the associated thread is a background thread. Listing 18.9 is a console application that uses the `OtherThread` class from listing 18.7 and demonstrates background threads.

Listing 18.9   Determines if the thread is a background thread (J#)

```
package BackgroundThread;
import System.Console;
public class ClassMain
{
    /** @attribute System.STAThread() */
    public static void main(String[] args) throws Exception
    {
        System.Console.WriteLine("Message          isAlive  isDaemon");
        OtherThread t;
        t=new OtherThread(5);
        displayStatus(t,"Before Start    ");

        Console.WriteLine("Other thread is Daemon? [Y/N]");
        String input = Console.ReadLine();
        if (input.toLowerCase().charAt(0) == 'y')
        {
            t.setDaemon(true);
        }

        t.start();
        Thread.sleep(1000) ;
        displayStatus(t,"After Start     ");
        Console.WriteLine("Main thread exiting");
    }
    private static void displayStatus(OtherThread t,String message)
    {
        String status = message + " ";
        status += t.isAlive() + "   ";
        status += t.isDaemon();
        Console.WriteLine(status);
    }

}
```

This program asks the user if he or she wishes the other thread to be a daemon thread. The user types in a string. If that string starts with a *Y* the other thread is set to be a daemon thread. Here's an example of the output when the user types a *Y*:

```
Message          isAlive  isDaemon
Before Start     false    false
Other thread is Daemon? [Y/N]
Y
*
After Start      true     true
Main thread exiting
*
```

Because of timing issues the main thread exits first. The key element is that when the main thread terminates the background thread is stopped. The following shows what happens when the user types in *N*:

```
Message          isAlive  isDaemon
Before Start     false    false
Other thread is Daemon? [Y/N]
N
*
After Start      true     false
Main thread exiting
*
*
*
*
```

Notice that the other thread continues to execute after the main thread has exited. The reason is that both the main thread and the other thread are foreground threads.

Suspending and resuming a thread

In chapter 5 we discussed suspending and resuming threads. J#'s versions of `suspend` and `resume` function much like their `System.Threading.Thread` counterparts. The only noticeable difference is that the J# methods do not raise exceptions when they are called from an incorrect state. For example, if a thread is not in the suspended state and the framework's `resume` is called, a `ThreadStateException` is raised. The J# methods do not raise exceptions based on thread state. Listing 18.10 contains the listing of a console application that allows the user to suspend and resume the other thread.

> **Listing 18.10 Allowing the user to suspend and resume the other thread interactively (J#)**

```
package PauseAndResume;
import System.Console;
public class ClassMain
{
    /** @attribute System.STAThread() */
```

```
public static void main(String[] args) throws Exception
{
    OtherThread t;
    t=new OtherThread(100);
    t.setDaemon(true);
    t.start();
    Console.WriteLine("q = Quit");
    Console.WriteLine("s = Suspend");
    Console.WriteLine("r = Resume");
    boolean keepGoing = true;
    while (keepGoing)
    {
        String input = Console.ReadLine();
        char inputChar = input.toLowerCase().charAt(0);
        switch(inputChar)
        {
            case 'q':
                keepGoing =false;
                break;
            case 's':
                t.suspend();
                break;
            case 'r':
                t.resume();
                break;
        }
    }
}
}
```

The following output shows that an exception isn't raised when the thread is running and resume is called:

```
q = Quit
s = Suspend
r = Resume
*
*
*
r*
*
r
*
```

Notice that the other thread is executing and resume is signaled. The suspend and resume methods are deprecated, meaning they will likely be removed from J# in future releases. Rather than having an external thread control the execution of a thread, it's better to have the thread itself control it using the wait and sleep statements. This removes the possibility that the thread is suspended at a point where it has a resource allocated, such as a synchronized region of code.

18.2 THE RUNNABLE INTERFACE

J#, along with C# and VB.NET, allows for inheritance from only one class. This single inheritance restriction greatly simplifies object-oriented development. There are times that it is desirable for a class to contain multiple types of reusable functionality. This is where the concept of an interface comes in. An interface is nothing more than a way of stating what methods and properties an object must implement if it claims to support an interface.

The Runnable interface in J# is used to create threads without deriving from the Thread class. If an object implements the Runnable interface it must contain a method named run that accepts no parameters and does not return a value. The instance of the object that supports the Runnable interface is passed to the constructor of the Thread class. The instance of the Thread class can then be used to start the thread, which will begin executing the run method. Listing 18.11 contains a base class that provides an Output method. This is intended to serve as an example of the need for interfaces, not to demonstrate object-oriented design. This class is overly simple in the hope that it will make the concepts clearer.

Listing 18.11   A very simple base class (J#)

```
package SimpleRunnable;
import System.Console;
public class BaseClass
{
    protected void Output(String message)
    {
        Console.WriteLine(message);
    }
}
```

Listing 18.12 contains a class that is derived from the BaseClass class. Since the DerivedClass class extends the BaseClass class, it cannot also extend the Thread class. Instead, it implements the Runnable interface.

Listing 18.12   The DerivedClass implements the Runnable interface (J#).

```
package SimpleRunnable;

public class DerivedClass extends  BaseClass implements Runnable
{
    public void run()
    {
        Output("Enter Second thread");
        try
        {
            Output(Thread.currentThread().getName());
        }
        catch(Exception ex)
        {
```

```
        Output(ex.getMessage());
    }
    for (int i=0;i<4;i++)
    {
        Output("*");
    }
    Output("Exit Second thread");
    }
}
```

Because the DerivedClass claims to implement the Runnable interface it must contain a function named run. The run function is the entry point for the new thread, just as it is when the class is derived from the Thread class. The run function is not called directly, but is invoked as a result of the start method being invoked on an instance of the Thread class.

Listing 18.13 contains the source code of a console application that creates an instance of the DerivedClass, associates it with an instance of the Thread class, and starts the new thread using the start method.

Listing 18.13   Allocates an instance of the Thread class and starts the new thread (J#)

```
package SimpleRunnable;
import System.Console;
public class ClassMain
{
    /** @attribute System.STAThread() */
    public static void main(String[] args)
    {
        Console.WriteLine("Enter main thread");          ❶ Implements
        DerivedClass derived;                               Runnable
        derived = new DerivedClass();
        Thread theNewThread;                              ❷ Is used to start
        theNewThread= new Thread(derived);                  the new thread
        theNewThread.setName("SecondThread");
        Console.WriteLine("Starting second thread");
        theNewThread.start();                            ❸ Starts the
        try                                                 new thread
        {
            Console.WriteLine("Main thread is joining second thread");
            theNewThread.join();                         ❹ Waits until the run
        }                                                   method terminates
        catch(InterruptedException ex)
        {
        }
        Console.WriteLine("Exit Main thread");
    }
}
```

① The main class starts by declaring an instance of `DerivedClass` named derived. Next we allocate a new instance of `DerivedClass`. `DerivedClass` does not support the `start`, `stop`, or `join` methods. To access those methods we must have an instance of the `Thread` class.

② The `theNewThread` class is an instance of the `Thread` class. Once an instance is allocated using the new statement, we can assign it a name, in this case SecondThread. Notice that we pass in the instance of `DerivedClass` to the thread. This is very similar to the use of the `ThreadStart` delegate in the `System.Threading` namespace in that it determines which method is invoked when the thread starts.

③ SecondThread is now ready to start execution. As we've discussed previously, the `start` method is used to start a new thread. The entry point for the new thread is the `run` method of the instance of the object that was passed into the `Thread`'s constructor.

④ The main thread pauses until SecondThread terminates, at the `join` statement. As we've discussed previously the `join` method puts the calling thread into a wait state until the thread associated with the instance of the `Thread` class terminates.

You're probably noticing that this is very similar to the way we create threads using the `System.Threading.Thread` class. Listing 18.14 shows the similarities between the C# implementation and the J# implementation using the `Runnable` interface.

Listing 18.14 Similarities between the Runnable interface and a ThreadStart delegate (C#)

```
using System;
using System.Threading;
namespace NoThreadInstanceExample
{
  class ClassMain
  {
    [STAThread]
    static void Main(string[] args)
    {
      Thread t;
      t=new Thread(new ThreadStart(run));
      t.Start();
      t.Join();
    }
    static void run()
    {
      for (int i=0;i< 4;i++)
      {
        Console.WriteLine("*");
      }
    }
  }
}
```

The `ThreadStart` delegate performs a duty similar to that of the `Runnable` interface. Recall that the `ThreadStart` delegate is used to associate a method with an instance of the `Thread` class. That method can be static, belong to the current instance of the class, or belong to some other class.

The `run` method of the instance of the class that supports the `Runnable` interface cannot be static. This means it must be an instance method. To state the obvious, that method must belong to the class that supports the `Runnable` interface. All this means is that the J# approach is slightly more restrictive than the delegate-based approach used by the framework. Since J# is a .NET language, there's no reason that the `System.Threading.Thread` class can't be used. Most likely the `Runnable` approach will be used when porting Java source code to the .NET environment.

18.3   CONCURRENCY CONTROL IN J#

Because of the nature of multithreaded development, concurrency control is a key in any language. J# contains a robust set of synchronization mechanisms to ensure that access to data elements is performed in a controlled fashion.

18.3.1   Synchronized regions

In chapter 7 we discussed creating regions of code that were protected by a lock. In C# we used the `lock` keyword and in Visual Basic .NET we used `SyncLock`. In J# the same operation is performed using the `synchronized` keyword. To see an example of why locks should be performed, consider the class contained in listing 18.15.

Listing 18.15   Prints a string, a character at a time pausing a tenth of a second between each (J#)

```
package SyncTest;
import System.Console;
public class UnSyncPrinter extends Thread
{
    private String whatToPrint;
    private int howManyTimes;
    public UnSyncPrinter (String whatToPrint,int howManyTimes)
    {
        this.whatToPrint = whatToPrint;
        this.howManyTimes = howManyTimes;
    }
    public void run()
    {
        int strLength;
        strLength=whatToPrint.length();
        for (int i=0;i< howManyTimes;i++)
        {
            for (int c=0;c< strLength;c++)
            {
                Console.Write(whatToPrint.charAt(c));
```

```
                    try
                    {
                        Thread.sleep(100);
                    }
                    catch(InterruptedException ex)
                    {
                    }
                }
            Console.Write("\r\n");
        }
    }
}
```

This class prints the string that's passed into the constructor onto the console one character at a time. Between each character the thread pauses for one tenth of a second. The number of lines printed is based on the value passed in to the constructor in the howManyTimes parameter.

This class contains no synchronization. When more than one instance of this class is created, the output of the two classes will be intertwined. Listing 18.16 contains a version of the class from listing 18.15 that provides synchronization.

Listing 18.16   SyncPrinter protects the output of each line with a synchronized region of code (J#).

```
package SyncTest;
import System.Console;
public class SyncPrinter extends Thread
{
    private String whatToPrint;
    private int howManyTimes;
    private Object lock;
        public SyncPrinter(Object lock,String whatToPrint,int howManyTimes)
        {
            this.lock=lock;
                this.whatToPrint = whatToPrint;
            this.howManyTimes = howManyTimes;
        }
    public void run()
    {
        int strLength;
        strLength=whatToPrint.length();
        for (int i=0;i< howManyTimes;i++)
        {
            synchronized(lock)
            {
                for (int c=0;c< strLength;c++)
                {
                    Console.Write(whatToPrint.charAt(c));
                    try
```

```
                {
                    Thread.sleep(100);
                }
                catch(InterruptedException ex)
                {
                }
            }
            Console.Write("\r\n");
        }
    }
}
```

Notice that listing 18.16 has an additional parameter passed to the constructor. Access to the synchronized region is controlled by the use of this object. Listing 18.17 contains the main class from a console application that demonstrates the importance of having synchronized regions.

```
package SyncTest;
import System.Console;

public class ClassSyncTest
{
    /** @attribute System.STAThread() */
    public static void main(String[] args)
    {
        Console.WriteLine("Unsynchronized");
        UnSyncPrinter one;
        UnSyncPrinter two;
        SyncPrinter three;
        SyncPrinter four;
        Object lockingObject=new Object();

        one=new UnSyncPrinter("abcdefghijklmnopqrst",5);
        two=new UnSyncPrinter("ABCDEFGHIJKLMNOPQRST",5);
        three=new SyncPrinter(lockingObject,"abcdefghijklmnopqrst",5);
        four=new SyncPrinter(lockingObject,"ABCDEFGHIJKLMNOPQRST",5);

        one.setName("one");
        two.setName("two");
        three.setName("three");
        four.setName("four");

        one.start();
        two.start();

        Console.WriteLine("Press Enter to Continue");
        Console.ReadLine();
        Console.WriteLine("Synchronized");
```

```
        three.start();
        four.start();

        Console.WriteLine("Press Enter to Continue");
        Console.ReadLine();
    }
}
```

Notice that the same instance of the `Object` is passed to each of the `SyncPrinter` constructors. This causes the access by both threads to be restricted by the common object. When the console application from listing 18.17 is executed, the following output is produced:

```
Unsynchronized
Press Enter to Continue
aAbBcCdDeEfFgGhHiIjJkKlLmMnNoOpPqQrRsStT
a
AbBcCdDeEfFgGhHiIjJkKlLmMnNoOpPqQrRsStT
a
AbBcCdDeEfFgGhHiIjJkKlLmMnNoOpPqQrRSStT
A
aBbCcDdEeFfgGhHiIjJkKlLmMnNoOpPqQrRsStT
a
AbBcCdDEeFfGgHhIiJjKkLlMmNnOoPpPqQrRrSsTt


Synchronized
Press Enter to Continue
abcdefghijklmnopqrst
ABCDEFGHIJKLMNOPQRST
abcdefghijklmnopqrst
ABCDEFGHIJKLMNOPQRST
abcdefghijklmnopqrst
ABCDEFGHIJKLMNOPQRST
abcdefghijklmnopqrst
ABCDEFGHIJKLMNOPQRST
abcdefghijklmnopqrst
ABCDEFGHIJKLMNOPQRST
```

The first portion of the output contains mixed upper- and lowercase characters. This occurs because each thread pauses before completing a line, allowing the other an opportunity to output its characters. Notice that the second portion of the output contains lines of only upper- or lowercase characters. This is because the synchronization block forces a thread to wait until the other has completed its output of a line before it can enter the region and begin outputting its line.

There are times that an entire method should be guarded by a synchronization mechanism. In the next section we discuss how to do that in J# and how it is accomplished in general in the framework.

18.3.2 Synchronized methods

There are times that access to an entire method should be synchronized. One way to accomplish this is to wrap the entire method body in a synchronized block, using `this` as the object to synchronize on. While this may function as desired it doesn't necessarily convey the programmer's intent. During maintenance some unsuspecting developer might mistakenly place one or more instructions outside the synchronized block only to introduce a bug that will be difficult to detect and repair.

Recall from section 7.1.1 that collections are not generally thread-safe. This means that if more than one thread interacts with a collection the odds are pretty high that some negative event will occur. J# contains numerous collections; for our example we'll use `ArrayList`. Listing 18.18 is a class that contains an instance of the `ArrayList` class. It serves as the recipient for data produced by multiple worker threads.

Listing 18.18 The Data class collects data produced by multiple threads (J#).

```
package SyncMethods;
import System.Console;
public class Data extends java.util.ArrayList
{
    private java.util.ArrayList list;
    public Data()
    {
        list = new java.util.ArrayList();
    }
    public void put(String data)                 ❶ Defines a method
    {                                               that is susceptible
        try                                         to race conditions
        {
            list.add(data);
        }
        catch(Exception ex)
        {
            Console.WriteLine(ex.getMessage());
        }
    }
    public void putSyncAll(String data)          ❷ Defines a method that
    {                                               uses a synchronized
        synchronized(this)                          region
        {
            try
            {
                list.add(data);
            }
            catch(Exception ex)
            {
                Console.WriteLine(ex.getMessage());
            }
        }
    }
```

```
    public synchronized void putSyncMethod(String data)    ❸ Defines a
    {                                                          synchronized
        try                                                    method
        {
            list.add(data);
        }
        catch(Exception ex)
        {
            Console.WriteLine(ex.getMessage());
        }
    }
    public int length()
    {
        return list.size();
    }
}
```

❶ In chapter 7 we discussed the impact of having shared collections manipulated by multiple threads without proper synchronization control. J# is no different. When multiple threads call the `put` function concurrently, eventually an `ArrayIndexOutOf-BoundsException` will be raised. The reason for this is the same as in other collections; one thread caused an area of memory to be allocated and another took it.

❷ Wrapping the entire function with a synchronized region will keep `ArrayIndex-OutOfBoundsException` from being raised. This approach doesn't convey the fact that the entire method must be protected with a synchronized region. Over time it's possible that other instructions will be added to the method, but not within the synchronized region. Perhaps some of those instructions don't need to be protected with the synchronized region, but eventually one that should be will be placed outside the region. When that occurs it will likely be very difficult to track down the cause of the new anomaly.

❸ When the `synchronized` keyword is applied to a method, invocation of the entire method is synchronized. This prevents other threads from accessing the method while another thread is in it. Not only does this successfully cause all invocations to be synchronized, but also it tells future developers that the method should be synchronized. While this could be accomplished using documentation, many developers don't document their code, and many don't read existing documentation until a problem has already occurred.

The .NET framework contains support for synchronizing access to an entire method. It is accomplished using `MethodImplOptions` from the `System.Runtime.CompilerServices` namespace. The following is a C# implementation of the J# `putSyncMethod` from listing 18.19:

```
[MethodImpl(MethodImplOptions.Synchronized)]
public  void putSyncMethod(String data)
{
    try
    {
        list.Add(data);
    }
    catch(Exception ex)
    {
        Console.WriteLine(ex.Message);
    }
}
```

Attributes are a powerful way of extending .NET languages. They allow for future expansion to languages. J# supports the use of attributes by using the @attribute statement within a comment block. For an example of using the @attribute statement look at listing 18.17. Prior to the static main method notice the line containing STAThread. This is equivalent to the [STAThread] attribute found in C# console applications.

18.3.3   The wait, notify, and notifyAll methods

The coordination of multiple threads is one of the more challenging elements of multithreaded development. In chapter 7 we discussed the .NET framework's Monitor class. Recall that the Monitor class allows a thread to enter a Wait state by calling the Wait method, until some other thread signals it using the Pulse and PulseAll methods or a timeout occurs.

J# includes similar functionality in the wait, notify, and notifyAll methods. Listing 18.19 contains a J# class that creates a worker thread that calls the wait method on an object that's passed to the constructor. The thread's processing suspends until some other thread calls notify or notifyAll.

> **Listing 18.19   Pauses until some other thread calls notify or notifyAll on the same key object (J#)**

```
package WaitNotify;
import System.Console;
public class Worker extends Thread
{
    private Object key;
    public Worker(Object key)
    {
        this.key=key;
    }
    public void run()
    {
        String name;
        name=Thread.currentThread().getName();
        Console.WriteLine("Wait:" + name);
```

```
        try
        {
            synchronized(key)
            {
                key.wait();
            }
        }
        catch(InterruptedException ex)
        {
            Console.WriteLine(ex.getMessage());
        }
        catch(Exception ex)
        {
            Console.WriteLine(ex.toString());
        }
        Console.WriteLine("Exit:" + name);
    }
}
```

Notice that the wait method is invoked inside a synchronized region of code. The reason for this is the same as the reason that Monitor.Wait must be invoked from within a synchronized region of code: to avoid race conditions. Listing 18.20 contains the main class that utilizes the Worker class.

Listing 18.20   Creates three instances all sharing the same key (J#)

```
package WaitNotify;
import System.Console;
public class ClassMain
{
    /** @attribute System.STAThread() */
    public static void main(String[] args)
    {
        Object key= new Object();
        Worker one = new Worker(key);
        one.setName("one");
        one.start();

        Worker two = new Worker(key);
        two.setName("two");
        two.start();

        Worker three= new Worker(key);
        three.setName("three");
        three.start();

        try
        {
            Console.WriteLine("Waiting one second\r\n");
            Thread.sleep(1000);
            Console.WriteLine("");
```

```
            synchronized(key)
            {
                Console.WriteLine("Calling notify");
                key.notify();
            }

            Console.WriteLine("Waiting one second\r\n");
            Thread.sleep(1000);
            Console.WriteLine("");
            synchronized(key)
            {
                Console.WriteLine("Calling notifyAll");
                key.notifyAll();
            }
        }
        catch(Exception ex)
        {
            Console.WriteLine(ex.getMessage());
        }
        Console.ReadLine();
    }
}
```

The output from listing 18.20 is as follows:

```
Waiting one second

Wait:one
Wait:two
Wait:three

Calling notify
Waiting one second

Exit:one

Calling notifyAll
Exit:two
Exit:three
```

Notice that when notify is invoked, only one thread, in this case the thread named "one," exits the wait state and terminates. When the notifyAll method is invoked the threads named "two" and "three" exit the wait state and terminate. This behavior is identical to that of the Pulse and PulseAll methods of the framework's Monitor class.

Sometimes it's helpful to compare something new to something familiar. Listing 18.21 is a C# version of the Worker class from listing 18.20.

Listing 18.21 The C# version of the Worker class is very similar to the J# version.

```
using System;
using System.Threading;
namespace WaitNotify
```

```
{
    public class Worker
    {
      private Thread theThread;
      private object key;
      private string name;
          public Worker(object key)
          {
          this.key= key;
          }
      public void run()
      {
          String name;
          name=Thread.CurrentThread.Name;
          Console.WriteLine("Wait:" + name);
          try
          {
              lock(key)
              {
                  Monitor.Wait(key);
              }
          }
          catch(Exception ex)
          {
              Console.WriteLine(ex.ToString());
          }
          Console.WriteLine("Exit:" + name);
      }
      public void start()
      {
          theThread = new Thread(new ThreadStart(run));
          theThread.Name=name;
          theThread.Start();
      }
      public void setName(string name)
      {
          this.name = name;
      }
    }
}
```

Notice that the C# version of the Worker class contains the start and setName functions. Since C# doesn't allow subclassing the Thread class we must provide a means for starting a thread in the Worker class. These methods could have been named anything, but for consistency with the J# version of the Worker class the names start and setName were chosen. Listing 18.22 contains the C# version of the Main class.

Listing 18.22 The Main class is virtually identical to that of listing 18.21 (C#).

```
using System;
using System.Threading;

namespace WaitNotify
{
    class Class1
    {
        [STAThread]
        static void Main(string[] args)
        {
            object key= new object();
            Worker one = new Worker(key);
            one.setName("one");
            one.start();

            Worker two = new Worker(key);
            two.setName("two");
            two.start();

            Worker three= new Worker(key);
            three.setName("three");
            three.start();
            try
            {
                Console.WriteLine("Waiting one second\r\n");
                Thread.Sleep(1000);
                Console.WriteLine("");
                lock(key)
                {
                    Console.WriteLine("Calling Pulse");
                    Monitor.Pulse(key);
                }

                Console.WriteLine("Waiting one second\r\n");
                Thread.Sleep(1000);
                Console.WriteLine("");
                lock(key)
                {
                    Console.WriteLine("Calling PulseAll");
                    Monitor.PulseAll(key);
                }
            }
            catch(Exception ex)
            {
                Console.WriteLine(ex.ToString());
            }
            Console.ReadLine();
        }
    }
}
```

The output produced by the C# version of the program is virtually identical to that produced by the J# version.

18.4 SUMMARY

J# is a .NET implementation of the Java language. It is based on the Java Development Kit (JDK) version 1.1.4. The J# language supports multithreaded development. J# allows two means of creating threads: implementing the `Runnable` interface and subclassing the `Thread` class. This is a departure from the `ThreadStart` delegate-based approach used by C# and VB.NET.

J# provides a means to leverage existing code, while taking advantage of functionality available under the .NET runtime. This allows applications to be ported to the environment without requiring a total rewrite. This includes multithreaded applications.

In this chapter we've seen that the majority of J# methods have a framework equivalent. The methods do not behave the same, but are similar enough to make the transition from J# to other framework languages relatively easy.

index

W

wait 313, 323
WaitAll 142, 144, 147, 149–151, 155
   restrictions 151
   VB.NET example 150
WaitAny 144, 147, 152, 155
WaitCallback 211, 197
WaitHandle 142–143, 145, 147, 149,
   184–186, 213
WaitOne 144–145, 147–148, 154–155
WaitOrTimerCallback 184–185, 213
WaitSleepJoin 65, 67, 74, 76–77, 82,
   85, 126, 133–134, 146–147, 226–227,
   229, 231
WaitTimeout 144, 152, 155
web pages 193

web site monitor 70, 96, 242
WebClient 71, 73, 79, 81, 193, 300, 305
   DownloadData 71
WebSiteMonitor 303
Win32 258, 292
Windows. *See* Microsoft Windows
Windows Forms 78, 214–216, 245–266, 276, 286
   not thread-safe 16, 118
   deadlock example 256
   timers 193, 235–240
WM_TIMER 209, 235–238
WorkItem 211
WriterSeqNum 177–179

X

XML Web Service 26

MANNING PUBLICATIONS CO.
.NET Developer's Library

Microsoft .NET for Programmers
BY FERGAL GRIMES
January 2002, Softbound, 386 pp.
ISBN 1930110-19-7
Price: $39.95 • Ebook $17.47

A programmer's guide to .NET

For ordering information visit www.manning.com

MANNING PUBLICATIONS CO.
.NET Developer's Library

Windows Forms Programming with C#
BY ERIK BROWN
April 2002, Softbound, 752 pp.
ISBN 1930110-28-6
Price: $49.95 • Ebook $24.97

A practical guide to creating Windows applications with .NET

For ordering information visit www.manning.com

MANNING PUBLICATIONS CO.
.NET Developer's Library

ADO.NET Programming
BY ARLEN FELDMAN
July 2002, Softbound, 592 pages
ISBN 1930110-29-4
Price: $39.95 • Ebook $22.47

A practical guide to ADO.NET

For ordering information visit www.manning.com

MANNING PUBLICATIONS CO.
.NET Developer's Library

NET Remoting
BY DON W. BROWNING
January 2003
Softbound, 350 pp.
ISBN 1930110-57-X
Price: $44.95 • Ebook $22.47

A guide to .NET's powerful and elegant distributed applications framework.

For ordering information visit www.manning.com